PLACING THE SOUTH

BOOKS BY MICHAEL O'BRIEN

The Idea of the American South, 1920–1941 (1979)
All Clever Men, Who Make Their Way: Critical Discourse in the Old South (ed. 1982)
A Character of Hugh Legaré (1985)
Intellectual Life in Antebellum Charleston (coed. with David Moltke-Hansen, 1986)
Rethinking the South: Essays in Intellectual History (1988)
An Evening When Alone: Four Journals of Single Women in the South, 1827–67 (ed. 1993)
Conjectures of Order: Intellectual Life and the American South, 1810–1860, 2 vols. (2004)
Henry Adams and the Southern Question (2005)
Cosmopolitismo e Località (2006)

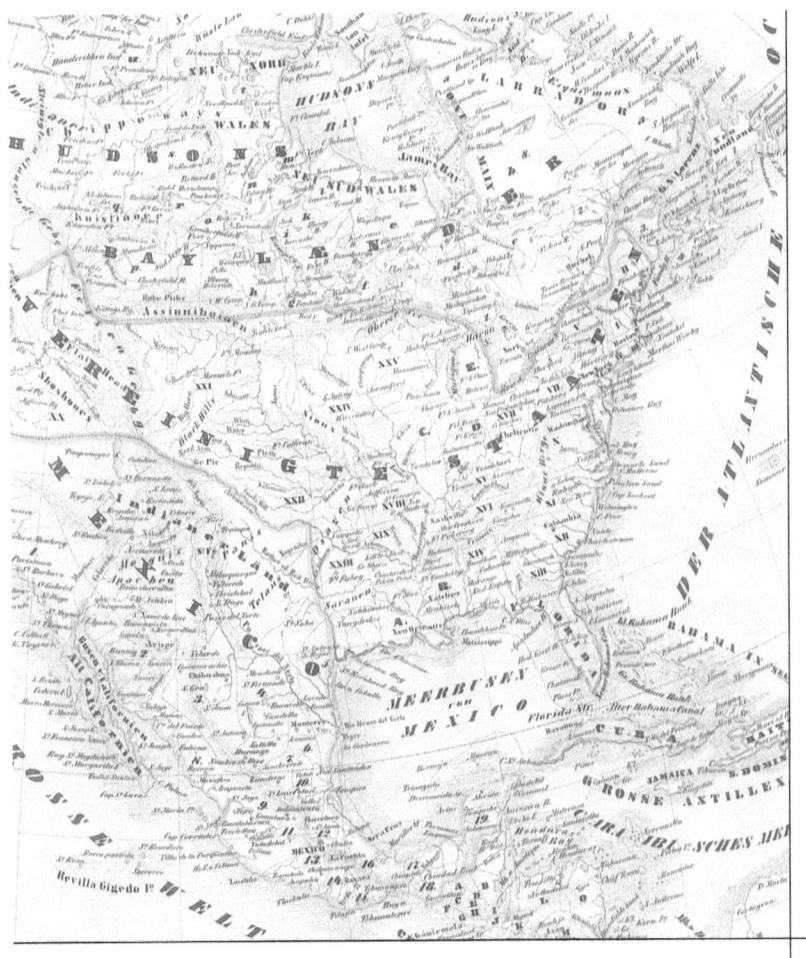

PLACING THE SOUTH

MICHAEL O'BRIEN

UNIVERSITY PRESS OF MISSISSIPPI
JACKSON

www.upress.state.ms.us

The University Press of Mississippi is a member of the
Association of American University Presses.

Illustration: Marco Berra, *Nord America* (Prague, 1840) (copy in author's possession)

Collection Copyright © 2007 by Michael O'Brien
All rights reserved
Manufactured in the United States of America
∞
Library of Congress Cataloging-in-Publication Data

O'Brien, Michael, 1948–
 Placing the South / Michael O'Brien. — 1st ed.
  p. cm.
 Includes bibliographical references and index.
 ISBN-13: 978-1-57806-934-7 (cloth : alk. paper)
 ISBN-10: 1-57806-934-3 (cloth : alk. paper) 1. Southern States—
Civilization. 2. Cosmopolitanism—Southern States. 3. Regionalism—
Southern States. 4. Southern States—Politics and government. 5. Political
culture—Southern States. 6. Political science—Southern States. 7. Southern
States—Intellectual life. 8. American literature—Southern States—History and
criticism. 9. Literary form. 10. Authors, American—Southern States. I. Title.
 F209.O27 2007
 975—dc22   2006019446

CONTENTS

Preface — vii

PLACING

Regions and Transnationalism — 3
The South in the Modern World — 10
Britain and the South — 26

IDEOLOGIES

Freedom — 41
Imperialism — 48
Unionism — 53
Race — 72

FORMS

Autobiography — 79
Biography — 86
Intellectual History — 100
Southern History — 123
Southern Literature — 142

WRITERS

Thomas Jefferson — 149
William Gilmore Simms — 153
Mary Chesnut — 159

DuBose Heyward	180
Allen Tate	194
W. J. Cash	197
C. Vann Woodward	205
William R. Taylor	213
Eugene Genovese	222
Edward Ayers	234
V. S. Naipaul	237
John Shelton Reed	245
Bill Clinton	251
Index	259

PREFACE

This volume offers a selection of essays and reviews published between 1985 and 2005. These pieces mostly address American culture, especially its Southern region, and habitually offer a comparative analysis, doubtless because the author, during these years, lived and moved between several states and communities within Europe (Britain, Luxembourg, the West Country, East Anglia) and the United States (Arkansas, Alabama, Ohio). Among scholars and critics of the South, such a perambulating standpoint used to be an oddity, was indeed regarded as a treason against the South's traditional culture, but has grown less so, as the South and the world have freshly and anxiously intermingled. In this world of oscillating migrations, such an experience is not especially peculiar, but it does have intellectual consequences. For my own part, it has compelled a stance on how the moving target of place might be understood, a sympathy with modes of understanding which prefer hybridity, and an interest in how disparate worlds converse. As the reader will come to discern, in thinking about how locality and the world have interconnected, I have developed a resistance to the nation-state and its attendant ideologies, and a preference for what transcends nationality, by being on a smaller scale and a larger. Villages and the world are places worth inhabiting, for each speaks to our shared humanity and neither possesses great coercive power. There is little to be said for the nation-state except administrative convenience, though that little, vexingly, is not unimportant in a world needing organization more than passion.

My sense of this has evolved over the years. When I took a professorship at Miami University in 1987 and was asked to give an inaugural address, I argued for a modified version of cosmopolitanism. It was a natural-enough choice, given that I was an Englishman, speaking to an Ohioan audience. The incongruity required an explanation, which was partly economic, the academic diaspora from Margaret Thatcher's Britain, partly philosophical, that shallow commitment to nationality not uncommon in my British generation, which had refused to stand in cinemas for the national anthem and little cared whether God would save the Queen, not only because God seemed an uninteresting possibility. In 1987, however, atavistic nationalities were on the rise. Mrs. Thatcher had recently manipulated ancestral memories of maritime sacrifice during her Falklands War, and Ronald Reagan was idly assembling the materials for the Molotov cocktail which was to become modern American nationalism. But it was also a moment when, more dimly, multiculturalism was being invented. On both scores, I was uneasy about these paradigms of belonging. "We all, it seems to be argued, have a cultural home, to which we are called," I then observed. "Our homes can have more than a geographical locale: feminism has been informed by the same impulse, as have black nationalism and homosexual rights. A place to belong is no mean thing in our time. But I am not alone in reflecting that, when the great call for the gathering of the clans goes out, I will be bemused to know my tartan. My own case is one among many. Few of us have a single culture: there are those we are born into, those we learn, those we choose, those we invent, those we have thrust upon us, those we acquire by love and friendship."[1]

Then the logical alternative seemed to be cosmopolitanism, the tradition of the Enlightenment and its lofty preference for the urban, the comparative, the skeptical, and the universal. One might turn to the letter sent by Denis Diderot to David Hume, when the latter returned from Paris to Edinburgh in 1768, and read: "My dear David, you belong to all the nations of the earth and you never ask a man for his place of birth. I flatter myself that I am like you, a citizen of the great city of the world."[2] There was Leibniz, too: "I am indifferent to that which constitutes a German or a Frenchman, because I will only the good of all mankind."[3] Yet one did have a place of birth, the world did not form a city, and indifference to nationality was a risk.

So the Enlightenment ideal was only partially available. The democratization of intellect, the decay of a stable theory of human nature, the abandonment of natural science as a model, and, less obviously, the expansion of the cosmopolis had long since altered the moral and intellectual equation. The generations of Voltaire and Hume, though they had urged interest in an exoticism like China, had confined the cosmopolis to western Europe and, at a pinch, its American hinterland. The Enlightenment had chosen among cultures confined within a relatively narrow range, in order to effect the order of reason. It was not clear that the global international order of 1987 provided more than "an eclectic disorder," which would later come conventionally to be called postmodern and transnational.[4] Sadly, the double obligation of the eighteenth-century cosmopolitan—to abjure prejudice and pursue enlightenment—had often degenerated into merely a desire to spurn the provincial. Nothing then (less so now) tended to denote the cosmopolitan faster than this abhorrence, the sneer at Wigan or the Midi or Iowa. Once the cosmopolis had been a place to gather for conversation: in 1987, at best, it was a moveable feast, going from city to city, in but pointedly never of the provincial. Instead, as Thomas Bender had recently argued, what passed for place among the intelligentsia were universities, specializations, communities of discourse.[5]

This was not enough. It seemed desirable to rehabilitate both the cosmopolis and locality as a conjoined influence on the intelligentsia, which was, willingly or not, fraily the heir of the Enlightened vision, yet inhabited particular places, worth acknowledging. So the only cosmopolitanism which could work was based, not on rejection of the local, but on respect for it: a knowledge of several provinces which became in turn its own idiosyncratic province. As such, it must be confessed, the name of cosmopolis, of the universal city, could scarcely be justified. Voltaire once remarked of the traffic of ideas between Italy, France, and England: "I do not know which of the three nations deserves the preference, but happy the man who is able to savour their different excellencies."[6] Happy and better, Voltaire might have added. One could no longer be confident about better—but in a zeal to escape the charge of arrogance, in the desire to redefine culture from Matthew Arnold's sense to that of Clifford Geertz, one had to remember that, if not better, the culture of the intelligentsia was inescapably different, it having been fashioned out of other cultures, all subjected to a measure of skepticism. This was what Hegel had meant by his definition of a cultured person as "one who knows how to impress the stamp of universality upon all his actions, who has renounced his particularity, and who acts in accordance with universal principles."[7] That is, culture was thought, which by its nature stepped beyond particularity and alienated.

Or so I thought in 1987. Mostly, I still think these things and seem now to have more company. Anthony Appiah has coined a phrase, "rooted cosmopolitanism," to describe the stance.[8] But the context since the 1980s has drastically changed and the following pieces show them changing. Then, though thinking much about the internal social dynamics of American and European culture and their nuanced differences, I presumed a rough sympathy, along the lines of the post-1945 world, and this sense informed

PREFACE ix

many of the following pieces, written in the 1980s and 1990s. Those written since 2001 are different, as the gap between the United States and Europe has widened, as European impatience with American culture and policy has grown, and as many Americans have grown violently hostile to transnationalism, to different gods, and to the godless. A recent book by an unreconstructed American nationalist, Samuel P. Huntington in *Who Are We? America's Great Debate,* is dismissive of the so-called "ampersands" who have dual citizenship.[9] The dismissal is reciprocal, at least from this dual citizen, who would be happy to see the following unrepentantly regarded as "ampersand studies."

However, hybridity takes many forms. States have boundaries, but so do genres. A genre is more admirable than a state, but can be a tyranny, too. Among historians, intellectual historians are perhaps most prone to transgressing genres, because their subject matters—literature, philosophy, political thought, historiography, and so forth—are shaped by genre and, to cope with this, as historians their rhetoric needs to be nimble.

These two impulses towards hybridity—in politics and society, in literary form—explain this book's structure. The first section ("Placing") has three pieces intended to show how a comparative analysis might work when applied to the American South, by looking at how regionalism has recently been conceptualized in world culture, how the modern South has acquired a pertinence for those outside the United States, and how (as a case study) the cultural relationship between Britain and the South has worked. The second section ("Ideologies") scrutinizes political ideas—freedom, imperialism, nationalism, racial ideology—which have informed American culture, mostly in the nineteenth century, by way of extending the case against nationalism. The third section ("Forms") looks at genre, at how the South has been constructed and reconstructed by literary forms, in this instance by autobiography, biography, history, and literary history. The last section ("Writers") is a straightforward collection of critical appreciations of authors—political thinkers, novelists, poets, critics, historians, sociologists—who have been important to Southern culture.

It must be stressed that, for the most part, these are works of criticism, often tied to a specific book, writer, or occasion. Over the years, I have preferred the schizophrenic practice of writing, on the one hand, books where historiographical debate is only implicit and, on the other, essays and reviews which intimately, even polemically, engage contemporary issues and writers. That is, in essays and reviews, I have tried to work out the stance latterly applied to writing my own history. Such a critical practice is more respected by literary scholars than by historians, especially American historians, who tend to be diffidently genteel. Yet the literary criticism of history is a deeply serious venture, which assesses that compelling mixture of splendid accomplishment and uneasy failure, intrinsic to the enterprise of history. This mixture the critic can help to identify, by acting either as a rapidly judging advance scout for new readers, or as the retrospective student of an inherited intellectual landscape. But the venture is more-than-usually incestuous. A drama critic need not be an actor, a literary critic may never write a novel, but it is very rare for a historical critic not to be a historian, whose criticism must therefore mingle dispassion with complicity.

So, the menu of this book consists of essays, review-essays, reviews, and a few conference papers previously unpublished. For the most part, the original essays and review-essays had annotation, but this was rarely the case with reviews and papers. So, for the reader's convenience, I have added footnotes. In general, I have cited the works I then used, but have not hesitated to cite superior editions, especially of original sources, if they have been published subsequently. In the reviews, I have occasionally restored passages or expressions excised by editors, if I was helpless before and regretted their changes. (The *Times Literary Supplement* is much given to altering texts, usually with a shrewd eye for what works in prose, but also for what fits on a page.) Throughout, I have eliminated repetitions and corrected misprints, misquotations, casual errors of fact, and bad grammar. Apart from these small matters, however, I have made no effort to re-write substance or style, conceived *in medias res*.

I need to express my thanks to the following for permission to reprint these pieces: the *American Historical Review*, Berg, Blackwell, *Comparative Studies in Society and History*, the *Historical Journal* and Cambridge University Press, the *Journal of American History*, the *Journal of Southern History*, the *Mississippi Quarterly*, the *South Carolina Historical Magazine*, *Southern Cultures*, the University Press of Mississippi, the University of North Carolina Press, the University of Virginia Press, and the *Virginia Magazine of History and Biography*. The *Times Literary Supplement* does not require its authors to seek such a license, but this is an appropriate place to thank its editors—for many years, it was Adolf Wood, lately mostly David Horspool—for inviting me so often to write and for their adroit attention to style and cogency of expression. I need also to thank Andrew Wylie, my literary agent, for arranging this publication.

NOTES

1. Michael O'Brien, "On Transcending the Mollusk: Cosmopolitanism and Historical Discourse," *Gettysburg Review* 1 (Summer 1988): 461.

2. Diderot to Hume, 22 February 1768, quoted in Thomas J. Schlereth, *The Cosmopolitan Ideal in Enlightenment Thought: Its Form and Function in the Ideas of Franklin, Hume, and Voltaire, 1694–1790* (Notre Dame, IN: University of Notre Dame Press, 1977), 1.

3. Leibniz to Giles Filleau des Billetes, 21 October 1697, quoted in Schlereth, *Cosmopolitan Ideal*, xxiv–xxv.

4. O'Brien, "Transcending the Mollusk," 459.

5. Thomas Bender, "The Cultures of Intellectual Life: The City and the Professions," in *New Directions in American Intellectual History*, ed. John Higham and Paul K. Conkin (Baltimore, MD: Johns Hopkins University Press, 1979), 181–95.

6. Voltaire, "Sur Mr. Pope et quelques autres poètes fameux," in *Lettres philosophiques*, ed. Gustave Lanson (Paris: Hachette, 1917), 2: 139, quoted in Schlereth, *Cosmopolitan Ideal*, 18.

7. Georg Wilhelm Friedrich Hegel, *Lectures on the Philosophy of World History: Introduction: Reason in History*, trans. H. B. Nisbet, introd. by Duncan Forbes (Cambridge: Cambridge University Press, 1975), 56–57.

8. Kwame Anthony Appiah, *The Ethics of Identity* (Princeton, NJ: Princeton University Press, 2005), esp. 213–72.

9. Samuel P. Huntington, *Who Are We? America's Great Debate* (2004; London: Free Press, 2005), 207–16.

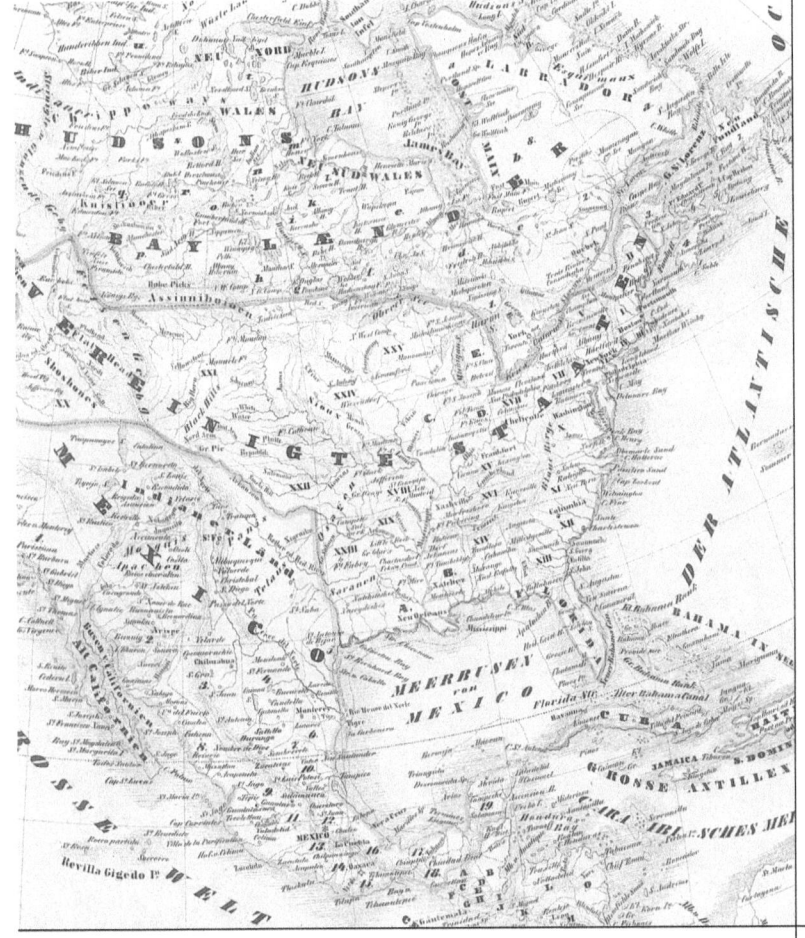

PLACING

First published as Michael O'Brien, "On Observing the Quicksand," *American Historical Review* 104 (October 1999): 1202–7, as a part of the "AHR Forum: Bringing Regionalism Back to History." Reprinted by permission. The articles, on which I was asked to comment, were Celia Applegate, "A Europe of Regions: Reflections on the Historiography of Sub-National Places in Modern Times," *American Historical Review* 104 (October 1999): 1157–82, and Kären Wigen, "Culture, Power, and Place: The New Landscapes of East Asian Regionalism," *American Historical Review* 104 (October 1999): 1183–1201.

Forty or so years ago, "the regional historian [was] likely to be oppressed by a sense of his unimportance" and to believe his moment was passing before the pressure of sweeping nationalisms.[1] Feeling unimportant is something of a character trait for Southerners in American culture, but this pessimism proved not to be prescient, although the vitality of the regionalist idea has remained conflicted and uneven. Of late, historians of the American West have grown more interested in the idea and the midwesterners show signs of life, but the New Englanders are mostly indifferent, and those in the "middle states" long since gave up the ghost. As usual, the Southerners have been most eager, most endowed with regional organizations, study centers, periodicals, publishers, tourist pilgrimages, and bric-à-brac. Indeed the South seems often to be looked to by other regions as a model of how to invent and sustain an identity, when the western by comparison seems diffuse and the midwestern etiolated.[2] So a historian of the American South comes to these articles on European and Asian regionalism with mixed feelings; one is greatly pleased to see such intelligent synthesis, but mildly puzzled at the notion that all this is news. In Mississippi, regionalism is not "a less-than-familiar perspective."

Professor Applegate skillfully rehearses the multifarious ways in which regionalism can be understood. Many echo how Southern history has been configured. Seeing locality as a safely subsidiary form of nationalism was the meaning of Henry Grady's "New South" and the "local-color" school of the late nineteenth century, while Howard Odum and his disciples around the 1930s published big, fat books on American and Southern regionalisms. Earlier there had been Southerners, like John C. Calhoun, who spoke of "Southern rights" but were Unionist, and who thought localism to be an underpinning of a federal nationality. There had been others, secessionists like Jefferson Davis, who concluded that

American nationalism had failed and who grounded a new state upon a different landscape of localities. Abraham Lincoln in the Gettysburg Address described the South as the site of the reactionary and counter-revolutionary, and many Southerners have thought him right and watched their neighbors for the un-American thing. That national politics is an aggregation of particularist politics was something James Madison knew and V. O. Key's *Southern Politics in State and Nation* argued in 1949. C. Vann Woodward's *Origins of the New South, 1877–1913* (1951) contended that the South became a colonial economy of the North. William Faulkner grasped the problem of "multiplicity and fragmentation" and there is a whole literature on "the idea of the South," which might be described as "constructivist." Placing the South in the story of modernization has been going on for thirty years or more, as have books on the invention of nationality, tradition, and region, mostly before Eric Hobsbawm and Terence Ranger. Southerners have even had the concept of the "post-Southern" for about twenty years, and they begin to have an intimation of a connection between regionalism and multiculturalism. Black Southerners and white Southerners, in their differing but interconnected ways, know a little of regionality as victimhood, the latter having buried their dead at Shiloh, the former having cut down their strange fruit. As to the tension between professionalized scholars and local érudits, most Southernists have a file of letters from vigilant women in Vicksburg and annoyed men in Alabama, who are not slow to correct one's misunderstandings of General Sherman or great-great-uncle Beauregard.[3]

So it is tempting to say that Southerners have been there, done that, and got lots of T-shirts, with images of Monticello, Appalachian springs, Robert Johnson, the Stars and Bars, and Delta weddings. In fact, they might be slightly dismayed to discover how trendy Southern understandings might be. They have found it energizing to be out of step; they have discovered many opportunities for indignation; and they realize that regions die without a certain quota of misanthropy about the opinions held of them somewhere else. Indeed this Southern habit of mind is now so old that it may be drifting into senescence. If Applegate is right that regionalism is all the rage in Europe (and I think her only half-right), it is a little tired in the American South, and the intellectual conviction of its pertinence is probably weaker now than a half-century ago; it may have become more subtle, analytically more sophisticated, but this may be the Owl of Minerva at dusk. My own recent experience is that it is hard to persuade people that region is a profitable way to structure American history, when race, class, and gender compete as useful categories of analysis, more firmly lodged in minds. Not unexpectedly, we do not now have Southern history, so much as we have (for example) women's history which happens to be located in the South. Identities have to be alert to survive.

One thing a Southern historian has learned is that, if one moves "region" from the realm of "objective" reality to what Professor Wigen calls the "subjective expressions of regional belonging," one has to give perception a history. It helps to interrogate how the idea of "region" has evolved.[4] As both authors suggest, it is a very vague and flexible term, but its commodiousness runs very deep. The word, after all, arises from the Latin *regere*, to rule, and early came to mean a place capable of being governed. But almost anything can be governed, from a cow to an Empire. So "region" did not necessarily mean a political domain, and size was irrelevant, as it often was in premodern usages; a "continent" might once have meant something large like Asia, but also something tiny, a spit of land. But bodies, too, had regions (arms, kidneys, the seats of humors), and so did the unearthly. John Milton's Satan asks in the Hall of Pandemonium, "Is this the Region, this the Soil, the Clime ... That we must change for Heav'n[?]"[5]

All this persists until very late. If anything, the word tended to become vaguer, the further it drifted from its Latin root. One can see this in American usage in the nineteenth century, including that of the South. Thomas Dew, president of the College of William and Mary, wrote in 1841, "Perhaps the most royal road to woman's heart is through the region of the intellect."[6] Striking is that, of the many usages of the word, the scarcest is the one deployed in these essays. Historians casually refer to the South as a "region" before the Civil War, but the term is anachronistic and was not then deployed by Southerners to describe the whole South. It meant something smaller, the Piney Woods or the Blue Ridge mountains or the city of Charleston. So George Frederick Holmes in 1849 spoke of "the tide-water region of Virginia," as we still might.[7] This usage was relational but had little implication of dependence; one might have regions without a whole, and parts might relate without one having sovereignty. With no core, there is no periphery. It had been the hope of the American political experiment to achieve Union without centralization, and most antebellum Southerners understood the United States precisely as a collectivity of parts in which none, especially not the federal government, was dominant, but all were freely cooperative. It was the death of this political idea in the Civil War which made it possible to describe the South as a "region," for it reconfigured the United States as a nation-state, with subsidiary divisions. But even in the late nineteenth century, the usage of "region" was uncommon and did not become usual until after the First World War.[8]

This chronology seems to accord with, at least, British usage. By imitation from the French, "regionalism" begins to appear in the 1880s, though infrequently and (as the *Edinburgh Review* put it) "inharmoniously." The *Oxford English Dictionary* gives the first reference to Applegate's primary meaning of region—"a relatively large subdivision of a country for economic, administrative or cultural purposes that frequently implies an alternative system to centralized organization"—in *The Future of Local Government* by G. D. H. Cole, the English socialist, in 1921.[9] Planning was important here; countries needed scientific management, and regions were rational units of governance, clever mediations between what a sensible planner might want and the inconvenient atavisms of awkward Bretons, Catalans, or Georgians. Howard Odum and Harry Estill Moore spoke in *American Regionalism* (1938) of "the new science of the region" and of "practical planning."[10] But one could not have this sense of region until after the consolidation of the nation-state, which was the long work of the nineteenth century and continued to our own day. Nor could one have that other sense of region, which is relevant to its Asian usage, as an geographical aggregation of nations within a world system. Upward and downward, region came to radiate from the nation.[11]

All this suggests a caution. Applegate confines herself to the period after 1945, by which time "regions" and "regionalism" had become accepted, if disputed categories. Yet many of her historical actors refuse the label, even now. Very few Scots would accept a description of Scotland as a "region," including those who do not vote for the Scottish Nationalist Party. I am half-Scottish and would not, perhaps the more so as the other half is Cornish and remembers not only Culloden but also the rebellion of 1497, when the English and Henry VII defeated a Cornish army on Blackheath. (True, I had to look up the date, but grievances are the more forceful for being vague.) Wigen's essay rightly speaks of very old historical Asian identities, hard to fit into these newfangled categories, but it is scarcely less so in Europe. The trouble is that continuities are so mixed with instabilities, not especially but markedly in our own times. New nations appear only to disappear, enclaves raise flags, bombs explode. Asia has changed immensely in the last several generations; in Tibet, India, Vietnam, Hong Kong, the lineaments of political identities have shifted and nationality itself has been invented. In Europe, the Soviet Union has come and gone, Italy develops fissures, the Balkans struggle into uncertain forms, the map of central and Eastern Europe is almost unrecognizable from what it was a generation ago. Even in Britain, that Burkean place, it becomes doubtful that the United Kingdom will remain united for much longer; Ulster's fate is uncertain, a Scottish parliament has reappeared, and the English do not know who they are; newspapers publish subtle articles about the legality of secession, just like in Canada, just like once in South Carolina.[12] Meanwhile, the European Union reconfigures itself with complicated and little-understood swiftness and, at the very least, seems to have rendered the idea of national sovereignty moot, without quite establishing a greater European federal nationality, though its possibility tends to sanction conjectural talk of European parts as "regions."

Applegate and Wigen, of course, know all this, better than I do. Yet their analyses quieten it all, because the language of regionalism is a language of stability and limited volatilities. Those who use it tend to be saying, "Yes, we belong one to another, we connect, but let's discuss the terms of belonging." They admirably deal in the nuances of stability, what have been or ought to be the relationships between core and periphery, the nation-state and its regions, the strong and the weak, but they presume that there should be or has been a reciprocal relationship. Applegate more than Wigen flings this presumption into the far past, into times when the modern word "regionalism" would have been meaningless to those then living. Her tone is mildly irritated or amused with those who seek to upset matters. She smiles at "the thicket of Basques, Slovenes" etc., and frowns at "murderous separatist movements." But as we know, one man or woman's political murder is another's act of patriotism. Applegate is for the big picture and wants to "productively stabilize our perceptions of European history," which is hard to do, when the damn people keep rearranging Europe and do not agree on its structure, when *their* perceptions are unstable, quicksilver. She wants us to think big, when all the regionalists want to think small. There is a dissonance.

Perhaps part of the problem is that writing from within American culture about Europe and Asia tends to suggest a stabler world than anyone in Belfast, Split, Lhasa, Seoul, or Saint Petersburg/Petrograd/Leningrad/Saint Petersburg might be experiencing. The United States is one of the few places in the world where the nation-state seems incontestable. Hardly anywhere else on the planet has a polity over two hundred years old and boundaries stable for more than a century. And this attitude is present, despite the fact that only about a third of the states of the Union are there by free consent. Perhaps one day the Chicanos will want to expel the Americans from the lands seized from Mexico in the 1840s or the Inuits may rise up to claim the Alaska bought without their consent, just as Louisiana was purchased. There are, to be sure, fringe groups who want a Southern nation and do "not hesitate to advocate secession and self-rule for the Southern states."[13] At Civil War battle reenactments, there are booths which sell charming little images of Lincoln with a red bullethole in his forehead, on which are emblazoned the ancient slogan, "Sic Semper Tyrannis." But, on the whole, the American republic has managed to turn empire into a stable, consensual polity. So, in the United States, region accepts the permanence of the nation-state, though even here the strength of regionalism is roughly in proportion to a history of a problematic relationship to the federal government. Hence this is, perhaps, a good place to conceptualize regionalism, but a poor place from which to imagine what region might mean elsewhere. Indeed, I suspect that the new availability of the language of regionalism in Europe and Asia may be partly due to the cultural influence of the United States, whose political language is now so broadly available and serves to reinforce the regionalist concept at the same moment that it has validated the efficiency of supermarkets. Applegate and Wigen are certainly discerning an indigenous movement in foreign cultures, but they may also be listening to an echo of American ideology.[14] For Americans seem to stand on solid ground, but most people in the world write about these matters as the quicksand approaches, recedes, or closes about them.

NOTES

    1. "The Irony of Southern History," (1952) in C. Vann Woodward, *The Burden of Southern History*, rev. ed. (1960; Baton Rouge: Louisiana State University Press, 1968), 187.
    2. For a brief overview, see Edward L. Ayers et al., *All Over the Map: Rethinking American Regions* (Baltimore, MD: Johns Hopkins University Press, 1996).
    3. Documenting all these standpoints would amount to a bibliography of modern Southern historical literature, but, by way of illustration, see: on Grady and local color, Wayne Mixon, *Southern Writers and the New South Movement, 1865–1913* (Chapel Hill: University of North Carolina Press, 1980); on Odum, as well as a Southern "constructivism," Michael O'Brien, *The Idea of the American South, 1920–1941* (Baltimore, MD: Johns Hopkins University Press, 1979); on Calhoun, Irving H. Bartlett, *John C. Calhoun: A Biography* (New York: W. W. Norton, 1993); on Davis and nationalism, Paul D. Escott, *After Secession: Jefferson Davis and the Failure of Confederate Nationalism* (Baton Rouge: Louisiana State University Press, 1978); on Lincoln, Garry Wills, *Lincoln at Gettysburg: The Words That Remade America* (New York: Simon & Schuster, 1992); on Madison, Lance Banning, *The Sacred Fire of Liberty: James Madison and the Founding of the Federal Republic* (Ithaca, NY: Cornell University Press, 1995); on Key, Milton C. Cummings, ed., *V. O. Key, Jr., and the Study of*

American Politics (Washington, DC: American Political Science Association, 1988); on internal colonialism, Gavin Wright, *Old South, New South: Revolutions in the Southern Economy Since the Civil War* (New York: Basic Books, 1986); on Faulkner, Daniel J. Singal, *William Faulkner: The Making of a Modernist* (Chapel Hill: University of North Carolina Press, 1997); on modernization, Jack Temple Kirby, *Rural Worlds Lost: The American South, 1920–1960* (Baton Rouge: Louisiana State University Press, 1987); on inventing the South, Frank E. Vandiver, ed., *The Idea of the South: Pursuit of a Central Theme* (Chicago, IL: University of Chicago Press, 1964); on the postmodern, Lewis P. Simpson, "The Closure of History in a Postsouthern America," in Lewis P. Simpson, *The Brazen Face of History: Studies in the Literary Consciousness in America* (Baton Rouge: Louisiana State University Press, 1980), 255–76; on multiculturalism, William L. Andrews et al., *The Literature of the American South: A Norton Anthology* (New York: W. W. Norton, 1998).

4. I confine myself to its usage in the English and American languages, though clearly there are formidable problems in dealing, as these essays do, with other cultures, whose languages use other words to describe what is here translated into "region" and so necessarily mean different things.

5. John Milton, *Paradise Lost*, Book 1, lines 242–44.

6. Thomas R. Dew to B. Franklin Dew, 10 May 1841, Dew Family Mss, Special Collections Department, Earl Gregg Swem Library, College of William and Mary, Williamsburg.

7. George Frederick Holmes to William Campbell Preston, 6 March 1849, Preston Family Papers, Virginia Historical Society, Richmond.

8. It is my impression that it was much used by newly national businesses, to categorize their divisional organizations. But also significant were the various scientific disciplines like geology, which were concerned to map the American landscape; the U.S. Geological Survey divided the country into regions.

9. *The Oxford English Dictionary*, 2d ed., 20 vols. (Oxford: Clarendon Press, 1989), 18:510–12.

10. Howard W. Odum and Harry Estill Moore, *American Regionalism: A Cultural-Historical Approach to National Integration* (1938; Gloucester, MA: Peter Smith, 1966), 3.

11. The invention of the region, in turn, mandated the invention of the "subregional." On this, see Michael O'Brien, "Finding the Outfield: Subregionalism and the American South," *Historical Journal* 38 (December 1995): 1047–56.

12. See, for example, "England, Whose England: It May Not Come Naturally, But Devolution Is Going to Force The English To Come To Terms With a Nebulous Sense of Identity," *Financial Times* (30 September 1998): 14.

13. Michael Hill, "The Southern League Mission Statement," which can be read at the website of the Southern League of Georgia at http://www.mindspring.com.

14. A recent American article about England, for example, speaks of "the other regions that make up Britain—Scotland, Wales and Northern Ireland": Warren Hoge, "Has England Lost Its Identity? Or Just Its Clichés?" *New York Times* (14 October, 1998): A4. The *Financial Times* article cited above, however, nowhere applies the words "region" or "regionalism" to Scotland, Wales, and Northern Ireland—it speaks of "the smaller parts of the UK"—but only to a conjectural administrative division of England into "regions whose dimensions no one can agree upon."

Michael O'Brien, "The Apprehension of the South in Modern Culture," *Southern Cultures* 4 (Winter 1998): 3–18; this was my contribution to a special issue, edited by myself, on "The South in the World." Reprinted by permission.

When I went to the University of Cambridge as an undergraduate in 1966, the South was deemed there to be a very minor part of the puzzle of American culture. American literature was Henry James, Melville, Emerson, Hemingway, Fitzgerald, but mostly Henry James. Of Southern authors only Faulkner had a significant hearing, though he was seen as a steamy exoticism, a sort of Henri Rousseau with a knowledge of the sexual utility of corncobs, not as one of the foremost modernists. As for history, the South was relevant to understanding the coming of the Civil War, as a problem to be deprecated, but little more. American history was told as a succession of whiggish reform movements, of Jeffersonian and Jacksonian democracy, of Populism, Progressivism, and the New Deal. The South did not fit in, except as the occasional obstacle. To be interested in the South then was to be against the grain. Matters are very different now, not only in Cambridge but elsewhere in Europe, even in Japan. The existence of the Southern Studies Forum as a branch of the European Association for American Studies—as far as I know, the only affiliation of that association devoted to a component part or aspect of American culture—is testimony to a growth of interest, evidenced by four conferences and three volumes of proceedings.[1] There are scholars in Odense who write about Walker Percy, in Berlin who concern themselves with John Esten Cooke, in Vienna who read Flannery O'Connor, in Genoa who are experts on women's clubs in Charleston, in Newcastle who do the history of rhythm and blues, in Australia who write on Southern Baptists. When I was in Chapel Hill, North Carolina, in November of 1997, a whole conference of Japanese scholars had descended upon the place. In the summer of 1998, there was a meeting at the University of Warwick titled "New Orleans in Europe," with no less than thirty speakers. What is going on?

Of course, much is explicable by the powerful cultural position of the United States in the postwar world, the more so since the collapse of the Soviet alternative. Self-evidently, the world grows crowded with American popular and high culture. Coca-Cola, Levi jeans, baseball caps, T-shirts, CNN, Elvis, Duke Ellington, Bill Gates, all these are familiar almost everywhere. This influence has deepened in the last twenty years. In 1973 my wife and I caught a bus in the eastern part of Crete, in the Lasithi region beyond Sitia and towards Kato Zakros. Behind us a small girl sat down, evidently on her way to school. She looked on us with wonder, as though we had come from another world, as indeed we had. With kindness towards strangers, she offered a part of the food she had for her lunch, and we, awkwardly and mutely, accepted it. I find it hard to imagine such a scene happening now, for the child would probably be wearing an outfit emblazoned with a Chicago Bulls logo.

The ancient condescensions of European culture have perceptibly weakened. I do not mean that Parisian intellectuals have swapped their Haut-Médoc for Dr. Pepper. I do mean that the presence of American culture in the formative years of European intellectuals has made it natural to take seriously interpreters of America who make that culture intelligible because they help to explain not only what America is, but what Europe is. For American culture is part of the fabric of European culture in ways that it was not in the nineteenth century, or far less so. That intermingling is, no doubt, deeply contentious, but it is at least arguable that American culture is now very close to being central to world culture and many—whether scientists, philosophers, historians, musicians, or literary critics—whether they admit to it or not, behave as though the United States were pivotal. And this occurs despite the fact that both sides are somewhat in denial about the phenomenon: the world for its old anti-American instincts, America because so much of its eschatology is founded upon a sense of being at the end of things, of time and space, not in the middle of things.

It so happens that a disproportionate amount of American popular culture, at least, is Southern. Jazz, blues, rhythm and blues, rock music, country and western, much in those genres is Southern or part of a Southern cultural diaspora, not only in Chicago and New York with Louis Armstrong and Duke Ellington, but in Paris with Sidney Bechet. Consider that Hollywood has, ever since D. W. Griffith, abundantly transmitted images of the South, as has American television. These things were and are part of a European upbringing. Southern literature has been one of the more vital components of modern American literature, while Southern historical literature had something of a golden age from about the late 1950s to the mid-1980s and made a decent case that to know the South was indispensable to understanding America.

Then again, the South has also been unusually prominent in American public affairs in recent decades. Viewed from the perspective of the century after 1865, this development is an oddity, but modern Europeans have not always realized this. They have watched Lyndon Johnson, Jimmy Carter, Bill Clinton, Dean Rusk, J. William Fulbright, Newt Gingrich, even the George Bush who scrupulously kept a hotel room in Houston, and concluded that the South matters. Moreover, the great moral struggle of the civil rights movement has exercised a peculiar fascination, and it is seen largely as a Southern story. Knowing Martin Luther King mandated knowing Selma, Birmingham, and Albany. When I caught a Greyhound bus from Washington to Alabama in 1968, the first time I ventured into Southern territory, I knew about the Freedom Riders and felt a frisson of tension. I saw peeling signs on walls in Tuscaloosa that read "For Colored Only" and knew what that meant, or thought I knew. I had seen it on television in Devon.

By such contemporary influences and impressions, Europeans were taught that the South was interesting, complicated, fecund, mobile, even as traditional American historiography told us that the South was backward, immoral, belated, inferior, frozen. Those old indigenous quarrels which go back to slavery and abolitionism were available to Europeans, but not compulsory, and there were no significant cultural penalties for resisting those stereotypes. Europeans did not always know the script. Knowledge came in too many pieces. No doubt, this is often true of the transmission of cultures. Much is fragmentary, accidental, driven by local considerations. The Chinese, for example, used to think the greatest American author was Jack London.

There was also the matter of moralities. Part of the old transatlantic dialogue was the contrast between European decadence and American innocence, with Americans asserting the veracity of the American Dream and Europeans shaking their heads at the folly of such an ambition. This was the Jamesian motif. As C. Vann Woodward long ago pointed out, the American Dream is, more accurately, a Northern dream, from which Southerners were excluded, with whose Puritan millennialism Southerners felt little historical sympathy.[2] Woodward thought that the South had more in common with European culture, that the North was the oddity. Even Henry James had some sense of this. When he visited the South in 1905, he felt himself again in Italy, that the antebellum mansions of Charleston were like so many Venetian palazzi guarded by the "ancient sallow crones" who populate *The Aspern Papers*.[3] Seen from Europe, Woodward's suggestion makes some sense, though a European might be more conscious of the American in the Southerner. When I first visited the South, I was often asked if I was reminded of England. As often, politely, I had to say, no.

As long as the South was a slaveholding culture, any sympathy between it and Europe was drastically constrained. This tension seen even in racial discourse. When in 1856 Josiah Nott had Henry Hotz of Mobile translate into English the racist work of Arthur de Gobineau, Hotz carefully removed Gobineau's strictures against slavery and his endorsement of a theory of American degeneration.[4] Gobineau noticed and complained to a friend: "Do you not wonder ... at my friends the Americans, who believe that I am encouraging them to bludgeon their Negroes, who praise me to the skies for that, but who are unwilling to translate the part of the work which concerns them?"[5] Segregation established sympathies between Europeans and Southerners because both were managers of exploited peoples and the United States was an elaboration of the imperial venture, but there was an awkward moment in the 1950s, especially, when many European intellectuals became anticolonialist and racially liberal, while officially the South had not. So one might argue that recent sympathies have been predicated on the death of the defense of segregation in the South, and that concomitantly much in European writing on the civil rights movement is a veiled contemplation of the end of empire and its legacy.[6]

Nonetheless, war, failure, prejudice, these *are* European things. Europeans can see themselves in Southern writing and history. William Alexander Percy's *Lanterns on the Levee* does read like Lampedusa's great novel of Sicily, *The Leopard*. By contrast, Europeans can find much in the history of the North which is a puzzle, for having such peace, such success, such a want of incident. Columbia, South Carolina, which was burned to the ground by Sherman, makes more sense to someone who, like me, grew up in a Plymouth flattened by the Luftwaffe, who played on bombsites and was taught, from as early as lessons could be taught, what to do upon coming across an unexploded bomb. When I was sixteen or so, I was in a group of schoolchildren who were shown a film about a midwestern state. It was Chamber of Commerce–like, showed many factories, growing suburbs, and leafy parks, all very upbeat. My friends and I looked upon these images with blank incomprehension. The question was in all our young English minds: if this place is so happy, why should it interest us? Our literary models were Eliot's *The Waste Land*, Osborne's *Look Back in Anger*, and Camus's *La Peste*; we wanted melancholy, despair, intractability, existential angst. We were not impressed with or experienced in hope, and so that impulse which so distinguished Northern attitudes towards the South, that sense that immorality (slavery, lynching, bigotry) made the South something untouchable and infecting, was less intelligible, at least then.

Mine was a postwar generation, fed stuntedly on powdered milk.[7] In my case, this effect was compounded by growing up in the working class, with its immense, necessary reservoir of stoicism, its skepticism of "them," its flickering community of strong women and of men lost in wars, colonies, and the pub round the corner, men whose idea of hope was a bookie's runner. In such a world, it was natural to believe that we are all more or less guilty, that we inherit guilt, build on it, transmit it. For to embrace human failing was to belong, for the broken people were the only ones available. We did not wish to live in a successful, innocent world, for such a place would be an offense against our understanding of humanity, a loss and a severing. Picket fences and well-mown lawns seemed a kind of spiritual death, as they do in Walker Percy's Will Barrett novels. So Southern literature, with all its Gothic elaboration, often seemed more congenial; Poe, after all, characteristically expressed his Southernism by telling grim stories set in European landscapes.[8] Other Europeans have their own stories, but it seems clear from the three volumes published under the auspices of the Southern Studies Forum that they are also drawn to the darker side—race, anti-Semitism, the instinct of Stoicism, sympathies with Fascism—and mostly seem unresponsive to attempts to lighten the burden of Southern history.

For me, at least, it took some while to notice the South in the image of America, which was at first more *On the Town* than *Absalom, Absalom!*, more a rumor of large refrigerators. Indeed, I suspect that one of the prime attractions of Southern culture for non-Americans used to be this sequence of knowing: first learning the alien qualities of American success, then discovering the buried culture of the South. For then the Southern story could be read as anti-American. To be interested in the South allowed one to be engaged by the United States but not implicated in its ideology, for Southerners themselves have been such vociferous critics of the Yankee. One might have one's American cake and not eat it. This is not an entirely attractive aspect of the problem, something which I mistrust in my own scholarship, but there is a deeper resonance. After all, the experience of being Americanized and being anti-American simultaneously, of accommodation and resistance, goes to the heart of a dilemma of many modern cultures. In that sense, the South has been available as one of the first victims of American political and cultural imperialism, and as an exemplum, for good and ill, of how to cope.

This congeniality is not an accident of history, a matter of chance sympathies. Conventional history argues that American culture broke loose from Europe in the early nineteenth century, probably when Emerson gave his address "The American Scholar," but that the South had a series of un-American cultural experiences.[9] According to this logic, Southerners have had a European-like experience, interpreted in ways congenial to Europeans but with little reference to them. You will look in vain in cultural histories of the United States for much evidence of European/Southern cultural exchange; all is George Ticknor in Göttingen, Emerson corresponding with Carlyle, Hemingway dining upon his moveable feast in Paris. Tellingly, even Woodward, in his 1990 lectures at the New York Public Library which became *The Old World's New World*, ignored the South.[10] In fact, the European/Southern exchange has been continuous since the colonial period, and European ideas have been peculiarly powerful in shaping Southerners' interpretations of their own experience. We will see this more clearly when we are as familiar with Joel Poinsett in Weimar in 1800, Hugh Legaré in Brussels in 1834, Basil Gildersleeve in Bonn in 1852, Caroline Carson in Rome in 1890, Robert Penn Warren in Oxford in 1930, and we have histories of the South's place in the world. Not all Southern culture has been centripetal, not all has been Faulkner's little postage stamp of Yoknapatawpha. Elizabeth Spencer's *The Light in the Piazza* of 1960 is set in Rome and continues a tradition commenced by John Izard Middleton, who wrote the first Southern Gothic short story, set in Italy, in 1810. William Alexander Percy's sense of declension is not only indigenous to his experience of Greenville, Mississippi, but influenced by his reading of the Matthew Arnold of "Dover Beach." Clearly, Northern cultural anger at Southern culture occurs because the latter has not always been convinced by the proposition that an American mind must be posited upon rejecting wholesale the influence of Europe, even if Mr. Jefferson said it must. Indeed, one could argue that Southerners have been distinctive, if not singular, among modern Americans for trying to separate the concept of culture from the idea of the nation. It is logical, though, that they should have done so, since they invented their own culture, but the nation, at least in its federal form, was reimposed upon many of them.

This question of the scope of the nation-state, too, seems to be part of the European, though probably not the Japanese, interest in the valency of Southern culture. We live in European times when the relationship between locality, region, nation, and a federation of negotiable coherence and scope is almost the most compelling issue before us. The nation-state is no longer self-evident, but how to construct a civilization upon other premises is deeply unclear. The study of the South offers a little help on this score, both before the Civil War, when it offered alternative visions of Union, and after, when it was obliged to negotiate with a nation-state of sorts, now deemed ineluctable but not always regarded as legitimate. The South's habit of complicating and inhibiting the process of nation-building used to be why the South was despised, and it is one reason now why it is studied. This is perhaps most evident in the work of Lothar Hönnighausen, who in recent years has been sponsoring at the University of Bonn a study of European and American regionalisms, and in the work of several Italian scholars who see parallels in the study of their own *Mezzogiorno*.

Concomitantly, we also live in times when social identity is seen as an invention. Clearly, this is an old theme of Southern history and thought. Indeed, though I am pleased to read the recent work inspired by Eric Hobsbawm and Terence Ranger's *The Invention of Tradition*, such as, for example, Larry Wolff's *Inventing Eastern Europe* or the essays collected in Roy Porter and Mikuláš Teich's *The National Question in Europe in Historical Context*, I read it with a sense of having seen all this before, that very little is being said which has not been long since explicated in Southern historical literature.[11]

So there are ample reasons to explain why the history and literature of the South might seem usefully available to foreigners. I do not want to make too much of this. Obviously much else in American culture has been resonant or pertinent, and less obviously this has been a study at the margins. That is, those abroad who study the United States tend not to be those with much intellectual authority within their own cultures. This is an old paradox. The European intellectuals whom Americans most listen to are those who seem most ignorant of the United States, however often they may pop over for visiting professorships. Indeed, I would hazard that the single greatest failure of the American Studies movement in Britain and Europe since the 1950s has been its inability to persuade our various cultures' leading intellectuals that a working knowledge of American history and culture is indispensable to the adequate formulation of modern aesthetic, philosophical, and historical understandings, that America is more than a footnote to Europe, or an amusing destination where one can take in a good jazz quartet and enlarge one's bank account.

Let me turn, more briefly, to the status of Southern culture within the United States. Peter Applebome, the former *New York Times* correspondent to the South, offers a bullish account of the status of Southern culture within the United States in his recent book called *Dixie Rising: How the South is Shaping American Values, Politics, and Culture*. Southern politicians, evangelical religion, and popular music, he argues, are taking over American culture at a time when the South is expanding economically and demographically. At one level, Applebome's view seems to fit my earlier notion about the South's place in international culture. But the American situation is more subtle, and, in fact, I am skeptical of Applebome's reading of the situation. As I have suggested elsewhere, Southern ideological exports tend to have their labels removed.[12] Southern religion becomes in California a blow-dried evangelicalism, the neo-Confederate becomes in Arizona generically conservative, the Arkansas governor becomes a president of multicultural vagueness, the old blunt talk by Cotton Ed Smith in 1938 about the "slew-footed, blue-gummed, kinky-headed Senegambian" becomes the oblique codes of the Willie Horton advertisement.[13] Even the Confederate flag, which shows up on leather jackets in Massachusetts, is stripped of Jefferson Davis, slavery, and Shiloh, and becomes only an indistinct symbol of defiance, to everything and nothing everywhere. If the South were to show up on the doorstep of American culture and openly say, I'm here, move over, imitate me, Southerners know that doors would slam in their faces. The nerve of those people, it would be said. Didn't they own slaves, lynch people, eat clay? Southerners know this deeper response, so they remain diffident about their legitimacy and hew to the old defensiveness, habitual since Lee did not give his sword to Grant. This is not the stuff of which hegemony is made. If their culture is expansive, it is little they planned, and something most of them have not noticed.

Indeed, if the state of literary and historical studies is any guide, then the South is less studied in American universities outside the South than it was a generation ago. Southern California is a strange exception, but there is little enough done in the Ivy League, and Woodward has (as yet) no senior successor at Yale. I am told that positions in Southern literature are becoming as scarce as those in Tudor-Stuart history, both regarded as something fusty and irrelevant which needs to be replaced by something newer, something multicultural. One might feel better about this if one did not suspect that this has been but the replacement of one marginal group by another. After 1900 or so, in the elite universities of the North, black Southerners were not represented, while white Southerners were accorded a small but distinct place at the edge of American culture, for being part of a great story—sectionalism, slavery, the Civil War, abolition, Reconstruction, the preservation of the Union—a story which needed to be told. Having a token Southerner on a Northern faculty, charged with explaining or apologizing for the South's oddity, made sense: witness William E. Dodd at Chicago, Ulrich B. Phillips at Michigan and then Yale. As early as 1886, Woodrow Wilson resentfully wrote to Richard Heath Dabney of Virginia, who had received a position in Indiana: "In a word, you have gotten into a chair whose incumbent is expected to present, not the scientific truth with reference to our Constitutional history, whether that truth be on the side of Webster or of Calhoun in the great historical argument, but 'Yankee sentiments'—sentiments agreeable to that eminent body of scholars, the Grand Army of the Republic."[14] The force of that story having faded, or rather having been subsumed in another great narrative, that of American racism, it has equally made sense that when that gray-haired white Southern professor retired, his successor as a representative of the margins would be an African American, of late preferably a woman. Did the change matter much for Northerners? Were not both, the white Southern male, the African American woman, from somewhere else? Worth a mention, a seat at the table, but just one, and not at the head.

Now, of course, much that has been or could be subsumed under the category of Southern survives into these new discourses, those of the African American or the black Atlantic or women's history or even postmodernist literary study. One can write essays on representations of the body in Faulkner while deploying French critical theory. But one does not need the idea of Southern culture to do this. Indeed, I suspect that most of the secondary writing on authors whom one might regard as Southern or who regarded themselves as Southern is done with indifference to that identity. Browse through the Modern Language Association's bibliographies, with their bulging sections on Poe, Faulkner, Chopin, Welty, and note how many articles are about odd fragments of these oeuvres to see the point. The author is broken loose from the psychic landmass which is the South; the book is broken loose from the author, who is declared dead, the chapter from the book, the paragraph from the chapter, the sentence from the paragraph, the word from the sentence. The South has been an irremediably contextual notion, and hence incompatible with poststructuralism. It has a better chance with postmodernism. Michael Kreyling, for one, has adopted (with a more upbeat tone than its coiner, Lewis Simpson, intended) the term *postsouthern*.[15] The term "post-" embodies some sense of time, even if time is dying or is manipulable, and the habit of mind which is characteristically postmodernist plays with the rigidities of time, place, and style by mingling them eclectically;

thereby time and place survive. As for the categories of multiculturalism, though nominally they could accommodate the idea of the Southern as one of the constituent elements in the great quilt of American culture, they seem very reluctant to do so, partly because multiculturalism is very reluctant to acknowledge historical guilt or responsibility, which is what Southerners do when they gather together. It is hard to imagine Southerners popping up at Berkeley and demanding a Southern Cultural Center in order to advance their sense of cultural self-esteem.

These are issues which are not merely relevant to the status of the South beyond its boundaries. They arise within the South itself. At one level, they always have. The idea of the South has always been only one of the synthesizing ideas available to those people who have lived in the southeastern United States since about 1820, to accept and use if they wished, to refuse if they wished. And I am not convinced that even at its apogee—which I would tentatively place at around 1880—that a majority of those people ever accepted "Southern" as the social identity most explanatory of their lives and individualities. The South has always been an effort of will, and I see odd pieces of evidence that the will is slackening, especially when even Southerners live in times when the idea of the synthetic is mistrusted and when we are told that identity is something we are free to invent. The question naturally arises: is "Southern" something still worth inventing, and reinventing, when American culture makes so many other, more pressing demands on the stamina of invention? Is there much left over from inventing gender, or race, or postethnicity to be spared for the South? The South begins to become a sort of voluntary lifestyle. The new Norton anthology of Southern literature, obviously not anxious to plunge into prescriptive discussions of what is "Southern," asserts that "what makes a southerner in these days, and by implication what would qualify as southern literature in this postmodern era, is less a matter of birth or origin or even lived experience, than of deliberate affiliation, attitude, style, and that elusive quality known today as 'voice.'"[16] And this may be how Southern identity will begin to perish, not with a bang but a whimper, because it has ceased to explain enough, or other discourses have come along which explain the same things differently.

Superficially contrary to this, institutionally, the idea of Southern culture is doing pretty well within the southeastern United States, however isolated the idea may begin to be in the rest of American culture. There are as many periodicals, academic courses and positions, publishers, scholarly organizations, cultural study centers as there ever were, certainly more than there were in 1930, perhaps even more than in 1980. The new prosperity has fattened up the cultural industry of "Southern," which has much to do with the recent visibility of Southern scholars in places like London and Sydney. It takes money to clamber on a plane to Cambridge, Bonn, or Genoa, whether it comes from one's own pocket or that of an obliging dean. It is also easier to clamber on that plane, whether one is leaving or arriving in the South, than it used to be. One no longer has to go through New York. This omission is a fact of fundamental cultural significance and a small sign of a great truth, that the world is beginning to become a traffic of cultural regions less dominated by hegemonic capitals.

It strikes me that what seems to be happening in the northern United States will, in due course, happen to the South's relationship with the non-American world, and for analogous reasons, and that this may be ominous. It helps to begin by asking what modern intellectual Southerners make of "abroad." The short answer is, not much, less than they did fifty years ago, incomparably less than they did 150 years ago. Modern Southerners have concerned themselves with establishing the legitimacy of the South in *American* culture and have wanted to be taken seriously in Boston and New York. This issue has swamped the older question of the cultural connection with Europe, a question which preoccupied many antebellum Southerners and lingered faintly in the writings of the Southern Agrarians. Modern Southerners have been proud of evidence of success, when Allen Tate or John Crowe Ransom won Guggenheim awards, or Robert Penn Warren won Pulitzer Prizes, or C. Vann Woodward went to Yale. The North has mattered and conveyed the summary judgments of belonging or exclusion. At least, it did. That cultural moment, which began when Lee surrendered at Appomattox, may be passing. Multiculturalism says that there are no single places of cultural judgment, there should be no canons. But even if there are, it is plausible to think that the South is as likely to be the judge as the judged.

So modern Southerners have not given much thought to earning the respect of Europe, let alone to commencing a conversation with it. (Interestingly, black Southerners are an exception, if we remember Richard Wright in Paris, but then the black Southern intellectual tradition has habitually been expatriate.) The idea that Europe might, one day, show up in Mississippi and tender its respect or express its interest without anyone asking for it was unexpected and remains puzzling, undigested. Southerners try to fit it into the old debates. Their newsletters boast of cultural exchanges between Ole Miss and Moscow, notice that Robert Johnson matters to Warsaw, but they still, at bottom, believe that no one cares about them, that they are despised, that they are marginal, that they have to fight for a place. In fact, they have had a place for several decades. They are not marginal, but as central as anyone else in a world which mistrusts centrality. The world comes to them, the world is interested in them, thinks there is something to be learned, with all due skepticism at their abundant shortcomings. On the whole, Southerners do not yet believe it.

So the basic tropes of modern Southern culture are centripetal. The centrifugal is regarded as a risk. This is who we are, Southerners say, and there is not much you can do about it, though we suspect you will want to do something. This is our religion, these our political values, this our literature, these our barbecue sauces. Let me tell about the South, a Southerner notoriously wants to insist. This used to be a rhetoric of cultural defensiveness, but often it has modulated into one of display. I once took English friends for an evening with intellectual Southerners, who did a lot of telling about the South as the evening went on. Afterwards, one of the visitors half-apologized for not having said much, adding acutely, "But it did not seem to be necessary." One of the more astute things that Allen Tate ever observed was that "the traditional Southern mode of discourse presupposes somebody at the other end silently listening: it is the rhetorical mode. Its historical rival is the dialectical mode, or the give and take between two minds, even if one mind, like the mind of Socrates, prevails. The Southerner has never been a dialectician."[17] As usual with Tate, this pronouncement is overdrawn; the "never" is historically imprecise and more strictly explains the postbellum mind better than the antebellum. But Tate does point to a common enough habit of expression and thought in the modern South, and the quotation has often been approvingly cited by Southern literary critics, who habitually identify with the speaker and never with the listener, whose only role is to be silent, to witness the display, to laugh or weep in the right places.

The three books sponsored by the Southern Studies Forum, which usefully contain essays by both Southerners and Europeans, express this relationship. On the whole, the Europeans tend to be dialectical, to move between theory and evidence, between the South and Europe, and to favor the comparative analysis, though it is done with very mixed success. The essays by Southerners, on the other hand, are almost completely indifferent to anything drawn from outside American or Southern culture. The rest of the world is an unnoticed silence, at best a listener, perhaps not even that. In 1977 Louis Rubin was commissioned by the United States Information Agency to prepare a series of talks to be given over the Voice of America which might explain the South to the world. (I presume this was intended to please the new President from Georgia.) In this, too, the world to which the talks are addressed is silent, is almost nowhere mentioned, is not taken account of.[18] Almost all the books which situate the South in a comparative framework—George Fredrickson's *White Supremacy*, Peter Kolchin's *Unfree Labor*—are not written by Southerners.[19] An inarticulate division of labor has developed; outsiders look after the place of the South in the modern world, while Southerners look after the South itself. But the two writings sit next to each other more often than they converse. This is not promising for a sustained relationship. Listeners have a way of drifting off to other tale-tellers once the tale is done and however good a story it is. Or they migrate to people who license the listener to be a talker listened to.

The explanation for this phenomenon is not clear. Part of it, no doubt, is a characteristic American introspection, the intellectual equivalent of the fact that in most American towns it is difficult to get foreign exchange and that 93 percent of Americans (or so I am informed by an advertisement now running in the British press) have no passport. Yet it would be hard to convict most American scholarship, in recent years, of being indifferent to external intellectual influences. Perhaps one might read this indifference as Southern self-confidence. One might say that Southerners know that they have a good act, and actors do not need to know precisely who is in the third row as long as the seats are full. Or one could posit the opposite theory that Southerners lack intellectual confidence. That, no doubt, is the explanation which would occur to most Northerners, but I doubt its cogency. There are Southerners who are comfortable with abstruse critical theory. Patricia Yaeger has likely forgotten more French theory than most French intellectuals have ever known, and Anne Goodwyn Jones is to publish a book called *Theory and the Good Old Boys*, in which she will stand for theory.[20] But most would testify that such an interest is regarded, by the majority of those who study the South, as somehow against the grain, as an un-Southern cultural activity. Put more epigrammatically, there is a marked tendency to think that the South and the abstract are intrinsically opposed. This, indeed, was the distinguishing claim and boast of a whole generation of Southern literary critics. We are particular, they are abstract.

It was never a very accurate description of the complicated texture of Southern thought and sensibility, which has been abstract as often as it has been particularist.

It is a nice point, whether cultures need to interact with other cultures to remain healthy. The French do not seem to think so, but the French have had interaction forced upon them and occasionally, as with Jules Michelet being influenced by German thought and by Giambattista Vico, have sought it out. It is my impression that Southern thought has been most innovative when most in dialogue with external ideas. James Madison reading Hume, Mary Chesnut reading Thackeray, Allen Tate reading Eliot, all these were Southern thinkers who used ideas from elsewhere, mated them with indigenous experience and concepts, and came up with something vital, in ways which transcended the merely neocolonial. It is also my impression that recent Southerners have lost the knack of this: the impressive growth of their indigenous cultural institutions has allowed their minds to wander from the usefulness of these dialogues because they have been less wanderers and scavengers on the landscape of ideas, and have become hosts, though often reluctant hosts. It is, for example, one of the more worrying aspects of recent history that there has been a quiet cultural warfare in Southern universities between native Southerners and the many more non-Southerners who have come to teach. Sometimes it has been not so quiet, but it has mostly been experienced more than articulated. The fault, no doubt, has been on both sides: Southern xenophobia and Northern condescension. Troublingly, there has developed a feeling among many Southerners, especially men, that the interests and theoretical preoccupations of the newcomers are somehow intrinsically hostile to the survival of the South, that a wall has to be built, and that the first bricks are laid by Southerners refusing to engage these ideas. This is a cultural error of the utmost significance. For good or ill, these are the discourses of modern thought, and if the South is to survive as a culture which matters, to the rest of the United States and elsewhere, it needs to make a place for itself within them. It does not have to swallow them whole. Indeed I am inclined to think that the South is one of the better places from which to articulate a courteous critique, and as good a place as any to fashion different understandings. But it has to join the conversation if it wishes to do more than declaim to an emptying auditorium. For the world is an opportunity which may assist in the survival of Southern identity, but only if Southerners gain in confidence, curiosity, and the willingness dialectically to listen and talk.

NOTES

1. Valeria Gennaro Lerda and Tjebbe Westendorp, eds., *The United States South: Regionalism and Identity*, Biblioteca di Cultura, no. 418 (Rome: Bulzoni Editore, 1991); Lothar Hönnighausen and Valeria Gennaro Lerda, eds., *Rewriting the South: History and Fiction*, Transatlantic Perspectives, no. 3 (Tübingen: Francke Verlag, 1993); Tony Badger, Walter Edgar, and Jan Norby Gretlund, eds., *Southern Landscapes*, Transatlantic Perspectives, no. 7 (Tübingen: Stauffenberg-Verlag, 1996).

2. "The Irony of Southern History," in Woodward, *The Burden of Southern History*, 197–211.

3. Henry James, *The American Scene*, ed. Leon Edel (1907; Bloomington: Indiana University Press, 1986), 403.

4. Arthur de Gobineau, *The Moral and Intellectual Diversity of the Races*, ed. and trans. Henry Hotz, appendix by Josiah C. Nott (Philadelphia, PA: J. B. Lippincott, 1856).

5. Michael Denis Biddiss, *Father of Racist Ideology: The Social and Political Thought of Count Gobineau* (New York: Weybright and Talley, 1970), 147.

6. See Mike Sewell, "British Responses to Martin Luther King, Jr and the Civil Rights Movement, 1954–68," in *The Making of Martin Luther King and the Civil Rights Movement*, ed. Brian Ward and Tony Badger (Basingstoke: Macmillan, 1996), 194–212.

7. Brian Ward, "Elvis, Martin, and Mentors: The Making of Southern History in Britain," *Southern Cultures* 4 (Winter 1998): 50–71, portrays a very different British moment. Mine was much closer to the prewar world portrayed in Richard Hoggart, *A Local Habitation: Life and Times, Volume 1, 1918–40* (London: Chatto & Windus, 1988).

8. Or so Richard Gray convincingly suggests in "Edgar Allan Poe and the Problem of Regionalism," in Lerda and Westendorp, *United States South*, 75–92.

9. Louis Hartz, *The Liberal Tradition in America* (New York: Harcourt, Brace, and World, 1955).

10. C. Vann Woodward, *The Old World's New World* (New York: Oxford University Press, 1991). It is right to observe, however, that Woodward has encouraged the writing of comparative history; see C. Vann Woodward, ed., *The Comparative Approach to American History* (New York: Basic Books, 1968).

11. Eric Hobsbawm and Terence Ranger, eds., *The Invention of Tradition* (Cambridge: Cambridge University Press, 1983); Larry Wolff, *Inventing Eastern Europe: The Map of Civilization on the Mind of the Enlightenment* (Stanford, CA: Stanford University Press, 1994); Mikuláš Teich and Roy Porter, eds., *The National Question in Europe in Historical Context* (Cambridge: Cambridge University Press, 1993).

12. I draw here upon my review of Peter Applebome, *Dixie Rising: How the South is Shaping American Values, Politics, and Culture* (New York: Times Books, 1996) in the *Times Literary Supplement* (16 June 1997): 14.

13. William J. Cooper, Jr., and Thomas E. Terrill, *The American South: A History*, 2nd ed. (Boston, MA: McGraw-Hill, 1996), 659.

14. Woodrow Wilson to Richard Heath Dabney, 7 November 1886, quoted in Peter Novick, *That Noble Dream: The "Objectivity Question" and the American Historical Profession* (Cambridge: Cambridge University Press, 1988), 78.

15. Michael Kreyling, "The Fathers: A Postsouthern Narrative Reading," in Jefferson Humphries, ed., *Southern Literature and Literary Theory* (Athens: University of Georgia Press, 1990), 186–205; "The Closure of History in a Postsouthern America," in Simpson, *Brazen Face*, 255–76.

16. Andrews et al., *Literature of the American South*, xvi.

17. "A Southern Mode of the Imagination," (1959) in Allen Tate, *Essays of Four Decades* (1959; New York: William Morrow, 1970), 583.

18. Louis D. Rubin, Jr., *The American South: Portrait of a Culture* (Baton Rouge: Louisiana State University Press, 1980). I am conscious that this assertion may be too sweeping and speaks only to

an emphasis; James Cobb, for example, has taken an interest in modernization theory; see James C. Cobb, *The Most Southern Place on Earth: The Mississippi Delta and the Roots of Regional Identity* (New York: Oxford University Press, 1992).

19. George M. Fredrickson, *White Supremacy: A Comparative Study of American and South African History* (New York: Oxford University Press, 1981); Peter Kolchin, *Unfree Labor: American Slavery and Russian Serfdom* (Cambridge, MA: Harvard University Press, Belknap, 1987).

20. Patricia S. Yaeger, *Honey-Mad Women: Emancipatory Strategies in Women's Writing* (New York: Columbia University Press, 1988); Patricia Yaeger, ed., *The Geography of Identity* (Ann Arbor: University of Michigan Press, 1996).

BRITAIN AND THE SOUTH

First published as "Afterword: On the Irrelevance of Knights," in Joseph P. Ward, ed., *Britain and the American South: From Colonialism to Rock and Roll* (Jackson: University Press of Mississippi, 2003), 215–27; it was originally given as concluding remarks to the 26th Annual Porter L. Fortune, Jr., History Symposium at the University of Mississippi in October 2001.

If the originating symposium for this book had been held about a hundred years ago in Oxford, Mississippi, it would have looked very different. Almost certainly, it would have been a celebration of Anglo-Saxon unity. There would have been much talk of civilization and German forests, the white man's burden, England's green and pleasant land, Southern manners and hospitality, and the inestimable gift of the English language. Perhaps there might have been a concert, where they would have played Edward Elgar's *Land of Hope and Glory*, which had recently been written. Perhaps LeRoy Percy might have come over from Greenville, reminisced about Harry Hotspur, and quoted Shakespeare about summoning spirits from the vasty deep. Perhaps there might have been talk of a shared democracy, though (considering the recent disfranchisement movement in Mississippi) perhaps not. The talismanic meaning of there being an Oxford, both here and there, would almost inevitably have been invoked.

Whatever one might think of that vision—and it is hard to think well of it—it would have had an intellectual coherence, a unity of myth, a rationale. All that has gone now. For now there are no Anglo-Saxons, there or here, save in the imagination of a few French intellectuals and politicians. This being so, what gives coherence to the topic of Britain and the American South in 2003, instead of 1903?

First a caveat, to do with the matter of Britain. Almost everyone is familiar with the difficulty of the term, *the South*. Many a Porter Fortune Symposium has gotten itself into a knot over what, if anything, that phrase means. But the instability of the phrase, *Britain*, is also pertinent. For, at best, *Britain* is a geographical expression, the name of an island. There is also something wider called *Great Britain*, which is an archipelago or collection of islands. At different times, on those islands, there have been various polities—Wessex, Mercia, Fife, England, Wales, Scotland, Ireland, the Isle of Man, Sark, Northern Ireland, the Irish Free State, Eire—which have fluctuated in their relationships, have come and gone, and interacted asymmetrically.[1] At best, of late, there has been something which (excluding Eire) can be regarded as a federal structure, a unity of kingdoms as the United States is a unity of republics, though the United Kingdom is a federation of dazzling illogicality, of almost Austro-Hungarian confusion. This illogicality has deepened in recent years, with the advent of the European Union above the nation-state (if that is what the United Kingdom is), the coming of Scottish and Welsh devolution below or beside it, and the regular appearing and disappearing of Northern Ireland as a polity. The result is that the British have little idea of who they are and are getting more confused by the year.

An anecdote illustrates the point. Some years ago, in the early 1990s, I acquired American citizenship. I was then living in Ohio. The U.S. Congress had begun to be unpleasant towards resident aliens, so my immigration lawyer advised that having dual citizenship would offer more safety. So off I trotted to the federal courthouse in Cincinnati, there to be sworn in by a judge, who explained the meaning of the American republic with much inaccuracy. That was not unexpected. But a strange scene was enacted. The Clerk of the Court required of the immigrants, seated in rows on hard benches, that when she called out our names, we should each stand up, repeat our names, state our country of origin, and then sit down. I happened to be about the second or third person to be called. I had to decide quickly what was my country of origin. This was not self-evident. I decided that, legally, I was from the United Kingdom. I had a fleeting memory that, on the Security Council in the United Nations, that was the name on the little plaque in front of the British ambassador. So I stood up, said my name, announced "the United Kingdom," and resumed my seat. I suppose I should have said "the United Kingdom of Great Britain and Northern Ireland," which has been the country's official name since 1927, but that would have been pedantic, even for a historian. Others followed, but very rapidly (because it seemed redundant) they stopped repeating their names, so they only stood up and said their countries. Nigeria, India, Cambodia, Nicaragua, and so forth, were shouted out in a roll call of allegiances foresworn. But I noticed that those from the British Isles were indecisive. A few said "England." Someone agreed with me on the "United Kingdom." Somebody said "Britain." A defiant old lady said "Great Britain," with an emphasis which betokened a want of enthusiasm for her new passport. No one, I noticed, said Scotland or Wales, but that may have been a fluke, that no one came from there, or it is possible that "Britain" is what you say at such an event, if you are not English. Someone from Ulster would have been much vexed to know what to say and, I suppose, their response might have depended on their religion—"Britain" for the Protestant, "Ireland" for the Catholic. My own decision was, after all, arbitrary. Where you think you come from need not be a legal matter. Legally, there is nowhere called the South, though many imagine it to be a place they come from.

I mention this story because these scholarly essays are, because of this historical complexity, necessarily wavering in what they understand to be contrapuntal to the South. The colonialists speak almost exclusively of England. Anglicization is Max Edelson's topic, the Church of England that of Franklin Lambert, the transmission of English concepts of property and power that of Holly Brewer. Almost nowhere does one find discussion of the Scots, the Welsh, and the Irish. Perhaps the omission of the Welsh is not an immense loss, for they came in very small numbers, but one of those Welsh families was called Jefferson, so their influence was not insignificant. (One might read the *Summary View of the of the Rights of British America* as a very Welsh document.) But the Irish and the Scots are another matter. One could, quite easily, have put together parallel books on the Southern connection to Scotland and to Ireland, with papers on Presbyterianism, Scottish philosophy, Irish laborers, Adam Smith and classical economics, the North-South divide in British culture, and the ideology of Unionism.

The later essays in this volume, logically, tend to be more acquainted with the construct of Britain and draw their evidence from more than England. Even so, Marcus Wood gives us an essay on English print satire, not Scottish. Richard Blackett talks at length about Liverpool, but seems here to have little interest in Glasgow, Cork, or Cardiff, though they, too, had opinions about the Confederacy and were all, in 1863, British places.[2] (Though it is worth conceding that Liverpool was more than a place where only the English lived.) Hugh Wilford does, perhaps, best in escaping the English hegemony, because he is peculiarly interested in the Labour Party, which had great strength in the "Celtic fringe," so Welsh and Scottish names occur in his discussion: Aneurin Bevan, a Miners Gala in Cardiff and so on, pop up. And Brian Ward knows what Scottish schoolchildren thought of Elvis Presley and knows that Lonnie Donegan came from Glasgow.

I mention this matter, not much to observe a lacuna, but mostly to indicate that both the South and Britain have been moving targets, not fixed points, each a mix of cultures much in flux. As a result, the Southern/British connections one might identify have come and gone, and changed in their nature. For example, since there was no "South" before the nineteenth century, in any meaningful sense, Edelson, Lambert, and Brewer rightly and inescapably deal with South Carolina and Virginia, not with the wider South. That they relate these colonies, at least after the Act of Union in 1707, to England and not Britain may be less inescapable. But the case made by Linda Colley that the eighteenth century made a British nation needs to be regarded with much skepticism.[3] Yet even the matter of England is not straightforward. Jamestown, 1607, and all that do not stand now, as they did in 1903. The old narrative of American history saw English culture as foundational, as making the presumptions which survived and civilized the infusion of other immigrant cultures, which is why many years ago American history departments always had an English medieval historian and a Tudor-Stuart historian, people who had read Frederic Maitland and knew about the Rough Wooing. Arthur M. Schlesinger, Jr., seems still to believe this story, but he is now in a hopeless minority among historians, if less so among the general public.[4] As a number of the essays, especially that of Kathryn Braund, indicate, colonial culture is not now understood as an inception, but as a convergence. The South, to use the anachronistic term, was in 1650 or 1750 a space into which (from different directions) many differing cultures—Indian, Spanish, French, English, Dutch, African—had moved and a space wherein they struggled for power, interacted, and changed one another. To be sure, those of English origin and descent gained the greatest social power, but it was shared with other Europeans (Germans, Sephardic Jews, Huguenots, Scots, Scotch-Irish).

Further, it is not always clear what one might usefully understand as English, when one considers how disparate in the seventeenth century was custom, law, language, and economic behavior in places so different as East Anglia, London, Yorkshire, or Cornwall.[5] What is more clear, especially from the Edelson and Lambert essays, is that the invention of Englishness was, in part and often unsuccessfully, a venture of the colonial mind.[6] This accords with recent developments in British historiography, which has grown very interested in how the imperial experience dialectically formed metropolitan understandings.[7] It will be pertinent to add that the invention of Englishness was in the nineteenth century also to be a venture of the Southern postcolonial mind, one of the ways by which Southerners came to configure what they imagined they had been, as a predicate to understanding what they had become and might yet be.

Let me try to suggest a chronology, though scarcely a framework, for the cultural understandings implicated in the Southern/British equation. I discern four phases: the colonial period from 1607 to 1776; that from 1776 to the early 1840s; that from the early 1840s to the end of the Second World War; then, lastly, the late twentieth century. But, before sketching these, it will be important to reiterate—the theme appears in many of these essays—that often Britain and the South have had little to do with one another and, when they have, have usually demonstrated remarkable ignorance and obtuseness about the other. Both are large and complicated cultures, with many preoccupations and interests, with many other exogenous cultures to address, at those moments when the outward gaze was required. So much has been oblique.

One might think, with some justice, that this obtuseness was less evident in the earliest period, when the colonies were crowded with migrants from the British Isles, but even then the metropolis seems to have been vague about what they did in Virginia, where it was, and whether it mattered. Holly Brewer's essay, though it plausibly argues for a continuity with late medieval and early modern English legal culture and reasoning, suggests that Virginia had much independence and discretion, that continuity should be understood as an invention, as well as a fate. Still, it is very clear that, up to the 1770s, the Southern/British connection was powerful and significant, though more so for the settlers, less for the metropolitan British. For the next seventy years or so, that connection palpably weakened. The South is more remarkable for Anglophobia than Anglophilia in the late eighteenth and early nineteenth centuries. Aside from the political struggle, the little matter of British troops burning the White House and the Battle of New Orleans, the growing British patronage of the antislavery movement drove a great wedge between the two cultures, as Richard Blackett shows. Marcus Wood, too, gives compelling evidence for this mutual dislike and, indeed, his essay makes much intelligible in the British response to the South even in the twentieth century, when the idea of the lazy, ignorant, violent, and cruel Southerner persists, even unto the days of Jerry Lee Lewis.

But, even if earlier the British had not placed themselves in the forefront of the antislavery movement and there had been harmony between Britain and the South over slavery, I suspect that Anglophobia would have been powerful, anyway. The independent South was in a postcolonial phase and very anxious to fashion its cultural meaning out of local materials, but also to look beyond Britain to other cultural influences—the North, France, Germany, Italy, and elsewhere. John Randolph, who was a fierce Anglophile, was very much an oddity in the 1820s and 1830s. Very few Southern intellectuals and political leaders spent much time in Britain in the early decades of the nineteenth century. A partial exception to this, however, needs to be noted. Scottish culture, in both its Enlightenment and Romantic incarnations—Adam Smith, Thomas Reid, Walter Scott—remained attractive for Southerners, but this was only a confirmation of Anglophobia, for the Scots offered the precedent of a provincial society which, by commerce and intellect, had made a powerful society which compelled respect, and (as a not incidental bonus) one which was antipathetic to the English.

This Anglophobia began to change in about the 1840s, though partially. Slavery remained a deep irritant, of course. But the Webster-Ashburton Treaty of 1842 removed Britain as a political and military competitor in the Southern part of North America and the South, perhaps the most aggressively imperialist part of the United States, took advantage of the opportunities thus licensed.

Though even after 1783 British writers had never ceased to be popular, because they offered nostalgia for a vanished order (reading Laurence Sterne) or provided guides to new ideas (reading the *Edinburgh Review*), the newer crop were read with closer sympathy. This change was subtle, but palpable. Thackeray, Dickens, Tennyson, Carlyle, all the mid-Victorians, evoked a sympathetic response in Southerners like John Pendleton Kennedy, John R. Thompson, and William Henry Trescot. Thackeray came and admired the South (then caroused with Trescot at the Café de Paris), Kennedy went to London and corresponded with Macaulay, Thompson visited Carlyle in Cheyne Row, Josiah Nott became an Honorary Fellow of the Anthropological Society of London.[8] These people liked each other, took one another to gentleman's clubs, were capital fellows together. The world was being made that eventually produced Woodrow Wilson, the Southerner who was a Gladstonian, and Walter Hines Page, the North Carolinian who became Ambassador to the Court of Saint James and insisted that the United States and Britain should stand together as English-speaking bulwarks against the ravages of Teutonic evil.[9]

Imperialism and race were at the center of the transformation. Both Britain and the South had by 1850 accepted a sense of themselves as imperial and racialist cultures. This was a contested matter in both places, but the British who eventually proclaimed their Queen as Empress of India and the Southerners who planted the American flag on the ramparts of Mexico City knew with clarity that they had an expansionist mission, which involved remaking the world in their image. They also knew that this process involved subjugating and exploiting assorted alien peoples. Slavery was, before the Civil War, a difficulty in retarding a sense of comity, but one that many in the British and Southern intelligentsias were doing their best, even before 1860, to diminish. The proslavery argument had arrived at the point, by the mid-1850s, of seeing slavery as only an incidental variant on systems of labor and racial control, and writers like Carlyle were speaking freely of the "nigger question." With emancipation, there was little to inhibit a rampant sense of comity.

Here one must note the pertinence of a development within the South. By far the most important inhibitor of the Anglo-Saxon myth before 1865 was the very heterogeneity of the Southern population. Huguenots, Jews, Scots, Acadians, Scotch-Irish, Germans—let alone African Americans and Native Americans—had no particular reason to embrace the idea that the South was an Anglo-Saxon culture; they were more remarkable in 1830 for cultivating their own ethnic and racial identities. But, by the end of the nineteenth century, the secular trends of cultural assimilation, especially high levels of intermarriage, when combined with the wrenching experiences of the Civil War and Reconstruction, and then the racial bonding impelled by the formalization of segregation, made Southern identity itself more central to those who lived in the southeastern United States. Being Southern had been far less important before 1860, but after 1865 it became imperative to find a historical grounding for the idea of a unitary Southern culture. Of the various available myths, the English one was most available. A significant nuance here is that the Civil War was to give Virginia an especial cultural authority in the postwar era and, even before 1860, for obvious reasons the Virginians had been more susceptible to the English myth. Hence, after 1880 or so, the narrative from Jamestown was freshly pertinent. So eventually we get that dreadful pageant about the lost colony of Roanoke, so eventually Mr. Rockefeller thought it important that Williamsburg be remade, so Virginian heiresses started showing up in London to marry lords, who were very glad to be so married and began to think well of the College of William and Mary, as they made their way to the bank. If one wished to write a history of this phase, one would go from Thomas Carlyle to Winston Churchill, from John Pendleton Kennedy to John Crowe Ransom. In this story, T. S. Eliot and Allen Tate would need to feature largely, and figures like Lady Astor.

The era since 1945 has been very different, largely because Britain began to enter a post-imperial phase. The South, of course, did not and has still not entered such a phase. The United States has waxed as a great imperial power—indeed, the greatest of such powers—and Southerners, as politicians and cultural agents, as Lyndon Johnson and Elvis Presley, have been immensely significant in that process. Hence an asymmetry has developed, which is worth exploring briefly, for Southern interest in Britain has lessened, while British interest in the South has grown.

It is my impression that, even now, some Southerners have retained a sanitized version of the Anglo-Saxon myth. Certainly, in the last thirty-odd years of traveling in the South, I have frequently encountered a puzzlingly warm Anglophilia, though it seems to be a upper-middle-class phenomenon, issuing from people who collect antiques and remember Mrs. Miniver. I have not encountered it much in diners and gas stations, though often in Charlestonian drawing rooms. But this Anglophilia, as elsewhere in American culture, has been steadily receding. Certainly, I have never found it wise, when around Southerners, to presume any particular knowledge of British literature or politics, which (if I had lived in 1850 or 1940) I might once safely have assumed. This is not to say I have not encountered such knowledge, but the modern dynamics of Southern society no longer naturally produce it. There is no particular reason, any more, why it should, other than the accessibility offered by a shared language. But English, of course, is no longer just a possession of what Churchill called the English-speaking peoples.

On the other hand, as Brian Ward and Hugh Wilford help us to see, British interest in the South is greater than it was, certainly in academic circles, but in popular culture, too. Though this phenomenon has nuances peculiar to Britain, I would see this as a local variant on the widespread influence of American culture in the modern world. We could look at German or Hindi or Australian culture and see similar patterns, see country-and-western singers and jazz musicians and rock musicians in Hamburg, New Delhi, and Sydney, see bemused academics in Tokyo and Cairo trying to grapple with Faulkner's prose. It is possible that the British are a touch more aware of the distinction between Southerners and other Americans than are some other cultures—the French may be more aware, though—but I have had enough experiences in Britain to make me doubtful even of that. So it is symptomatic that, in this book, the earlier essays tend to be concerned with what the South thought of Britain, but the later essays deal with what Britain thinks of the South; cultural authority first moved from east to west, but now often runs from west to east.

In this recent phase, race has remained central, though differently. Race used to be an idea propounded in Britain, but mostly an experience elsewhere. Gravely complacent men in London institutions once drew up charts of human evolution, in which it was explained how Leamington Spa and Tunbridge Wells were superior to Kandahar and Lagos, yet those men had little occasion at home to encounter an Afghan or a Nigerian. But the eventual harvest of Empire brought many "non-white" peoples to Britain— Jamaicans and Kenyans, Pakistanis and Chinese—and Britain is now, though less so than the United States, a multicultural society. Notting Hill riots and Notting Hill festivals have changed understandings. To comprehend these fresh realities, some Britons have grown interested in the Southern experience, in slavery, segregation, and civil rights, in William Faulkner and Louis Armstrong. But it will be important to stress that this is part of a wider interest, in African history, in the Indian experience, and in diasporas. There has been a widespread sense that the indigenous intellectual and aesthetic traditions of British culture do not help much in the endeavor of understanding race. Jane Austen is no longer enough. Even *Othello* is not enough.

But now a different sort of Briton is involved in this dialogue. This is no longer just a conversation among white people. In truth, it never was, though the whites seldom noticed. Olaudah Equiano, Frederick Douglass, William Wells Brown, and Alexander Crummell, all once had significant British experiences. Equiano passed from southern Nigeria to the West Indies and Virginia, but ended up as a Methodist married to an Englishwoman and living in London. Douglass went from a Maryland plantation to refuge in the North, but his visits to Britain famously provided him with a comparative perspective on American racism. Brown went from slavery in Kentucky and Missouri to Canada and, eventually, to writing travel accounts of Britain. Crummell, a Northern free black, studied at the University of Cambridge, before becoming an Episcopalian missionary in Liberia and a minister back in the United States, where he wrote extensively on Southern society.[10]

It is an incident in the life of Crummell which catches the ambivalence of Victorian Britain about race, the confused impulses which led many to oppose the Confederacy and many to support it. A story of Crummell's graduation at Cambridge in 1853 is told in A. C. Benson's life of his father. It begins, "On a certain Degree day in 1850 or thereabouts, a West African undergraduate named Crummell, of Queens', a man of colour, appeared in the Senate House to take his degree." No doubt, it is symptomatic that an English clergyman—Benson himself was relaying an anecdote furnished by Rev. J. Bowman of New Southgate—would presume that a black attendant at Cambridge would come from Africa, not from the United States. It continues, "A boisterous individual in the gallery called out 'Three groans for the Queens' nigger.'" Here Victorian racism is palpable. But, "A pale slim undergraduate, very youthful-looking, in the front of the gallery... became scarlet with indignation, and shouted in a voice which re-echoed through the building, 'Shame, shame! Three groans for you, Sir!' and immediately afterwards, 'Three cheers for Crummell!' This was taken up in all directions... and the original offender had to stoop down to hide himself from the storm of groans and hisses that broke out all around him." The defender was E. W. Benson of Trinity College, who went on to become Archbishop of Canterbury.[11] The message of the story is complacent, but it is doubtful that these cheers for Alexander Crummell signaled a transcendence of racism, merely that an English gentleman should not stoop to cheap insults of even inferiors. The young men of Cambridge, who went forth from the Senate House in 1853 to quash the Indian Mutiny and to govern their Empire, were not remarkable for advancing racial equality.

The triangulation of Africa, the Americas, and western Europe goes to the heart of the Southern/British equation. It was the British attitude towards and experience of Africa (and Asia beyond) which predicated much in their understanding of the South. The British saw in the South a caricature of what they feared they themselves might be in South Africa and elsewhere, or an affirmation of what they felt they needed to be to sustain their mastery, or a complacent reassurance that a British empire was a more moral thing than a Southern one. Concomitantly, the white Southern experience of African Americans structured much in how the former envisioned a pertinence for the British experience. For white Southerners, Britain became a sort of historical touchstone. To claim the title of Anglo-Saxon in 1890 was to assert that slavery had made no difference, that there was nothing in being Southern which needed an explanation drawn from the longstanding presence of adjacent Africans. In that sense, the British idea for Southerners served the great purpose of self-denial.

Many people have worked to efface that self-denial. Not insignificant, of late, has been the distinguished body of writing by those from the Caribbean and Africa, who are resident in Britain as migrants or the children of migrants, for whom the South has sometimes provided a point of reference, if one enfolded in the wider pattern of the black, brown, and beige Atlantic. I am thinking of Paul Gilroy, of course, but also figures like V. S. Naipaul, Caryl Phillips, and, in an earlier generation, the great C. L. R. James. One of the youngest of these is Gary Younge, a journalist for the *Guardian* in London, who in 1999 published a book called *No Place Like Home: A Black Briton's Journey Through the American South*.[12] Richard Blackett himself—born in

Trinidad, educated in Manchester, living in Nashville—can partly be seen as contributing to this tradition.

Here the asymmetry between British perceptions of the South and Southern perceptions of Britain is most marked. On the whole, in recent times, elite Southerners have drawn from Britain an image of conservative hierarchy, but have not often been nourished by the radical side of British society. As Ransom put it in 1930, "England was . . . the model employed by the South, in so far as Southern culture was not quite indigenous. And there is in the South even today an Anglophile sentiment quite anomalous in the American scene. . . . The customs and institutions of England seem to the American observer very fixed and ancient."[13] This sympathy, of course, marked a change from those expressed by many Southerners in the eighteenth and early nineteenth centuries, when the Commonwealth republican tradition of James Harrington and Algernon Sidney had been resonant in places like Virginia and South Carolina. To be sure, there have been a few modern instances of Southerners turning a little to the left by having learned something from Britain. Rupert Vance was influenced by Patrick Geddes, who was among the founders of British sociology and urban planning; the Highlander Folk School and Black Mountain College were nourished by the British workers' education movement (and the Scandinavian); and the musicological researches of John Lomax were much impelled by the antecedent work of British students of "folk music."[14] Still, the mainstream has been more conservative. Today at golf tournaments on Hilton Head Island, they play the bagpipes, but not many people are interested in Scottish socialism. The British, on the other hand, after their imperial phase, have mostly turned to the dissident elements in Southern culture, to jazz, the blues, rock music, and radical political activism. The University of Newcastle takes a singular pride in having awarded an honorary degree to Martin Luther King, Jr., in 1967. Oddly, then, the South may have done much to make Britain a more eclectic, even humane place, but I doubt that British influence on the South has been so salutary.

Since this is 2003 and not 1903, LeRoy Percy cannot speak his piece and rebuke the observations above. Instead he lies in his grave in Greenville, and over him broods the bronze statue of an English knight, leaning on his broadsword and encased in chain mail and armor. Upon the tomb are written words from Matthew Arnold's poem "The Last Word," which speaks of battle, loss, and honorable death. To Leroy's son, William Alexander Percy, who commissioned the statue and the tomb in the early 1930s, the chivalric and English iconography seemed apposite, even moving.[15] It would be pleasant to reflect that, today, the imagery has become irrelevant. It would be still more agreeable to imagine a time when a Southern tomb might be guarded by the statue of a Tolpuddle Martyr. But that seems an improbability.

NOTES

1. On these matters, Alexander Grant and Keith J. Stringer, eds., *Uniting the Kingdom? The Making of British History* (London: Routledge, 1995) is helpful.
2. In his book on the Britain and the Civil War, however, Blackett is very attentive to these matters. See R. J. M. Blackett, *Divided Hearts: Britain and the American Civil War* (Baton Rouge: Louisiana State University Press, 2001).
3. Linda Colley, *Britons: Forging a Nation, 1707–1837* (New Haven, CT: Yale University Press, 1992).
4. See Arthur M. Schlesinger, Jr., *The Disuniting of America: Reflections on a Multicultural Society* (New York: W. W. Norton, 1992).
5. Pertinent is Keith Wrightson, *English Society, 1580–1680* (London: Unwin Hyman, 1982).
6. This would seem to support the suggestion of Anderson that nationalism was a venture of Creole culture: see Benedict Anderson, *Imagined Communities: Reflections on the Origin and Spread of Nationalism*, revised and enlarged ed. (1983; London: Verso, 1991).
7. On literary culture, see Alan Richardson and Sonia Hofkosh, eds., *Romanticism, Race, and Imperial Culture, 1780–1834* (Bloomington: Indiana University Press, 1996). More broadly, the two relevant volumes of the *Oxford History of the British Empire* are pertinent: P. J. Marshall, ed., Alaine Low, asst. ed, *The Oxford History of the British Empire: Volume II: The Eighteenth Century* (Oxford: Oxford University Press, 1998); and Andrew Porter, ed., Alaine Low, asst. ed, *The Oxford History of the British Empire: Volume III: The Nineteenth Century* (Oxford: Oxford University Press, 1999).
8. On Thackeray, see James Grant Wilson, *Thackeray in the United States, 1852–3, 1855–6: Including a Record of a Variety of Thackerayana*, 2 vols. (1904; New York: Haskell House, 1970), 1: 128, 278–96, 347–48; on Trescot, see William Henry Trescot to William Porcher Miles, 4 December 1853, William Porcher Miles Papers, Southern Historical Collection, University of North Carolina, Chapel Hill; on Thompson, entry for 4 October 1864, John R. Thompson Diary, Thompson Papers, Alderman Library, University of Virginia, Charlottesville; on Kennedy, entries during March and April 1856, John Pendleton Kennedy Journal, and Thomas Babington Macaulay to John Pendleton Kennedy. 23 February 1856, both in Kennedy Papers, Peabody Library, Baltimore; on Nott, see the list of fellows of the Society appended to its edition of Johann Friedrich Blumenbach, *The Anthropological Treatises of Johann Friedrich Blumenbach*, ed. Thomas Bendyshe (London: Longman, Green, Longman, Roberts, & Green, 1865).
9. On Wilson's Anglophilia, see John A. Thompson, *Woodrow Wilson* (London: Longman, 2002), 15–42; on Page, Burton J. Hendrick, *The Life and Letters of Walter H. Page*, 3 vols. (London: William Heinemann, 1923).
10. Olaudah Equiano, *The Interesting Narrative and Other Writings*, ed. and introd. by Vincent Carretta (New York: Penguin, 1995); Alan J. Rice and Martin Crawford, eds., *Liberating Sojourn: Frederick Douglass & Transatlantic Reform* (Athens: University of Georgia Press, 1999); Paul Jefferson, ed., *The Travels of William Wells Brown* (New York: Markus Wiener Publishing, 1991); Wilson Jeremiah Moses, *Alexander Crummell: A Study of Civilization and Discontent* (New York: Oxford University Press, 1989); J. R. Oldfield, ed., *Civilization and Black Progress: Selected Writings*

of Alexander Crummell on the South, Southern Texts Society (Charlottesville: University Press of Virginia, 1995).

11. Arthur Christopher Benson, *The Life of Edward White Benson, Sometime Archbishop of Canterbury*, new edition, abridged (London: Macmillan, 1901), 43–44.

12. See Paul Gilroy, *The Black Atlantic: Modernity and Double Consciousness* (London: Verso, 1993), but especially Paul Gilroy, *Small Acts: Thoughts on the Politics of Black Cultures* (London: Serpent's Tail, 1993); V. S. Naipaul, *A Turn in the South* (New York: Alfred A. Knopf, 1989); Caryl Phillips, *The Final Passage* (London: Faber, 1985), a novel of Caribbean migration to Britain, and Caryl Phillips, *Cambridge* (London: Bloomsbury, 1991), another on English involvement in Caribbean slavery; C. L. R. James, *American Civilization*, ed. Anna Grimshaw and Keith Hart (Oxford: Blackwell, 1993); Gary Younge, *No Place Like Home: A Black Briton's Journey Through the American South* (London: Picador, 1999).

13. John Crowe Ransom, "Reconstructed but Unregenerate," in *Twelve Southerners, I'll Take My Stand: The South and the Agrarian Tradition* (1930; Baton Rouge: Louisiana State University Press, 1977), 3–4.

14. John Shelton Reed and Daniel Joseph Singal, eds., *Regionalism and the South: Selected Papers of Rupert Vance* (Chapel Hill: University of North Carolina Press, 1982), 44, 46, 313, 318; Martin Duberman, *Black Mountain: An Exploration in Community* (Garden City, NY: Anchor Books, 1973); Henry D. Shapiro, *Appalachia on Our Mind: The Southern Mountains and the Mountaineers in the American Consciousness, 1870–1920* (Chapel Hill: University of North Carolina Press, 1978), 231–43; John Lomax, *Adventures of a Ballad Hunter* (New York: Macmillan, 1947).

15. Bertram Wyatt-Brown, *The House of Percy: Honor, Melancholy, and Imagination in a Southern Family* (New York: Oxford University Press, 1994), 3–5.

IDEOLOGIES

A review of David Hackett Fischer, *Liberty and Freedom: A Visual History of America's Founding Ideas* (New York: Oxford University Press, 2004), in the *Times Literary Supplement* (May 27, 2005): 5–6.

Alexis de Tocqueville once observed that, in the United States, liberty and freedom were *habitudes du coeur*. True to this, David Hackett Fischer believes that understanding American democracy will be incomplete if confined to written texts, because, though the *Federalist Papers* and the Gettysburg Address were consequential, most Americans learned these heartfelt habits by other means. Fischer illustrates this contention by an anecdote about Captain Preston, an aged veteran of the battle at Concord and Lexington who was interviewed in 1843 by a young scholar. Preston was puzzled to be asked about the Stamp Act, the tea tax, the writings of John Locke, topics of which he knew and cared little. In turn puzzled, the young man asked, "Well, then, what was the matter?" And Preston replied, "Young man, what we meant in going for those Redcoats was this: we always had been free, and we meant to be free always. They didn't mean we should."[1] But how did Captain Preston come by this instinctive meaning?

Fischer is convinced that Americans were formed by the visual images of liberty and freedom around them, that what they saw expressed what they were, but also formed what they wished to become. So this is a book, richly illustrated, of the icons of American political ideology: the Liberty Tree and Liberty Pole, the Liberty Bell, national and state flags ("Don't Tread on Me"), Miss Liberty, Uncle Sam, the Statue of Liberty, the Pledge of Allegiance, Yankee Doodle, and the many forms of material and popular culture which carried such images—cartoons, furniture, pottery, and the like. Formally, the work is a companion piece for an exhibition, which is now in Richmond at the Virginia Historical Society, its organizers, and will in due course migrate to Pittsburgh, Atlanta, Lexington in Massachusetts, and St. Louis until ending in 2007.

Also, more elusively, this is the second volume of Fischer's proposed four on *America: A Cultural History*, though thematically it is the third. The first was *Albion's Seed: Four British Folkways in America* (1989), which argued that four British regional cultures (East Anglia, southern England, the north Midlands, and north Britain) transmitted their values to four American regional cultures (New England, Virginia, the middle states, and the Appalachian backcountry). Still in preparation are *American*

Plantations: African and European Folkways in the New World, which will presumably extend the argument of *Albion's Seed* to the migrations of Africans and continental Europeans, at least in the colonial period, and *Deep Change: The Rhythms of American History*. Fischer likes continuity, the big picture, the sweep of time. Of course, most American historians like the small picture, the fragment, the arrested development and think the moment is long past when a historian can paint like Benjamin West. Many American readers, however, like patriotic tableaux, which Fischer of late has been supplying in narrative profusion, with books on *Paul Revere's Ride* ("In our mind's eye we tend to see Paul Revere at a distance, mounted on horseback, galloping through the dark of night") and *Washington's Crossing* ("It was March 17, 1776, the mud season in New England. A Continental officer of high rank was guiding his horse through the potholed streets of Cambridge, Massachusetts").[2]

Fischer begins here, not with horses, but the crisp announcement that liberty and freedom are different. "Liberty" comes from the Latin (*libertas, liber*) and meant "unbounded, unrestricted, and released from constraint," and this meaning descended to colonial Americans from the southern European, classical tradition. "Freedom" comes from "the Norse *fri*, the German *frei*" and implied being "joined to a tribe of free people by ties of kinship and rights of belonging," and was exclusive by being inclusive; those within the tribe could be free, but those beyond it need not be. So, according to Fischer, "North European traditions centered on freedom as a form of belonging and rights of connection to a community of free people. They imply tribal membership, and the existence of inalienable rights among all freeborn people. The Mediterranean tradition of liberty is an idea of separation and independence. It is an idea of hierarchy, in the variable possession of privileges that might be given or taken away by a higher power."[3]

This is not a promising beginning. There seems little or no evidence that anyone in the eighteenth century or, indeed, much earlier made this distinction. In *Liberty before Liberalism* (1998), a study of early modern political thought, Quentin Skinner observes, for example, "I have deliberately used the terms freedom and liberty interchangeably. . . . [A]mong the writers I am considering, nothing of philosophical importance is felt to hang on the differences." As evidence, he quotes Hobbes's *Leviathan*, which speaks indifferently of "LIBERTY, or FREEDOME." Certainly, Fischer's insistence that liberty is individualist and freedom communal seems little cogent, since self and society (to use anachronistic terms) were mingled in both the traditions he ventures. The Roman conception of liberty, at least, presumed the indispensable context of the *respublica*, and the neo-Roman paradigm—to use Skinner's coinage for James Harrington and his ilk—further presumed that, as Skinner puts it, "what it means for an individual citizen to possess or lose their liberty must be imbedded within an account of what it means for a civil association to be free." That is, in the neo-Roman tradition, liberty was not the space which lay beyond the constraints of the state or the will of another, but the shared condition of free citizens in a free state, and only possible in that condition.[4]

Fischer knows the Hobbesian passage, too, but characterizes Hobbes as etymologically ill-informed and, worse, "entirely absorbed in the refinement of his own abstractions" and so a man who failed to notice how "older tensions of meaning persisted in the folk memory of English-speaking people." This is bold, but Fischer seldom lacks for boldness in dispatching his opponents, high and low. Indeed, this gift for polemical violence is part of the fun of reading him, though the violence has an impersonal quality, as though his prose is a windscreen wiper which chances to swat scarcely noticed flies. Many historians end up splattered on Fischer's Buick in this way, but especially intellectual historians, who are singled out as practitioners of a deficient "text-and-context method."[5]

Fortunately, for this intellectual historian, Fischer's distinction only intermittently survives the book's introduction, indeed is semi-retracted even there. Rather, he quickly settles into a rapid rhythm. He selects an image, provides an illustration or two, and tells the story of how the image was started and received, preferably with references to ancient folk customs and beliefs. He starts with the Liberty Tree, an icon born in Boston in 1765, when the effigy of a Stamp Tax collector was found hanging from an elm tree, on which was subsequently placed a copper plate reading "The Tree of Liberty." Thereafter Liberty Trees appeared throughout New England and spread into the South, as far as Savannah, though elms were inessential. (Oaks were popular.) Fischer goes on to the Liberty Pole, erected by Whigs in New York in 1766 and taking the form of a ship's mast, on which was placed a board which read, "George 3rd, Pitt—and Liberty," but also assorted decorations (a flag of Saint George, a weather vane inscribed "Liberty," a liberty cap). He then tells the story of the Liberty Bell ordered from England for the Pennsylvania State House in the early 1750s, on which was inscribed, by Quaker insistence, "Proclaim liberty throughout all the land unto all the inhabitants thereof." And so Fischer proceeds to the modern day, though he lingers in the late eighteenth century with his collection of American eagles, rattlesnakes, and freedom birds, until he winds his way to Rosie the Riveter, the gloved fist of Black Power, and the World Trade Center.

On the whole, the narrative works. Fischer has a lean, brisk style, and he likes a good story. The illustrations are ample and fascinating, if occasionally too small for discerning intricate images. The chapters hurry by, because often brief, some as short as two pages, if Fischer is only doing his duty by an icon. This pace is agreeable, though occasionally the book feels like a Sears-Roebuck catalogue, and often *Liberty and Freedom* is hard to tell from a standard American history textbook, which also tends to have many color illustrations and dwell on the theme of liberty and freedom. This tendency towards the conventional might have been avoided, no doubt, if Fischer had been by training an art historian or critic, or even a scholar of popular culture. But he is no Gombrich, that is, he has no especial technique for seeing how images generate their own meaning, but rather he reads images in the light of standard interpretations of American ideology and follows the usual chronology, defined by political events. Images do not have their own chronology, nor have they been allowed to generate any ordering for this book. Presumably, the catalogue would look very different if Fischer had asked, not what images of freedom and liberty have Americans had, but, what images have Americans produced to describe their social and political condition? In such a cultural history, Aunt Jemima would matter as much as Uncle Sam, and the theme of liberty and freedom would have been less insistent. (Not many cultural historians, one suspects, would recognize Fischer's work as cultural history.) To be sure, Fischer understands that the idea of liberty takes many forms, not always benign. So, slaveholders and the Ku Klux Klan had their own images of freedom, rightly if glancingly presented here. But Fischer seems less receptive to the notion that images are themselves unstable, unusable for the purposes he intends. Often he imposes meaning by brute force.

Take, for example, his exegesis on the many meanings of the Liberty Tree. An elm, he starts by saying, was "a symbol of great age," and "early Christians worshiped beneath elms that became emblems of eternal life." But elms were also "symbols of community" used for public gatherings. Further, "old trees of many species . . . symbolized ancient folk-rights of freedom and liberty": so, the oaks of Sherwood Forest, the oak used as a symbol by Jack Cade's Rebellion, the Norfolk Rising of 1549 where justice was dispensed under "the Oak of Reformation," the Charter Oak of Connecticut. But, then, too, there was the Royal Oak, in which Charles II had hid after the battle of Worcester, not to mention the colonial Massachusetts military colors which had borne a green tree, sometimes "cradled in the arms of a cross of St. George." Last, in some versions, the tree denoted nature, the wilderness where men sought their freedom.[6]

All very confusing, one might think, these trees which denoted the qualities of being aged, Christian, free, Reformed, royalist, Anglican, republican, and natural, all at once or serially. But these contradictions do not worry Fischer, who insists that, "All of these meanings came together in a vision of liberty and freedom that was unique to New England." He tries to show how, but seems only to deepen the confusion. The Liberty Tree was "a political instrument for uniting the communities of New England in the Patriot cause." On the other hand, in 1766 after the repeal of the Stamp Act, the tree was "transformed into a symbol of loyalty to the Crown and decorated with Union Jacks." The Patriots back in control, it became a place to which dissidents were brought and where they were intimidated, with an intolerance so marked that, when Loyalists came back to power in 1775, they cut the tree down in revenge. Still, the tree began to appear on American militia flags, on powder horns and the like, often combined with other images, described as "folk symbols, firmly rooted in New England's ancestral ways" and embodying "a carefully balanced idea of individual and collective rights."[7]

This is how the book proceeds. Fischer is too good a historian not to notice that his images are vagrant, but too relentless a synthesizer to resist asserting a stability of meaning. On the whole, that meaning is disappointingly conventional, though Fischer seems indecisive about where he stands ideologically. (Being in favor of liberty does not clarify much.) Mostly, by Fischer, Americans are seen as decent people, doing their best to be free and to give liberty to others, and, if they sometimes failed with Indians, slaves, and immigrants, these were temporary problems, which all these images helped to solve. So, "Every now and then, these ideas have faded a little. But events intervened to make them strong again." Occasionally, the continuing revolution has met a reverse, but "these retreats have been short-lived and insubstantial." There have been fleeting troubles with anti-democratic Federalists, proslavery advocates, and "some writers on the academic left ... who tried to suppress free expression in the universities by imposing 'speech codes' and a repressive regime of 'political correctness,'" but the events of September 11, 2001, helped to make "American ideas of liberty and freedom ... stronger than ever before." Hence Fischer cannot significantly entertain the proposition that his images might have worsened matters, precisely because

Americans were so convinced that their actions must serve freedom, when often they did not, indeed could not.[8]

It is, of course, the case that Fischer's intellectual enthusiasm for folk customs puts him in some odd company. Reading Fischer is, too often, uncomfortably like reading a Romantic like August von Schlegel, who also stressed the difference between southern Europe and the Gothic tradition and whose imagination once wandered in ancient German forests, and like reading William Graham Sumner the conservative Social Darwinist, who first coined the term *folkways* in 1906. (Though, in *Albion's Seed*, Fischer was keen to distinguish himself from Sumner, if unconvincingly.) This Burkean sympathy for the organic shows itself in Fischer's hostility to "formal texts, philosophical abstractions, learned discourses, and ideological controversies" and preference for "customs, traditions, and folk beliefs."[9] But the rationalist tradition does have the advantage that it mitigates exceptionalism, common in the Romantic tradition. In the world imagined by the Enlightenment, ideas can and should travel. But Fischer, though he seems to think that the world will share the American experience of moving inexorably towards more freedom and liberty—though why is not explained—seems little to think that the American example has much power, because so intricately embedded in what is customary and local.

Hence, to square this impossible circle, Fischer tries to show some of the world's cultures making their own way towards "the promise of a better world to come." In his last pages, he does a lightning tour of recent democratic movements in China, India, and Poland, to show that each of these societies has indigenous traditions of liberty and freedom, which Americans mistakenly read as evidence of American influence. This final gesture is worthwhile, but very out of joint with what precedes, which includes praise for Wilsonian democracy as the offer of "a great and noble idea of a free and open world," admirable for its "universal quality." Fischer's section on the American Revolution ends, likewise, with a jarring story about how, in China in 1786, news of the American Revolution galvanized local opinion into a respect for liberty. We are told that, "In Asia, Africa, and Europe, ideas of American liberty and freedom became a vision of a better world." The contemporary resonance of that remark is unlikely to be accidental and unlikely to appeal to non-American readers, for many of whom the sound of American shots heard round the world summons up different images, not of Liberty Trees, but of those cowering in doorways and dragging corpses from rubble.

NOTES

1. David Hackett Fischer, *Liberty and Freedom: A Visual History of America's Founding Ideas* (New York: Oxford University Press, 2004), 1–2.

2. David Hackett Fischer, *Paul Revere's Ride* (New York: Oxford University Press, 1994), 3; David Hackett Fischer, *Washington's Crossing* (New York: Oxford University Press, 2004), 7.

3. Fischer, *Liberty and Freedom*, 5, 10. For this analysis, Fischer draws extensively on Hanna Fenichel Pitkin, "Are Freedom and Liberty Twins?" *Political Theory* 16 (November 1988): 523–52.

4. Quentin Skinner, *Liberty Before Liberalism* (Cambridge: Cambridge University Press, 1998), 17–18, 23.

5. Fischer, *Liberty and Freedom*, 12, 3.

6. Ibid., 24–26.

7. Ibid., 26, 35.

8. Ibid., 718, 721.

9. David Hackett Fischer, *Albion's Seed: Four British Folkways in America* (New York: Oxford University Press, 1989), 7–11; Fischer, *Liberty and Freedom*, 716. Cf. Augustus William Schlegel, *A Course of Lectures on Dramatic Art and Literature*, trans. John Black (London: Henry G. Bohn, 1846), 17–29.

IMPERIALISM

A review of Charles A. Cerami, *Jefferson's Great Gamble: The Remarkable Story of Jefferson, Napoleon and the Men Behind the Louisiana Purchase* (Naperville, IL: Sourcebooks, 2003), Thomas J. Fleming, *The Louisiana Purchase* (Hoboken, NJ: John Wiley, 2003), and Jon Kukla, *A Wilderness So Immense: The Louisiana Purchase and the Destiny of America* (New York: Alfred A. Knopf, 2003), in the *Times Literary Supplement* (February 20, 2004): 9–10.

Last year saw the bicentenary of the Louisiana Purchase. In Paris on May 2, 1803, James Monroe and Robert Livingston signed a treaty which gave 60 million francs to the French government and a further 20 millions to Americans who had claims against the French, in exchange for the 875,000 square miles of the Louisiana territory, which today embraces the wedge of thirteen states which runs north from Louisiana to Minnesota and west to Montana. Formal possession was taken in New Orleans on December 20, when the American flag was raised in front of the Cabildo, to the applause of a handful of Americans and amid the glum silence of numerous French and Spanish (perhaps even the odd Native American). Some months later, a parade was held in New York City and a white silk banner was displayed, on which was written, "Extension of the Empire of Freedom in the Peaceful, Honorable, and Glorious Acquisition of the Immense and Fertile Region of Louisiana."[1]

These three books, all written by Americans, roughly endorse the sentiments of the banner, though they are a little uncertain about "honorable" and less insistent on "glorious" than might have been the case a few generations ago. Still, the oldest narrative seems mostly intact: that the Louisiana Purchase was a brilliant diplomatic coup which saved North America from the bloody fate of Europe, advanced the extension of liberty from sea to shining sea, built an edifice of American economic power upon the ideological foundations laid in 1776, and so made possible the American destiny of making the world safe for democracy. In the case of Fleming and Cerami, this traditionalism is not surprising; they are popular historians who must please the opinions of the average American reader, who is not disposed to challenge the idea that American expansion was beneficent or to interrogate whether an "empire of freedom" is an oxymoron. Jon Kukla, on the other hand, is a serious scholar of intelligence and imagination, and his reluctance to break new ground is more disappointing.

Fleming's book is brief, tidy, unannotated, unadventurous, but competently written and sure footed. Cerami's text is longer, more prone to errors of fact (John Randolph rather than Edmund Randolph is said to be Secretary of State in 1794), more profligate with adjectives (as in "a wild, stomping rush towards the west") and keener on what Americans in the nineteenth century called eagle-screaming, that is, aggressive patriotism.[2] But Cerami has more flair in describing his dramatis personae and his characterizations, if usually melodramatic, are often shrewd. Traditionally, character has ruled in studies of the Louisiana Purchase. Henry Adams, even when writing as a scientific historian in the 1880s and providing what is still the best diplomatic history of the affair, grasped that this ought to be told as a morality play about human frailty, ambition, and luck. Jefferson the velvet hypocrite, Madison the reserved strategist, Napoleon the impetuous demiurge, Talleyrand the languid Mephistopheles, and Joseph Bonaparte the comic relief; these do make a good story, especially if one throws in Toussaint L'Ouverture freezing to death in a French fortress, James Wilkinson playing the Spanish double agent, and Pauline Bonaparte copulating with random enthusiasm in France and Haiti. All these solve an old problem of narrative, that so many of the early republic's historical actors were dull. There is Aaron Burr, of course, who by furnishing amorality and perhaps even treason has helped many (especially Gore Vidal) to get through this Sunday school of a history. And Alexander Hamilton was, to be sure, adulterous and wittily hated the mob. But the rest are disappointingly moral. A perennial attraction of the Louisiana Purchase, therefore, has been that it licences the historian to incorporate a goodly number of European and Caribbean roués, cut-throats, megalomaniacs, and swindlers to enliven an American story, but still allows the display of virtue defeating vice, which is what an American story is supposed to show.

There is disagreement about the appropriate chronology, however. Fleming is most rigorous; for the most part, he starts in 1801 and concludes in about 1804, and so confines himself to the immediate diplomacy. Cerami starts at roughly the same time but carries on to 1815 and the Battle of New Orleans, because he is keen to see the purchase as an episode in the history of the American West. Kukla is most leisurely; he commences with Jefferson in Paris in 1786, takes 200 pages to reach 1801, and ends, like Fleming, at 1804. About the diplomacy itself, there is little disagreement, indeed little need for advance on Adams's analysis. In 1801, the United States wanted access to the Mississippi River and New Orleans, and had moved from pressing the Spanish for trading concessions to thinking that possession of New Orleans and West Florida would be necessary. In the 1790s, the Spanish had no great interest in Louisiana, acquired by them in 1764 from the French, and saw it as an unprofitable northern extension to their greater American empire, but of some value as a bargaining chip in slowing their deteriorating position in European politics. The French, who reacquired the colony in 1800, were mostly concerned with the profits of their Caribbean possessions, but were indecisive about whether Louisiana was worth the trouble, except as a buffer zone. Napoleon was most indecisive. When he was resolved to crush the Haitian slave revolt and re-establish slavery, he thought Louisiana might be a springboard for a wider ambition in the Americas. It was when his armies failed in Haiti and he needed money for his whirling European plans, that he suddenly, unexpectedly, and casually tossed Louisiana to the Americans, not without the thought that a stronger America might mean a weaker Britain. For the most part, the crucial decisions were made by Europeans for European reasons, though the Americans kept up what pressure they could manage. Jefferson threatened France with making an Anglo-American alliance, if Napoleon would not sell New Orleans, and Madison spoke darkly of "collisions."[3] In the short term, this amounted to little more than bluster. But both Madrid and Paris realized that it would be difficult to muster enough military and demographic power to resist the long-term danger of American migration.

The game was oddly abstract, as great games often are. The huge geographical reach of "Louisiana" was unimportant, even to the Americans, who would have been happy to get New Orleans alone, were reluctant to contemplate the prospect of North Dakota, and only took it all because it was on offer, was cheap, and might come in handy. No one was sure where Louisiana was. Livingston once pressed Talleyrand on what exactly the United States had bought. Talleyrand said, "You must take it as we received it," and added, with indifference, "I can give you no direction. You have made a noble bargain for yourselves, and I suppose you will make the most of it." Napoleon gave more mischievous advice: "If an obscurity did not already exist, it would perhaps be a good policy to put one there."[4] It was advice the United States took for many decades, when squabbling with Spain over the boundary of Florida and with Mexico over Texas.

Kukla's is the most satisfying, but also the most frustrating of the books on offer. He has a deep knowledge of the secondary literature, at least of American history, and a working knowledge of French and Spanish historiography. He does not seem to have noticed postcolonial history, which would seem a logical place to find fresh insight. But he writes well, if in that romantic vein much favored by American historians with an eye on a wider readership ("The skies over Paris were cloudy on Wednesday, January 25, 1786, and the early morning temperature was 42 degrees" and the like). He is more prone to demotic flourishes than is usual; "Bourbons on the Rocks" is one chapter heading. By way of amplifying his gift for description, he has opted with great enthusiasm for the policy of telling stories about crazy Europeans. He is inclined to allow narrative to carry analysis, with the result that a reader can be unclear what is being argued. I infer that he believes the purchase is best understood as the last phase of a longer story of how Spain, France, and the United States interacted in North America. Certainly, he is not much interested in the social and political consequences of the purchase, except in briefly suggesting that the ethnic complexity of Louisiana commenced "a long encounter with diversity that has forced us, and that should inspire us, to think and live far differently than the Founders expected."[5]

Still, I am not sure that these works add much except drama to what has long been the standard account, Alexander DeConde's *This Affair of Louisiana* (1976). Indeed they mark something of a retrogression, since DeConde was usefully clear that the acquisition of Louisiana was an imperial venture and, as such, part of a pattern. He saw that American imperialism did not start with William McKinley and Theodore Roosevelt but had been essential to the creation of the United States from its inception. This imperialism was not ineluctable. Jefferson himself had once suggested that it would matter nothing to the overall fate of liberty if North America came to be populated by a number of "sister republics," of which the United States would be but one.[6] Upon this logic, he might have worked to accomplish the independence of Louisiana as a Creole republic. But, as president, he came to presume that the existence of adjacent polities was, de facto, a threat and so American liberty could only be guaranteed by American imperialism, and hence that republicanism required the un-republican aggression of "collisions."

Since Jefferson was little capable of using the language of *realpolitik*, he squared the circle by speaking of the "empire of liberty." His opponents were not persuaded; they pointed out that a republic, if it meant anything, meant the consent of the governed, and the governed of Louisiana had never given their consent. Nor, in due course, would most of the inhabitants of Florida, Texas, California, Hawaii, Alaska, Iraq, and so forth, all of which were bought or conquered in the name of liberty without consent. Jefferson's was a thin argument then and a thinner one now.

NOTES

1. Jon Kukla, *A Wilderness So Immense: The Louisiana Purchase and the Destiny of America* (New York: Alfred A. Knopf. 2003), 334.

2. Charles A. Cerami, *Jefferson's Great Gamble: The Remarkable Story of Jefferson, Napoleon and the Men Behind the Louisiana Purchase* (Naperville, IL: Sourcebooks, 2003), 1.

3. Thomas J. Fleming, *The Louisiana Purchase* (Hoboken, NJ: John Wiley, 2003), 14.

4. Kukla, *Wilderness So Immense*, 327; Cerami, *Jefferson's Great Gamble*, 180.

5. Kukla, *Wilderness So Immense*, 6, 339.

6. On this, see Robert W. Tucker and David C. Hendrickson, *Empire of Liberty: The Statecraft of Thomas Jefferson* (New York: Oxford University Press, 1990), 157–71.

These two pieces are: 1) a commentary on Peter Kolchin, "Considering Reconstruction in Comparative Perspective," Southern Intellectual History Circle, Historical Society of Pennsylvania, February 2003; and 2) a review-essay, published as Michael O'Brien, "The Iron Machine: From Lincoln to Disfranchisement," *Historical Journal* 46 (March 2003): 219–29, which considered Gabor Boritt, ed., *The Lincoln Enigma: The Changing Faces of an American Icon* (New York: Oxford University Press, 2001), Allen C. Guelzo, *Abraham Lincoln: Redeemer President* (Grand Rapids, MI: William B. Eerdmans, 1999), David W. Blight, *Race and Reunion: The Civil War in American Memory* (Cambridge, MA: Harvard University Press, Belknap Press, 2001), Dan R. Frost, *Thinking Confederates: Academia and the Idea of Progress in the New South* (Knoxville: University of Tennessee Press, 2000), J. William Harris, *Deep Souths: Delta, Piedmont, and Sea Island Society in the Age of Segregation* (Baltimore, MD: Johns Hopkins University Press, 2001), and Michael Perman, *Struggle for Mastery: Disfranchisement in the South, 1888–1908* (Chapel Hill: University of North Carolina Press, 2001). Reprinted by permission.

Peter Kolchin observes that Reconstruction involved "two separate processes—the rebuilding of relations between the Rebel states and the Union, and the rebuilding of southern social relations in the wake of slavery's demise." Much of his paper is preoccupied with the latter. Most of what he says about the former—the matter of reconstructing nationality—deals with the issue of leniency versus harshness; whether or not Southerners were better or worse treated than the losers of other civil wars. One cannot quarrel with his claim that Southerners got off very lightly. But, if you take seriously the obligation to undertake a comparative analysis of Reconstruction, one must also consider the comparative historical problem of rebuilding a union, to the understanding of which his comparison with Russia gives little help.

There are neutral and un-neutral ways to approach this question. The neutral way is to ask, what happened in societies where there was a civil war and then a restoration, in which the prewar political structure was retained, if a little modified by the experience? There are many examples: England in the seventeenth century, China after the Taiping Rebellion in the mid-nineteenth century, Spain in the early and Nigeria in the late twentieth century, these come immediately to mind. Such histories suggest that restorations were usually marked by the establishment of a conservative social and political order, that it has been very rare for the experience of civil war to eventuate in a more liberal order. In the case of Reconstruction in the United States, the episode of Radical Reconstruction has had a way of disguising this fact—if it is a fact—since fleetingly there was a liberal experiment, a moment which has much tantalized those historians with a willing heart, who like to see in Reconstruction a promise and not a negation. But what came to pass in 1877 and later, in both the South and the North, seems the more logical consequence of restoration. Repression is the usual aftermath of civil wars and a sort of repression is what the United States got. Arguably, it had a more conservative, more oligarchical, less democratic civil order in 1900 than it had in 1830. The only exception to this observation—and a grave exception, which may wreck the observation—is that the United States had also shed slavery. Nonetheless, it is clear that the order of 1900 arose, with a cold logic, from the restoration. Piecing together the Union required a series of deals and understandings between its influential citizens, North and South, which mostly turned on sacrificing and repressing its less influential citizens and non-citizens.

It follows, too, that one should interrogate those polities which experienced civil wars, but did not see a restoration. The revolt of the Netherlands in the seventeenth century, the separation of the Netherlands and Belgium in the 1830s, the independence of the Irish Free State, the division between the People's Republic of China and Taiwan, the separation of Pakistan and Bangladesh, these come to mind. The creation of the United States, itself the product of a civil war where the old order died, would be relevant. Here it is harder to see a firm tendency, except to observe that much hinged on the political and social complexion of what was shed and what was retained. It is arguable that the United Kingdom was more liberal in the mid-twentieth century than it might have been with the retention of southern Ireland—remembering the conservative Catholicism of Eire. Likewise, the Netherlands has been the more liberal for the loss of Belgium. But there have been less frequent situations where the reverse happened, when a conservative state lost touch with a liberal province. Most notable, perhaps, is the American Revolution, though the instance is more opaque than Americans like to think, since it is not self-evident which polity was the more liberal in 1790—Britain with its oligarchical politics or the United States with slavery.

The un-neutral way of considering the comparative problem of nationality and Reconstruction is to enquire, was it a good idea that the United States was restored in 1865? Traditionally, almost the only people to have asked this question have been the neo-Confederates. For all I know,

Trent Lott may go to birthday parties in Mississippi and observe that Grant's surrendering to Lee would have spared us all a lot of trouble.[1] But a social democrat might as easily ask the question, though American social democrats (that beleaguered minority) have preferred a different one. They have not asked, has the survival of the United States served social democracy? They have asked, how do we make the United States into a social democracy, how do we finish the revolution? But their presumption is that the revolution is capable of being finished, that this political structure is inherently capable of a liberal completion. Frankly, I have ceased to believe that conjecture, if I ever did believe it. My own sense is that the outcome of the Civil War left the United States committed to a reactionary constitutional and social system, and (above all) left it committed to the premise of size and power, and to an amended version of Thomas Jefferson's "empire of liberty," that impossible vision. For empires cannot be free, and freedom is not a rationale for empire. My prejudice is to believe that humane societies are almost invariably small ones, that it is better to be Denmark than the United States, that the American ambition—immensely accelerated by the restoration of the Union—to be the greatest nation on earth has not served the purposes of civilization and may not even have served the interests of Americans. The world would probably be a better place if, in North America, there were today seven or eight polities, instead of two. It would be probably a better place for those who live in North America, but almost certainly a better place for those who do not live in North America, who now live lives menaced by the power accomplished in 1865.

My reasoning has, of course, many grave difficulties, both historical and conceptual. What of the ending of slavery, you might rightly ask? What, in the longer run, of the American role in the Second World War, perhaps even in the Cold War? What, a few of you might even ask, of the beneficence of capitalism? Even those of you as critical of American society as I seem to be might want to echo, in speaking of the American constitution and the Civil War, what Chou-En-Lai famously replied, when asked what he thought of the French Revolution, "It is too early to tell."[2]

I raise this question, mostly because a conference on Reconstruction ought to pause and interrogate this fundamental issue, instead of presuming it. But I also raise it, partly to make a point about American political thought. In the late eighteenth century and up until 1860, Americans not only considered how the American political economy might work in its details—should it have high or low tariffs? should it permit or abolish slavery? were national banks constitutional? and so forth—but also whether the existence of this particular constitutional structure was justifiable. That is to say, people articulated a vision of society and asked if this or that constitutional structure would best enable its realization. William Lloyd Garrison used to burn copies of the United States Constitution, upon the defensible reasoning that the yoking together of a slave and a free society poisoned the latter. A consequence of the Civil War and Reconstruction was to make the matter of the Constitution undiscussable, except at the margins—whether to add or disavow this or that amendment. Americans were to lose the habit of imagining a world beyond what had been imagined in 1787, because they had paid so horrendous a price between 1861 and 1865 for salvaging that world. This constriction of imagination was not a gain, for them, for us. To be sure, this is a matter of grave doubt. But the doubt lessens, the further you get away from the United States. If I were living in the Gaza Strip, I would not be doubtful. I would know that the survival of the United States has not furnished forth mankind's last, best hope, and shows no sign of being able to do so.

• • •

There are four presidents carved on Mount Rushmore: George Washington, Thomas Jefferson, Abraham Lincoln, and Theodore Roosevelt. The case of George W. Bush would seem to suggest that modern Americans do not like their presidents to be complex. If so, among the granite faces, only Washington and Roosevelt answer to this need. The former possessed what his admirers called republican simplicity, what his enemies (and even some personal friends) thought might be a lack of intellectual nimbleness. The latter had a violence of conviction so wondrous in its clarity that numerous psychologists have been enlisted to find something beneath its surface. Jefferson, by contrast, was dizzyingly complex, but he is also inaccessible, especially to modernists who find an eighteenth-century sensibility eerily polished and cold. Abraham Lincoln, however, was satisfyingly messed up. A broken family, a lost lover, an unhappy marriage, dead children, plus years of thwarted ambition, nightmares, melancholy, and suicidal impulse, all combine to make a man of nervous inadequacy, someone whom Oprah Winfrey would be glad to have back, again and again, as an icon of the perennial crises of masculinity.

Not that the Lincoln scholars are at peace with this image. For there is the other Lincoln, the marble man inside the monument. This second

Lincoln is permitted only moments of doubt, though as a martyred Christ-figure, it is obligatory that he have those moments, for by them he shares fallibility and vindicates the humanity of American nationality. But how to navigate between these two Lincolns, the depressive who needs Prozac and the kindly doctor who prescribes it, is not self-evident.

The essays in *The Lincoln Enigma* tack in different directions, though mostly towards Lincoln the well-balanced, if troubled physician. The book derives from a symposium held in 2000 at the Civil War Institute of Gettysburg College. Gabor Boritt, who is that Institute's director, is keen to have us respect Lincoln, to know for example that Lincoln was not gay (a popular notion of late), just someone who, living roughly in frontier taverns, spent a lot of time in bed with men. Nor was he much of a racist, just someone who, in the way of nineteenth-century Americans, liked minstrel shows, wanted to ship blacks back to Africa, and made jokes about "niggers," but who also lamented the fate of the "poor creatures" trapped in slavery and became their emancipator.[3] The former refutation is fairly easy, but the latter is very hard. Boritt points to timing: Lincoln endorsed colonization before about 1862, but then switched to finding a place for freedmen in the United States. Boritt indicates, too, a sort of psychological sleight-of-hand. The early Lincoln desired the end of slavery, while knowing the depth of American racism, and squared the circle by promoting a Liberian solution which most people knew to be impractical, but whose impossibility the normally empirical Lincoln refused to examine. This is not much of a defense. Better is Boritt's evidence that Lincoln treated blacks with courteous humanity, a quality which much impressed Frederick Douglass, and that Lincoln went about as far as white Americans of his generation ever went (if one forgets Thaddeus Stevens), which was far short of conferring full civil rights on freedmen.

Likewise defensive, Douglas Wilson wants us to know that Lincoln, as a young man, was not a failure. He was honest, independent, ambitious, strong-willed, and tender-hearted, someone who refused to drink or smoke with the men, and someone who would attend to a bird with a broken wing. He was a fatalist, who had come to the conclusion that a man needed both logic and a sense of humor, the qualities (it has been traditional to believe) so necessary in surviving his botched marriage. That Mary Lincoln was a monstrous harridan, short, fat, proslavery, spendthrift, and bullying, is one of the cosier legends of American history. But Lincoln's memoirists and historians have almost all been men, usually misogynist, or so Jean Baker plausibly believes. Rather, she sees a marriage which mostly worked and was marked by tenderness, sexuality, companionship, and the shared interests of parenthood and politics. This cheerful news is, however, a little disturbed by Robert V. Bruce, who considers Lincoln's long fascination with death and mortality. Evidently, there were many bad poems, which Lincoln read and may have written, about time's empty passage, and "wretched life," and "mossy marbles" in churchyards, and fast-flying clouds. He knew Poe's "The Raven" by heart.[4]

Other essays speak to Lincoln the president and commander-in-chief. Gerald J. Prokopowicz suggests that Lincoln had fantasies of leading his armies in the field and, indeed, had some gifts as a strategist, but wisely understood that he would have made a terrible general. David Donald revisits the old saw that, if Lincoln and Jefferson Davis had swapped presidential places, the Confederacy would have won the war.[5] Donald sees more similarity in their gifts and positions than is usual, but the usual differences in their temperaments. Above all, he stresses Lincoln's commitment to the use of executive power, about which Davis was diffident. Allen C. Guelzo, by contrast, is anxious to exonerate Lincoln from the charge of setting aside the Constitution, especially out of an exaggerated regard for the principles of the Declaration of Independence. William C. Harris seems to endorse this view of Lincoln's moderation, at least as it affected his offer of peace terms to the South as late as early 1865, when he was willing to offer $400 million to owners in compensation for the ending of slavery.

All this is very miscellaneous. More intriguing are several dozen illustrations, which show the various ways in which Lincoln the icon has been portrayed in American art. All are benign: Lincoln the liberator by Thomas Hart Benton in 1955, Lincoln in the snow showing a child how to chop wood by Horace Pippin in 1943, the young Lincoln standing tall with an axe and a book by Norman Rockwell in 1963, Lincoln on horseback, or in an army tent, or wrapped in the flag, or reading to his son, or weeping for the death of Kennedy in a cartoon, and so forth. With the partial exceptions of some caricatures by David Levine and Jo Davidson's bust of the "Man of Sorrows," American art does not seem to prefer Lincoln the neurotic. Everywhere he is shown as adequate, paternal, square-jawed, tall, though also invariably unsmiling, despite his deserved reputation for jokes and stories. If, as Boritt claims, Lincoln is "the quintessential American, the nation's best face to itself and to the world," this lack of shadowing is troublesome, if not surprising.[6] For this nice man, who in American art seems just to walk across the lawn to bring a cheesecake to new neighbors, unwillingly killed half the seed of America, one by one. To his credit, Lincoln knew this of himself, if his artists have not.

I am not sure that Allen C. Guelzo's *Abraham Lincoln: Redeemer President* quite knows it, either, though Guelzo is much interested in Lincoln's religious identity and is aware of the bloody, sacrificial dimension of Christianity, which Lincoln came to invoke in his Second Inaugural. His book claims to be an intellectual biography, though it is wisely more than that, since Lincoln's reflective writings were few and his political actions many. The overall portrait is of a complicated, subtle, somewhat evasive man of ideas, who much stressed the accidents which had formed his life, but who quietly worked to make his fortune, not only as a politician, but as a corporate lawyer. As an economic thinker, Lincoln was a liberal capitalist in the mode of Henry Clay, though the residue of his parents' Calvinism made him (not very consistently) a skeptic about the freedom of the will and a believer in the doctrine of necessity. As we have seen, he had Romantic literary tastes, though oddly they seem to have been confined to poetry; he claimed never to have finished a novel and even *Ivanhoe* was left half-read. Rather, he inclined to Tom Paine and the Enlightenment, to Jeremy Bentham and utilitarianism, to "Reason, all-conquering Reason," while being a Victorian rationalist, that is, someone troubled by the problem of faith. Guelzo makes much of Lincoln's hard-scrabble origins, the early death of his mother, the warmth of his stepmother, and the callousness of his father. He stresses that Lincoln did not take the usual way to resolve these anxieties, but as a young man stayed resolutely skeptic, someone who disbelieved in redemption, punishment for sin, the afterlife, and the soul, but who incongruously suspected God and/or Providence of predestining human affairs without bothering about justice. In his "deep streak of despair, disappointment, and worthlessness," perhaps he had Tennysonian leanings, but Lincoln was very un-Victorian in his manner of expression, for he strove always for the plain style, for clarity and concision, dryness and logic. Nowhere was this more evident, of course, than in his Gettysburg Address.[7]

All this describes a man painfully isolated, of whom it is said that even his jokes and stories were told "to whistle off sadness and [were] no evidences of sociality." Later, this taste for solitude was of some use to a man obliged to sustain a national effort by force of will, against brutal oppositions foreign and domestic, to which almost anyone else would have capitulated, just to stop the pain. For Lincoln assumed that pain was ineluctable.

As his secretary, William Herndon, was to paraphrase Lincoln's view of the human condition: "[Man] is simply a *simple tool*, a mere cog in the wheel, a part, a small part of this vast iron machine, that strikes and cuts, grinds and mashes, all things, including man, that resist it."[8] Guelzo argues convincingly that this bleakness occasioned compassion in Lincoln, that he looked about him to see others being rended by the machine and felt sorrow. Less clear is how such a view could lead to action, to compassion becoming reform—to help slaves or anyone. And the case seems to be that it did not, that Lincoln had to await events, to survive the machine until it moved to a different place, to the Emancipation Proclamation or to Robert E. Lee's surrender at Appomattox Courthouse, and then to Ford's Theater where the machine finally killed him.

Guelzo's is a satisfying portrait, perhaps because he has been a scholar of Jonathan Edwards, so is more conscious of the intellectual and political contexts which preceded and made Lincoln, but less concerned with the retrospective usefulness of Lincoln as a national icon, which leads to so much special pleading in *The Lincoln Enigma*. Guelzo's Lincoln is bleak, tentative, and necessarily inconsistent, for no one could function in life, let alone politics, with so stark and passive a vision. But the portrait does create an irony, for it gives us a Lincoln who seems to have expected little to change, who was always surprised by abruptness—he did not expect secession, for example—but who experienced and himself created immense changes, if much against his will.

David Blight's *Race and Reunion* is, however, peculiarly drawn to the retrospective, to how Americans made sense of the Civil War between 1865 and that moment in 1913 when Woodrow Wilson, the Virginian, retraced Lincoln's steps from Washington to Gettysburg, in order to mark the fiftieth anniversary of the battle. This is not a novel theme, but the historiography of civic memory has much altered in recent years, especially in indicating ways to capture memory, by looking at monuments, ceremonies, historical organizations, histories, and popular culture. So Blight gives us many anniversaries, obelisks, novels, parades, and orations. He offers three broad traditions of memory: Southern, Unionist, and African American. The last of these was best articulated by Frederick Douglass and exemplified later by W. E. B. Du Bois. In Douglass's view, expressed in late 1863, "The mission of this war is National regeneration." Its meaning lay in the ending of slavery, but also in the establishment of equality, in making "a country which shall not brand the Declaration of Independence as a lie."[9] White Southerners, to the contrary, accepted the verdict of the war on the practicality of slavery and the inevitability of nationality, but otherwise continued to insist on the wisdom of racial hierarchy, the necessity of local political and social control, and the worth of Southern culture: no regeneration here, and not much equality. In this view, the Civil War was a sort of moral draw, in which the North won some things, the South some others. The Unionist/Northern perspective, on the other hand, was reluctant to disavow victory, to embrace the notion that somehow the South had not lost, had not deserved to lose, and that Lee's Miserables could be regarded as a peer of the Grand Army of the Republic; it took satisfaction in ending slavery, but was much less interested in equality, except as a way to annoy and subordinate former traitors.

Blight's story is of how the white Southerners and Northerners managed to effect a shared narrative, at the expense of the black "emancipationist" vision, of how race became the balm to heal white animosities. This is scarcely a new argument, but it is worked out with much skill, good sense, and sympathy. Blight is perhaps most original in recovering the black retrospection on the war. From as far back as Paul Buck's *The Road to Reunion* (1937), we have known about the white dialectic, but less has been written about, for example, the ten thousand blacks who went to the site of a Confederate prison for Union soldiers in northern Charleston in the spring of 1865 to decorate the graves of the Union dead. But the book is not trapped in its tripartite analysis. Blight knows that William Tecumseh Sherman remembered the war differently from a Northern prisoner-of-war, that Alexander Crummell dissented from Douglass, that Alexander Stephens was more reluctant than Henry Grady to move to a New South. He knows, too, that for many, the meaning of the war lay less in its politics—whether slavery should have ended or not, whether the old Constitution was killed, whether segregation was necessary—but in the experience of combat itself. So he makes intelligent use of, for example, Walt Whitman's evocation in *Specimen Days* of the "hundred unnamed lights and shades of camp," the myriad experiences at the "marrow of the tragedy" which would never be written. Blight especially recurs to Oliver Wendell Holmes's 1895 address to Harvard's graduates on "The Soldier's Faith," where the young were urged to eschew comfort, to risk manliness, and to seek "combat and pain," and so escape the banalities of commerce and "the doubts of civil life." This was a message more thrilling than rational, indeed thrilling because irrational. As Holmes put it, "But in the midst of doubt, in the collapse of creeds, there is one thing that I do not doubt . . . and that is that the faith is true and adorable which leads a soldier to throw away his life in obedience to a blindly accepted duty, in a cause which he little understands, in a plan of campaign of which he does not see the use."[10] Perhaps Matthew Arnold might have been spared the despair of Dover Beach in 1867, if he had had the good sense to run off to a meaningless Battle of the Wilderness in 1864?

The social order which emerged in the South by 1900 has not lacked for recent historians, who have gone to much trouble to destroy the warm reconciliations of 1913, to make ironic and ominous the photographs of ancient veterans, Blue and Gray, who once stiffly shook hands and shared platforms. Nationality is an accomplishment which modern Americans tend to take for granted—they grow peculiar in this regard—but they are insistently alert to the difficulty of racial understanding and justice, acutely aware that there are not too many photographs of black and white Americans shaking hands at ceremonies declaring social peace in the race conflict.

Dan R. Frost's *Thinking Confederates* makes only a modest contribution to comprehending the New South. His is a study in futility. When the war was over, the venture of Southern higher education was resumed and obliged to consider the lessons of defeat. Before 1861, most colleges had confined themselves to the liberal arts and a contempt for the vocational. Frost makes a decent case that the generation, many in it veterans, which took control of Southern universities during and after Reconstruction tried hard to restructure curricula to make a place for engineering, chemistry, scientific agriculture, geology, and the like, because they believed that defeat had been occasioned by the North's superior use of science and industry. (They were to nod knowingly when reports of the Prussian defeat of France reached Virginia.) So their presumption became that Southern progress could only come from a body of experts, influential on public policy, which was itself to be newly energetic in structuring the political economy of the region. This was not merely to offer techniques, but also the ideology of progress itself, which Frost thinks was etiolated in the Old South. I suspect he is more right about the novelty of technical education than he is about the originality of ideas of progress, which were abundant enough before 1861. Still, he does show convincingly that these reformers had little success, at least in making Southern colleges into advanced centers of technical study. Such study is, of course, expensive. No Southern state had the means to fund this, even when it had the will or interest. In 1898, it was calculated that nine Northern universities had scientific equipment worth $211,000, while nine of their Southern counterparts had just $41,587.

One reason why there was little money is that Southern states were usually paying for two parallel, segregated educational systems, at both the school and college level. But social and economic problems ran deeper even than the costs occasioned by racial animosity, though it is a temptation to use the rise, persistence, and fall of segregation as a master narrative for modern Southern history. J. William Harris's *Deep Souths*, perhaps unintentionally, shows why this temptation might be worth resisting, because the narrative can splinter into irreconcilable fragments. He does not reach the end—he stops in 1939—but he deals with the beginning and middle phases of the system of racial segregation, which came to be called Jim Crow. But he is also concerned to examine the diversity of Southern experience, at least in the Deep South. His book juggles the history of three subregions: the Sea Islands and rice coast of Georgia, the eastern Piedmont of the same state, and the Mississippi-Yazoo Delta. It is not entirely clear why these are singled out, other than that each was once the subject of distinguished books: William Alexander Percy's *Lanterns on the Levee*, Arthur Raper's *Tenants of the Almighty*, and *Drums and Shadows* (an oral history by the Georgia Writers Project). At any rate, Harris wishes to "show readers that there is more than one South to tell about," even more than one Deep South.[11] This uninteresting desire has led, however, to an unexpectedly rich book.

The narrative splits into three phases, 1876–96, 1897–1918, and 1919–39. Within each phase, Harris moves between his three places, to ask of each more or less the same historical questions about the intersections of black and white experience. How was the land issue settled? How was segregation established and administered? What was the effect of Populism? How did economic fortunes change? How did war intrude? As one might guess, he gets very different answers for each place.

In general, it was best (though not good) to be African American on the Georgia coast. Antebellum plantations there had cultivated cotton or rice, the latter of which required very large slave forces, tightly disciplined to maintain the necessary, elaborate infrastructure of banks, ditches, canals, trunks, and floodgates which sustained the water levels appropriate to each moment of the crop's cycle. When the slaves became free, discipline collapsed, the labor force dissipated, the dykes disintegrated, and the rice ceased to be profitable. (Cotton did a little better, but not much.) It took about twenty years for this conclusion to become inescapable, but in time the old masters threw in their hand, to abandon the poor, but quasi-independent black peasants who sometimes owned their own land, but often were tenants, but who were mostly uninterested in cash crops and preferred subsistence farming, leavened by hunting, fishing, and oyster-gathering, and by occasional days of working for wages on adjacent plantations. In general, here a black was likely to own land (52 percent of black farmers were owners in 1910) and to have a vote, and less likely to face racial violence, especially in the form of lynching. On the other hand, blacks' economic marginality left whites free to explore other options: lumber, turpentine, commercial fishing, eventually the hotels, golf courses, and winter homes which came to cater to Northern travelers and resident aliens.

It was middling to be in the Georgia Piedmont. There the old cotton plantations held on and blacks tended to be farm laborers or sharecroppers, a condition which came gradually to be shared by many whites, who had previously owned land. But land was not greatly concentrated in a few hands, there were many smaller farms which grew cotton, and a very few blacks came to be owners (but only 4.7 percent of black farmers in 1910), usually of very small plots. Being thus integrated in the economy, blacks were more vulnerable to being blamed for the usually bad economic conditions. Still, they did better than in the Delta. Harris has charts (a little hard to read) which seem to show that from 1883 to 1930, lynchings in the Delta ran at about three or four times the rate in the Piedmont.

No one will surprised to learn that it was worst in Mississippi. The Delta was, even in 1860, still a semi-frontier, with many large plantations but much land undeveloped. There were formidable costs associated with development, not least the building and maintenance of the levees which kept the Mississippi River at bay. So the future belonged to those who could command capital, buy extensive acres, clear them, and then plant cotton on a large scale. Obviously no blacks fell into this category, nor did many local whites, and the Delta even in the late nineteenth century was much farmed by foreign and Northern investors, the ancestors of the agri-businesses which today dominate the landscape. In general, the region lacked a significant number of white small farmers, even of tenants and sharecroppers. Rich planters and poor blacks faced each other with unusual starkness. In such a system, African Americans were usually laborers, often sharecroppers, but in the former capacity a little better placed than in the Georgia Piedmont. In 1880, a black laborer in the Delta could earn seventy-five cents a day, compared to fifty cents in the Piedmont, and so Mississippi was a place to which many migrated, often at the behest of white recruiters. (Hence Yazoo became a station on the way from, say, Alabama to Chicago.) But one traveled there at no little risk. The ferocity of racial violence, directed by the small number of poorer whites against blacks, was extraordinary: lynchings were only the most Gothic part of the Delta's broad, deep culture of beatings, burnings, and physical intimidation.

Deep Souths is unusual. We have had not a few comparative studies of the South and other countries (South Africa, Brazil, Russia, Prussia, Italy)[12] and, more rarely than one might expect, of the South and the northern United States.[13] Almost all Southern historians are sensitive to local variations within a given state, for these have especially driven politics. So a scholar of Alabama familiarly deals with the Black Belt, the hill country, the Wiregrass region, and so forth. But rigorous comparative studies of different subregions of the wider South are extremely rare. Unrigorous assertions about the border South as compared to the Black Belt, the Tidewater against the upcountry, are common enough—I have made them myself—indeed indispensable to recent interpretations of the South's political economy.[14] But Harris, in effect, deconstructs the presumption that subregions where African Americans were a very large proportion of the population can be grouped together, that there is something called "the Deep South" available as a stable point of reference. This is an insight worth keeping in mind. However, I am not sure that Harris's narrative form helps the reader to keep to this, to maintain a focus on the comparative dimension. His book is agreeably written and he has a nice touch in telling stories which make the economic and social abstractions concrete, but his division of the three places into three periods means that the reader is made to hop with great rapidity from dyke to levee, from red clay soil to oyster banks, from Tom Watson to LeRoy Percy, and it is easy to lose a thread not frequently reiterated. In a way, as valuable is to contemplate the many tables which Harris has provided in an appendix, which provide a detailed survey of many things of importance: population, agricultural production, lynchings, voting patterns, scales of ownership/tenancy/sharecropping, farm sizes, and occupations, many arranged according to race.

Michael Perman deals with a more familiar historical problem, the process by which Southern blacks, given the vote during Reconstruction, had it taken away by the turn of the century. Within this, Perman suggests two phases. That from the mid-1870s to the mid-1890s was marked by voter fraud and manipulation, that is, by intimidation, violence, the alteration of ballots, and laws intended to gerrymander constituencies. The second from 1890 to 1908 (Perman's subject matter) was marked by voter elimination, the use of state constitutions to re-structure the electorate. It is important to Perman to see these phases as distinct. The first mooted no principles, but was a series of improvised measures, often local, that nowhere changed the fundaments of the state. The second was a sort of systematic moral reform, intended as a final settlement of issues previously messy, dishonest, and inconsistent. In this argument, Perman does not greatly differ from those made by C. Vann Woodward and J. Morgan Kousser many years ago.[15] But there has long been unclarity over who initiated disfranchisement and especially over whether the sharp drop in the size of the white electorate was intended, or merely a by-product of the elimination of black voters. Woodward, the Populist sympathizer, suspected that elite Southerners were as (if not more) interested in removing white radicals from the rolls.

Perman does the obvious thing, which oddly no one has bothered to do before. He takes each state in turn, beginning with Tennessee in 1889 and ending with Georgia in 1908, and carefully logs the sequence of events: who called constitutional conventions (or passed amendments) and why, what was the political context, who resisted or wanted change, what options were offered and adopted, what were the political consequences for the electorates and the parties. In addition, he intersperses chapters which monitor the evolving attitude of Washington (the presidency, Congress, the Supreme Court) to the process gathering pace, in evident subversion of the Fourteenth and Fifteenth Amendments. Hence, if you are someone interested in gender and Jim Crow, or intertextuality in racial ideology, or any number of new theoretical perspectives, you would be well advised to give *Struggle for Mastery* a miss. This is political history of an old-fashioned sort, a narrative of what votes were taken, what politicians said and did, what people intended. But it is a very able and clear history, which adds to our understanding.

Perman sees much diversity, but also a pattern. Events in one state influenced the next in the chain, but each reform necessarily occurred within the idiosyncrasies of a local political economy, while also being structured by the exigencies of a specific moment (before the depression of the 1890s, during it, after the Populist crisis, etc.). Perman stresses the solemnity and complexity of the process: solemn, because there was a sense that illegal cheating was no way to run a government, but that legal cheating would be better; complex, because revising whole constitutions (as was done in Mississippi, South Carolina, Louisiana, Alabama, and Virginia) was a long-winded process and even submitting constitutional amendments (done in all the other states) was not easy, since it mandated a scrutiny of the whole texture of political life. On the other hand, the South had a long tradition of constitutional revision. Conventions had been common before the Civil War, the establishment of the Confederacy had required more tinkering, and then the course of Reconstruction had sometimes required conventions in quick succession. So these were people with the knack. Indeed this frequency somewhat undercuts Perman's insistence that disfranchisement by constitutional means signified a qualitative shift, a formality of graver import. Someone attending a convention in 1895 had no especial reason to expect that the outcome of the deliberations would last much beyond a generation and might, in fact, anticipate more provisionality even than that.

First, a little about the diversity. In Mississippi and South Carolina, upcountry farmers initiated disfranchisement, but in the former the Black Belt much resisted, while in the latter the low country bought in. In both states, the Republicans had long since dwindled to a nullity, so this was overwhelmingly a debate within the Democratic party. In Louisiana and North Carolina, however, the Populist revolt had led to a Populist-Republican fusion which had taken power in the latter state and severely diminished Democratic control in the former: there, disfranchisement was explicitly a move by Democrats to destroy the electoral bases for Populist-Republican success. Something similar happened in Maryland, though there events happened in the early 1900s, so the Populists were no longer a factor. In other states (Alabama, Virginia), in contradistinction, disfranchisement was a move by progressive factions who believed that the existence or threat of the black vote strengthened conservative power. But here the liberals were outflanked by conservatives, who came to realize that the same mechanisms which disfranchised blacks would also disfranchise whites, and so understood that granting the reformers' wish would thwart what the reformers desired. (So these states answer to Woodward's model.) In Texas and Georgia, on the other hand, the progressives sponsored disfranchisement, but they also maintained control of the process.

What tended to be standard were the means. Though many strategies were proposed, including giving votes to women, a limited number of techniques emerged, the more readily seen to be efficacious the later in the cycle a state fell and the more experience had accumulated. (One must remember, of course, that the U.S. Constitution forbade anything so explicit as constitutional clauses which said, "No black person may vote in the state of Alabama," and hence indirection was of the essence.) First, there was the introduction of the secret, so-called Australian ballot, which came to replace *viva voce* voting or ballots provided by parties: its efficacy lay in the ability of election officials to disqualify ballots, *in camera*, and more generally in its drastically reducing the number of people capable of discerning the plausibility of election returns, formerly evident when voting had been public. Second, there was the poll tax, the requirement that voters pay for the right to vote, usually much in advance. Third, there were various qualifying tests, especially one requiring a voter to show an "understanding" of the state's constitution. All of these, in fact, did not in themselves discriminate between black and white voters, for a black might be more literate than a white or be more able and anxious to pay his poll tax. Much depended upon shifting power into the hands of registrars, who could arbitrarily declare a Harvard Ph.D. illiterate or neglect to notice a poll tax unpaid by a white man, or be closed on the day someone wished to register. Hence Democratic party control of election officials was at the heart of the matter.

Perman stresses that, though the impulse for disfranchisement often came from white-majority areas, no such reform was possible unless the white leaders of the black-majority areas gave their consent. This was not immediately forthcoming, not least because planters often (if unstably) controlled the votes of their black tenants, employees, and sharecroppers. So consent was given only when planters were confident that the changes would not diminish both their local and statewide power, indeed would enhance it. Further, these reforms had no especial mandate from the existing electorate, but were engineered by the party elites. So there was no planter conspiracy, but rather a process which many factions strove to work to their advantage, but which the planters did rather better at managing. In the end, everyone white agreed on the desirability of disfranchising blacks. Some hoped that poorer whites, too, especially if they were Republicans, would be eliminated, but most thought the new rules could be implemented in such a way as to sustain the white electorate. The great drops in white voting came as a surprise to many, if a pleasant surprise to the Black Belt, as well as to those urban and middle class reformers who thought the electoral process would be the healthier for the absence of poor illiterates.

Especially illuminating are the chapters where Perman notices Washington's response to all this fiddling. The failure of the Lodge Force Bill in 1892 is familiar to historians, but few have looked beyond it. When the Democrats took over control of the presidency and Congress in 1893, they promptly repealed federal election laws on the books since the early 1870s, though against only token Republican opposition. Thereafter, the Republicans in power could only venture punishing the South retroactively for its misdeeds by invoking the Fourteenth Amendment, which gave Washington the power to reduce a state's representation, in proportion to those disfranchised. (So, if a state had four members of the House of Representatives and disfranchised a quarter of its electorate, it might go down to three members.) Certainly there was a moral case. As voters disappeared from Southern rolls but federal representation stayed unaltered, the remaining Southern voters came to exercise a grotesquely inflated influence. As a senator from Wisconsin indignantly observed even in 1890, why should "378,897 voters in the South elect twenty-six members of the Congress and 353,691 voters elect only nine in Wisconsin"?[16] The presidency of William McKinley gave little answer to this cogent question, but only made polite noises towards the South, still more polite during and after a Spanish-American War launched from Southern soil towards Cuba. Something a little better was managed late in 1900, when the results of that year's census reached Congress, and it had to decide how to adjust representation. Edgar D. Crumpacker of Indiana, among others not blessed with a name from a William Dean Howells novel, made an effort to reduce the representations of those states which had enacted formal disfranchisement measures. They lost, but there was a serious airing of the issues. Nonetheless even many Republicans felt it was pointless to agitate this matter. Some even entertained the hope that a Republican party, bleached lily-white, might be able to make more headway in the South, which indeed it came to do, though not for another half century and more.

It is usual for historians to look on this episode of disfranchisement through the lens of the late twentieth century. To this, Perman forms no exception. But there may be more merit in setting it against the early nineteenth. Few in South Carolina in 1830 would have been surprised at the events of the 1890s. In Southern political culture before 1860, the Federalist impulse which regarded the people as a great beast had never quite abated, though it became increasingly difficult to say such things in the open. Moreover, slavery had placed its own asterisk against the notion of democracy, so that even Jacksonians had never had to commit themselves to a franchise open to all men, and certainly many Whigs had not done so, even for white men. Radical Reconstruction called everyone's bluff. Suddenly white Southerners were asked to be serious democrats, without regard to race, class, or religion, but keeping only to gender as an exclusionary principle. That they could not do so, was not only because they were racists, but also because few of them had ever been unmitigated democrats, however much they might have chanted the names of Jefferson and Jackson. Their democracy had been instrumental; they had been willing to give votes to people whom they trusted, as a way to share power not to diminish it. Little wonder that in the brutal economic and social times of the 1890s, this tentative sense of trust so rapidly disintegrated. Little surprise, too, that the Democrat who introduced the 1893 legislation to repeal federal oversight of elections was a Virginian named Henry St. George Tucker, who was the great nephew of Nathaniel Beverley Tucker, himself the half-brother of John Randolph of Roanoke.[17] It was Beverley Tucker who used to speak to the College of William and Mary's law students of democracy's "rabble, drunk with flattery and alcohol, [who] unite to plunder and oppress the middle classes, and shout the praises of parties and demagogues." And John Randolph, who was among the most conservative and charismatic of Virginian politicians, a man who saw little reason to move beyond the constitution Virginia had had in the mid-eighteenth century, in 1829 had famously insisted, "I would not live under King Numbers." Seventy-five years later, a Tucker could look out on a Virginia where only about a quarter of adult males were voting and reflect that his ancestor would feel vindicated.[18]

NOTES

1. This allusion is to the (then recent) occasion, when the Majority Leader of the United States Senate had observed, at a farewell birthday party for Strom Thurmond: "I want to say this about my state. When Strom Thurmond ran for president, we voted for him. We're proud of it. And if the rest of the country had followed our lead, we wouldn't have had all these problems over all these years, either."

2. This has been variously attributed to meetings of Chou-En-Lai with French journalists, Henry Kissinger, Richard Nixon, and Tony Benn, so may safely be regarded as apocryphal.

3. Gabor Boritt, ed., *The Lincoln Enigma: The Changing Faces of an American Icon* (New York: Oxford University Press, 2001), 6.

4. Ibid., 142, 134.

5. I would quote from this essay, but it is prefaced with the strange and impractical admonishment: "This essay may not be duplicated, printed, published, or quoted without the previous written consent of the author" (72). But is one allowed to quote the proscription?

6. Boritt, *Lincoln Enigma*, 210.

7. Allen C. Guelzo, *Abraham Lincoln: Redeemer President* (Grand Rapids, MI: William B. Eerdsman, 1999), 19, 110.

8. Ibid., 110, 118.

9. David W. Blight, *Race and Reunion: The Civil War in American Memory* (Cambridge, MA; Harvard University Press, Belknap, 2001), 18.

10. Ibid., 209–10.

11. J. William Harris, *Deep Souths: Delta, Piedmont, and Sea Island Society in the Age of Segregation* (Baltimore, MD: Johns Hopkins University Press, 2001), 5.

12. George M. Fredrickson, *White Supremacy: A Comparative Study of American and South African History* (New York: Oxford University Press, 1981); Carl N. Degler, *Neither Black Nor White: Slavery and Race Relations in Brazil and the United States* (New York: Macmillan, 1971); Peter Kolchin, *Unfree Labor: American Slavery and Russian Serfdom* (Cambridge, MA: Harvard University Press, Belknap, 1987); Shearer Davis Bowman, *Masters & Lords: Mid-19th-Century U.S. Planters and Prussian Junkers* (New York: Oxford University Press, 1993); Enrico Dal Lago and Rick Halpern, eds., *The American South and the Italian Mezzogiorno: Essays in Comparative History* (New York: Palgrave, 2002).

13. Of late, notably, the *Valley of the Shadow* project at the University of Virginia, which has been comparing Augusta County, Virginia, and Franklin County, Pennsylvania. This is mostly a website (http://www.iath.virginia.edu/vshadow2/), where many original sources can be found. See also Edward L. Ayers and Ann S. Rubin, *The Valley of the Shadow: Two Communities in the American Civil War – the Eve of War* (New York: W. W. Norton, 2000), which has a CD-Rom.

14. For example, William W. Freehling has recently been much preoccupied with the issue of the border states in the origins and course of the Civil War: see William W. Freehling, *The South vs. the South: How Anti-Confederate Southerners Shaped the Course of the Civil War* (New York: Oxford University Press, 2001).

15. C. Vann Woodward, *Origins of the New South, 1877–1913* (Baton Rouge: Louisiana State University Press, 1951); J. Morgan Kousser, *The Shaping of Southern Politics: Suffrage Restriction and the Establishment of the One-Party South, 1880–1910* (New Haven, CT: Yale University Press, 1974).

16. Michael Perman, *Struggle for Mastery: Disfranchisement in the South, 1888–1908* (Chapel Hill: University of North Carolina Press, 2001), 117.

17. Perman, *Struggle for Mastery*, 45; on Henry St. George Tucker, see W. Hamilton Bryson, *Legal Education in Virginia, 1779–1979: A Biographical Approach* (Charlottesville: University Press of Virginia, 1982), 615–23.

18. Nathaniel Beverley Tucker, *A Series of Lectures on the Science of Government, Intended to Prepare the Student for the Study of the Constitution of the United States* (Philadelphia, PA: Carey and Hart, 1845), 44; *Proceedings and Debates of the Virginia State Convention, of 1829–30* (Richmond, VA: Samuel Shepherd, 1830), 321. For the statistics, see Kousser, *Shaping of Southern Politics*, 226.

RACE

A review of Jane Dailey, *Before Jim Crow: The Politics of Race in Postemancipation Virginia* (Chapel Hill: University of North Carolina Press, 2000), Stephen David Kantrowitz, *Ben Tillman and the Reconstruction of White Supremacy* (Chapel Hill: University of North Carolina Press, 2000), and Jane Dailey, Glenda Elizabeth Gilmore, and Bryant Simon, eds., *Jumpin' Jim Crow: Southern Politics from Civil War to Civil Rights* (Princeton, NJ: Princeton University Press, 2000), in the *Times Literary Supplement* (May 25, 2001): 13–14.

Things are not always what they seem. In the presidential election of 2000, about seven hundred thousand people in Florida were deemed ineligible to vote, though they were over eighteen, American citizens, and residents. As is now well known, they were identified in lists sent out to election boards by the Florida secretary of state, Katherine Harris, she of the tight smile and determined air. The formal justification was that all these were felons and, by Floridian law, no felon serving or having served a prison sentence can vote, unless they have petitioned for the restoration of their civil rights. The informal justification, the source of her Republican anxiety to enforce the law, was of course that the poor (white, black, and brown) disproportionately vote Democratic and populate penitentiaries. Though African Americans constitute 14 percent of Florida's population, they make up 55 percent of its prison inmates, and about 31 percent of the black men in Florida over the age of 18 have been convicted of a felony, and so seldom trouble election officials.

This looks like the old game, which has been played in the South since the late nineteenth century: the statute which superficially looks neutral, but is carefully designed to exclude from the electorate those who might oppose the will of white elites. In fact, it may not be the old game (or not in inception), though the officials of the American Civil Liberties Union who are suing the state of Florida for racial discrimination would prefer that it was so. For, in fact, the law dates from 1868, when a constitutional convention inserted into the state's fundamental law, as Article XIV, Section 2, wording to the effect that the mad might not vote, but neither could "any person convicted of felony be qualified to vote at any election unless restored to civil rights."[1]

There had been no such clause in the Confederate Constitution of 1860, and that of 1868 was written by Radical Republicans, in a convention where 40 percent of the members were black. It seems likely that the clause was not aimed at freedmen, who when slaves had existed mostly outside of the legal system and who had barely begun to populate jails by 1868, but at the white Southerners who had, over the years, had the most traffic with sheriffs, judges, and warders. In this fact is the cold truth that whoever controls a political system will wish to rig the electorate to suit its purposes, but also that in our beginnings are not necessarily our ends, for what was intended in 1868 is not what this clause did in 2000. Those American jurists (including Chief Justice Rehnquist) who assert that intent should govern judicial interpretation would make a sad muddle of the law if they took 1868 as the basis for construing 2000. But, then, as we also know, in *George W. Bush, et al., Petitioners v. Albert Gore, Jr., et al. on a writ of certiorari to the Florida Supreme Court*, they did make a sad muddle.

These new books on the origins and course of the Jim Crow system would not, I think, be much surprised at the above. Their insistent message is that the pattern of Southern racial and political relations since 1865 has been fluid, unpredictable, and seldom linear. In this contention is a partial return to arguments made by C. Vann Woodward in *The Strange Career of Jim Crow* in 1955. (In fact, *Jumpin' Jim Crow* has a preface by Woodward, written not long before his death.) He had been anxious to claim that segregation had been slow to develop in the late nineteenth century, had been much impelled by internal political squabbles among whites, and (being contingent) need not be regarded as fixed. Over the years, these hopeful contentions were much battered by critics and events. Segregation was shown to have had antebellum origins and to have been sometimes preferred by the black community in the 1860s and 1870s, but also to have been imbedded in a broader system of violence and repression, besides which Woodward's gesture of hope seemed frail, even quixotic. The metanarrative of Southern history which emerged from the civil rights movement came to define the period from 1954 to the death of Martin Luther King, Jr., as a peculiarly heroic moment, a definitive advancement, before which there had been darkness, after which there was light. Segregation was understood as a more-or-less inevitable product of the Southern white refusal of Radical Reconstruction, a rejection which had produced a starkly efficient and little-contested "Jim Crow era."

There has been restlessness with this narrative for several years, mostly from younger scholars. Some are politely bored with older people who preen themselves on having marched at Selma and who suggest tactlessly that the young are a lesser breed, come to dine after the feast. The "movement" was peculiarly a religious experience, imagining a "beloved community," and the warming sound of the hymns has faded. Many have noticed that the Voting Rights Act of 1965 and desegregation did not erase racism, and did not even remove much de facto segregation. Some black intellectuals have become mildly nostalgic about the lost communities of the South, prefer Malcolm X to King, John Coltrane to Louis Armstrong, and many (not merely African Americans) urge what is now called diversity, which can often look uncomfortably like what used to be called voluntary segregation. Others observe that much happened before 1954, that Jim Crow was never a perfected system, since the Southern world was always more subtle and shifting than could be strictly legislated and policed. It is not so much that today there is a clear case for pessimism or optimism about, what Thomas Holt has recently called, in an echo of W. E. B. Du Bois, "the problem of race in the twenty-first century." One day the police set up roadblocks to interrogate black voters on their way to the polls, and the American world feels like 1948. The next day a black man becomes U.S. secretary of state and one knows it is no longer 1948. Rather, the tone is one of uncertainty. As a consequence, historians seem to be drawn to moments, whose leitmotif is unclarity. As Nancy MacLean puts it in her shrewd essay on the Leo Frank case in *Jumpin' Jim Crow*, "change and contestation, not stasis and consensus, constituted the very essence of early-twentieth-century southern history," a moment usually regarded as least contested, but now promoted to the status of the conflicted.[2]

Narrating opacity has its risks, on the whole avoided here. Jane Dailey's *Before Jim Crow* is an elegant, often sardonic study of the Readjuster movement in Virginia in the 1870s and 1880s. This was a liberal biracial coalition of black and white Republicans, plus assorted white Democrats, who sought to "readjust," that is, repudiate the state debts which Virginian conservatives had thought it essential to repay, even at the cost of starving the public school system. For a few heady years, the Readjusters held the governorship, the state legislature, and most of the state's congressional delegation, including its two senators. They foundered on the sexual politics of race, when they appointed two black men to the Richmond school board and whites reacted badly to the prospect of African Americans controlling white female teachers. Compared to Dailey's work, Steven Kantrowitz's *Ben Tillman and the Reconstruction of White Supremacy* is longer, bleaker, and more ambitious. "Pitchfork Ben," the South Carolinian governor and senator, used to be regarded as a sort of honorary Populist, the advocate of the poor white man, but in Kantrowitz's account he is portrayed as a cruel terrorist, a wealthy man affecting folksiness, a coward of violent words and little action, and an abrupt patriarch. (The politics of households loom large in all of these books.) Dailey and Kantrowitz show, then, the two sides of the coin: the Readjusters suggest what might have been, Tillman what mostly was. As historians, though, they might usefully have swapped topics, for Dailey's skepticism seems often at odds with her upbeat message, while Kantrowitz has the outraged air of a man vexed to be sharing a book with so many brutes. Such ambivalence is carried through in *Jumpin' Jim Crow*, which collects valuable essays by many of the brighter young historians who are studying the South from the mid-1870s to the 1930s. As its introduction explains, by them "white supremacy is not seen as an overwhelming force ... [but] a precarious balancing act, pulled in all directions by class, gender, and racial tensions." They wish to "denaturalize white supremacy," to expose its contingency, and to show the absence of inevitability. There is the fairly clear implication that we should take heart from these assertions.[3]

Perhaps we should. It is hard not to respect this recrudescence of the Woodwardian attention to "forgotten alternatives." But the tone of these books is too indecisive to be utterly convincing. No doubt, everything is contingent, nothing is inevitable. The philosophers of history, before and after Isaiah Berlin, have been much divided on the matter of inevitability, but we live in times disposed towards placing philosophy in the service of what Richard Rorty calls "social hope."[4] Yet the analytical choice does not lie between inevitability and contingency, but between degrees of contingency. As far as I can see, the historical record is clear, and it favors less, not more contingency. In every Southern state in the thirty years or so after Reconstruction, biracialism failed, disfranchisement was accomplished, segregation was established, a systematic policy of cruel discrimination was followed. The details vary, no doubt. In one state, biracialism lasted longer; in another, disfranchisement came earlier; in a third, more were lynched; in a fourth, the demagogues were especially hypocritical. But the pattern is much the same. The lights gradually went out. This looks about as close to inevitability as human experience gets. These historians ask us to look at a glass which was, at best, 20 percent full and, from this sight, take doubtful courage. But one does not have to be much of a pessimist to observe that it looks 80 percent empty.

NOTES

1. The text is online at http://www.law.fsu.edu/crc/conhist/1868con.html.
2. Thomas C. Holt, *The Problem of Race in the Twenty-First Century* (Cambridge, MA: Harvard University Press, 2000); Jane Dailey, Glenda Elizabeth Gilmore, and Bryant Simon, *Jumpin' Jim Crow: Southern Politics from Civil War to Civil Rights* (Princeton, NJ: Princeton University Press, 2000), 186.
3. Dailey, Gilmore, and Simon, *Jumpin' Jim Crow*, 4.
4. Richard Rorty, *Philosophy and Social Hope* (Harmondsworth: Penguin, 1999). For a sampling, see Isaiah Berlin, "Historical Inevitability," in *Four Essays on Liberty* (Oxford: Oxford University Press, 1969), 41–117; Karl R. Popper, *The Poverty of Historicism* (London: Routledge & Paul, 1957); Sidney Hook, ed., *Determinism and Freedom in the Age of Modern Science: A Philosophical Symposium* (New York: New York University Press, 1958); Bernard Berofsky, ed., *Free Will and Determinism* (New York: Harper & Row, 1966); Raymond Aron, *Introduction to the Philosophy of History: An Essay on the Limits of Historical Objectivity* (London: Weidenfeld and Nicolson, 1961); Arthur C. Danto, *Analytical Philosophy of History* (Cambridge: Cambridge University Press, 1968); and Maurice Mandelbaum, *The Anatomy of Historical Knowledge* (Baltimore, MD: Johns Hopkins University Press, 1977).

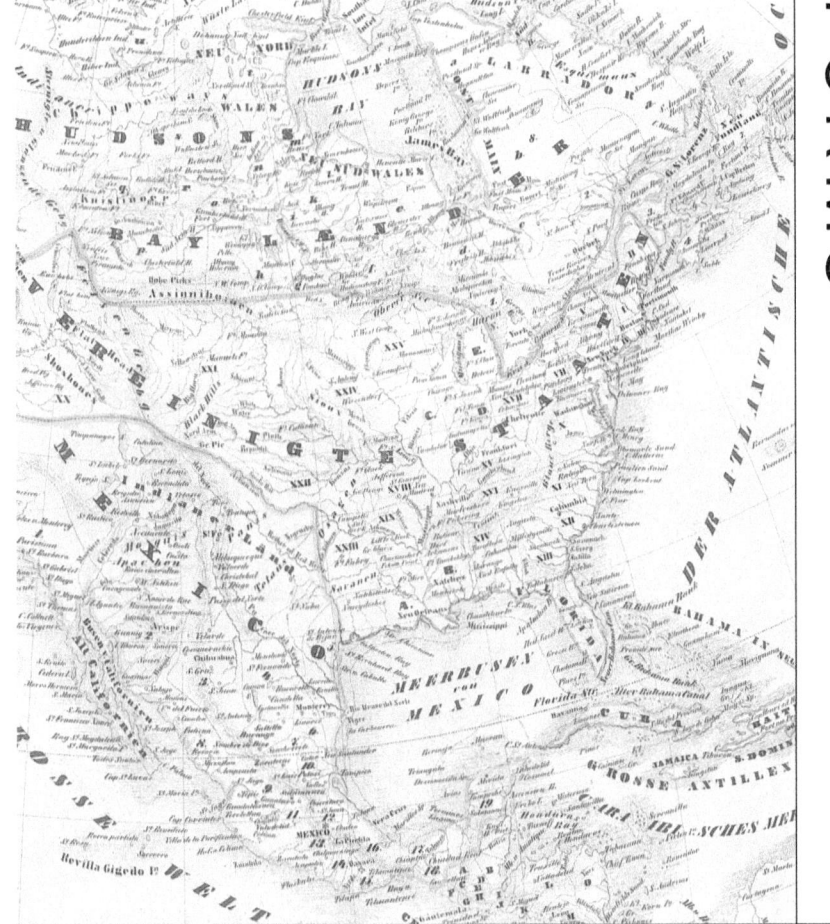

FORMS

Michael O'Brien, "Of Cats, Historians, and Gardeners," *Journal of American History* 89 (June 2002): 48–53, a contribution to the "Round Table: Self and Subject," in which contributors were asked to comment on whether historians should talk about themselves in narratives. Copyright © Organization of American Historians. All rights reserved. Reprinted by permission.

Let me try a preface in two ways.

One warm, rainy, English afternoon, I was sitting in my college room and thinking about death. My cat had just died. He had grown very old, straggly, weak, and much dependent. In his last days, he had taken to crying out in the night and I had become used to getting up, seeking him out, and putting him on the pillow next to my head, where it had been his custom to sleep when younger. It did not seem to help, at least not him. Nineteen years is old for a cat, so it was not unexpected. Still, loss is loss. As it happened, as the rain beat against the high window which looks out on the chapel, I was beginning to write about a death elsewhere, to be included in this book on politics and the rituals of mourning in Alamance County, North Carolina, in the 1830s. I had recently been sent an unexpected manuscript, the diary of a young woman whose husband had been drowned in a freshet, a disaster which she herself had survived, if only just. For ten months, she kept anguished, detailed records of what happened, how she felt, how death was negotiated. It was all there, sharp and unremitting. The body ("wrinkled and bloated"), the laying-out ("Aunt Betty came"), the prayers ("Oh Lord, our help in ages past"), the taking of the baby to the body ("Sally did not understand"), the poverty which followed ("I asked Mr Jones to help with the pigs, but he said he was busy"), her thinking about widowhood and its unexpected freedom ("the bed is empty, which is sometimes a pleasure").[1] Somehow, it helped in understanding the diary of Jemima O'Rourke, that Georg (named when I was young and Hegelian) had just died, that it was raining. The implications were not simple. In ancient Egypt, the death of Georg would have been more important than the drowning of David O'Rourke, for a cat was divine. In medieval Bosnia, cats were killed and buried in small, oak coffins, placed inside that of their newly deceased masters and carried clockwise around the church. (Dissidents did it anti-clockwise and there had been a small war over it in 1327.) So, I began to see how death is cultural, but also how we privilege a man's death in ways specific to time and place. Then I noticed, obscurely placed in the diary, a discussion of the death of a cow called Phyllida. (She had fallen off a bank and crushed a goat.) When I had first looked at the manuscript, my eye had slid over the incident. But now I saw how hierarchy was working in Jemima's imagination. How we understand death in nature, too, is cultural. Only a few days earlier, the college had been obliged to slaughter one of the deer in the Deer Park, because it showed symptoms of foot-and-mouth disease, and the death had prompted me to wonder why Bert, the college gardener, who had recently had a bad cold, was permitted to live . . .

Well, one could run on in this vein for quite a while. Let me try it again.

For several decades, historians have been interested in the cultural dynamics of mourning, death, and cultural hierarchy. The French historian, Pierre du Chatelet, whose study of La Vendée was so instrumental in showing how class and gender have structured ritual responses to death, has reminded us that the cultures of death and the patterns of politics are interconnected.[2] Yet American historians have been slow to apply his insights to the fate of American republicanism after 1776, despite the very large literature which the topic has generated. Death as a theme has been neglected, though even a quick look at the original sources will show that Americans in the early republic were very concerned, even obsessed, with how death was interwoven with the political scene. "I would rather see the u states die than yield to the barbrous opression of the British yoke," wrote Andrew Jackson on the eve of the Battle of New Orleans.[3] Death and the republic went hand in hand, which is understandable as a perspective in a society where death was not hidden, where bodies were laid out openly in parlors, where life was short, where parents lost children with sickening frequency, where cattle had their throats cut in the yard to provide dinner, where violence and politics were intermingled. Jackson himself killed several men in duels and his political rhetoric was soaked in the imagery of blood, power, and death. Yet it has become clear that, though it is helpful to study the speeches of political leaders, the dynamics of republican death are best understood at the local level. There, one can see how men and women responded to the immediacy of death, how it affected their worldview, and how in turn it helped to structure the politics of households and the state. For this reason, this book will concentrate on Alamance County, North Carolina, during the nineteenth century. This county offers an abundance of rich sources: the legal records of probate courts, the documents produced by the churches, the rhetoric of a complex and shifting political scene, a rich trove of diaries and letters, including (unusually) some written by yeomen women. Preeminent is the diary of Jemima O'Rourke...

What difference does it make, the one narrative or the other?

One difference is obvious. In the first narrative, the historian is given a life, a place, and a texture, and there the story begins. Thereby the past is drawn into the life of the historian. Seen in one light, this has the merit of honesty. As a practical matter, one might think, this is how historical narrative does happen: first the historian, then the history. Another difference may be less obvious. This narrative asks for sympathy and invites the reader to know the historian, who shares confidences, pain, doubt, or ambition, things which readers know, too. It has become a premise that readers like the confessional and the intimate in a world where the marketing techniques of publishers pay deference to the cultural logic of Oprah Winfrey. A historian, too, might wish for celebrity, perhaps not the giddy intoxication of being hunted by paparazzi, but the lesser charms of appearing on a PBS show, of testifying to a congressional committee, of having an agent, of requiring five-thousand-dollars-plus-expenses for a lecture, of buying a summer home in Maine, and of helping in the revival of narrative. (Few seem to be interested in reviving narrative, unless a large check is involved.) The confessional can be a move into the market, can be a raised voice claiming attention. Indeed Colin Campbell has made a plausible case that the emergence of consumerism was a predicate for the Romantic ethic, which lies at the root of these issues.[4]

Of course, seen in another, neoclassical light, history does not begin with the historian, but with the past. The world makes events, leaves evidence of what occurred, and the historian comes along and tries to make sense of it. The historian is retrospective, not only to the past, but to other historians. This presumption informs the second narrative, which mimics the standard rhetoric—the evocation of the formative historian, the nature of the debate, the analytical decision, then the nature of the sources. In it, nowhere does the historian speak of self. Yet this, too, could be understood as a deflected narcissism. For the account does not, in fact, begin with the past of Alamance County, but with another historian. Only eventually do Andrew Jackson and Jemima O'Rourke appear, as a sort of vindication of someone at the Collège de France. The author borrows intellectual authority from the profession of history, at large. Still, everyone in the second narrative is, formally at least, not the author, but other people in the past. By such an impersonal voice, the illusion is created that the past makes the narrative, that we can in some measure be true to something beyond self and prior to self.

Philosophically, almost everything is in favor of the first narrative. From David Hume to Ludwig Wittgenstein and beyond, it has been cogently demonstrated that there is no escape from self, no objectivity, no past, only fractured words in the present, which flits unstably by. Clearly, the confessional is epistemologically defensible, or as defensible as any pattern of words, and (almost certainly) less deceptive than the simulation of dispassion. Of late, there are those who even find the confessional to be morally cogent, who have therapeutic theories about the self-exploration of social and individual identities, and who think that history might serve the great purpose of health, as though a convention of the Organization of American Historians were a sort of exercise room, where smoking is forbidden and exercise bikes are compulsory. Their theoretical ancestor among philosophers of history is, perhaps, Wilhelm Dilthey, who in about 1910 observed that knowing the world and knowing self were dialectically interdependent: "The understanding of other persons and their expressions of life is based upon both the lived experience and understanding of oneself, and their continual interaction."[5]

Yet, despite this sanction from philosophy, there is something disquieting about the confessional historian, if the center of the historical enterprise is not the historian, but those whom she or he narrates. It will seem that every sentence spent on the historian distracts attention from the others, the people in the past. Partly, this is a matter of scale. The historian is one person, but the past is thousands and more, a myriad of documents, a confusion of voices, besides which the historian is very small beer. A historian might want us to be interested in what his grandfather used to say about Confederate veterans, in how the sun shone when she once went to view the battlefield, in what someone once told him at a Civil War round table. But is this not inconsequential compared to what happened at Gettysburg? Is not the battle's reality diminished if we can gain an entrance to the battlefield only through the tiny doorway of the historian's self? Yet, for good or ill, that is the only doorway we have. Much hinges on whether one wishes to celebrate the good or hide the ill.

Since any history is a negotiation between the historian and the people of the past, there is a balance of power involved. In practice, the historian, if not omnipotent, has a power difficult to constrain. She or he is everywhere in the narrative, in the tone of voice, in the expression of significance, and in the choice of evidence. Those narrated speak only when asked to, say only what the historian wishes to have known, and (unless it is a work of recent history) are unable to respond, being dead. A wise historian knows of this corrupting authority and tries to work against its grain by lending sympathy to the dead, even to those for whom he or she feels little sympathy. (The historian must have the gift of hypocrisy.) Does it not further overbalance matters if the historian, besides having the usual advantages, also claims the spotlight and says, look at Margaret Fuller, but first look at me?

Then, there is a rhetorical problem. The trouble with the confessional is that it tries to be friendly, reduces things to an individual scale, and wishes to forge a bond between author and reader. It need not be so, but the American version tends to speak with the pleasant cadences of *All Things Considered* and is usually sentimental, and hence inflexible as a rhetoric. Considering that history itself is very often unfriendly, works on a scale which swamps the individual, and snaps bonds with regularity, this tone is limiting. For history is not, on the whole, someone one would wish to know, just a host of somebodies one needs to know, as a matter of urgent human knowledge.

Lastly, there is an asymmetry. When a scholarly history is written, there are procedures. One must provide a scholarly apparatus by which the reader may judge competence and probity. But a personal past is, by comparison, irresponsible. No ethic requires even the historian to undertake research into the accuracy of memory, from which there is little appeal. I tell you a story, of what happened to me when I was thirteen, of an encounter in an archive, or an intellectual confrontation when someone waved a poker at me. Or I remember a family legend, something my Uncle Bill once told me about his entering Buchenwald. How can I know if he told it aright, or even if I am accurate in my retelling, it being long ago and a Christmas party when both he and I were the worse for wear? By convention, historical narrative requires what men and women take for proof. But the self lacks rigor and has difficulty in passing the ordinary tests, by which historical narrative has consented to be judged. It may not be the lesser for being unrigorous, but it is available on different terms.

Still, these need not be cold choices, all one thing or the other. History is a mix of genres, more than a single one, and takes many forms: the long narrative, the biography, the article, the essay, the book review, the conference paper, the job talk. For those moments when one is unusually conscious of having contemporary interlocutors, the confessional may be a valuable device, which can decorate a prolegomenon, point a moral, or raise a laugh. And there is no reason why a historian should not write an autobiography or a memoir, though—Edward Gibbon, W. E. B. Du Bois, and Jill Ker Conway aside—the record is not encouraging.[6] Historians seem to bungle the self-reflective moment and, on the whole, live dull, inconspicuous lives. Compared to novelists and poets, they tend to be genteel, unwilling to narrate their own jagged hatreds, betrayals, sexual passions, and ugly experience, though happy enough to narrate those of others. Rather, historians like to show themselves as virtuous and competent, the prudent guardians of reform and hope, the users of inoffensive language. (The skeptical historian, contemplating the matter of Sally Hemings, may venture of Thomas Jefferson that he might have been a hypocrite, not that he was a fucking son-of-a-bitch.) This primness offers thin encouragement that the cultivation of self will yield much of literary range, comparable to Allen Ginsberg's *Howl* or Ewan McGregor's *Trainspotting*, though we might hope for a peer of Vladimir Nabokov's *Speak, Memory*.

On the other hand, if it is a tenable contention that the world is too crowded with prim authorities, nothing will strip history of its authority more readily than a steady supply of confessing historians, who have nothing to proclaim but their Emersonian self-trust, "impervious to the incidence of evil," especially in themselves.[7]

Yet none of this bears on the private awareness of the historian, only whether that awareness is made public. As to that private dimension, I presume it is crucial, but also that it will necessarily take many forms, for some historians are introspective, some not; some believe in iron repression, some in the weekly trip to the analyst; some are consumed with family and place, some dislike their parents and prefer anywhere but home; some believe in loyalty to a nation, race, gender, or sexuality, some think loyalty an oppression. That is as individuals prefer, and these tastes will necessarily affect narratives. Whether a narrative is the better, however, for *exposing* self-awareness—as opposed to being written *with* self-awareness—is complex. Henry Adams once said of the Gothic cathedral and, by implication, himself: "The delight of its aspirations is flung up to the sky. The pathos of its self-distrust and anguish of doubt is buried in the earth as its last secret."[8] Adams himself omitted what may have been his life's greatest event from *The Education of Henry Adams*, but it is doubtful if his memoir would be the better if he had told of the morning when he found his wife dying on the carpet. Secrets may interest readers and may drive authors, but a secret revealed grows rapidly dull. Worse, the therapeutic act might cure, and what is the use of a psychologically healthy author? And what would the confessing historian, if these habits became habitual, do in a second book? Find more family memories, more insights from personal experience? The poor historian will be obliged to blunder into the quagmire which has consumed so many modern novelists, whose first book deals with childhood and youth, whose second book deals with becoming a novelist, whose third book deals with the problem of having deadlines which arrive more rapidly than personal experience accumulates.

So it is not wrong that the historian tap personal experience when writing, because self is inescapable. Throughout this essay, for example, I have drawn on my own experience. But would it advance my analytical case to tell you where and how?

Though I will say, in case you are worried, that the college gardener is fine.

NOTES

1. Entries for 3 and 4 March, 12 May, 27 November 1833, Jemima O'Rourke Diary, Alamance County Historical Society, Graham, NC.

2. See Pierre du Chatelet, *La Crise de la mort: La Vendée, le deuil, et le destin de la république, 1789–1914* (Paris: Gallimard, 1982). Useful is *The Historical Poetics of Death: Pierre du Chatelet and His Critics*, ed. Andrew Porcher (Columbia: University of South Carolina Press, 1997), though it is preoccupied with modern Europe and has only one article on American history, oddly on the colonial period.

3. Andrew Jackson to Jean Baptiste Gayarré, 18 February 1815, in Harold D. Moser et al., *The Papers of Andrew Jackson: Volume III, 1814–1815* (Knoxville: University of Tennessee Press, 1991), 349.

4. Colin Campbell, *The Romantic Ethic and the Spirit of Modern Consumerism* (Oxford: Basil Blackwell, 1987).

5. Wilhelm Dilthey, "The Understanding of Other Persons and Their Expressions of Life," in *Descriptive Psychology and Historical Understanding*, trans. R. M. Zaner and K. L. Heiges (The Hague: Martinus Nijhoff, 1977), 123.

6. Edward Gibbon, *Memoirs of My Life*, ed. Georges Bonnard (New York: Funk & Wagnalls, 1969); W. E. B. Du Bois, *Dusk of Dawn: An Essay Toward an Autobiography of a Race Concept* (New York: Harcourt, Brace, 1940); Jill Ker Conway, *The Road from Coorain* (New York: Alfred A. Knopf, 1989).

7. George Santayana, "The Genteel Tradition in American Philosophy," (1913) in David A. Hollinger and Charles Capper, eds., *The American Intellectual Tradition*, 4th ed., 2 vols. (New York: Oxford University Press, 2001), 2:98.

8. Henry Adams, *Mont Saint Michel and Chartres* (1905), in Henry Adams, *Novels, Mont Saint Michel, The Education*, ed. Ernest Samuels and Jayne N. Samuels (New York: Library of America, 1983), 695.

BIOGRAPHY

Michael O'Brien, "Biography and the Old South: A Review Essay," *Virginia Magazine of History and Biography* 93 (October 1985): 375–88. Reprinted by permission.

In the last several years there have been an unusual number of biographies of antebellum Southerners.[1] But then there has been a general revival of biography. We know this because there now exist those ominous mausoleums, a journal and a center for study, both far off in Hawaii, where Leon Edel has issued *Principia Biographica*, which uses his own life of Henry James as the exemplum of modern practice. And there have been conferences and treatises. Rarely there have been controversies, because biographers (unlike historians) tend to be amiable people who like mainly to talk about their subjects or the hazards of their research and seldom bother with theory.[2] At one level, biography is the easiest, least problematical of forms, because the biographer is granted freely what is almost the historian's hardest task, defining and keeping within bounds his subject matter. Any historian can feel the wisdom of Charles Beard, who once instructed Eric Goldman, "Tell them, tell them that the old man says that writing any history is just pulling a tomcat by its tail across a Brussels carpet."[3] By comparison, nothing could be simpler than biography: get the subject born, carry him through life, get him buried, stop.

It is not that biography has not had problems. This age is not Carlylean, but suspicious of greatness. The flood of Napoleonic biographies which Pieter Geyl had once to study and stem has diminished. Instead of everyone haggling over the great lives, we seem to prefer the system of allowing one unfortunate soul to write the multivolume "definitive" biography while the rest do "minor" lives. In Southern history the biographies of the preeminent—John C. Calhoun, Thomas Jefferson, Jefferson Davis—are all from an older generation, and there seems to be no one scrambling to repeat the task for this generation. Robert Remini's recent three-volume life of Andrew Jackson is almost an oddity.

And there are troubling conceptual difficulties for biography in the recent temper. We have embraced the doctrines of utilitarianism and relevance, and it is hard to define how far a life is useful. We have granted the preeminence of sociology and psychology, thus making the public an extension of the private and the private justifiable by its illumination of the public. Thereby we have derogated character from both without and within, and left very little in between. Indeed, modernism has so weakened the doctrine of the solidity of character that it is difficult to find in the chronology of a life a sufficient still point from which the biographer may radiate. Most recently linguistics has detached language from flesh and bone, so that the texts of a life serve only deconstruction.

If biographers stopped to reflect on such matters, they would grow palsied. Fortunately, they almost never do. What passes for theory among biographers is a dinky toy compared to the armored vehicles of the semioticians, which rumble past the shuttered windows of ordinary historians. Whether to write biography is not a problem. Unfortunately, how to write it is, and on this score there is little ground for complacency.

This is not a golden age of Southern biography, but there are some good recent lives. Elisabeth Muhlenfeld is succinct and precise about Mary Chesnut. Lester Stephens has done a good job with some very intractable and technical material, and Joseph LeConte does—rather ponderously, because he was a rather solemn and ponderous man—appear before us. Drew Gilpin Faust presents an absorbing, didactic, and sociologically interesting portrait of James Henry Hammond. Norma Lois Peterson has resurrected a neglected figure, Littleton Waller Tazewell, and done him justice. Ray Mathis, largely by intruding so little upon an exegesis of the diaries of John Horry Dent, has evoked the life of an Alabama planter and a rather unedifying individual. Dickson J. Preston, though he sometimes writes with a freedom which justifies his book being prefaced by James Michener, has done a remarkable piece of detective work on Frederick Douglass's early life. These works, and the rest, cast a good deal of light on the history of the Old South.

They teach, for one thing, the variety of antebellum lives. These people moved with great freedom: Mary Chesnut the diarist from South Carolina to Mississippi and back; John Horry Dent the planter from South Carolina to Alabama and back to Georgia; Joseph LeConte the geologist from Georgia to South Carolina, back to Georgia, and on to California; Frederick Barnard the mathematician from New England to Alabama and back to New York; Renato Beluche the privateer from New Orleans to Colombia and all over the Caribbean basin; John M. Brooke the sailor from Virginia to West Africa and Japan, and back to Virginia; Lucy Audubon the schoolmistress from England to Cincinnati, down to Louisiana, back to England, and over to New York; Ashbel Smith the doctor from Connecticut to North Carolina, over to France, back to Texas, over to England, and back to Texas; Sul Ross the soldier from Iowa to Texas; Frederick Douglass the abolitionist from Maryland to New York, over to England, back to New York, and down to Haiti; Free Frank the entrepreneur from South Carolina to Kentucky, and finally to Illinois. There are, to be sure, settled lives—Littleton Waller Tazewell in Norfolk, John Taylor in Caroline County, James Henry Hammond in South Carolina, Thomas R. R. Cobb in Georgia, Charles Fraser in Charleston, W. W. Holden in North Carolina—but they are less definitive than Southern historians might once have thought. But then recent Southern historiography has become almost dominated by an interest in the elements of change and mobility in the region's history, and biography—which records social history willy-nilly, just by recording lives—is likely to embody the new enthusiasm.

Intellectual history, also a recent and modest feature of Southern historical literature, has been miscellaneously served by these works. Chesnut, LeConte, Hammond, Ruffin, Taylor, Tazewell, Cobb, Barnard—these will all need to be weighed by Southern intellectual historians, just as Charles Fraser needs to be assessed by those who are interested in the aesthetic history of the region. Perhaps only Robert Shalhope has self-consciously made a contribution to intellectual history (discernible if only by his referring to Quentin Skinner and Thomas Kuhn in his first few pages), but the rest help by not narrowing their emphasis as drastically as Shalhope, who shrinks John Taylor's private life to occasional paragraphs to leave room for exegesis of the Virginian's thought. Biographers' lack of narrow focus helps because life, thought, and politics were so interwoven in the Old South that it is doubtful an exclusive intellectual history, such as is practiced upon the intellectuals of the twentieth century, is practicable or desirable. Certainly these lives moved easily between the realms of thought and politics, society and self, with the themes of republican ideology and slavery predominating. The Old South was dotted with small knots of literati who talked, wrote, and agitated, with occasional knowledge of each other. The communities varied in richness: abundant in Chesnut's low country, adequate in Tazewell's Tidewater, barely sufficient in Cobb's Georgia, thin in Barnard's Tuscaloosa. But the virtue of biography is to remind us of variety, idiosyncrasy, exceptions. Barnard peering through a telescope, LeConte digging up rocks, Brooke inventing a deep-sea sounding lead, Fraser painting miniatures, Chesnut reading Balzac—these are hard to jam into a general interpretation.

Biographies are written from an abundance of mixed motives. The strongest impulse seems to be the desire to institutionalize the man, to express esteem at best, importance at least: this is the literary equivalent of naming a dormitory after someone. Publication secures a harmless if modest apotheosis. Local pride and filiopietism, always so important in American historiography—the most balkanized of disciplines, the more so with the decentralization of American publishing—are here in abundance. Texas, Virginia, and Georgia are memorialized. With even more particularism, the local worthies of Texas A&M University, Sul Ross and Ashbel Smith, are dusted off (though, I note, they will soon face a serious challenge from the new Mercer University Press, which threatens a "Great Mercerians" series). In such books, the fact of a life is more crucial than its details. This is demonstrated with comic precision by Professor Jane Lucas De Grummond's biography of Renato Beluche (a sort of poor man's Jean Laffite), about whom it seems we know almost nothing. The author helpfully explains, with illustrations, how she traveled the Caribbean finding that almost nothing, before carrying on with her task, which consists of explaining what everyone else was doing in the places where she thinks Beluche was. But, for less bold spirits, the details have usually to be there. They are laid out with the staid and flat protectiveness of the introductions to academic lecturers; biographers, like introducers, seem to be terrified that the audience will be insufficiently impressed, or rather they believe that it is wise to persuade the audience of the merit of the lecturer, in case it proves less than self-evident in the case of the lecture.

But praise is biography's oldest tradition. As Momigliano has shown, the genre itself was the heir of the encomium. Yet Polybius and Plutarch also made a clear distinction between history and biography: the first dealt with the public, the second with the private; the first with the state, the second with the individual (though, even then, the individual might be regarded as a type).[4] Biography bore a special moral responsibility, because it showed the possibilities of individual greatness as well as the dangers of misjudged ambition: biography defined models. This function is in disarray.

It is a curiosity of modern biography and historicism that we have reversed Burke, who declared to the electors of Bristol in 1780: "Crimes are the acts of individuals, and not of denominations; and therefore arbitrarily to class men under general descriptions, in order to proscribe and punish them in the lump for a presumed delinquency, of which perhaps but a part, perhaps none at all, are guilty, is indeed a compendious method, and saves a world of trouble about proof; but such a method, instead of being law, is an act of unnatural rebellion against the legal dominion of reason and justice."[5]

Today we seem to find it very easy to judge denominations but very hard to judge individuals. Take, for example, Drew Gilpin Faust's biography of James Henry Hammond. Hammond was an odd man, to say the least, avaricious, intelligent, constrained, ambitious, sensual, proud, and timid. He whored around, like most of his contemporaries, mostly with his slaves, which complicated his family life, because his wife resented his energetic and proximate couplings; eventually she left him. Lord Acton would have been severe about the private morality and vices of James Henry Hammond. Yet all of this—not least, some great freedoms with his nieces—Faust recounts with unprejudiced candor, scarcely thinking any of it a moral issue. Yet her biography is a condemnation of Hammond. His fault, which leads to much huffing and puffing, is that he embodied his society in desiring a mastery of his environment, particularly of his slaves. He is charged before the bar of history not with being himself, but with being everyone else. Burke is reversed: society is chargeable, the individual not. Is this not a peculiar logic?

Yet it is not easy to settle the working relationship between history and biography, especially now that sociology has so overwhelmed the annalistic tradition of political narrative. For example, recent historiography has been embattled over the issue of social recognition of the poor, the black, and the female, and by those heats much useful history has been written. Biography has begun to be implicated in the struggle. So we have here some biographies which exist largely as extensions of the general historiographical debate and are couched in those terms.

Free Frank, a slave in South Carolina and Kentucky, is chronicled by Juliet E. K. Walker as he gains his manumission by energetic entrepreneurship, moves to Illinois, gradually buys his family into freedom, and establishes a township. The message of the biography, like that of recent work, is the dignity and variety of the antebellum black experience. Similarly Lucy Audubon, wife of the artist, is studied in the spirit of feminist historiography, as a person-in-her-own-right. As contributions to the wider debate, these are useful books. But as biographies, they are failures, though for differing reasons.

It is a truism that the records of antebellum slaves are comparatively scanty, so historians must dig energetically to resurrect them: sometimes literally dig, because archaeology has been pressed into service, splendidly so in Charles Joyner's recent *Down by the Riverside*. As the new works of Michael P. Johnson, James L. Roark, and Willard B. Gatewood, Jr., show, the caste of free blacks has proven less inaccessible once someone decided to look.[6] Silence is a handicap for social history, but for biography it is almost fatal. Biography since Lytton Strachey has become intimate, impossible without records which allow access to the private. The "public" biography is now almost extinct, and Folk and Shaw's study of W. W. Holden appears almost a freak for utterly neglecting all but the public record. Unfortunately, Free Frank was illiterate and conducted a successful capitalist life by documents to which he could only put his mark. Most of his family and contemporaries were similarly handicapped. The natural consequence is that—apart from a few inferable characteristics, such as family loyalty and affection and a passion for material advancement—we know very little about Free Frank. That being so, he becomes an abstraction, and biography is vitiated by the abstract.

The case of Lucy Audubon is different, as it is with most antebellum women, who were the very custodians of literacy. We have her letters and can plot her feelings, which were mostly disgruntled, because John J. Audubon, whatever his virtues as an artist, was a wretched provider, a childlike and mostly absent husband. The problem is that, despite Carolyn E. DeLatte's protestations, I found Lucy Audubon quite uninteresting as a person and never shed the feeling that I would not be reading about her if she had not been married to Audubon. Which is not to gainsay a biography inspired by feminism, but to ask that the women brought to our attention genuinely merit and gain our interest. This is a test Mary Chesnut has no difficulty in passing. I did not read Muhlenfeld thinking, "What is Senator Chesnut up to?" But I pined for Audubon's reappearances to save me from Lucy Audubon.

These are troublesome issues for the student of biography. Recent historiography has flourished so remarkably because it has become the battlefield of ideology, of the struggles between darkness and light, right and wrong, justice and oppression. These struggles have shaped debates, given form and energy to narratives, and engaged readers. It is, no doubt, an odd notion that present justice can be served by the adjustment of the past, but it is an oddity endemic to our culture. Studying the past for its own sake is a heterodoxy today, which is perhaps as well, for there is little question that the implicit effect of such antiquarianism, however erudite or literate, is conservative. Such detachment can only occur if the social composition of the class of historians is restricted. English historical literature earlier in this century was remarkable for a tone of dispassionate indifference to contemporary society (save in a whiggism which was so entrenched, woolly, and general as to have become redundant) and for remarkable works of re-creation of the past. It could be so because history was a virtual monopoly of middle-class Oxbridge dons, content with the status quo. Of late, the monopoly has been broken and the literature has grown more vigorous, more interesting, and more presentist, even if there is a lingering aftertaste absent from an

American historical literature, which has almost always been a battleground of sections, classes, ethnic groups, races, and religions.

The real difficulty is that the rhetoric and logic of a biography are not well served by ideological conflict. If recent historiography has flourished by being against something and for something else, biography has been weakened. Biography "begins in praise," as Robert Gittings has remarked (drawing upon not Momigliano but his own experience in writing on John Keats and Thomas Hardy). Biography is partly vindication, though we now mistrust the exemplary, so that rogues and saints have become equal.[7] It is a dialogue between author and subject and has the peculiar rhetorical difficulty of abjuring the Manichaean. This is why biography is easy to bungle, because it is exceptionally difficult to maintain a balanced narrative of any impetus, when both author and subject are drawn up on the same side and engaged in an intimate dialogue. There are, it is true, rare cases where the author creates conflict by attacking his subject, as with Richard Aldington's life of T. E. Lawrence, but the effect is almost never happy, because the reader witnesses the massacre of the life, and his attention is directed to the anger of the biographer. Few can match the immense rages of Dean Swift, which alone can justify such a venture. Great lives, because they beget many biographies, will better bear such squabbling. Minor lives cannot, because they are not likely to be done more than once, or once every few generations, and the opportunity cannot be wasted upon a mere tirade. Yet one must be careful. Though few things date more rapidly than anger, panegyric is one that does. Lytton Strachey fled the Victorian biography, not just because of length, but from weariness at such acres of virtue. Biography may begin in praise, but it is unwise to end with it. Praise (or respect for the life lived) initiates the desire to re-create; it should not dictate the rhythms of judgment.

Biography, then, is not very amenable to being used in dubious historiographical battle. A life is too messy, too singular, too circumscribed, to be pounded into a shape fit for the general issues of historical debate. By such brutality the reader feels manipulated; worse, he feels the life itself is being messed around; worst, he begins to suspect the biographer thinks the life itself insufficient, that it needs bolstering by the wider issue of society, that he regards the life as just an artifact, like a potsherd, picked up to reconstruct the ur-pot. It is striking how, in general historical narrative, we mind this less, if only because we understand that the historian has a great many lives to juggle and cannot bestow singular care upon each. But in a biography, such brutality is peculiarly offensive.

The paradox runs deeper. In recent historical narrative, the voice of the narrator is very strong and the narrative itself decidedly, if implicitly, ahistorical. Present and past, historiography, theory, and history are jumbled up. No historian is now offended to see a name from 1985 and one from 1716 in the same sentence, to see Max Weber, Immanuel Wallerstein, and John Law confounded. In that very limited sense, we have returned to the voice of the eighteenth century, which saw no oddity in the modern philosopher and the ancient Roman inhabiting adjacent clauses, and for the same reasons: we have again grown interested in judgment and less engaged by the ambition of verisimilitude. Walter Bagehot's reproach that Gibbon did not know how to enter into men's hearts, and Dame C. V. Wedgwood's that the Roman historian could not sympathize with an attitude of mind not his own, are indictments which can be liberally made against modern historiography, which seems concerned to fend off the identities of the past, because it wishes to mold the future.[8]

Yet in biography the act of dramatic reenactment is paramount, and this has been so at least since Strachey. This has the odd consequence that in this most intimate of ventures, the strictest anonymity is enjoined upon the narrator. Robert Gittings has spoken with justified horror of the violation of this rule, when instead the narrative is cluttered up by argument with other historians or earlier biographers:

> There is one very long biography of Robert Browning where, in spite of argument being placed in footnote and appendix, it is duplicated by being retained in the text as well. Even the names of the academic authorities to be controverted appear among the historic characters of the Browning story, and, even more incredibly, not only their names but their academic titles.... In one instance, it even appears that Elizabeth Barrett and Robert Browning are somehow accompanied closely in their love-affair, elopement, and honeymoon, not merely by a College Dean but, as would appear from the text that names him, no less than a Dean Emeritus.[9]

In the books at hand are a good many modern American professors wandering around the plantations of the Old South, where they conspicuously study oratory from beside the hustings, take notes at a slave whipping, hurl insults at Eugene Genovese or give bouquets to J. G. A. Pocock, the one apparently on his way to a black prayer meeting, the other to the library of James Madison. Professor De Grummond, the Richard Cobb of Lake Pontchartrain, carries this implication to its logical conclusion by offering us four photographs of herself, to only two of her subject.

Verisimilitude is a quaint and Romantic ambition, to which contemporary historians are unused. Obliged to it by the genre of biography, they are inclined to lose their bearings, blunder into orotund nineteenth-century phrases and sentences, and suddenly find themselves very interested in landscape and weather, Wordsworthian matters which elsewhere never occur to or detain them. Opening sentences are especially suspect. Here is a sampling. "One late October day in 1829 a travel-weary party returning home from more than a year's sojourn in Europe, topped a crest on the deeply rutted red clay road that led to Barboursville, a quiet hamlet located in the central Virginia Piedmont's Orange County." "Late in the evening of May 18 1861, Mary Boykin Chesnut was in a hotel room in Montgomery, Alabama. The day had been a warm one, particularly for a woman dressed in the heavy looped and frilled fashions of the period, so she was glad to sit by lamplight and enjoy the cool air brought by darkness." "On a ridge high above the Savannah River stands Redcliffe, presiding over carefully planned avenues of magnolias and groves of hickory and pine that slope down towards Augusta, visible more than five miles away." "Flowing gently through the lowlands of Liberty County, Georgia, the shallow waters of the little South Newport River meander in their crooked channel until they merge with their northern counterpart and then glide imperceptibly into a maze of swamps and tidal creeks, emptying finally into the inlet on the southern fringe of St. Catherines Sound." "The town of Sheffield lies among the Berkshire hills in southwestern Massachusetts, about twelve miles above the Connecticut line and fifteen miles below Great Barrington. Just southwest of it rises one of the taller peaks of the Berkshires, Mount Everett, with a height of 2,624 feet; just northwest lies a considerable lake, Mill Pond."[10] I shall desist, being appointed a reviewer for the readers of this journal, not a flagellist of them. But it is a matter of some curiosity why so many think biography must begin with pastoral. Ulrich B. Phillips may have been wrong to observe, "Let us begin by discussing the weather," but it is a mandate Southern biographers have taken seriously.[11]

One mandate those biographers have disdained is that of psychobiography. Only Robert Brugger's life of Beverley Tucker has deliberately deployed a psychological theory to explicate his subject's life, and Brugger has been little emulated.[12] Psychobiography is, no doubt, often a mess and rightly mistrusted, because it makes the life a test case of some Viennese or Manhattan hobby horse. But, at its best, psychobiography can have the merit of focusing attention upon the life, to the exclusion of the extraneous. It can even, it has been argued, choose its psychological theory on the basis of what best explains the particular life. The old notion of character is the predecessor of the modern theory of the psyche. Yet psychobiography presumes an intimacy with mind and emotions beyond even the knowledge of him who lived the life. More, it complicates the challenge of dramatic reenactment, by jumbling together nineteenth-century lives and late twentieth-century jargon. Robert Browning's traveling party swells beyond deans emeriti to include couches, Freud's complete works, and hermeneutical expositors, all heaving themselves over the Brenner Pass.

Making morality only social, or replacing ethics with psychology, has abolished the old theory of biography. Perhaps the reluctance to judge would not matter, did it not lead to a reluctance to define and to the apparently natural, but mistaken, belief that events explain a life and that, if you get the events in the right order, the reader and the writer will be enabled to understand the subject. It is a mistake, because it is the necessary strategy of biography to believe that character generates or interacts with events, so events by themselves will not suffice. The biographer must assume the responsibility of deciding character, which is his most hazardous and important task. For biography is the realization of character, its crystallization and evolution.

This fact has slipped from view for honest reasons. There is an inescapable burden of ahistoricism in biography, which is why some prefer to see history and biography as different genres. That the subject lived in a past which is different from our present is, of course, crucial; no biographer is any good who does not deal with this. Yet—the paradox is evident to anyone who has written a biography and is often attested—the biographer and his subject must, in some sense, become contemporaries, because biography is so intimate a venture. This may be one reason why biography is often done so well by historians untrained by the schools; they have no difficulty with this aspect of the genre, because they were never told of the problem, whereas professional historians feel compromised by the deliberate choosing of ahistoricism.

This requirement of intimacy is also why Momigliano's reminder is apposite, that biography and fiction were historically and are still closely allied. After all, we cannot know character. It rests in emotions and motives which are incompetently revealed by documentary evidence. Yet character must be asserted, and the usual method is anecdote, because it embodies the characteristic.[13] It is a mark of how reluctant biographers have become to define that there is scarcely an anecdote in these books, only facts.

On one score the reviewer can be happy. That these are minor lives has, at least, spared him from enduring that standing vice of modern biography, literary elephantiasis. Lytton Strachey long ago performed drastic surgery upon the Monypennies and Buckles of English biography, and he was imitated in the United States, though more for the tone of sarcasm than the aesthetic of brevity. But the lesson has again been lost. We again sink beneath the useless lumber of definitive lives. "Blotner on Faulkner"—the phrase alone is enough to set an honest reader twitching with horror and to thinking of benumbed days in the corridors of the Vatican Museums or the Louvre.[14] Naturally literary biographers are our worst offenders, because they are besotted men, breathing the brain-numbing incense of literary fame and clutching at every last fact which drifts by them in their stupor. But presidential biographers come a close second. Flexner on Washington, Malone on Jefferson, Brant on Madison, Remini on Jackson, Link on Wilson—these are awful monuments, terrible to behold, exhausting to read. Indeed, to be blunt, they are almost never read, except by that impecunious slave, the reviewer, who feels he has stolen a march by the free acquisition of such a poundage, useful for standing on when reaching for real books.

It is sometimes said that such leviathans are useful compendia of facts, and they are. But that is to miss the point. Biography is narrative and judgment, kept in honest tension. Documentation is quite another art, less favored in our day, which has made an idol of the monograph. If one asks, "Where are the documents of antebellum lives?" the answer is discouraging. There are exceptions: Rayburn Moore's new edition of Hayne letters, C. Vann Woodward's Mary Chesnut, Carol Bleser's Hammond family letters, the remarkable edition of Calhoun papers, the diary of Edmund Ruffin.[15] But, generally speaking, we are short of the basic texts, especially of correspondence. Publishers embrace the brisk monograph; they look horror-stricken at the suggestion of a text. So we are without certain obvious tools: to name but a few, the essays of George Frederick Holmes, the writings of Louisa McCord, the political and social essays of William Gilmore Simms, the speeches of John Randolph, the works and letters of Hugh Legaré, the correspondence of Basil Gildersleeve, the writings of Thomas Cooper, the social and theological essays of James Henley Thornwell, and the letters of

Edmund Ruffin. Each generation of Southern historians must begin afresh at the archives. It was an old custom, but sound, that the biographer performed the double task—the biography, which was his narrative and judgment, and the correspondence, which showed the sources upon which judgment was made and permitted the contrary judgments of others. We have lent too much to the former and, by neglecting the latter, made biography padded and unwieldily. Biographies, after all, last only a generation or so. Texts, if accurately done, are permanently useful. They permit the student freedom to pick and choose, to go to the sources, to avoid a steady diet of what Hugh Legaré used to call "eleemosynary scraps."[16] Here, as elsewhere, Americans have until recently resisted the idea of a canon, fit to be permanently embodied by texts. Where is the South's Camden Society?

This neglect is the more unfortunate because the Old South's epistolary achievement was not inconsiderable. Antebellum Southerners spent much of their time writing letters, and many did it well. A society large and mobile, with a literate elite, the growing ethic of domesticity, the interests of politics, and the necessity of watchfulness in a slave society, naturally generated a great mass of letters. Mary Chesnut's diary, though idiosyncratic in its development, was the natural product of an antebellum tradition of self-commentary, which historians have just begun to reconstruct. Indeed, this abundance of biographies would be impossible without such a tradition. It has been often said that Southerners are accustomed to talking, to assuming a listener, with the implication that the chief resource of their understanding and accounting of reality has been oral. But letters and diaries are themselves a manner of speaking with a listener, whether it be a son, a cousin, a political ally, or oneself. The archives are heavy with such conversations, to which we are beginning to listen. It is evident they do not speak with one voice.

NOTES

1. The biographies reviewed in this essay include: Charles D. Lowery, *James Barbour, a Jeffersonian Republican* (Tuscaloosa: University of Alabama Press, 1984); Elisabeth Muhlenfeld, *Mary Boykin Chesnut: A Biography* (Baton Rouge: Louisiana State University Press, 1981); Drew Gilpin Faust, *James Henry Hammond and the Old South: A Design for Mastery* (Baton Rouge: Louisiana State University Press, 1982); Lester D. Stephens, *Joseph LeConte: Gentle Prophet of Evolution* (Baton Rouge: Louisiana State University Press, 1982); Dickson J. Preston, *Young Frederick Douglass: The Maryland Years* (Baltimore, MA: Johns Hopkins University Press, 1980); Nathan Irvin Huggins, *Slave and Citizen: The Life of Frederick Douglass* (Boston, MA: Little, Brown, 1980); Martha R. Severens and Charles L. Wyrick, Jr., eds., *Charles Fraser of Charleston: Essays on the Man,*

His Art and His Times (Charleston, SC: Carolina Art Association, 1983); Norma Lois Peterson, *Littleton Waller Tazewell* (Charlottesville: University Press of Virginia, 1983); William J. Chute, *Damn Yankee! The First Career of Frederick A. P. Barnard: Educator, Scientist, Idealist* (Port Washington, NY: Kennikat Press, 1978); Ray Mathis, *John Horry Dent: South Carolina Aristocrat on the Alabama Frontier* (Tuscaloosa: University of Alabama Press, 1979); Jane Lucas De Grummond, *Renato Beluche: Smuggler, Privateer, and Patriot, 1780–1860* (Baton Rouge: Louisiana State University Press, 1983); George M. Brooke, Jr., *John M. Brooke: Naval Scientist and Educator* (Charlottesville: University Press of Virginia, 1980); Robert E. Shalhope, *John Taylor of Caroline: Pastoral Republican* (Columbia: University of South Carolina Press, 1980); Juliet E. K. Walker, *Free Frank: A Black Pioneer on the Antebellum Frontier* (Lexington: University Press of Kentucky, 1983); Carolyn E. DeLatte, *Lucy Audubon: A Biography* (Baton Rouge: Louisiana State University Press, 1982); Edgar E. Folk and Bynum Shaw, *W. W. Holden: A Political Biography* (Winston-Salem, NC: John F. Blair, 1982); Elizabeth Silverthorne, *Ashbel Smith of Texas: Pioneer, Patriot, Statesman, 1805–1886* (College Station: Texas A&M University Press, 1982); Judith Ann Benner, *Sul Ross: Soldier, Statesman, Educator* (College Station: Texas A&M University Press, 1983); William B. McCash, *Thomas R. R. Cobb: The Making of a Southern Nationalist* (Macon, GA: Mercer University Press, 1983); Betty L. Mitchell, *Edmund Ruffin: A Biography* (Bloomington: Indiana University Press, 1981); W. Hamilton Bryson, *Legal Education in Virginia, 1779–1979: A Biographical Approach* (Charlottesville: University Press of Virginia, 1982); Robert M. Bain, ed., *Southern Writers: A Biographical Dictionary* (Baton Rouge: Louisiana State University Press, 1979).

2. See, for example, Richard D. Altick, *Lives and Letters: A History of Literary Biographies in England and America* (New York: Alfred A. Knopf, 1965); Anthony M. Friedson, ed., *New Directions in Biography* (Honolulu: University Press of Hawaii, 1981); Marc Pachter, ed., *Telling Lives: The Biographer's Art* (Philadelphia: University of Pennsylvania Press, 1981); Leon Edel, *Literary Biography* (1959; Bloomington: Indiana University Press, 1973); John Arthur Garraty, *The Nature of Biography*. (New York: Alfred A. Knopf, 1957); Dennis W. Petrie, *Ultimately Fiction: Design in Modern American Literary Biography* (West Lafayette, IN: Purdue University Press, 1981); James Lowry Clifford, *From Puzzles to Portraits: Problems of a Literary Biographer* (Chapel Hill: University of North Carolina Press, 1970); James Lowry Clifford, ed., *Biography as an Art: Selected Criticism, 1560–1960* (New York: Oxford University Press, 1962).

3. Eric F. Goldman, *Rendezvous with Destiny: A History of Modern American Reform* (New York: Alfred A. Knopf, 1952), xi.

4. Arnoldo Momigliano, *The Development of Greek Biography: Four Lectures* (Cambridge, MA: Harvard University Press, 1971), 12–13, 15.

5. "Speech at the Guildhall in Bristol, Previous to the Late Election in That City, Upon Certain Points Relative to His Parliamentary Conduct, 1780," in *The Works of the Right Honorable Edmund Burke*, 3rd ed., 12 vols. (Boston, MA: Little, Brown, 1869), 2:418.

6. Michael P. Johnson and James L. Roark, eds., *No Chariot Let Down: Charleston's Free People of Color on the Eve of the Civil War* (Chapel Hill: University of North Carolina Press, 1984); Willard B. Gatewood, Jr., ed., *Free Man of Color: The Autobiography of Willis Augustus Hodges* (Knoxville: University of Tennessee Press, 1982).

7. Robert Gittings, *The Nature of Biography* (Seattle: University of Washington Press, 1978), 19.

8. "Edward Gibbon," in Walter Bagehot, *Literary Studies*, 2 vols. (London: J. M. Dent, 1911), 2:1–48; C. V. Wedgwood, *The Sense of the Past: Thirteen Studies in the Theory and Practice of History* (1960; New York: Collier Books, 1967), 106–36.

9. Gittings, *Nature of Biography*, 66–67.

10. Lowery, *James Barbour*, 1; Muhlenfeld, *Mary Boykin Chesnut*, 3; Faust, *Design for Mastery*, 1; Stephens, *Joseph LeConte: Gentle Prophet of Evolution*, 1; Chute, *Damn Yankee!* 3. The other common gambit is the ordering of ancestors, which at least has the merit of chronology.

11. Ulrich Bonnell Phillips, *Life and Labor in the Old South* (1929; Boston, MA: Little, Brown, 1963), 3.

12. Robert J. Brugger, *Beverley Tucker: Heart Over Head in the Old South* (Baltimore, MD: Johns Hopkins University Press, 1978); see also Robert J. Brugger, ed., *Our Selves/Our Past: Psychological Approaches to American History* (Baltimore, MD: Johns Hopkins University Press, 1981).

13. Momigliano, *Greek Biography*, 56–57, 76.

14. Joseph Leo Blotner, *Faulkner: A Biography*, 2 vols. (New York: Random House, 1974).

15. Rayburn S. Moore, ed., *A Man of Letters in the Nineteenth-Century South: Selected Letters of Paul Hamilton Hayne* (Baton Rouge: Louisiana State University Press, 1982); C. Vann Woodward, ed., *Mary Chesnut's Civil War* (New Haven, CT: Yale University Press, 1981); Carol Bleser, ed., *The Hammonds of Redcliffe* (New York: Oxford University Press, 1981); Robert L. Meriwether et al., eds, *The Papers of John C. Calhoun*, 28 vols. (Columbia: University of South Carolina Press, 1959–2003); William Kauffman Scarborough, ed., *The Diary of Edmund Ruffin*, 3 vols. (Baton Rouge: Louisiana State University Press, 1972–89).

16. "Classical Learning," in Mary Swinton Legaré, ed., *Writings of Hugh Swinton Legaré*, 2 vols. (Charleston, SC: Burges & James, 1845–46), 2:49.

INTELLECTUAL HISTORY

These two pieces are, firstly, Michael O'Brien, "Southern Intellectual History," in *A Companion to American Thought*, ed. Richard Wightman Fox and James T. Kloppenberg (Cambridge, MA: Blackwell Publishing, 1995), 647–50, reprinted by permission, and, secondly, the previously unpublished keynote address to the sixth annual meeting of the Southern Intellectual History Circle at the University of Mississippi in 1993.

The tradition of identifying a distinctive pattern of intellectuality in the American South dates from the early nineteenth century, but the practice of a sub-discipline called "Southern intellectual history" is a very recent phenomenon. To understand this, it helps to consider the circumstances under which these terms—"Southern" and "intellectual"—converged and became attached to the discipline of history.

There were cultures in what we now call the South for centuries before the category of "the South" was invented in the early nineteenth century. Though many things later named as characteristics of the South—agrarianism, slavery, white supremacy, manners—existed before 1800, these were disparately described; the colonial plantation societies of Virginia and the Carolinas were understood in relation to others of their ilk, like Barbados, as parts of British imperial culture. Only after 1776 and 1789 and the creation of a Federal Union was there anything reliably to be "south" of, and only after the abolition of slavery in the Northern states did the South come to have a distinguishing social institution; the tensions implicit in federalism drove many of the ideas formative of Southern ideology. Northerners began to criticize slave society as a pernicious social anachronism. Concomitantly Southern critical thinkers, partly as a means to understand slave society, began to define a role for themselves as custodians of culture, and thereby invented a culture to guard; they were the equivalent of those Romantic thinkers in Europe, like Mazzini in Italy, who rested their case as thinkers upon a mutually reinforcing bond with a nation, imaginatively defined. Up to 1861, the nature of Southern society was in dispute. Controversy centered upon the centrality of slavery, whether it disqualified the South from a role in modern and progressive society, and whether the reality and depth of Southern culture necessarily mandated a political independence which alone could guarantee that reality. This discourse, which identified the "South" with historical change, was reinforced by the influence of Romanticism and, in particular, by historicism, with its central claim that human nature assumed different forms in different times and places, and that there were characteristic and evolving social configurations, of which nations and races were the most formative. The South was increasingly nominated and accepted as such a configuration.

At the same time, the words "intellect" and "intellectual" were undergoing a significant change. The adjective had long existed and, by the late eighteenth century, denoted a quality roughly equivalent to "rational" or "pertaining to the understanding"; it was often used by those influenced by the psychological categories of Scottish Common Sense philosophy. Thus Hugh Blair Grigsby of Virginia might write in his diary for 1828 that a debating society was "well designed to whet the intellect and amuse the fancy of those who composed it," and thereby he distinguished separable components of the mind.[1] Professions thought peculiarly to require rationality, especially the law or the academy, were distinguished by a larger admixture of such intellect. By extension, a country might have an intellect, that is, a significant quality of rationality in the conduct and comprehension of its affairs; hence Frederick Grimke in 1838 asked Hugh Legaré, a fellow South Carolinian, to estimate "the intellect of that country [Germany]."[2] By this he meant, what are the significant products of rationality in Germany and how should we appraise them? The South being increasingly regarded as a cultural nation, it too might have such an intellectual quotient. So in October 1847, a writer in the *Southern Quarterly Review* could speak of "the activity of Southern intellect."[3] In 1858 James Johnston Pettigrew of North Carolina, in approved Romantic manner, could say that "the intellect of the south is like its land."[4]

It was argued that intellect mattered in the directing of society. In 1854, for example, Oscar Lieber observed to his father Francis Lieber that graduates of the South Carolina College were "above the average of intellect of the country," a good thing since such graduates would come to form the state's elite.[5] Similarly, in 1859 Basil Manly, Jr., of Richmond argued that cities were peculiarly important because in them congregated "more of the living, controlling intellect of the land." Hence there were increasingly frequent attempts to understand the characteristic pattern of Southern intellect. George Fitzhugh argued in 1857, for example, that twenty years earlier "the South had no thought—no opinions of her own." By this he meant that the South had only recently justified and constructed the educational and literary institutions by which her culture might be sustained. "It is all important that we should write our own books," he said.[6]

The attempt to define "us," the necessarily circular venture of self-definition, has provided the essential subject matter of Southern thought ever since. Broadly speaking, the movement has been from an exclusive definition to one which is inclusive; at first, in Fitzhugh's usage, "we" were white males of the planting class, though almost simultaneously the circle was extended outwards to white women of the same class; it tentatively reached non-slaveholders before the Civil War, then more successfully whites of every class after Reconstruction and, finally and ambivalently in our own day, African Americans, who now sometimes claim the title of Southerner, sometimes refuse it. "Southern" was thus one of the more expansive social identities of modern times. Intellectuals have concerned themselves with administering the processes of the identity, adjusting or exploiting its tensions, negotiating and understanding the many harrowing social transformations which have especially afflicted the South. However, before the Civil War, there was little sense of a usable noun, "the intellectual," or of a class of people called "intellectuals" or "the intelligentsia" who might be the subject matter of a history: in the South, as elsewhere, that is a later development.

The formal study of Southern thought began systematically only after the Civil War. A twelve-volume study of the *The South in the Building of the Nation* was published in 1909, of which the seventh volume, edited by John Bell Henneman, was entitled *History of the Literary and Intellectual Life of the South*. Its contents define the then-current definition of intellectual life: there are chapters on genre (poetry, historical studies, "English studies," classical scholarship, mathematics, astronomy, the physical sciences, natural history, philosophy), on professions (the law, medicine, music, the press, librarianship), and on a few miscellaneous categories (folklore, humor, Louisiana). There is, by way of an afterthought, a concluding chapter on "The Literary and Intellectual Progress of the Negro." There is a general chapter on the "Intellectual Tendencies of the South," whose emphasis, consonant with the orientation of the volumes towards the "New South," was on accomplishments, the South's return to the nation, the importance of science, the growth of education and industry; throughout there is a disparagement of "the barrenness of the Old South in the field of literature," which is explained by the tendency of slavery to promote intolerance. But the New South's fracturing of such an "artificial unity of thought and speech" would nevertheless leave the South with an identity, since it would retain customs which mark "its peculiarities as a province."[7] In short, Romantic nationalism would survive, minus separatist politics, but Southern culture was now "provincial" or "regional," with the clear implication that there was a metropolitan culture somewhere else to whose status the South should now aspire.

The title of this volume posited a conjunction between literature and intellectual life which has been very important in the South, because literary scholars were the first, and have always been the most zealous, to establish a canon for Southern thought-qua-literature. This had been done only fitfully before the Civil War, but commenced more briskly afterwards in books such as James Wood Davidson's *The Living Writers of the South* (1869) and Louise Manly's *Southern Literature from 1579–1895* (1895). This work was summarized in the sixteen-volume anthology, *The Library of Southern Literature* (1907), which was the joint work of academics and "amateurs." Later a more singly academic tradition of Southern literary history emerged; this tradition culminated in Jay B. Hubbell's *The South in American Literature, 1607–1900* (1954), was sustained by many monographs and anthologies, and renewed in our own day by *The History of Southern Literature* (1985).[8] A weaker second to this tradition was that of the history of Southern political thought, which flourished most vigorously from the end of the nineteenth century to the Second World War; its notable landmarks were Ulrich B. Phillips's *Georgia and State Rights* (1902); Frank Owsley's *States Rights in the Confederacy* (1925); and Jesse Carpenter's *The South as a Conscious Minority, 1789–1861* (1930).[9]

The idea of gathering together such discrete enquiries under the rubric of "intellectual history" came slowly, however, and evolved from a very different intellectual genealogy, external to the South. Its ancestor is the systematic history of philosophy, written first by philosophers such as G. W. F. Hegel or Dugald Stewart as a way of understanding earlier and mistaken metaphysics, later by non-philosophers as a way of conveying the accomplishments of human intelligence. By the mid-twentieth century this latter tradition had transmogrified into the "history of ideas," a term popularized by Arthur O. Lovejoy. In 1938 he had pointed out the need to draw together discrete traditions of intellectual enquiry; the histories of philosophy, science, language, religion, literature, fine arts, economic theory, and education, as well as folklore studies, comparative literature, political and social history, and the "historical part of sociology."[10] This school concentrated more on the logical content and relationship of ideas themselves, less on the intellectuals who held them and their social context; philosophy was its core discipline, with social and political history on the periphery.

The precise moment at which "intellectual history" was born has not been satisfactorily established. Perry Miller has been credited with using the phrase first in 1939 in the preface to *The New England Mind: The Seventeenth Century*, when he wrote of "the intellectual history of New England."[11] In fact, it is much older. Hugh Legaré in 1828 wrote of "a philosophical inquirer into the intellectual history of the species."[12] But this was a phrase, not a program for a scholarly discipline, as was the case with Miller. By the 1940s works in Southern intellectual history had begun to appear, first with Clement Eaton's *The Freedom-of-Thought Struggle in the Old South* (1940), later with Rollin Osterweis's *Romanticism and Nationalism in the Old South* (1948), written as a Yale dissertation under Ralph Gabriel. Eaton later added other studies: *The Mind of the Old South* (1964) and *The Waning of the Old South Civilization* (1968). Sometimes such books were inspired by the so-called "American Studies" approach, as with William R. Taylor's *Cavalier and Yankee: The Old South and American National Character* (1961). Collaterally, some literary scholars were broadening their methodology to write intellectual history: notable was Richard Beale Davis, whose *Intellectual Life in Jefferson's Virginia, 1790–1830* (1964) was later to be surpassed in length by his *Intellectual Life in the Colonial South* (1978).[13]

However, a self-conscious sub-discipline of "Southern intellectual history" is a product of approximately the last twenty years. These books have marked characteristics, being poised between the traditional preoccupations of Southern history and the discipline of intellectual history. That is, they are influenced by modern theories, many of them non-Southern in origin (Freud, Geertz, Rorty, Skinner, Gramsci, and many others), some of them indigenous (Calhoun, Tate, Weaver); likewise they often employ paradigms—the Enlightenment, Romanticism, Victorianism, modernism—current in European and American intellectual history. But these books are also connected to the traditional preoccupations of Southern historiography; the nature of slave society and proslavery thought, the origins of the Civil War, the problems of biracialism, the broad issues of social and political history. This is so, because those intellectuals who designated themselves as Southerners or (more loosely but distinguishably) those who resided in the South were formed by and meditated upon these issues. This preoccupation with political and social history is the more marked because the traditional formative influence upon intellectual history elsewhere, philosophy, has been notably absent in the South, which has not produced a body of abstract metaphysics.

Intellectual history, as a discipline, has never been securely established, mostly because its topics—works of the intellect and people called intellectuals—have been notoriously hard to define and, awkwardly for a democratic culture like that of the United States, intrinsically elitist. The willingness to affirm the existence and significance of intellectual elites, by the culture which surrounds intellectuals and even by intellectuals themselves (many of whom deny the title which others wish to give them), has made intellectual history an uncertain venture. This familiar problem has been compounded for Southern intellectual history by two skepticisms, one Northern, the other Southern. Northerners, the most imperial force in American culture, who compelled the South back into the Union at the point of a bayonet, have been inclined to view Southerners as backward and unintelligent and hence to see Southern intellectuality as an oxymoron. For their part Southerners have evolved a culture which has stressed social unity and organicism; this impulse has been partly driven by the scarring impulses of racism but also by the need to survive together in a world which—with little ambiguity between 1861 and 1865 and thereafter—expressed hostility to the Southern way of life. Such a culture has resisted the premise that intellectuals form a distinct class, but has instead striven to make them ideological voices, elaborators of ideas commonly held. Many Southern intellectuals have accepted this role, but many others, embracing the familiar modern obligation of alienation as evidence of intellectuality, have resisted it. This tension between being Southern and belonging, and being intellectual and singular, has formed a characteristic motif.

...

When the members of the Southern Intellectual History Circle met in Nashville last year, we discussed what might be our main topic for debate in Oxford in 1993. I hazarded the observation that, though we had been meeting for several years and the study of Southern intellectual history had been proliferating in a modest way for longer, we have given little thought to what relationship, if any, all this study might have to what is conventionally called "American intellectual history." Our purposes have been mainly introspective, properly concerned with what we might be contributing to the understanding of Southern history and literature. For the most part, we have let our role in the wider discourse of American history take care of itself. After I said this, the others nodded sagely at me and, to my dismay, said I should go away, do that thinking, and come back when I had something to say. I now wish that someone else had volunteered and I could be just one of the happy few whose task would be confined to criticizing the volunteer. For, the more I have thought about this problem in the last few months, the less sure I have grown about its dimensions and validity. Hence almost all of what follows is tentative, deliberately intended to promote debate and invite rejoinder. I do believe most of what I am about to say, but with varying degrees of firmness.

There seemed to be several ways of constructing this talk. The most ambitious would be to summarize some of the conclusions which recent scholars of Southern thought have reached, enquire what impact these have had upon the broader understanding of American thought, and offer an inclusive reconstruction of American intellectual history. This would be to play Jack Greene, who has done such a thing for American colonial history by building upon the formidable body of work upon Southern and Caribbean society to seize control of early American history. With remarkable temerity, he has tried, perhaps even succeeded in banishing New England to marginality. It would be possible, though far more difficult and tendentious, to do the same for American intellectual history. The argument, I suppose, would run something like this. Southerners in the colonial and early national period hammered out a guardedly optimistic, partly bleak assessment of the potentialities for a progressive improvement of human society; struggled with the related problems of democracy, republicanism, and social hierarchy; thought through the tension between tradition and cultural independence; and arrived by 1850 at a mature body of intellectual thought which, though forged by the necessities of a slave society, survived the Civil War, and (though only intermittently influential outside its borders) has offered a permanently useful understanding, not of American hopes, but of American reality. New England, by comparison, had by 1850 and Emerson pursued a more millennial path, which, though achieving a certain prominence between 1840 and the late nineteenth century, eventually ran bluntly into the realities of a complicated modern society and was obliged to retrace the paths which Southerners had long since traveled. It would be a simple matter to demonstrate, for example, that the social philosophy of a via media described by James Kloppenberg in his admirable book about the turn of the twentieth century is anticipated in much antebellum Southern thought.[14] In such an interpretation, New Englanders would be portrayed as influential but unselfaware clowns, Southerners as bleak, astute if often repulsive realists.

I could do this. But the elbowing aside of ineffectual New Englanders— playing, as it were, Bill Clinton to Michael Dukakis—though something not a few Southerners would be happy to see happen, strikes me as a vulgarly imperial thing to do, and probably unwise. For one thing, if it is to be done, a Southerner not an Englishman needs to do it. For another, as the old advice has it, if you strike at a king, you must kill him. I am not sure Southern thought has quite the firepower to kill this particular king.

So I turn to a more modest venture. I want to consider what relationship, if any, exists between those who now write about Southern thought and those who write about the minds of the other Americans, for whom those within Southern discourse have no satisfactory term and with whom they have had only an intermittent relationship. "American" serves ill, because it implies a counterpoint of "Southern" and "American," in which "Southern" is excluded from the definition of "American." "Yankee" is a cheap and unsatisfactory jibe, though not unfamiliar around here. "Northern" is more polite, but this excludes western. For the moment, let me call them "American," because that is who they think they are. Both sides in this matter are entitled to their illusions.

My main contention this evening will be that the last generation has not seen the establishment of a satisfactory working relationship between these two groups. Mostly, I want to explore why this has been so. I offer no solutions. Indeed, if my analysis is correct, I doubt that the problem is soluble.

Let me first discuss the obvious issue, before considering its only modest usefulness. That American intellectual history has, since its inception and with the possible exception of Vernon Parrington, neglected and misunderstood the intellectual culture of the South seems to me beyond dispute. There is scarcely an old book and, more worryingly, scarcely a new one passing itself off as American intellectual history, which is not more-or-less awful on the South. Generally speaking, the backbone of these books is still New England-ish and New York-ish, and the South is accorded the odd paragraph, the odd page or two.[15] On the whole, I have come to prefer the books which never mention the South to the ones which do. In the former case, one can mentally adjust, change the adjective in their titles from "American" to "Northern," or reconsider "America" as "William James and a few of his friends." Thereby, many of these works are rendered serviceable enough. But the books which gesture towards the South tend to be the most vexing, since they convey the message that comprehending the South requires reading only one or two secondary works (*A Sacred Circle* or *The War Within*) and one or two primary texts (*Cannibals All!* or *Light in August*).[16] Authors want a few serviceable generalizations and no confusing cross-currents. Indeed it is chastening for this group to reflect that, after the writing and intellectual effort of the last twenty years and longer, the situation in general works on American intellectual culture is little improved in quantity since 1960.

Two or three generations ago, outbursts of indignation like the one I have just simulated were common enough among intellectual Southerners. It was the rhetoric of Frank Owsley. It was the voice of that generation of Southern literary critics who demanded that a Southern author be nominated as a great American novelist: with Faulkner they succeeded, with Simms they are still trying. On the whole, however, this indignation has been unsuccessful, no matter what generation has attempted it. It has failed, because it has proceeded upon false premises. There is, of course, no dispassionate center to American culture, to which reason can appeal or which indignation can intimidate.

At least, there is no putative center to which a regional culture can appeal. Obviously, recent American culture has responded with remarkable rapidity to the reason and indignation of African Americans, of women, and other social groups. Indeed, instructively, the aspects of Southern thought which have entered the mainstream, if such there be, are figures like Harriet Jacobs and Frederick Douglass, and (less thoroughly) women like Mary Chesnut. But they have done so, in the main, by being disembodied from any precise, historically specific idea of Southern identity and culture. And that these writers might be regarded as Southern has been mostly irrelevant to the motives which drove their canonization, though it has not been irrelevant to some of its consequences. Indeed we live at an interesting and ironical moment when, for many non-Southerners, black voices loom larger in the definition of the South than white ones. Certainly most undergraduates know Douglass or Jacobs or Martin Luther King better than they know Calhoun, and as well as they know Jefferson.

That African Americans and women have fared differently from white Southerners is a commentary, not only on the moral plausibility of their indignation—after all, the white Southerner did not come to his minor place at the table with unstained hands—but on the strategic fact that women and blacks are social constituencies within Northern culture, whereas the South is a place elsewhere. This is the South's weakness in breaking into the definitions of Americanism, but also, of course, a strength. After all, the South is a rich and large culture, which commands more resources than perhaps at any point in its history. If no one mentioned the South ever again in a New York book or a Chicago periodical, if courses in Southern literature and history vanished utterly from Ivy League universities, would it matter?

A little, no doubt. As a non-Southerner myself, I would be sorry to see the contributions of non-Southerners diminish and vanish. But does the South need non-Southerners? Hugh Legaré once said this of American sensitivity to foreign opinion:

> For all our hyperbolical vauntings about our own superiority to the rest of mankind, we do too much refer to ... [foreign] criticism, and suffer ourselves at once to be governed and to be made unhappy by it. We have too much national vanity, and too little of the far nobler feeling of national pride.... Instead of clipping and paring away our energies to suit ourselves to the taste of foreigners, let us give them free scope, and trust to the sympathies of our neighbours, our friends, our brethren. What Frenchman expects to be admired at London, or cares a straw about the opinions of English and Scotch censors? For him the whole world lies between the Alps, the Pyrenees, and the ocean.[17]

Yet it obviously does matter to some Southerners. Though they do inhabit a spiritual nation between the Atlantic, the Gulf of Mexico and the places where (according to John Reed) the word "Dixie" begins to disappear from the Yellow Pages, Southerners are also Americans.[18] It matters because American culture has never been centralized to the degree that French or English intellectual life has been, and has worked more like German culture, with multiple foci, many minor, some major, with a few which have asserted centrality and, on occasion, commanded a grudging and incomplete assent from other localities. The game of claiming centrality is one that, for a century and longer, Southerners have been inhibited in playing, however much they played it with gusto before 1861. Appomattox made the North the imperial power and gave Southerners a permanent mistrust of cultural imperialism, at least beyond Southern borders and within the United States. Hence the Southern role in the American cultural game has been essentially defensive, not claiming centrality, only trying to deny centrality to someone else.

There is, no doubt, something ridiculous about books which bear bold and comprehensive titles like *The Rise of American Philosophy* and tiny subtitles like *Cambridge, Massachusetts, 1860–1930*.[19] (From this universalist parochialism, I suppose even Boston and Waltham might feel excluded.) No Southerner would have the gall to call a book, say, *The Origins of American Thought*, and subtitle it *Charleston, 1789–1860*, which could be contrived to make as much sense. However, Southerners should not feel too complacent. As the old English verse—which contains the wisest critique of the concept of hegemony which I know of—has it, "Greater fleas have lesser fleas, / Upon their backs to bite 'em / And lesser fleas have smaller fleas / And so ad infinitum." For nothing is more common than books entitled *Social Origins of the New South*, which turn out to be about a few counties in Alabama.[20] The South too is an invented and aggressive identity, in fact, one of the imperial identities of modern times, for many years expanding, adding more and more social groups. Being thus synthetic, the South is vulnerable to disaggregation. If the act of will should falter, or if the terms of synthesis should shift, this group and that group can fall away, or slide into differing syntheses. Others are better equipped than I to analyze whether those who inhabit modern society in the southeastern United States are, on the whole, less or more prone than their parents or grandparents to using the concept of the South as a means of identity. My crude guess is that the identity has crested and may be on the wane.

But the South is not just a function of social identity. For intellectuals, it has worked by being plausibly connected to genre. Thus we have had, not just the novel but the Southern novel, not just history but Southern history. This has partly been a function of intentions, that is, the novelist intends a fiction as a contribution to the genres of Southern literature, but also of audience, that is, the reader wills the book into a certain category. Membership in the canon of Southern literature has been firmest when intention and reception have been congruent.

Let me take the case of Southern literary criticism to illustrate what I mean, to illustrate how a genre can be born and, by the same token, how it might become moribund or die. After all, the possibility of the genre of Southern literary criticism has rested upon the interweaved notions that there is a society called the South, that literary texts ought to be socially and biographically situated, and that text, self, and society evolve historically. This has been the mystic trinity of Southern literary criticism since about the 1830s: the text, the history, the South. Obviously, these propositions coalesced at an identifiable historical moment. Before the invention of the idea of the South in the early nineteenth century, literary criticism was practiced by some of the inhabitants of Williamsburg or Charleston in 1780 or 1810 in the light of those intellectual premises which were intelligible to them. Neo-Aristotelianism, Scottish common sense philosophy, whatever school of literary criticism you may have chosen then, they were notable for a slighting of history and place. As late as the 1830s, at the South Carolina College, for example, there was no tidy category of literature assigned to a single professor. Robert Henry and Henry Junius Nott taught belles lettres, with the latter holding a chair in the "Elements of Criticism, Logic, and Philosophy." If one consults Nott's reports for 1835 on what he was teaching his classes in what we should call literature, one finds three categories of analysis: genre (epic, fable, drama), language (Latin, Greek, English, French, German, Spanish and Italian), and logic.[21] That is, Nott was interested in the internal structures of literature and language, especially as they related to philosophy. Within the academy, texts mattered most (within the various traditions of rhetoric), history a little, South not at all.

At the same time, however, historicism was finding its way into the study of belles lettres in ways which would eventually supersede Nott's methodology, though it is important to stress that Romantic literary criticism started where Nott left off. A look at Romantic literary theorists like the Schlegels shows that the crucial connection between literature and society was made out of an attempt to find a history to explain genre. One can see this connection being fashioned within Southern culture itself during the 1820s. One can see it, for example, in an essay which Thomas Smith Grimké, the Charleston lawyer and essayist, published in two parts in 1828 and 1829 about the origin of rhyming in poetry. The argument of the essay was that rhyme did not exist in the ancient world, but that "the modern world" owed its invention mainly to the "Christian Latin poets of the fourth century, and to their successors."[22] Grimké was richly informed by the body of critical discourse which was making the transition out of Lord Kames's world; he had put together his argument from the body of late Enlightenment and early Romantic literary history and criticism. Hence Grimké was able to make the central claim of historicism, that ancient and modern were different, discontinuous. He writes, for example,

> A dictionary of rhymes would be as unintelligible to a Greek or Roman poet, as an English orator would esteem it useless to have instructions, like those of Dionysius of Halicarnassus, explanatory of the compositions of prose sentences from poetical feet. The very fact then, that the character and objects of such a lexicon ... would be incomprehensible to a classic poet, demonstrates the existence of a state of things in modern poetry, entirely unknown to the ancients. Whence has arisen this state of things: in other

words, to whom, to what age, to what country, do we owe the invention of rhyme?[23]

This last sentence, this last question, was the crucial question that arose when literature was situated in the mutabilities of time and society. "Whence has arisen this state of things ... to whom, to what age, to what country, do we owe" a particular form of literature? That is, Grimké was beginning to connect genre and form with history, language, and culture. He was molded by a critical discourse in which ideas of nationality, concepts of North and South, were crucially deployed. That, in this essay, the American South is nowhere mentioned is of minor importance. There were plenty of people waiting to take that small step, to slot the worlds of South Carolina and Mississippi into the typology designed to elucidate the Troubadours. Here Grimké (though not Grimké alone) began a critical tradition which, with significant variations, survives to our own day. After all, the form of Grimké's essential question—"Whence has arisen this state of things ... to whom, to what age, to what country, do we owe" a particular form of literature?—is the question of Allen Tate's essays on the Southern mode of the imagination.[24] Answering that question has been the essential chess game of Southern literary criticism.

If one follows the chronological pattern, one can see that in 1800 one did not have the category of the South at all, either for society or literature. In 1830, it was possible to believe in the South as a political or even a social construct, without believing that such a construct had necessary implications for literary analysis. In 1850, some people had constructed the modern trinity of South, text, and history.

Obviously, today, that trinity is in deep trouble, during a time when poststructuralism has tried to sever the connections between texts and society, and postmodernism has ventured to reduce history to a matter of eclectic lifestyles. Multiculturalism, on the other hand, being extremely old-fashioned cultural nationalism is, at one level, logically compatible with the analytical premises of Southern discourse. Indeed one could make a case, tongue in cheek, for Southerners as among the first American multiculturalists. If my intention were solely to annoy Eugene Genovese, I would now do so. Certainly, on the American scene, white Southerners have modestly pled the necessity of diversity. I attended a lecture by Cathy Davidson, editor of *American Literature* a year or more ago at the Modern Language Association, a lecture mostly concerned with stressing how far back ideological and literary wrangling went in the history of the periodical, *pace* those who think our present age peculiarly vicious and "ideological." She observed that the only piece of affirmative action required by the founding constitution of *American Literature* is not ethnic, not racial, not gender-specific, but regional: each of the regions must be represented on its editorial board. This will not surprise anyone who remembers that the periodical was founded in 1929 by Jay B. Hubbell, whose very reminiscences are entitled *South and Southwest*.[25] But, it must be said, Southerners were multiculturalists by necessity, not instinct; they were compelled into a revulsion from hegemony by the defeat sealed at Appomattox.

Nonetheless it is useful to remind ourselves that forms of cultural discrimination—I use the word in its strict sense, as the process of choice—are very mutable. Hubbell's mandate of regional balance was itself discriminating against older forms of choice. When professors were hired at American colleges in the early nineteenth century, for example, what mattered most then was religion. Was the candidate a Presbyterian, a Methodist, a Baptist, an Episcopalian? Did they have the denominational balance right? was the question which bothered electors at state universities in 1840.

The extent to which these older, and equally bitter, identities and contentions have changed was illustrated to me, on a recent visit to hear a panel discussion at my university's English Department. A member of the audience was complaining that Miami University was relentlessly homogeneous, was, she said, "95 percent WASP." In the interests of accuracy, I observed that this could not be so, since about 45 percent of the student body was Roman Catholic. I was gazed upon with blank stupefaction. The student's lips palpably moved through the acronym and stumbled across the word, "Protestant." She paused, waved her hand in impatience at the irrelevance of the religious distinction, said something about all of these people being "European-Americans," and moved on. She did not even notice "Anglo-Saxon," the remnant of an older system of classification which has happily passed to its last reward. "Caucasian," I observe from the federal forms which I habitually deface, is still with us.

At another level, however, I have serious doubts about whether the idea of the South would survive a rigorous multiculturalism. This is not because, as I have already suggested, the South lacks an available multiplicity of social groups, for it does not. It is not even because it is hard to hold together in one's mind, say, traditional white Southern conservatives and Chicanos and gays and Hindu motel owners in Arkansas, though it is. It is because Southern identity has worked historically by social groups agreeing to converge upon a definition of identity, consenting to accept and bargain a normative definition of the collectivity. Southerners are people who can find a way to say, "The South is . . ." or "Southerners are . . ." What Southerners have said, what the South is, what Southerners are, has varied hugely over time and through place; that has never been the point. Rather, it has been the willingness to believe in and assert a mutuality that has marked the South's reality. Those who believe in multiculturalism, it seems to me, characteristically abrogate that willingness, are interested in centrifugal identities, see mutuality as hegemony, are skeptical of every social organism but their own. For all that, it is possible to imagine a multiculturalism which would find a place for the South. Social identities seldom die. More often they diminish in emotional urgency and are layered over. We could have a South which was hyphenated, made up of black Southerners, Mississippi Chinese Southerners, female Southerners, Cherokee Southerners, and as many more social groups as proved interested in buying shares in the enterprise.

These three analytical movements—poststructuralism, postmodernism, and multiculturalism—have engrossed much intellectual endeavor in the last decade or so. Insofar as Southern discourse has a difficult time being reconciled to any of them, it is not hard to understand why this has been an inauspicious time for Southern intellectual culture to be taken seriously, or to be noticed by the Americans. For American intellectual historians themselves have been having a complicated and more sustained relationship with these same analytical movements, so much so that they have had little time or need to notice such Southerners, diffident applicants to the American canon as they are. Moreover, I would hazard that American intellectual history in the last generation has not been expansive, but rather static, perhaps even shrinking, and more than usually prone to introspection.

At the Wingspread Conference of 1977, the meeting which generated the important volume of essays, *New Directions in American Intellectual History*, there was much brave talk about intellectual history making a comeback against the dominance of the "new" social history. This does not seem to me to have happened. Which is not to say we have not seen very good books about particular topics—Kloppenberg's *Uncertain Victory*, Bender's *New York Intellect*, Ross's *The Origins of American Social Science*, among others— but none of them occupy a central place in the discourse of modern American historians.[26] We do not even have a book which works as a textbook survey of American intellectual history. More precise was the prediction of 1977 that the old metanarratives of Perry Miller and Merle Curti were done for, that instead we would only be persuaded by smaller narratives.

Where American intellectual historians have been doing a land-office business, by a development unanticipated in 1977, is in offering themselves as interpreters and referees of critical theory. They have been popping up here to explain Foucault and there to identify the "linguistic turn." They have been roaming around the pages of *American Historical Review* to explain to the lumpenproletariat of diplomatic and political historians why authors are now considered dead (except those who write for the *American Historical Review*) and all meanings are now meaningless (except those announced in the *American Historical Review*).[27] Above all, they have been tendering theoretical advice to the social historians, whose facts did not turn out to be self-evident, except to those who did not need the facts for evidence. Indeed it is symptomatic that the only work of American intellectual history which can be regarded as having had a widespread influence, Peter Novick's *That Noble Dream*, is a social history of the philosophical enterprise of the American historical profession.[28]

This has been a useful mediating role, discharging what has long been a responsibility of intellectual historians or historians of ideas, the explaining of philosophy to ordinary historians. But, frankly, this has been done often in belated haste. The taste for critical theory was not created by intellectual historians and only noticed by them after its progress in literary studies. To some extent, indeed, the prominence of theory has diminished the distinctiveness of the enterprise of intellectual history. I remember, when writing my first book in the mid-1970s, I felt rather daring and insecure about importing Hegelianism into Southern history, asserting the formative role of ideas, and pointing to the crucial role of language in creating social identity. Culture, I said, is an invented thing. At the time, I was thought distinctly peculiar. I looked over my shoulder lest the empiricists come to arrest me in the night. Today these are propositions which are the commonplaces of the classroom. For all I know, they are believed by the young man who delivers my pizza. Taking pot shots at positivists was once a satisfying sport, but no more; there are not too many fish left in the barrel. In fact, of late, most of us have become the fish in someone else's barrel, as more ambitious versions of philosophical idealism have exposed us as closet empiricists. Few are more grumpy than the skeptic who has been philosophically outflanked by a more radical skeptic.[29]

I do not quarrel with the usefulness of such a mediating role. But I am obliged to observe that the energies spent in this manner have been diverted from the production of the narratives to which theory was once supposed to be prolegomena, more especially as the theories have often denied the possibility of coherent narrative. For, to have lived through the historiography of the last decade has been like living in a Tom Stoppard play. On our rehearsal stage, we settle down for the game of enacting a history, but someone knocks a pawn to the ground, removes a rook and substitutes a checkers piece, switches opponents on us, or declares bleakly that, though we have five minutes for a move, the clock will run backwards. Someone swings on a trapeze above our heads. There is a body under the table, which may be us. Under such circumstances, the game has made little progress, is indeed irrelevant. For the game is more for the drama critic than the actor, more for the rehearsal than the performance, more for Beckett than garbage cans. What matters is establishing process, discussing identity with the other actors. The rest, the play before the public, is silence.

But the times have also been inauspicious for redefining a relationship between Southern culture and American culture, because—oddly, and with the very important and partial exceptions of African Americans and women—the canons of American intellectual history have been surprisingly inert in the last generation. Everywhere I seem to see this conservatism, and it comes from differing schools, from poststructuralists and contextualists alike. Look at Dominick LaCapra, who, on the rare occasions when he does write about someone other than himself and his immediate contemporaries, writes about Sartre, Marx, and Wittgenstein.[30] Look at Hayden White, a better historian and a quieter epistemologist, who gives us the likes of Michelet, Ranke, Tocqueville, Burckhardt, Hegel, Marx, Nietzsche, and Croce.[31] Look at the first edition of David Hollinger and Charles Capper's anthology, *The American Intellectual Tradition*: with the logical exception of the very last section and a very few female voices, there is scarcely a name here which would not have been considered canonical a generation ago.[32]

Timidity has arisen for different reasons in these schools. For contextualists, there has been the desire to hold on to the integrity of intellectual history as a discipline. This has bred a tendency to hold on to the safe topics. The logic seems to be, If we continue to write about what we used to write about, when all agreed on our integrity, might we not insure the continuance of that integrity? This merely professional instinct has compounded a basic difficulty of contextualism, evident in its most distinguished practitioners, J. G. A. Pocock and Quentin Skinner. Their habit is usually to move from well-established texts—Machiavelli, More, Harrington, Hobbes, Locke—to less familiar contexts, in order to return to the same texts, newly understood. As a technique, it is almost incapable of generating new texts, of seeing the possibility of new canons, of demoting the canonical to the uncanonical. For someone like Pocock, a man of deep cultural conservatism, a man entranced by the shape and modulations of intellectual tradition, this is no accident. Moreover, their idea of context is so often narrowly confined to the world of books, that they have seldom been able to establish a conversation with social historians.

For poststructuralists, however, an inattention to the matter of canons has arisen partly by accident. If the intention is to concentrate energy on the play around the text, any old text will do if it has some complexity. The established canon has that, so it serves. Or, if someone else changes the canon, that will serve too, although this is not preferred. Newly canonized texts tend to be regarded with restless moral earnestness. Since the methodology of deconstruction is intentionally playful at the same time that the social ideology of its practitioners is proclaimed to be radical, this sets up tensions which have been best avoided. Fun and games with Jules Michelet is one thing, cracking jokes about Harriet Jacobs would be altogether another thing. Nonetheless the essential game of deconstruction is skill, and all that is essential is that the reader share the text, so that he or she can better appreciate the virtuosity of the deconstruction. If I dismember with panache and wit Eliot's *The Waste Land*, connoisseurship by the reader of what I have done is possible. If I am ingeniously clever with one of the lesser Latin works of Johann Gottlieb Heineccius, the range of appreciation available to the reader is starkly reduced. Best to stick to the familiar. Only the New Historicists, with their taste for quirky Renaissance texts, seem to be abjuring this counsel.

The exceptions to this inertia help to establish the rule. Feminism preeminently, and black scholarship secondarily, have permanently altered what we read, because they have had a powerful sense of what matters beyond reading. But these works have, in the last generation, appeared before us, less as intellectual history, more as aspects of black history or women's history. They have been defined more by the shared identity of authors and audience, less by methodology. In such circumstances, at a time when subjects take root in social groups, American intellectual history has been peculiarly disadvantaged, for it does not have a social constituency with any clout, except something amorphous called the intelligentsia, a group whose identity and location is a matter of some obscurity, especially in an American culture whose democratic ethic mistrusts the concept of an intellectual elite. The tendency to explore the intellectual history of women within the paradigms of women's history has left American intellectual history as a mostly male subject, both as to its practitioners and its subject matter. At least, it has had difficulty expanding its natural domain to include women. This is not a promising state of affairs. Feminists have already pointed out the inadequacy of Novick's *That Noble Dream* on matters of gender, but most male intellectual historians have done little better.[33]

Indeed American intellectual history has grown, if anything, more High Church and abstract during recent times, which have been marked by the opposite tendencies, particularism and a taste for the concrete.[34] In the discipline of history, the times are Low Church, even Broad Church. A generation or two ago, American intellectual history had, at least, the utility of joining in the forlorn chase for the American national character and was often taught in courses which bore the brave title, "American social and intellectual history," whose contents were somehow never very social or, for that matter, never very intellectual. This turn towards the abstract, even the metaphysical, has further compounded the difficulty confronted by Southern intellectual history in finding a place in the discourse of American intellectual history, because Southern thought has been little concerned with abstract philosophical issues: the South has had no William James and no Charles Sanders Pierce, but rather has produced a rich tradition of social and literary thinkers.

Only one methodology, it has seemed to me, has offered even a promise of a common ground for Southern intellectual historians and the Americans. I remember being exceptionally attracted by discourse theory, when I read a version of it in the papers given at the Wingspread Conference by David Hollinger and Thomas Bender.[35] As my language so far has betrayed, I am still attracted by it. But its potential for decentralizing American intellectual history has not been fully worked out. We have no reliable catalogue of these discourses, and only a few histories of them.[36] The roots of the methodology in Foucault's thought meant that more attention has been focused upon the centripetal concepts of power and hegemony, and far less upon the centrifugal realities of culture. Thomas Bender, for example, has been notable for championing the idea of local discourses. But even he has been able to write that, "An adequate account of the life of the mind in America requires an understanding of why and how one or another of these cultures [of intellectual life] achieves hegemony," which begs the question of whether any did achieve hegemony, which I doubt.[37] In truth, I am not sure that a thorough application of discourse theory would reintegrate American intellectual history, so much as abolish it. We would have a bundle of discourses, held together by little more than the Library of Congress cataloguing system. The idea of American culture, though it has badly needed disaggregating, has more life in it than that. For there are certain ideas which pervade and connect all of these local cultures: democracy, republicanism, race, God, gender, and many others. If there is a sense in which any one locality has exercised hegemony over American culture, it has lain in the process by which certain groups have disproportionately defined the meaning of these general concepts and excluded others from the opportunity differently to define them. Whether Southerners are free to define the history of the proslavery argument or the Agrarians is an important issue, but an equally important one is whether intellectual Southerners are granted equal access to defining the general ideological constructs of American culture, not to control the definition but to influence it.

However, I would like to stress that these spheres—the local and the national, even the international—ought to be coequal. We often talk as though the cultural nation is primary, and localities are secondary, to be fitted together into a jigsaw which will form a single pattern. There is precious little historical evidence for this, perhaps in any nation, let alone the United States. Rather, I think we reason locally—and by local, I mean not only geographical areas but discrete social groups—and turn to national or cosmopolitan reasoning because no locality can encompass who we are or want to be.[38] This is both the occasion for and the problem with discourse theory. For we each belong to several discourses, our words jaggedly enter into several conversations, and "America" or "England" or "France" or "the South" is the name we give to the intersections of some of the conversations. But, it is important to stress, at these intersections, there is no coherence of conversation, which is why it is unlikely that Southern intellectual historians and American intellectual historians will manage fully to understand each other. For we are standing in a room choked with people, where our words are half-heard by more than those we address, we hear more than those we most listen to, we have no standpoint from which to reconstruct the totality of the conversations, many of which are disordered even by those who participate in them. This is the normal human situation, at least in large cultures blessed or cursed by freedom of communication. It is a situation, however, which runs against the temperamental grain of intellectual history. Because of the discipline's origins in philosophy, we have a marked preference for the synthetic, for proceeding from the many to the few or the one. We like to sum up, to reduce multiplicity to a paradigm or a thought. This is a useful instinct, as long as it has no chance of succeeding. For we need to recognize that, though we have obligations in extracting such order from the babble as narrative requires, nothing but our vanity would be served if a single voice came to silence the room.

NOTES

1. Entry for 22 November 1828, Hugh Blair Grigsby Diary, Hugh Blair Grigsby Papers, Virginia Historical Society, Richmond.

2. Frederick Grimke to Hugh Swinton Legaré, 18 May 1838, Hugh Swinton Legaré Papers in the Harry L. and Mary K. Dalton Collection, Manuscripts and Special Collections Department, William R. Perkins Library, Duke University, Durham.

3. "Critical Notices—Presbyterian Review," *Southern Quarterly Review* 12 (October 1847): 535.

4. James Johnston Pettigrew to James C. Johnston, 3 June 1858, Hayes Collection, Southern Historical Collection, Wilson Library, University of North Carolina, Chapel Hill.

5. Oscar Lieber to Francis Lieber, undated [folder suggests 1854], Francis Lieber Papers, Henry E. Huntington Library, San Marino, CA.

6. Basil Manly, Jr., to Charles Manly, 7 January 1859, Manly Family Papers, W. S. Hoole Special Collections Library, University of Alabama, Tuscaloosa; George Fitzhugh, "Southern Thought," *De Bow's Review* 23 (October 1857): 337, 341.

7. John Bell Henneman, ed., *History of the Literary and Intellectual Life of the South* (Richmond, VA: Southern Historical Society, 1909), xxxviii, xlii, xli.

8. James Wood Davidson, *The Living Writers of the South* (New York: Carleton, 1869); Louise Manly, *Southern Literature from 1579–1895: A Comprehensive Review, with Copious Extracts and Criticisms* (Richmond, VA: B. F. Johnson, 1895); Edwin Anderson Alderman and Joel Chandler Harris, eds., *Library of Southern Literature*, comp. Lucian Lamar Knight (New Orleans, LA: Martin & Hoyt, 1907); Jay B. Hubbell, *The South in American Literature, 1607–1900* (Durham, NC: Duke University Press, 1954); Louis D. Rubin, Jr., et al., *The History of Southern Literature* (Baton Rouge: Louisiana State University Press, 1985).

9. Ulrich B. Phillips, *Georgia and State Rights: A Study of the Political History of Georgia from the Revolution to the Civil War, with Particular Regard to Federal Relations* (Washington, DC: U.S. Government Printing Office, 1902); Frank Lawrence Owsley, *State Rights in the Confederacy* (Chicago, IL: University of Chicago Press, 1925); Jesse T. Carpenter, *The South as a Conscious Minority, 1789–1861: A Study in Political Thought* (New York: New York University Press, 1930).

10. Arthur O. Lovejoy, *Essays in the History of Ideas* (1948; New York: G. P. Putnam's Sons, 1960), 2.

11. Perry Miller, *The New England Mind: The Seventeenth Century* (New York: Macmillan, 1939), vii.

12. Hugh Swinton Legaré, "Classical Learning," *Southern Review* 1 (February 1828): 41.

13. Clement Eaton, *Freedom of Thought in the Old South* (Durham, NC: Duke University Press, 1940); Clement Eaton, *The Mind of the Old South* (Baton Rouge: Louisiana State University Press, 1964); Clement Eaton, *The Waning of the Old South Civilization* (Athens: University of Georgia Press, 1968); Rollin G. Osterweis, *Romanticism and Nationalism in the Old South* (New Haven, CT: Yale University Press, 1949); William R. Taylor, *Cavalier and Yankee: The Old South and American National*

Character (New York: Braziller, 1961); Richard Beale Davis, *Intellectual Life in Jefferson's Virginia, 1790–1830* (Chapel Hill: University of North Carolina Press, 1964); Richard Beale Davis, *Intellectual Life in the Colonial South, 1585–1763*, 3 vols. (Knoxville: University of Tennessee Press, 1978).

14. James T. Kloppenberg, *Uncertain Victory: Social Democracy and Progressivism in European and American Thought, 1870–1920* (New York: Oxford University Press, 1986).

15. From the standpoint of New York, however, Boston can be the ogre: see Thomas Bender, *Intellect and Public Life: Essays on the Social History of Academic Intellectuals in the United States* (Baltimore, MD: Johns Hopkins University Press, 1993), xvi.

16. Drew Gilpin Faust, *A Sacred Circle: The Dilemma of the Intellectual in the Old South, 1840–1860* (Baltimore, MD: Johns Hopkins University Press, 1977); Daniel J. Singal, *The War Within: From Victorian to Modernist Thought in the South, 1919–1945* (Chapel Hill: University of North Carolina Press, 1982); George Fitzhugh, *Cannibals All! or Slaves Without Masters*, ed. C. Vann Woodward (Cambridge, MA: Harvard University Press, Belknap, 1960); William Faulkner, *Light in August* (New York: H. Smith & R. Haas, 1932).

17. Hugh Swinton Legaré, "Hall's Travels in North-America," *Southern Review* 4 (November 1829): 322–23.

18. John Shelton Reed, *The Enduring South: Subcultural Persistence in Mass Society* (Lexington, MA: Lexington Books, 1972).

19. Bruce Kuklick, *The Rise of American Philosophy: Cambridge, Massachusetts, 1860–1930* (New Haven, CT: Yale University Press, 1977).

20. Jonathan Wiener, *Social Origins of the New South: Alabama, 1860–1885* (Baton Rouge: Louisiana State University Press, 1978).

21. Henry Junius Nott to George McDuffie, 25 November 1835, Henry J. Nott Papers, South Caroliniana Library, University of South Carolina, Columbia.

22. Thomas Smith Grimké, "Origin of Rhyme," *Southern Review* 3 (February 1829): 157.

23. Thomas Smith Grimké, "Origin of Rhyme," *Southern Review* 2 (August 1828): 33–34. The prominence of historicism in the antebellum South offers a good example of the misunderstandings that can arise when American intellectual historians ignore Southern evidence. Dorothy Ross has argued that historicism does not come to American culture until the late nineteenth century, a claim that is unintelligible to anyone acquainted with Southern sources; see Dorothy Ross, "Historical Consciousness in Nineteenth-Century America," *American Historical Review* 89 (October 1984): 909–28.

24. Allen Tate, "A Southern Mode of the Imagination," in *Essays of Four Decades* (1959; New York: William Morrow, 1970), 577–92.

25. Jay B. Hubbell, *South and Southwest: Literary Essays and Reminiscences* (Durham, NC: Duke University Press, 1965).

26. John Higham and Paul K. Conkin, eds., *New Directions in American Intellectual History* (Baltimore, MD: Johns Hopkins University Press, 1979); Kloppenberg, *Uncertain Victory*; Thomas Bender, *New York Intellect: A History of Intellectual Life in New York City, from 1750 to the Beginning of Our Own Time* (Baltimore, MD: Johns Hopkins University Press, 1987); Dorothy Ross, *The Origins of American Social Science* (Cambridge: Cambridge University Press, 1991).

27. James T. Kloppenberg, "Deconstruction and Hermeneutic Strategies for Intellectual History: The Recent Work of Dominick LaCapra and David Hollinger," *Intellectual History Newsletter* 9 (1987): 3–22; Dominick LaCapra, "Of Lumpers and Readers," *Intellectual History Newsletter* 10 (1988): 3–10; James T. Kloppenberg, "Reply to LaCapra's 'Of Lumpers and Readers,'" *Intellectual History Newsletter* 10 (1988): 11; John Toews, "Intellectual History After the Linguistic Turn: The Autonomy of Meaning and the Irreducibility of Experience," *American Historical Review* 92 (October 1987): 879–907; James T. Kloppenberg, "Objectivity and Historicism: A Century of American Historical Knowing," *American Historical Review* 94 (September 1989): 1011–30; David Harlan, "Intellectual

History and the Return of Literature," *American Historical Review* 94 (June 1989): 581–609; David A. Hollinger, "The Return of the Prodigal: The Persistence of Historical Knowing," *American Historical Review* 94 (June 1989): 610–21; David Harlan, "Reply to David Hollinger," *American Historical Review* 94 (June 1989): 622–26; Donald R. Kelley, "'History of Ideas': Canon and Variations," *Intellectual History Newsletter* 11 (1989): 28–38; Dominick LaCapra, "Canons and Their Discontents," *Intellectual History Newsletter* 13 (1991): 3–14; David A. Hollinger, "Discourse About Discourse About Discourse About Discourse? A Response to Dominick LaCapra," *Intellectual History Newsletter* 13 (1991): 15–18.

28. Thomas L. Haskell, "Objectivity is not Neutrality: Rhetoric vs. Practice in Peter Novick's *That Noble Dream*," *History and Theory* 29, no. 2 (1990): 129–57; J. H. Hexter et al., "AHR Forum: Peter Novick's *That Noble Dream*: The Objectivity Question and the Future of the Historical Profession," *American Historical Review* 96 (June 1991): 675–708.

29. See, for example, the recent exchange between Richard King and Alun Munslow, in which the former is accused of offering "a stalwart defence of empiricism": Richard H. King, "The Discipline of Fact / the Freedom of Fiction?" *Journal of American Studies* 25 (August 1991): 171–88; Alun Munslow, "A Reply to Richard King, 'The Discipline of Fact / the Freedom of Fiction?,'" *Journal of American Studies* 26 (April 1992): 90–93.

30. Dominick LaCapra, *Rethinking Intellectual History: Texts, Contexts, Language* (Ithaca, NY: Cornell University Press, 1983); Dominick LaCapra, *History, Politics, and the Novel* (Ithaca, NY: Cornell University Press, 1987).

31. Hayden White, *Metahistory: The Historical Imagination in Nineteenth-Century Europe* (Baltimore, MD: Johns Hopkins University Press, 1973); Hayden White, *Tropics of Discourse: Essays in Cultural Criticism* (Baltimore, MD: Johns Hopkins University Press, 1978); Hayden White, *The Content of the Form: Narrative Discourse and Historical Representation* (Baltimore, MD: Johns Hopkins University Press, 1987).

32. David A. Hollinger and Charles Capper, eds., *The American Intellectual Tradition*, 2 vols. (New York: Oxford University Press, 1989).

33. Among the several hundred names mentioned, for example, in the collected essays of one of the more influential of American intellectual historians, I count only five women (Hannah Arendt, Mary McCarthy, Margaret Mead, Gertrude Stein, Virginia Woolf): see David A. Hollinger, *In the American Province: Studies in the History and Historiography of Ideas* (Bloomington: Indiana University Press, 1985). In 1979, when the Intellectual History Group published a directory of those who subscribed to its *Newsletter*, there were 34 female names among the 281 listed; this amounted to 12 percent. If one looks at the last six issues of the *Intellectual History Newsletter*, one finds that no woman has published an article in it since 1987.

34. Though many—Richard Rorty comes to mind—have endorsed the particularist, this has been more by way of benediction, less by way of practice. See Richard Rorty, *Contingency, Irony, and Solidarity* (Cambridge: Cambridge University Press, 1989).

35. David A. Hollinger, "Historians and the Discourse of Intellectuals," and Thomas Bender, "The Cultures of Intellectual Life: The City and the Professions," in Higham and Conkin, *New Directions*, 42–63, 181–95.

36. Notable, however, have been Bender, *New York Intellect*, and Lawrence Buell, *New England Literary Culture: From Revolution Through Renaissance* (Cambridge: Cambridge University Press, 1986).

37. Bender, "The Cultures of Intellectual Life," reprinted in Bender, *Intellect and Public Life*, 5. Nor can he resist reaching for significances beyond the local: "What Lee Benson and many colonial historians have said about New York remains compelling: New York may be unique among the states, but in the very diversity that makes it unique it best represents the United States as a whole" (xvi).

38. I have discussed this further in Michael O'Brien, "On Transcending the Mollusk: Cosmopolitanism and Historical Discourse," *Gettysburg Review* 1 (Summer 1988): 457–68.

The first of these pieces is an entry on "Southern Historians," in *The New Encyclopedia of Southern Culture: Volume 3: History,* ed. Charles Reagan Wilson (Chapel Hill: University of North Carolina Press, 2006), 115–18. Copyright © 2006 by the University of North Carolina Press. Used by permission of the publisher. The second is a lecture to the Commonwealth Fund Conference at University College London in February 2000, subsequently published as Michael O'Brien, "Orpheus Turning: The Present State of Southern History," in *The State of U.S. History,* ed. Melvyn Stokes (Oxford: Berg, 2002), 307–24. Reprinted by permission.

The oldest tradition of historical literature in the South is that of state descriptions and history, which commenced before the settlement of Virginia with the pamphlets and books which promoted and inflated the virtues of colonization. It continued through the studies of Robert Beverley (*History and Present State of Virginia,* 1705), William Stith (*History of the First Discovery and Settlement of Virginia,* 1747), and Thomas Jefferson (*Notes on the State of Virginia,* 1785). In the Spanish and French colonies, there were comparable works. By the nineteenth century a considerable body of such writings existed, among them David Ramsay's *History of South Carolina* (1808), Charles Gayarré's *Histoire de la Louisiane* (1846), and Charles Campbell's *History of the Colony and Ancient Dominion of Virginia* (1860). Such history was an amateur undertaking, local in focus and patriotic in tone, sometimes though not often allied to the foundation of state historical societies. Before 1861, such organizations existed in nine states: Virginia (1831), North Carolina (1833), Louisiana (1836), Georgia (1839), Tennessee (1849), Alabama (1850), South Carolina (1855), Florida (1856), and Mississippi (1858).

Notable before the Civil War, however, was an absence of South-wide historiography, which had to wait until the late nineteenth century brought a generation of Southerners schooled by the experiences of war and Reconstruction. The first broader historical organization was the Southern Historical Society, founded in New Orleans in 1869 by ex-Confederates and dedicated to the vindication of the Lost Cause. Its successor, the Southern History Association, founded in Washington in 1896, was both more New South in persuasion and less bitter in tone; its publications appeared between 1896 and 1907. Insofar as professional historiography is an offshoot of urban modernity, it is no surprise that the Southern historical and educational industry should have commenced outside and on the borders of the South before moving into the region later. The earliest centers of academic Southern history were the Johns Hopkins University, where Herbert Baxter Adams taught Woodrow Wilson and William P. Trent; Columbia University, where William A. Dunning instructed students of Reconstruction such as Walter L. Fleming and J. G. de Roulhac Hamilton; and the University of Chicago, where William Dodd directed Frank L. Owsley's studies. The first course in Southern history was taught by James C. Ballagh at Johns Hopkins in 1896 and the first within the South by William K. Boyd at Trinity College (later Duke University) in 1907.

Usually under the direction of Northern graduates born in the South, an infrastructure of graduate programs, journals, archives, presses, and professional organizations was fashioned indigenously after 1920. About a hundred history doctorates, mostly on Southern topics, were granted by Southern universities between the world wars. In 1930 the Southern Historical Collection, the largest archive of regional documents, was founded at Chapel Hill. In 1934 the Southern Historical Association was organized and publication of its *Journal of Southern History* commenced in 1935. In the 1920s the University of North Carolina Press began to publish books on regional history and culture, and in 1937 the Louisiana State University Press began a multivolume *History of the South*.

Southern history, as both a professional and an amateur pursuit, has largely and consistently been written in the South by Southerners for Southerners and published by Southern journals and presses. Though a wider national and international interest was sparked by the civil rights movement, there is mixed evidence that this curiosity is in decline, perhaps more slowly in Europe where scholars sponsored in the 1980s the Southern Studies Forum as a subdivision of the European Association of American Studies, but more rapidly in the North. Nonetheless the study of Southern history forms an important and perhaps permanent subculture in American social discourse, one possessed of many private symbols and rituals. There is a healthy amateur industry, flourishing as tourism, cheerfully anecdotal political journalism, and military and genealogical antiquarianism; all are characterized by a warmth of nostalgia for hooped skirts, Earl Long's penchant for striptease artists, or grandfather's exploits at Shiloh.

Professional historians in the South are notable for being an accepted part of their society, often partisan about the South, formerly bitter against the North but recently—as a function of growing relative affluence—more amiable. Their specialities are social history (particularly of slavery and race relations), biography, and political history. Military history, once popular as a function of bitterness, is now in decline, at least among professional historians. Economic history has been a weaker tradition, and intellectual history (save as literary history) has been almost non-existent until very recently. Southern historians tend to divide by social persuasion (usually conservative, often liberal, rarely radical), by place of birth (Virginians, Tennesseans), by ancestry (yeoman, planter, Tidewater, Piedmont), and by gender (male, female, gay), rather than by theoretical persuasion (Marxist, Hegelian, postmodernist). However, the youngest generation of Southern historians shows a marked, if wary interest in theory.

Southern history is implicitly comparative, because scholars of Southern history assume a distinction from "northern" culture and occasionally offer formal comparisons with non-American cultures, as in the writings of Eugene D. Genovese (Japan and Sicily), Stanley Elkins (Latin America), Peter Kolchin (Russia), or C. Vann Woodward (Europe). More usually—and this is necessary to its function as social discourse—Southern history is inward looking. The old tradition of state history continues and constitutes the bulk of Southern historical literature, chiefly because archives and higher education are organized largely by states. So Southern history tends to be either the aggregate of state histories or, more commonly, narrative by synecdoche, in which a part is made to do service for the whole.

There is no known analysis of the social origins, recruitment patterns, or social habits of Southern historians as a tribe, but there are several works which study individual historians, by way of intellectual biography or as part of an attempt to plot historiographical changes.

• • •

> So much for the past and present. The future is called
> "perhaps," which is the only possible thing to call the future.
> And the important thing is not to allow that to scare you.
>
> —TENNESSEE WILLIAMS, preface to *Orpheus Descending*[1]

The present state of Southern history can be considered on various levels: its place in the American historical profession, its relationship to disciplines and methodologies, and the shifting of its philosophical rationale and narrative shape. Such a consideration is not usual. Recent Southern history has been little given to the synoptic view and to asking itself or others where the subject stands. While it used to be a grim and dispiriting ritual of the Southern Historical Association that its presidential address would define the South and offer a shape for its history, this habit has much abated.[2] The *Journal of Southern History* has a preference for microcosmic studies and (unlike the *Journal of American History*) an aversion to commissioning synthetic review-essays or special issues. And it is uncommon for general symposia on American history to include an essay on the South, since they tend to be organized by period (the American Revolution or the New Deal), methodology (economic history), or groups of national scope (immigrants, women).[3] Region tends to fall away, except when it is pertinent to these other matters, to the Civil War or labor relations or the non-ratification of the Equal Rights Amendment. In general, then, the Southern historian possesses fewer road maps than is usual within the American historical tradition.

First, the professional landscape. The writing of Southern history is moderately healthy, if numbers mean health. In 1936, when the Southern Historical Association first met in Birmingham, Alabama, it had 109 attendants. In Louisville in 1970, which was the first one I attended, there were 1744 people registered and the association had 2948 members. In Birmingham in 1998, the figures were 1453 and 3402, respectively.[4] So, in the last thirty years of the twentieth century, the SHA has acquired a few hundred more members, who want to see each other somewhat less than they used to. This relative stability is fairly impressive, given a proliferation of subdisciplines, conferences, and organizations, many of them Southern in focus.[5] In short, Southern history is one of the larger intellectual constituencies of American history, but perhaps about to shrink. It happened that the expansion of Southern history and literature in the American imagination in the 1950s and 1960s coincided with the sharp expansion of American higher education; that generation drawn to Southern history and subsequently employed begins to retire. It is very doubtful that these historians will be replaced, man or woman for man; hence it is probable that the number of Southern historians will have shrunk by a half in the first decade or two of the twenty-first century, though much will be written under different rubrics which might once have been called Southern history.[6]

However, for the moment, there seems to be little slackening in the production of Southern narratives. Young historians seem still to be drawn. The American Historical Association's database of dissertations-in-progress shows perhaps three hundred registered on Southern history, either on topics of regional scope, in state or local history, or in African American history of Southern emphasis.[7] The center of gravity for advanced graduate study has moved, however. In 1963, that center was arguably in New Haven, when C. Vann Woodward and David Potter were in their heyday. This was, in fact, a traditional pattern, when one recalls the earlier influence of William Archibald Dunning at Columbia, of Ulrich Phillips at Yale, of William Dodd at Chicago. Today it is hard to think of a Northern university with a comparable influence, though individual Ivy League universities have single figures of great note. Rather, the subject is decentralized, but is most studied in various Southern locations—Chapel Hill, Charlottesville, Atlanta, Oxford (Mississippi)—which sometimes have institutes specifically dedicated to Southern studies. It seems probable that the recent initiative of the National Endowment for the Humanities, whose head is a Mississippian, to fund regional study centers will accelerate this trend. Such a pattern is cause for concern, for it threatens that Southern history should become only a thing Southerners do in the South, but the worry may be less pressing than a comparable situation two generations ago might have elicited. Partly offsetting a decline in Northern is a rise in international interest.[8] And Southern universities are more cosmopolitan than they used to be, even if nativism is scarcely extinct, and there is a tendency for colleges to demonstrate a progress into worldliness by expunging the South from their curricula. It has been a while since any of us had any reason to remember the physical location of the *South Atlantic Quarterly* in the South.

One professional change is especially significant. The future of Southern history looks coequally female. Although men may still slightly outnumber women in new doctorates, the former are disproportionately crowded in subdisciplines, such as political and military history, of diminished influence. Southern history seems to be a subject which women find attractive, unlike diplomatic or (oddly) Native American history. With this process of recruitment going on since around 1980, a number of the senior positions in Southern history are now occupied by women, who tend to attract graduate students mostly female, sometimes male, but both much drawn to the history of gender. Usually the best attended session at the Southern Historical Association each year, except for the presidential address, is the annual session of the Southern Association for Women Historians. So a fascinating process of transformation and adaptation is in process, in which female Southern historians are not merely creating new topics, previously oblivious to the male tradition, but reconfiguring topics once thought distant from gender. Drew Faust's *Mothers of Invention* has made inroads on traditional understandings of the Civil War, for example.[9] In this process, several things are notable. Firstly, as one might expect, new women have meant new men. The definitive Southern males are no longer the ugly, but potent figures who sought and found mastery, like James Henry Hammond.[10] Rather, we are being given a series of ambivalent characters who commit suicide, have affairs with their chauffeurs, get murdered by their slaves, seem never to get the hang of patriarchy, and inveterately are plunged into crises of manhood.[11] Thomas Jefferson becomes, not a Founding Father, but the common-law husband of Sally Hemings, a man surreptitious and confused.[12] Even Pitchfork Ben Tillman now has masculine angst.[13] Secondly, the old cultural warfare between Southern intellectuals and the American "mainstream," in which the former complained of being marginalized, is being duplicated in the relationship between Southern and American women's history.[14] Thirdly, there is an imminent crisis of purpose and evidence, since women historians have mostly gone in search of a usable liberal tradition—what Jacquelyn Hall has called "a female anti-racist tradition"[15]—but very often encounter Southern conservative women defending slavery, sewing KKK sheets, nurturing Confederate veterans, refusing the suffrage, spitting at civil rights protesters.[16] Lastly, whether the female historians who are assuming the responsibility for the direction of Southern history and falling heir to its legacy will choose to address the full range of that history—economics, battles, county politics, ecology, intellectual culture and much else—will determine whether the history of the South will become or remain more than an episode in the history of gender.

 What of interdisciplinary relationships? These have mutated. A few generations ago, economics and sociology were potent influences, while psychology was of some moment, literature was preeminent, and anthropology persistently irrelevant. The history of slavery from as far back as Ulrich Phillips and as late as Robert Fogel had first been an economic problem, and the history of the New South in the hands of that Beardian, C. Vann Woodward, had been understood as largely a matter of colonial, economic dependency.[17] Southern historians were supposed then to know their statistics. A few know them still (Stanley Engerman, Gavin Wright, Peter Coclanis), but the band is much diminished.[18] Social history is a softer methodology, which has lost touch with the founding disciplines for which it once formed a convergence. Sociology, too, is a lost influence. John Shelton Reed is the last of the line of sociologists commencing in the 1920s with Howard Odum and

Rupert Vance, who insisted that studying the South first required a notion of social structure, and Reed is an empirical sociologist, not an interpreter of grand theory drawn from Marx, Durkheim, or Weber.[19] As to psychology, its status is peculiar. Southern history is often a Gothic genre, anxious and neurotic, so it has naturally been drawn to psychology. Occasionally, this has eventuated in historians who have drawn formally on psychological theory, notably Stanley Elkins and Richard King.[20] But usually it has led to historians who offer psychological readings of people or events, but without any specific allegiance to a Freud or Jung, but who use the common language which the psychological tradition has transmitted to the lay intellectual. Nonetheless, the implicit influence of psychology is great. The South is persistently regarded as stretched on a couch like a patient, repressing or confessing to incest, rape, murder, or to trouble about lovers, fathers, and mothers.

One great change lies in the linkage of history to fiction and poetry, and secondarily to literary criticism. There is no modern Southern novelist who means as much to this time as William Faulkner did to 1950, and no literary critic as influential as Allen Tate once was. Eudora Welty and the late Walker Percy have been important, but the younger generation of, for example, Lee Smith and Clyde Egerton have not had as marked an impact. The reasons for this are complex, but one may be that the postmodernist moment has been around in Southern literature for a generation and longer, and Southern historians seem to be very reluctant postmodernists.[21] On the other hand, paradoxically the relationship between historians and literary critics is much healthier. In the 1950s, the idea that the critic should read history (beyond the odd volume of Woodward) was only intermittently entertained, however much talk there was of the importance and burden of history. The South's recent literary critics are immeasurably better read in historical literature.[22] Concomitantly, as intellectual history is now more significant as a subdiscipline, some Southern historians are more conversant with literary theory and practice, and have themselves often been literary critics.[23]

What is new as an influence is popular culture. The Center for the Study of Southern Culture at the University of Mississippi has peculiarly fostered studies of country music, the blues, sports, and material culture; these can be found embodied in a great *Encyclopedia of Southern Culture*.[24] The Center for the Study of the American South in Chapel Hill has likewise sponsored a semi-academic, semi-popular periodical called *Southern Cultures*, where one habitually finds (amid more solemn topics lightly narrated) essays on sororities, cooking, and basketball.[25] Woodward's generation, though it defended the integrity of the populist tradition, was mandarin by instinct, and so less likely to write about Hank Williams and Goo Goo Clusters. If Allen Tate and Donald Davidson defined the elite and vernacular polarities of the Southern Agrarian tradition, it is not Tate the follower of T. S. Eliot, but Davidson the librettist of a hillbilly opera who better presaged the modern Southern sensibility, at least among men. Academic women seem more resistant to these democratic allures.

Lastly, there is the matter of how Southern and African American history relate. Once Negro history was largely a subset of Southern history, especially when it was written by white Southerners like Ulrich Phillips. In time, largely following the demographic patterns of outmigration, writing about the experience of black Americans outside the orbit of the South came to be as important as that within; the former is now, almost certainly, more important. The African American experience is too large a topic with too weighty a moral authority to be contained within a narrative of Southern history. Indeed it has sought a partial release from the confines even of American history. African American intellectual life, at least as it is embodied in what has become its headquarters at the Du Bois Institute at Harvard, has been imaginatively reaching out to an international experience.[26] Henry Louis Gates makes television documentaries about Africa, but not about Alabama. The South appears very little in his work.[27] He once summarized his purpose as the attempt to comprehend "a late twentieth-century world profoundly fissured by nationality, ethnicity, race, class, and gender."[28] In that list, the word region does not occur. On the surface, this is a casual, unthinking omission, but I suspect it has a deep structure. Gates has been interested in what can take and has taken black Americans away from what has imprisoned them, physically by acts of expatriation as narrated in slave narratives, intellectually by deftly deconstructing the crude atavisms of race. Whatever else this may mean, it seems to mean looking away from what was the experience of most black Americans for most of American history, that is, the South. There is unfinished business here, something not confronted and, in the case of Gates's memoir *Colored People*, even sentimentalized.

This pattern is broader than the Du Bois Institute. African American history in the last two generations has been an expansive field, while Southern history has been fairly static, changing but not appreciably having more impact on the American imagination, indeed probably declining. Black history drives a Mercedes, Southern history the family Buick. So, if anything, the old relationship is beginning to reverse itself. Black history is no longer a subset of Southern history, but Southern history begins to be a subset of black history, at least as it is understood and taught outside the South. This is a practical question: all departments have to have a black historian, but a Southern historian is a luxury, so increasingly and only sometimes Southern history is given to the African American scholar to do. For the moment, this is a promising development, even if it will tend to make much of Southern history (the part remote from the black experience) marginal and unintelligible, but that is an old story, denoting little change. If you are a backcountry Southerner, it does not much matter if Southern history is narrated by the descendant of a slaveholder or a slave; neither will be much bothered with you. The promise resides in the sophisticated debate about identity and multiculturalism, to be found especially in the work of Anthony Appiah, which ought to affect the debate about Southern culture and identity.[29] The South is going from being single to being multiple and stands (as usual) in peril of dissipating. But this has been true of black identity in the last generation, too, as integration was ambivalently attempted. Black Americans and Ghanaians, among others, have hazarded ways to salvage what is usable in the idea of race out of the bitter authoritarianism of racism. By their logic and desire, identity becomes a cultural role. But we have many identities and roles.[30]

The Southern/African American equation is the sharpest instance of a wider phenomenon. For what has grown more opaque in the last generation is the scope of "Southern." Logically, to write Southern history, one needs to know who the Southerners are. As far as historical narrative went, this used to be simple. Southerners were the descendants of the Europeans who colonized the southeastern corner of what is now the United States and was briefly the Confederacy, the people who owned or consented to the ownership of slaves, those who ordered the system of Jim Crow. There were prettier ways of describing them, which they themselves preferred, and the community encompassed many anguished dissidents, mostly ineffective. But, to count as a Southerner, it helped to be a man, white, born in the South or (if expatriate) publicly troubled by the exile, preferably in a work of fiction. In general, one could be a woman and Southern, but only in an ancillary way, but (with rare exceptions) one could not be black and Southern, nor Native American and Southern. To be thought Southern after 1865 usually required two qualifications: to have social power within the region, but to be marginal in the nation; the injustice of the latter was used to justify the necessity of the former.

The last few generations have left this standpoint in hopeless confusion. Once the South was understood to have made Southerners, by whatever mechanism the historian or sociologist preferred to describe, whether it was by the land or poverty or shared experience. In practice, of course, it only made certain people Southerners, though regionalism was in theory an inclusive premise.[31] But the experiences of the post-Second World War economic transformation and the civil rights movement upset this reasoning. Urbanization killed off the Agrarian definition of the Southern way of life, by making modernity too ubiquitous to be excluded from the formation of identity. Then around 1965, for the first time, polling data showed a significant number of blacks in the South being willing to describe themselves as Southern. This did for Ulrich Phillips's presumption that Southernness was white supremacy. Further, outmigration and inmigration scrambled the argument that "Southern" was occasioned by descent and residence. Was a black Mississippian migrant in Detroit a Southerner? Were his or her children, if they stayed in the North or chose to move to Texas? Was someone from Minnesota who moved to North Carolina a Southerner? What of the Mississippi Chinese and the Melungeons? In our time, diversity is not supposed to preclude sharing. But such reasoning does vitiate the arguments of C. Vann Woodward. For, if you arrived late to Southern culture, if you did not share the old experiences of war and poverty, did not Woodward imply that you could not be Southern? Were not midwestern migrants to North Carolina among those driving the machinery of the "Bulldozer Revolution"?[32]

These confusions will be familiar to students of migration and the nation-state in the modern world, whose burgeoning literature ought to influence how we understand the South, since they offer dizzyingly and clumsily an "appreciation of the practices of identity-formation in a world (modern, late-capitalist, postmodern, *fin-de-siècle*, supermodern) where processes of globalization (creolization, compression, hybridity, synchronicity) have made traditional conceptions of individuals as members of fixed and separate societies and cultures redundant."[33] Yet the question of whether the child of a Turkish migrant in Heidelberg is a German is, whatever else it is, firstly a legal question. Though Southern identity is an outgrowth of the discourses of nationalism, the South is not a nation-state, has no fixed boundaries, issues no passports, collects no taxes. The South is a willingness of the heart. Or so the last generation of the twentieth century was disposed to think. In the collapse of the essentialist presumptions of the old intellectual order, there was a turn in the 1970s towards self-consciousness as the workable premise for constructing Southern history, towards understanding "culture [as] a form of narrative or discourse."[34] A Southerner possessed an identity; of late he is often understood to be someone nurtured by patterns of social memory.[35] This was, in its day, an elegant solution to the problem. It was the solution to be offered elsewhere, a little later, which has given us so many books on nationalism and inventing tradition, and has now worked its way back even to that most un-Hegelian of discourses, British history.[36] The European version of deconstructing the project of Romantic nationalism arose from the crisis of citizenship occasioned by the collapse of eastern Europe and the coalescence of the European Union, the successive challenges to nationality caused by fragmentation, integration, and migration. The Southern version arose from the crisis of citizenship which the American racial crisis occasioned, plus migration. When the world is a kaleidoscope of shifting forms, modern people tend to fall back on what they know or can imagine they have, a self. The civil rights movement itself, by initiating or reiterating the premise that the personal is political and transmitting it to feminism, doubtless helped to make this step plausible.

In retrospect, it was an impractical solution. Two kinds of Southern scholars had offered it. John Shelton Reed deployed the techniques of polling and the presumptions of social psychology to map the psychic configuration of the region, and thereby to offer a geography of feeling.[37] Various intellectual and literary historians explored how individual Southerners had fashioned their sense of Southern identity.[38] The former was a technique for a mass society, in which individuals matter little, while the latter could only cope with individuals. But the centerground of historical narrative has worked in a rougher, readier manner, especially in an era in which social history has been dominant. It requires workable generalizations for narratives of any scope; individuals who can be used to explain patterns, patterns which can be used to explain individuals. Idiosyncrasy is kept at arm's length. But the aggregate is suspect, too, since social history has of late abjured the homogeneous, mistrusted the idea of continuity, and favored the premise of conflict.[39] So, while in theory narratives about the South ought to confine themselves to those who have accepted the identity of Southern, this would exclude probably a majority of the people who have lived in the southeastern United States. Most importantly, it would exclude almost all African Americans before 1965, which is not a morally or politically acceptable hypothesis in our time. So a middle ground has had to be found, which is the Hegelian premise that self-perception is dialectically created by the self-perception of others, so even the un-Southern resident of the South forms part of Southern culture. The net effect, however, is disappointingly unrigorous. The South has become a space in time, on which anyone who has crowded is accounted part of the narrative, whether or not they knowingly chose to belong to that story. However much we praise discourse, we cannot afford to ground our history in it, because it is too quicksilver.

What of the subject matters of Southern history? The shape has changed markedly. Much arises from the familiar, wider shifts in historical methodologies: the rise of social history, the decline of political history, the emergence of feminism, the premise of multiculturalism, the significance of theory. Southern history, with small variations, followed and occasionally led the broader patterns of American historical literature in the last generation, if conservatively. In general, the South has had more social history, less theory, a more cautious feminism, and a more tentative multiculturalism.

As a genre, Southern history does not much predate the 1880s; history written before the Civil War concerned itself with the history of individual states, almost never the region. For much of the early days of the enterprise, the necessary preoccupation was with the period from Jamestown to 1877, when 1877 was only yesterday. Two moments merited intense scrutiny, the Revolutionary, Virginian moment centering on Washington, Madison, Jefferson, and Marshall, and then the origins and course of the Civil War. The colonial experience was thought to explain the antebellum one, with the latter (if you were a Southern liberal) being thought to be a defection from the civic virtues laid down in the seventeenth and eighteenth centuries or (if you were a conservative) a flowering. It is in the late nineteenth century that the anachronism of the colonial South is invented.

From the early 1950s to the early 1970s, from C. Vann Woodward's *Origins of the New South* to Eugene Genovese's *Roll, Jordan, Roll,* which was the high-water mark of Southern historical literature, perhaps the most significant development was that the colonial South began to drift away from the rest of the Southern narrative; this tendency has drastically accelerated.[40] In 1967, when essays in historiography were offered to Fletcher Green under the title of *Writing Southern History,* the two editors (neither of them colonialists) gave three chapters to the period before 1800.[41] When the effort was renewed in 1987 for Sanford Higginbotham as *Interpreting Southern History,* a single chapter was thought to be sufficient for everything before 1800.[42] The recent Norton anthology of Southern literature offers precisely three items from

Southern culture before Jefferson, 16 pages out of 1155.⁴³ This is unusually drastic, but symptomatic.

Why this falling away? No doubt, much arises from a foreshortening of historical memory, the falling away of classical and medieval history, the growing antiquity and remoteness of the early modern for many who think that they are expansive to think earlier than 1900. Our having passed the year 2000 is unlikely to help; soon, it will begin to seem that three centuries intercede between us and 1750. Moreover, what drove this yoking of colonial and antebellum was the sense that colonization mattered as the prelude to nation-making. Southern historians are less preoccupied now with the region's relationship to the nation, as the idea of the nation has lost its privileged status.⁴⁴ But some causes of this dissevering are institutional. Colonial history has become peculiarly the domain of the Institute for Early American History in Williamsburg, which has firm opinions about the chronological boundaries of its *imperium*. While, in one sense, the Institute has strengthened understanding of what could loosely be called Southern history by fostering so many studies of the Chesapeake and colonies southward, in another it did not, ironically by being so successful. Southern colonial history has become almost the narrative of American colonial history and succeeded, to a large extent, in displacing the premise of the Puritan origins of the American self. But in succeeding in becoming American, or even more in being transatlantic, Afro-Caribbean, and imperial, that history has ceased to be significantly Southern, except as an aside. So the best articles on colonial Georgia now go to the *William and Mary Quarterly*, not the *Journal of Southern History*, and the annual convention of the Southern Historical Association usually has thin submissions on topics before 1800. Jack Greene's work, for example, though it has rich implications for the antebellum South, is little used for these purposes by later historians and he himself seems indifferent to the possibility.⁴⁵ Only studies of slavery seem to be a partial exception, though a large one, to this unhealthy disjunction.⁴⁶

This has left the history of the Old South more firmly defined as antebellum, as something which matters because it looks towards and explains the Civil War; this is a specialized function to explain a large, diffuse, and complicated society or set of societies. Here we encounter an oddity. The dominant figure for the last generation and more has been Eugene Genovese. In theory, Genovese's work ought to have encouraged a sense of continuity with the colonial South, since he commenced with the premise that the Old South was premodern. In practice, he has been relatively indifferent to the colonial experience and, in effect, encouraged a tendency to isolate the Old South and make it self-contained and exceptionalist, though a sort of moral intensification of the problem of Western culture. For, like Woodward, Genovese has believed in the discontinuity of Southern history. But, whereas Genovese thought that everything changed in 1865, mostly for the worse, but was not very interested in what the postbellum South turned into, Woodward believed that everything changed in 1865, eventually for the better, but was not very interested in what had been before. The twin effect of these dominant influences was to slice Southern history down the middle. While there have been persistent efforts to establish a continuity between 1830 and 1900, these struggled against the tide. I think this is about to change. Woodward is now dead and it seems probable that his synthesis, which was eerily extended beyond a normal lifespan by his own longevity and iron will, will be abruptly reconsidered.

One reason is that the civil rights movement begins to displace the Civil War as the moral centerpiece of Southern history. Not that the writing of Civil War history is going to go away. But I suspect its constituency will be, more and more, the public which retains a puzzling fascination with the conflict, and so it will be as much an annex of public history as a scholarly venture in dialogue with the rest of Southern or American historiography. The urgent business of Southern history will be, rather, to reconfigure the period from the 1870s to the present day. This will mean that antebellum historians will face a choice: to be the last act in an early modern drama not much interested in them, or to make a case for the late antebellum South as the first act of the modern South, or at least as the crossing of the ways, to use Allen Tate's phrase. Even Genovese, now transformed into a Roman Catholic intellectual, has begun to respond to this pressure, by trying to annex the modern South to a conservative tradition commenced in the Old South, but I see little evidence that many beyond the small community of conservative historians are persuaded by this move.[47] Rather, precisely the interpretation which Genovese abominates is likely to happen. The Old South will be seen as fluid, multiple, contingent. The evidence already exists to make a decent case for this, in work like that of James Oakes, and it is a trend in works by younger scholars.[48] Nonetheless, inventing a semi–Old South as the prelude to the New South will be an optional extra for many. I doubt that the real excitement will be there, but later.[49]

We do not yet know what this new history of the New South will look like. For the moment, Woodward's understanding of the period from 1877 to 1913 remains unexpectedly canonical. Edward Ayers's *The Promise of the New South* hinted at possibilities, suggested vitalities, but did not supplant Woodward.[50] Indeed Ayers has explained that synthesis is no longer a historian's responsibility in a postmodern world.[51] Feminist scholars have offered intriguing work, but they too mistrust synthesis, at least beyond matters of gender.[52] Work on the period from 1913 to the late 1940s is episodic, while the historians of the civil rights movement are still struggling free of the perspectives generated by the movement itself. The celebratory barely begins to make way for the critical. Insofar as there is a clear direction, it seems to lie in making the civil rights movement less of a dramatic transformation, making the segregated South look more contested and less bleak, making the world partly fashioned by Martin Luther King, Jr., less of an improvement. The question of continuity, which once centered on 1865, increasingly centers on 1965. But there is much confusion and more guilt here, as yet unresolved, perhaps irresolvable. It is precisely this moral complexity, the tension between hope and realism, which will give the subject vitality. Yet this sense of social contestation wavers around a mean. As Laura Edwards has put it, "Recent scholarship uses the analytical lenses of gender, sexuality, and race to highlight fissures in southern society and the ability of ordinary southerners to disrupt the social order."[53] That is, the Gemeinschaft to Gesellschaft theme, once so popular, has been much battered. But there is a lingering sense that there has been a stable order somewhere to be disrupted, even as it becomes hard to locate.

As long as that sense lingers, the project of Southern history is likely to continue. When the South was invented in the early nineteenth century, it was conjectured as one instance of the patterns which human beings inherited in God's natural order and sustained by their imaginative free will: these shapes included societies, races, classes, and sexes. Like those other orders, the South's rationale was that it stood between man and chaos, whether that was threatened by Nat Turner, the Seminoles, Charles Sumner, Sarah Grimké, malaria, or David Hume. The project of the South has, therefore, flourished on the idea of peril, on the sense that the South stands always on the brink of dissipation. Each generation has redefined the order by identifying different perils. Postmodernism is as good a bogey man as any, if too amiable in tone to justify dread. But racial crisis is persistent, the genders are at odds, ethnicity is making a comeback, and religion is divisive, so on the whole, things are looking bad enough for the discourse to keep going. It will persist as long as a respectable number of the people in the southeastern

United States find the South to be a useful category of analysis. I suspect the proportion begins to decline, but for the moment it seems enough.

NOTES

1. Tennessee Williams, "The Past, the Present, and the Perhaps," in *The Rose Tattoo: Camino Real: Orpheus Descending* (Harmondsworth: Penguin Books, 1976), 241.

2. A partial exception is Paul K. Conkin, "Hot, Humid, and Sad," *Journal of Southern History* 64 (February 1998): 3–22.

3. See, for example, Eric Foner, ed., *The New American History* (Philadelphia, PA: Temple University Press, 1990), which has seven chapters divided by chronology, and six more on social history, women's history, African American history, labor history, ethnicity and immigration, and diplomatic history.

4. Bennett H. Wall, "Annual Report of the Secretary-Treasurer," *Journal of Southern History* 37 (May 1971): 248, 249; William F. Holmes, "Annual Report of the Secretary-Treasurer," *Journal of Southern History* 65 (May 1999): 367, 371. However, not everyone who attends the annual convention is a member of the SHA and the convention serves a few hundred European and Latin American historians, who are allocated a portion of the program. A formal purpose of the association is, not only to foster Southern history, but also the practice of history in the South.

5. The calendar of regular Southern conferences has grown very crowded; for example, the Porter Fortune Symposium at the University of Mississippi, the Southern Intellectual History Circle, the Saint George Tucker Society, the Southern Association of Women Historians, and the Society for the Study of Southern Literature.

6. I infer this from the statistics in Carl Abbott, "Tracing the Trends in U.S. Regional History," *Perspectives* 28 (February 1990): 4–8. In 1988, 63 percent of those who taught courses in Southern history were aged between forty and fifty-five.

7. See http://www.theaha.org/pubs/dissertations/.

8. On this, see Michael O'Brien, ed., "The South in the World," *Southern Cultures* 4 (Winter 1998): 1–83.

9. Drew Gilpin Faust, *Mothers of Invention: Women of the Slaveholding South in the American Civil War* (Chapel Hill: University of North Carolina Press, 1996). She is, however, the only woman historian among the fourteen contributors to James M. McPherson and William J. Cooper, Jr., eds., *Writing the Civil War: The Quest to Understand* (Columbia: University of South Carolina Press, 1998).

10. Faust, *Design for Mastery*.

11. Bertram Wyatt-Brown, *The House of Percy: Honor, Melancholy, and Imagination in a Southern Family* (New York: Oxford University Press, 1994); Melton A. McLaurin, *Celia: A Slave* (Athens: University of Georgia Press, 1991); William A. Link, "The Jordan Hatcher Case: Politics and 'a Spirit of Insubordination' in Antebellum Virginia," *Journal of Southern History* 64 (November 1998): 615–48; John Howard, *Men Like That: A Southern Queer History* (Chicago, IL: University of Chicago Press, 1999); Anne Goodwyn Jones, "The Work of Gender in the Southern Renaissance," in *Southern Writers and Their Worlds*, ed. Christopher Morris and Steven G. Reinhardt (College Station: Texas A&M University Press, 1996), 41–56; Ted Ownby, *Subduing Satan: Religion, Recreation, and Manhood in the Rural South, 1865–1920* (Chapel Hill: University of North Carolina Press, 1990).

12. Jan Ellen Lewis and Peter S. Onuf, eds., *Sally Hemings & Thomas Jefferson: History, Memory, and Civic Culture* (Charlottesville: University Press of Virginia, 1999).

13. Stephen Kantrowitz, *Ben Tillman and the Reconstruction of White Supremacy* (Chapel Hill: University of North Carolina Press, 2000).

14. See, especially, Catherine Clinton, ed., *Half Sisters of History: Southern Women and the American Past* (Durham, NC: Duke University Press, 1994), but also Jacquelyn Dowd Hall, "Open Secrets: Memory, Imagination, and the Refashioning of Southern Identity," *American Quarterly* 50 (March 1998): 109–24.

15. Hall, "Open Secrets," 122.

16. Younger women seem more disposed to grapple with this phenomenon. For example, Elna C. Green, "From Antisuffragism to Anti-Communism: The Conservative Career of Ida M. Darden," *Journal of Southern History* 65 (May 1999): 287–316, which speaks of "a growing body of literature on conservative women and female antifeminism" (287).

17. Ulrich Bonnell Phillips, *American Negro Slavery: A Survey of the Supply, Employment and Control of Negro Labor as Determined by the Plantation Regime*, foreword by Eugene D. Genovese (1918; Baton Rouge: Louisiana State University Press, 1966); Robert William Fogel and Stanley L. Engerman, *Time on the Cross: The Economics of American Negro Slavery* (Boston, MA: Little Brown, 1974); C. Vann Woodward, *Origins of the New South, 1877–1913* (Baton Rouge: Louisiana State University Press, 1951).

18. Stanley L. Engerman, ed., *The Terms of Labor: Slavery, Serfdom, and Free Labor* (Stanford, CA: Stanford University Press, 1999); Gavin Wright, *Old South, New South: Revolutions in the Southern Economy Since the Civil War* (New York: Basic Books, 1986); Peter A. Coclanis, *The Shadow of a Dream: Economic Life and Death in the South Carolina Low Country, 1670–1920* (New York: Oxford University Press, 1989).

19. For Reed on Vance, see John Shelton Reed and Daniel Joseph Singal, eds., *Regionalism and the South: Selected Papers of Rupert Vance* (Chapel Hill: University of North Carolina Press, 1982).

20. Stanley M. Elkins, *Slavery: A Problem in American Institutional & Intellectual Life*, introd. by Nathan Glazer (1959; New York: Grosset & Dunlap, 1963); Richard H. King, *A Southern Renaissance: The Cultural Awakening of the American South, 1930–1955* (New York: Oxford University Press, 1980).

21. Fred Hobson, *The Southern Writer in the Postmodern World* (Athens: University of Georgia Press, 1991).

22. An excellent example is Michael Kreyling, *Inventing Southern Literature* (Jackson: University Press of Mississippi, 1998).

23. On this, see Fred Hobson, "Of Canons and Cultural Wars: Southern Literature and Literary Scholarship After Midcentury," in *The Future of Southern Letters*, ed. Jefferson Humphries and John Lowe (New York: Oxford University Press, 1996), 72–86. It is now common for volumes of essays to contain historians and literary critics coequally: see, for example, Christopher Morris and Steven G. Reinhardt, eds., *Southern Writers and Their Worlds* (College Station: Texas A&M University Press, 1996), and Anne Goodwyn Jones and Susan V. Donaldson, eds., *Haunted Bodies: Gender and Southern Texts* (Charlottesville: University Press of Virginia, 1998).

24. Charles Reagan Wilson and William Ferris, eds., *Encyclopedia of Southern Culture* (Chapel Hill: University of North Carolina Press, 1989).

25. For historians who are interested in popular culture, see Charles Reagan Wilson, *Judgment and Grace in Dixie: Southern Faiths from Faulkner to Elvis* (Athens: University of Georgia Press, 1995), and James C. Cobb, *Redefining Southern Culture: Mind and Identity in the Modern South* (Athens: University of Georgia Press, 1999).

26. Anthony Appiah, Henry Louis Gates, Jr., and Michael Colin Vazquez, eds., *The Dictionary of Global Culture* (New York: Alfred A. Knopf, 1997).

27. Surprisingly, this is true even of his West Virginian memoir: Henry Louis Gates, Jr., *Colored People: A Memoir* (New York: Alfred A Knopf, 1994). But there is an anecdote about a basketball game in North Carolina, in which Gates reproves a white racist fan and Gates's father mockingly

stops him by saying, "Nigger, is you *crazy*? We am in de Souf'": Henry Louis Gates, Jr., *Loose Canons: Notes on the Culture Wars* (New York: Oxford University Press, 1992), 148.

28. Gates, *Loose Canons*, xv.

29. See especially, Kwame Anthony Appiah, *In My Father's House: Africa in the Philosophy of Culture* (New York: Oxford University Press, 1992), and Kwame Anthony Appiah and Amy Gutmann, *Color Conscious: The Political Morality of Race* (Princeton, NJ: Princeton University Press, 1996).

30. This parallels the argument for a lightly-held ethnicity in David A. Hollinger, *Postethnic America: Beyond Multiculturalism* (New York: Basic Books, 1995).

31. Valuable is David L. Carlton and Peter A. Coclanis, "Another 'Great Migration': From Region to Race in Southern Liberalism," *Southern Cultures* 3 (Winter 1997): 37–62, which argues that region is a weaker analytical premise now than in the 1930s, but race a more powerful one.

32. C. Vann Woodward, *The Burden of Southern History* (1960; Baton Rouge: Louisiana State University Press, 1968).

33. Nigel Rapport and Andrew Dawson, eds., *Migrants of Identity: Perceptions of Home in a World of Movement* (Oxford: Berg, 1998), 3. Useful is Saskia Sassen, *Globalization and Its Discontents: Essays on the New Mobility of People and Money* (New York: New Press, 1998).

34. Jefferson Humphries, "The Discourse of Southernness: Or How We Can Know There Will Still be Such a Thing as the South and Southern Literary Culture in the Twenty-First Century," in *The Future of Southern Letters*, ed. Jefferson Humphries and John Lowe (New York: Oxford University Press, 1996), 120.

35. On this, see Edward L. Ayers, "Memory and the South," *Southern Cultures* 2 (February 1995): 5–8, and Scot A. French, "What is Social Memory?" *Southern Cultures* 2 (February 1995): 9–18. For a feminist version, see Hall, "Open Secrets."

36. Most important have been Eric Hobsbawm and Terence Ranger, eds., *The Invention of Tradition* (Cambridge: Cambridge University Press, 1983) and Benedict Anderson, *Imagined Communities: Reflections on the Origin and Spread of Nationalism*, revised and enlarged ed. (1983; London: Verso, 1991). On British history, see Colin Kidd, *British Identities Before Nationalism: Ethnicity and Nationhood in the Atlantic World, 1600–1800* (Cambridge: Cambridge University Press, 1999).

37. First in John Shelton Reed, *The Enduring South: Subcultural Persistence in Mass Society*, foreword by Edwin M. Yoder, Jr., (1972; Chapel Hill: University of North Carolina Press, 1974), and then, somewhat more systematically, in idem., *Southerners: The Social Psychology of Sectionalism* (Chapel Hill: University of North Carolina Press, 1983).

38. For example, Michael O'Brien, *The Idea of the American South, 1920–1941* (Baltimore, MD: Johns Hopkins University Press, 1979); King, *A Southern Renaissance*; Singal, *The War Within*; Richard Gray, *Writing the South: Ideas of an American Region* (Cambridge: Cambridge University Press, 1986).

39. The hostile reaction to the work of David Hackett Fischer is evidence for this: see David Hackett Fischer, *Albion's Seed: Four British Folkways in America* (New York: Oxford University Press, 1989).

40. In this, I differ from the view expressed in John B. Boles, "The New Southern History," *Mississippi Quarterly* 45 (Fall 1992): 369–83.

41. Arthur S. Link and Rembert W. Patrick, eds., *Writing Southern History: Essays in Historiography in Honor of Fletcher M. Green* (Baton Rouge: Louisiana State University Press, 1965).

42. John B. Boles and Evelyn Thomas Nolen, eds., *Interpreting Southern History: Historiographical Essays in Honor of Sanford W. Higginbotham* (Baton Rouge: Louisiana State University Press, 1987).

43. William L. Andrews et al., eds., *The Literature of the American South: A Norton Anthology* (New York: W. W. Norton, 1998).

44. Among the last of the books with this concern, in a series (the New American Nation) peculiarly defined by the issue of nationalism, is Dewey W. Grantham, *The South in Modern America: A Region at Odds* (New York: Harper Collins, 1994).

45. See, especially, Jack P. Greene, *Pursuits of Happiness: The Social Development of Early Modern British Colonies and the Formation of American Culture* (Chapel Hill: University of North Carolina Press, 1988). A rare exception is Joyce E. Chaplin, *An Anxious Pursuit: Agricultural Innovation and Modernity in the Lower South, 1730–1815* (Chapel Hill: University of North Carolina Press, 1993).

46. Notably Ira Berlin, *Many Thousands Gone: The First Two Centuries of Slavery in North America* (Cambridge, MA: Harvard University Press, Belknap, 1998), and, on a more specialized topic, Sylvia R. Frey and Betty Wood, *Come Shouting to Zion: African-American Protestantism in the American South and British Caribbean to 1830* (Chapel Hill: University of North Carolina Press, 1998).

47. Eugene D. Genovese, *The Southern Tradition: The Achievement and Limitations of an American Conservatism* (Cambridge, MA: Harvard University Press, 1994). See also Elizabeth Fox-Genovese, "The Anxiety of History: The Southern Confrontation with Modernity," *Southern Cultures* (Inaugural issue 1993): 65–82.

48. James Oakes, *Slavery and Freedom: An Interpretation of the Old South* (New York: Alfred A. Knopf, 1990). See Jonathan Daniel Wells, *The Origins of the Southern Middle Class: Literature, Politics, and Economy, 1820–1880*, dissertation, University of Michigan (1998), and Beth Barton Schweiger, *The Gospel Working up: Progress and the Pulpit in Nineteenth Century America* (New York: Oxford University Press, 2000).

49. The AHA database suggests that dissertations are being written in a rough proportion of one colonial study for every two on the antebellum period, and every five on the years after 1877.

50. Edward L. Ayers, *The Promise of the New South: Life After Reconstruction* (New York: Oxford University Press, 1992).

51. Edward L. Ayers, "Narrating the New South," *Journal of Southern History* 61 (August 1995): 555–66.

52. Glenda Elizabeth Gilmore, *Gender and Jim Crow: Women and the Politics of White Supremacy in North Carolina, 1896–1920* (Chapel Hill: University of North Carolina Press, 1996), and Jane Dailey, "Deference and Violence in the Postbellum Urban South: Manners and Massacres in Danville, Virginia," *Journal of Southern History* 63 (August 1997): 552–90. For a later period, see Grace Elizabeth Hale, *Making Whiteness: The Culture of Segregation in the South, 1890–1940* (New York: Pantheon Books, 1998).

53. Laura F. Edwards, "Law, Domestic Violence, and the Limits of Patriarchal Authority in the Antebellum South," *Journal of Southern History* 65 (November 1999): 735.

SOUTHERN LITERATURE

A review of William L. Andrews et al., eds., *The Literature of the American South: A Norton Anthology* (New York, W. W. Norton, 1998), in the *Times Literary Supplement* (May 29, 1998): 32–33.

Anthologies, once regarded as mere book-making, have of late become anxiously monitored signifiers of the country's cultural politics. On the whole, the American South has been awkwardly placed in these controversies, since so much of its literature and history is perceived to have been tainted. Despising the South has been a chief way by which America has proved to itself that error belongs to someone else, not quite American. Indeed recent anthologies of American literature tend to expel Southern writers from their pages, upon the reasoning that such retrograde texts infect the moral health of young minds. So it is something of a surprise that Norton ("publisher of the most widely read literature anthologies in the English-speaking world") should think it viable to commission a Southern anthology, at all, when its stock-in-trade includes volumes of American postmodernist poetry, African American, and Native American literature, all topics which have increased in popularity on American campuses, at a time when classes in Southern literature have declined and seem set to decline further.[1]

William Andrews is alert to these issues. He and his fellow editors (Fred Hobson, Trudier Harris, Minrose Gwin) seem to have opted for repackaging the South to make it palatable to the postmodernist mind. They back away from prescriptions about the nature of "Southern." "What makes a southerner these days, and by implication what would qualify as southern literature in this postmodern era," Andrews suggests, "is less a matter of birth or origin or even lived experience, than of deliberate affiliation, attitude, style, and that elusive quality known today as 'voice.'" But how to decide a canon, when one has so few presumptions? "More than any other single factor, the most influential basis for our choice of writers and texts . . . has been our own accumulated experience of reading, studying, and teaching the literature of the American South . . . . [and] a reflection of what its editors know and like about their subject."[2] But do father and mother know best?

The evidence is mixed. The anthology has been divided into three main sections: "beginnings" to 1880, for which Andrews has been responsible, 1880 to 1940 handled by Hobson, then "the contemporary South" edited by Harris and Gwin. These are very unevenly divided: the first gets 243 pages for a span of about 250 years, the second 328 for sixty years, the third 572 for almost another sixty. Andrews acknowledges that the earlier period is only "sampled," whereas "one of the strengths of our anthology is the breadth of its comprehension of modernist and contemporary southern writing." Indeed the sampling is ruthless. The whole colonial period gets precisely three selections: John Smith, Ebenezer Cook, and William Byrd II. The period from the Revolution to the Civil War does a little better, but not much, with eleven authors: Thomas Jefferson, Benjamin Banneker, John Pendleton Kennedy, George Moses Horton, William Gilmore Simms, James Henry Hammond, Edgar Allan Poe, Johnson Jones Hooper, Harriet Jacobs, Frederick Douglass, and Henry Timrod. Two more (William Wells Brown and Mary Chesnut) hover between secession and 1880, though both were much formed before the war. All this is puzzling. The two areas of scholarship which, in recent years, have shown more signs of life, offered more original suggestions, and rediscovered more texts than any other in the intellectual and literary history of the South, have been the colonial and antebellum periods. The work of David Shields, for example, notably in *Civil Tongues and Polite Letters*, has changed our understandings. As for the antebellum years, there has been a marked tendency to expand the scope of Southern writing beyond belles lettres to social thought, theology, historical literature, and theories of the state. In one sense, Andrews is fully in the modern idiom, indeed has himself been a significant sponsor of it, by valuably including African American figures like Douglass, Jacobs, Banneker, and Horton. As these have been included in anthologies of American literature for several years—Douglass's *Narrative* now has the status in American high school and college classes once occupied by *The Scarlet Letter*—this may be an orthodox move, yet still a just one. However, this is one step forward, to one taken back. We are still peddled the hoary nonsense that the Old South was marked by "growing sectionalism, defensiveness, and insularity" articulated by the conservative, musty, and genteel. Being not-modern remains a term of reproach.[3]

Unfortunately, this trade-off is not accidental. Rightly constituting the Old South as biracial tends, at least here, to turn its literature into a dialogue about slavery and race, in which white writers (Jefferson, Hammond) give their version and black ones (Banneker, Horton, Jacobs, Douglass, and Brown) reply. The odd consequence is that the uninitiated can acquire the notion that, somehow, proslavery writers were in the minority. This is of a piece with the manner by which Vernon Burton, the historian, likes to startle audiences in his home state, by telling them that South Carolina won the Civil War, upon the impeccable reasoning that about two-thirds of the state's inhabitants were slaves; he was once nearly assaulted by someone outraged on behalf of vanquished ancestors. Such an effective irony and generous instinct can, however, be misleading. Here, the absorption in the great morality play of slavery leads the mind away from other pertinent concerns, even those which have preoccupied many recent anthologists. (Including Madison or Calhoun is probably a lost cause, although the *Heath Anthology of American Literature*, otherwise relentlessly trendy, manages to find space for the Tenth Federalist.) In *The Literature of the American South*, race does seem to trump gender, at least before the Civil War. No female writer speaks before Harriet Jacobs's slave narrative of 1861 and Chesnut's journal begun in the same year; both seem more present for reasons of race than gender. Where are Louisa McCord, Caroline Gilman, Augusta Evans, Susan Petigru King, Frances Ellen Watkins Harper, or, from an earlier time, Eliza Lucas Pinckney? Surely this exclusion cannot survive, when the second edition is considered.

No doubt, part of the difficulty arises from considerations of genre, where this anthology is fairly old-fashioned, not least in its having an additional section on "vernacular traditions," by which is meant music and storytelling, things like "Amazing Grace," blues lyrics, trickster stories, Native American origin stories, and Martin Luther King's "I Have A Dream" speech. (There is an accompanying CD.) The notion that a sophisticated literature rests on a folk tradition is as old, at least, as Percy's *Reliques* and, among Southerners, was much urged by Simms in the 1840s. It is likewise traditional that such things are served up, like *lagniappe*, on a dish safely distant from the un-vernacular main course. For the rest, fiction and poetry are thought to encompass most of Southern literature, with two plays and no little autobiography, it being so crucial to the African American literary tradition. Otherwise there are no diaries, letters, or all the rhetorical forms which literary scholars now take to be their domain. Of historians, who have of late been ambivalently readmitted to the ranks of the literary (even sometimes when not trying to write like Macaulay), only W. J. Cash makes it and even David Ramsay and C. Vann Woodward are excluded. Likewise, self-denyingly, literary critics are omitted: Allen Tate is included for "Ode to the Confederate Dead," but not "A Southern Mode of the Imagination." But anthologies tend to be a conservative form, however much they claim innovation, perhaps most so in retaining a suspicion of popular, as opposed to vernacular literature. Margaret Mitchell, easily the most influential Southern writer who has ever lived, remains stubbornly absent.

Andrews is right that the contemporary section is the anthology's best. It breathes a fresh spirit. Suddenly there is candor about sexuality, and the insistence on biracialism seems to be quickening, rather than constraining. Black writers have, as Harris and Gwin argue, been "reclaiming Southern soil," and certainly the period since the 1960s has been the only one in which "black Southerner" has not been an oxymoron, offensive to African Americans themselves, for whom the South had been an immurement and a danger, infrequently a self. But, as they also suggest, "that process of reclamation often means that racism, while ever-present, is not the dominant guiding force."[4] So the tone is more relaxed and various, even hopeful. No doubt, some chosen texts will prove mistaken, considering that there is an author here born only in 1963; some look a bit shaky, even now. Still, ageing New Critics used once to lament that all, after the "Southern Renaissance" and themselves, would be decline. The later pages of this anthology offer evidence to the contrary; there is vitality, even if the relevance of "Southern" grows attenuated. Perhaps the latter does not matter, except to the taxonomists of culture. But can the South survive without taxonomists?

NOTES

1. Andrews et al., *Literature of the American South*, xix.
2. Ibid., xvi–xvii.
3. Andrews et al., *Literature of the American South*, xviii, 6; see David S. Shields, *Civil Tongues and Polite Letters in British America* (Chapel Hill: University of North Carolina Press, 1997).
4. Andrews et al., *Literature of the American South*, 588–89.

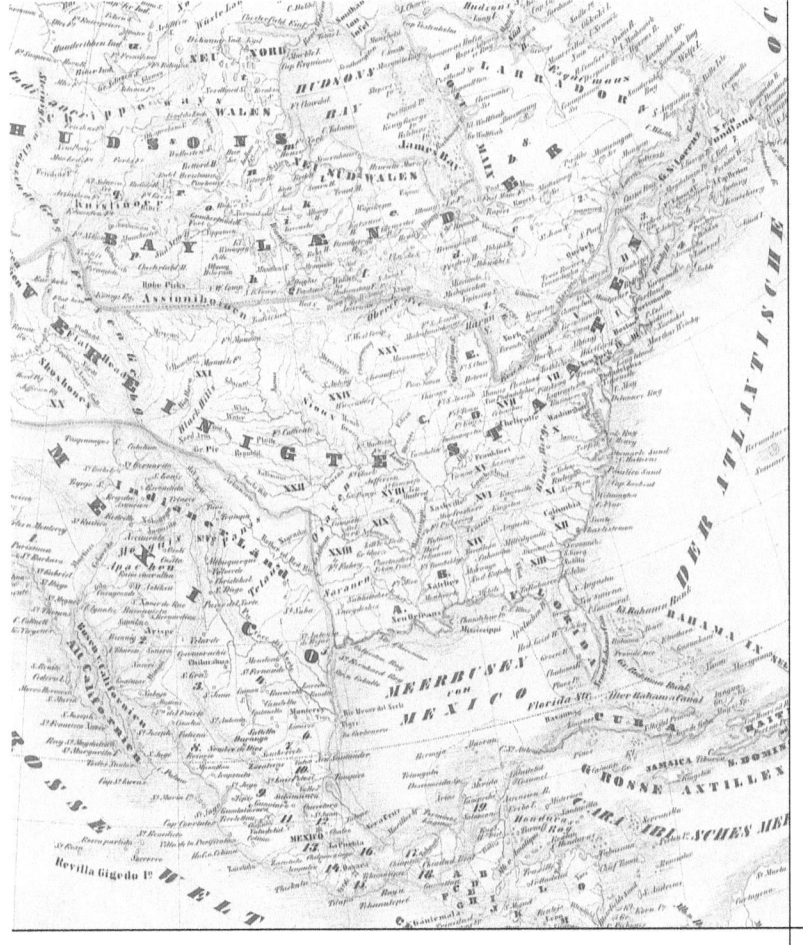

WRITERS

A review of Peter S. Onuf, ed., *Jeffersonian Legacies* (Charlottesville: University Press of Virginia, 1993) and Jay Fliegelman, *Declaring Independence: Jefferson, Natural Language, & the Culture of Performance* (Stanford, CA: Stanford University Press, 1993), in the *Times Literary Supplement* (January 21, 1994): 24.

In 1856, Henry S. Randall of New York was eager to vindicate Thomas Jefferson against the slanders of Charles Francis Adams, that "little twopenny *Boston* cliquist," who in defending the veracity of his grandfather John Adams had felt it necessary to indict Jefferson's honesty. Foraging for help, the biographer corresponded with those who had frequented Monticello. In Philadelphia was Robley Dunglison, a doctor whom Jefferson had brought from England in 1825 to be the first Professor of Medicine at the University of Virginia. What sort of man was Jefferson? Randall asked. Tolerant, decent, philanthropic, "sincerely attached to the excellent family that were clustered around him," Dunglison replied; "not a man who could be regarded as an eminent conversationalist," however, but "rather reserved." Tolerance had not meant flexibility, for he "had generally formed his own opinions on questions, and did not abandon them easily." He "could not be considered verily as an *adroit* man." He liked theories and could be dogged about those "even of a minor character," especially if they involved mathematics. "In architectural details, this was strikingly evinced. Palladius must be followed line and rule; and if a deviation would have added comfort & convenience, it must not be adopted; because [it] was sanctioned by high architectural authority. It was said—and said truly—that the outsides of the *pavilions*—as the habitations of the professors were called—received primary attention from him, whilst the insides must shift for themselves. This want of expansion applied, I think more or less, to his views on some other subjects."[1]

Clearly there was something inaccessible about Jefferson even in 1856, some disjunction between the public face and the private sensibility. Modern American historians remain troubled by this. In 1992, many of them gathered in Charlottesville to debate the great man on the 250th anniversary of his birth. The papers delivered then have been gathered into *Jeffersonian Legacies*, a primer for how the times view Mr. Jefferson.

Though several essays deal with the public man operating in Philadelphia or Paris, the most original and striking pieces in *Jeffersonian Legacies* concern the patriarch of Monticello. This directs attention to the slaveholder, who has always offered difficulties. Much old ground is gone over, notably by Paul Finkelman, who thrashes through Jefferson's published writings to show yet again the scale of his ambiguity on race and slavery. But recent efforts by the Thomas Jefferson Memorial Foundation to discover and elucidate the lives of the slaves who inhabited Jefferson's mountain have made possible a badly needed fresh approach. Lucia Stanton's essay demonstrates how little Jefferson grasped the personalities and experience of his servants, except as they fitted his plans. And this seems to exemplify a general truth about Jefferson, which Jan Lewis's study of his family life reinforces. Jefferson was a man who loved coldly, who used people for his comfort. He had no gift for realizing personality and noticing idiosyncrasy; he reached for the abstraction. Hence he was sometimes impractical. James Madison was not alone in shuddering at Jefferson's recommendation that each generation should have its own revolution, not least because the last one had been exhaustion enough. So many attempts to recover Jefferson's internal life—Rhys Isaac makes a brave effort to do so for Jefferson the young man—have foundered on Jefferson's sharp reticence and resistance to intimacy. These qualities were evident even in his writing, where he did have gifts. As Douglas L. Wilson's "Jefferson and the Republic of Letters" reminds us, Jefferson published little in his own name and then only under duress. "My great wish," he wrote in 1789, "is to go on in a strict but silent performance of my duty; to avoid attracting notice & to keep my name out of newspapers, because I find the pain of a little censure, even when it is unfounded, is more acute than the pleasure of much praise."[2] Strange doctrine for a Founding Father, a diplomat, a president, a maker of political parties and institutions, this desire to go unnoticed.

Jay Fliegelman has an improbable solution for the problem of Jefferson's elusive selfhood: the Virginian was the prisoner of eighteenth-century theories of rhetoric and of a particular vision of human representation. By 1776, there was "an intensified quest to discover (or theorize into existence) a natural spoken language that would be a corollary to natural law.... [A]n orator's primary obligation was no longer to communicate thoughts and feelings. Rather it was to display persuasively and spontaneously the experiencing of those thoughts and feelings."[3]

Sincerity mattered less than "the spectacle of sincerity." Such theories made many conscious of the slipperiness of self, Jefferson among them. All this is cleverly explained in a short but rambling book, which carries us away from the fact that the Declaration of Independence was intended to be read aloud and was hence an effort of oratory, to Jefferson's notions of rhythm, to the growing popularity of Windsor chairs, to the decline of the syllogism, to the fact that the American sculptor Patience Wright molded busts of the eminent with soft wax held between her thighs. *Declaring Independence* is a book as cluttered as Monticello was during Jefferson's heyday. One might go through it, intrigued by the mounds of stuff hauled back from Paris, London, and the West beyond the Blue Ridge Mountains, without noticing that Jefferson himself is seated quietly in his library, is reading a book and seems very reluctant to get up and declaim. After all, Jefferson always hated speaking in public, he whispered his first inaugural address, and refused to give his State of the Union messages in person. Fliegelman all but concedes this point: "I treat Jefferson less as the autonomous subject of this study than as a witness to, and conflicted participant in, a new affective understanding of the operations of language, one that reconceives all expression as a form of self-expression, as an opportunity as well as an imperative to externalize the self, to become self-evident." For "conflicted participant," read "Jefferson does not really fit my thesis." Moreover, it is a thesis which overestimates the originality of eighteenth-century theory by scanting classical and Renaissance emphases upon the "emotional credibility" of rhetoricians.[4]

But, at least, Fliegelman has tried to locate Jefferson in his age, however angularly. *Jeffersonian Legacies* is a more valuable book than *Declaring Independence*, but the former attends to residues, to our own time as much as 1800. Jefferson was bound, sooner or later, to be judged by a ruling assumption of the now not-so-younger generation of American historians: the personal is political, the political is personal. The poor man miserably fails the test of this pitiless idea. Viewing this abjectness, our moderns seem to recommend that he be hastily consigned to a therapist and be obliged to think through his life, until he is prepared to hug his children, demand that people call him "Tom," and pay as much attention to the insides of buildings as their outsides. Would it be possible for a Jefferson thus renovated to design a Palladian softball field, on which the little-leaguers of Monticello would democratically play? Could he learn to scream at the umpire, when his daughter Martha is thrown out at third base?

NOTES

1. Henry Stephens Randall to Hugh Blair Grigsby, 4 December 1856, in Frank J. Klingberg and Frank W. Klingberg, eds., *The Correspondence Between Henry Stephens Randall and Hugh Blair*

Grigsby, 1856–1861 (Berkeley: University of California Press, 1952), 69; Robley Dunglison to Henry S. Randall, 1 June 1856, Dunglison-Randall Letters, Alderman Library, University of Virginia, Charlottesville.

2. Thomas Jefferson to Francis Hopkinson, 13 March 1789, in Merrill D. Peterson, ed., *Thomas Jefferson: Writings* (New York: Library of America, 1984), 942.

3. Jay Fliegelman, *Declaring Independence: Jefferson, Natural Language, & the Culture of Performance* (Stanford, CA: Stanford University Press, 1993), 1–2.

4. Ibid., 2.

A review of John C. Guilds and Caroline Collins, eds., *William Gilmore Simms and the American Frontier* (Athens: University of Georgia Press, 1997) and Charles S. Watson, *From Nationalism to Secessionism: The Changing Fiction of William Gilmore Simms* (Westport, CT: Greenwood Press, 1993); published as Michael O'Brien, "William Gilmore Simms," *Southern Cultures* 5 (Summer 1999): 107–12. Reprinted by permission.

William Gilmore Simms has long been a critical problem and opportunity. In the fitfully vanishing days when literary canons were confidently negotiated, he was nominated as the Old South's candidate for its greatest man of letters. The hope was that the American schoolchild, in declaiming the names of the mighty, would chant "Irving, Cooper, Hawthorne, Melville, Simms, Twain" and not stumble over the word "Simms" in puzzlement, that *The Yemassee* and "How Sharp Snaffles Got His Capital and Wife" would be as routine as *The Scarlet Letter*, that Simms would be as familiar in our mouths as household words. This would be a final vindication, when all the wounds of Gettysburg would be healed, when we might get back to the collegial moment when Simms, Melville, and the men of Young America in the 1840s broke bread amiably together in the cause of an American national literature. This aspiration required some trimming, roughly upon the lines of New South ideology. New York was supposed to canonize Simms, if Southern critics carefully repackaged him by deprecating his sectionalism and his proslavery writings, by making him a proto-Faulkner who happened to fall into bad company and worse times. On the whole, Southerners have kept their half of the bargain and, for a generation and more, have tried to make his texts available, written his life, edited his letters, studied his criticism, and made their case. But New York never responded, as it had when a similar offer had been made at roughly the same time for the canonization of Faulkner.[1] Rather, Simms has appeared and disappeared in anthologies of American literature, been mentioned here and there, usually dismissively, has been rarely reprinted by metropolitan publishers, and has been thought never quite to have made the grade. Further, canons have moved on from the 1940s and 1950s, which is when the Simms brigade first made their big push. Irving and Cooper have been retired from the front, Hawthorne is in danger of court-martial for that remark about scribbling women, and canons themselves are supposed to have fallen silent, now that authors are dead.

So the Simms scholars seem often to be amassing ammunition for a war no one is fighting any more, to be poring over maps of countries which no longer exist. To claim that Simms is a great American novelist, to a critical generation which dismisses greatness, refuses nationality, and deconstructs genre, is somewhat like (to change the metaphor) applying for membership in a club whose building was demolished a generation ago; under such circumstances, one cannot even have the comforting indignity of a black ball.

Charles Watson stands as a mild representative of the old logic, in a brief book which has the merit of clarity. There are those things for which Simms should be honored; he was, in the beginning, a devoted nationalist, a democrat, an expansionist who shed a tear for the vanishing Native American, an energetic historian, an author of various genres, a precursor of Welty as a chronicler of place. Then there are the other things, the infections of states rights, proslavery, sectionalism. On the whole, all is deemed to have gone well until about the mid-1840s, when Simms was most in the midst of Young America, but then there is degeneration, until he is left standing in the midst of his burned plantation, and mourning the death of his son in war. In Watson's vision, Simms has the defect of his virtues; the course of events turned his passionate devotion to locality into a destructive impulse. Along the way, the reader is offered concise discussions of selected books by Simms, with some thematic chapters, including a valuable one on Simms's interest in Spanish history and culture.

Now and again, Watson courteously quarrels with some nuances of the old orthodoxy. He seems less enthusiastic about deprecating Simms's social criticism than once was usual. For a familiar part of the old tactics of rehabilitation was to define the political as unliterary, and so beyond the scope of relevant criticism, or to argue that Simms's worst beliefs were the conventional wisdom of his culture, for which he was not responsible; the critic should focus on what was original in Simms's oeuvres. Watson seems less convinced of this, without going so far as to repudiate the traditional framework.

Since the terms feature largely in Watson's book, it may be worthwhile briefly to comment on the words "section" and "region," and their ideological emanations, "sectionalism" and "regionalism." In twentieth-century usage, these words have come to have a fairly precise meaning. Both presuppose the primacy of the nation-state. "Regionalism" is that ideology which benignly identifies geographical and social diversity. "Sectionalism" is a term of abuse, used to describe those who use locality as a political weapon in resisting the various legitimate purposes of the federal government. These terms were much in use when the debate over Simms began in the 1940s and were, most directly, a product of the politics of the New Deal and a postwar era, moving contentiously towards desegregation and civil rights, when Calhoun's name was invoked by massive resisters. On the whole, regionalism was a word available to liberals and conservatives alike, but sectionalism tended to be used by liberals when condemning conservatives. So, for example, Fletcher Green in the 1950s wrote deprecatingly of growing evidence of "sectionalism," from within a Southern progressive tradition.[2] Charles Sydnor, in particular, helped to popularize a notion that "sectionalism" was the *bête noire* of the Union in his influential *The Development of Southern Sectionalism, 1819–1848* (1948), but Avery Craven too, with his Quaker hostility to war and disunion, followed much the same line.

However, there are formidable etymological difficulties in transposing these terms to Simms's day. For one thing, most people, even in the North, did not see the Union as being primary, with states or regions as subsidiary. That was not how the Union worked, not then. Rather, all its components (states, localities, the federal government, the various branches of government at all levels) were understood to be cooperatively coequal. As Madison gnomically put it in the thirty-ninth number of the *Federalist Papers*, "The act ... establishing the Constitution will not be a *national*, but a *federal* act." That is, the idea of the nation was predicated upon the idea of the federal, and it was not clear whether there was a nation-state, at all, let alone one which required a hierarchy of loyalties. Even passionate Unionists might concede this, and quarrels hinged more on the social questions (especially slavery) which flowed through these interpenetrating institutions, than on their legitimacy. Everyone believed in states' rights, everyone believed in federal rights, but there was disagreement on which rights adhered where, and over which issues. So, to say that Simms believed in states' rights does not distinguish him from Abraham Lincoln.

To this, one must add that the words "region" and "section," which one can certainly find in Simms's writings, did not then have the force they were to acquire in our century. They were, on the whole, innocuous words of vague scope, but usually confined to a geographical space far smaller than the whole South. They had roughly the force of "place" or "area" in our usage. Certainly, I have never seen the words "sectionalism" or "regionalism" in any antebellum Southern text, though I would be interested to be corrected on this score. So, when Simms argued that a "region" or a "section" was a valid grounding for literature, he was not necessarily making a political statement, or no more so than Eudora Welty in defending the utility of place. In his 1844 essay on the writings of Cornelius Mathews, which Watson uses partly to ground his evidence of Simms's growing sectionalism, Simms (as I read him) is not speaking of the South against the North when he writes, "The nature of the people of this region lacks the rigidity, the solemnity, the staid forms and exactions of the people on the slopes of the Atlantic." For "this region" is the "great back-bone, the central ridge of the country, following the course of its waters along the slopes of the western and south-western valleys," and hence there is a differentiation between roughly the Appalachians and the low country.[3] This usage is, indeed, a particular manifestation of a wider problem in reading early nineteenth-century texts. For this was the century which tried to systematize the American language, to give words precise meanings, and nothing required more effort than disciplining the tendency of early-modern English to give words a loose scope (to allow, for example, a word like "continent" to be applicable not only to Asia, but to a cow pasture). But the effort was barely launched in Simms's day.

One of the manifestations of the Simms crusade has been the establishment of the Simms Society. This seems to have been as much a product of how the cultural politics of the American Literature Association works than anything else; authors thought worthwhile (Henry Adams, Willa Cather, Robinson Jeffers [sic]) have their eponymous societies, which help in entitling the sponsors to a session at the annual convention. But the Simms Society also holds conferences, of which one was held at the University of Arkansas in 1993. Its revised proceedings constitute *William Gilmore Simms and the American Frontier*. It is a book much at odds with itself, which is an encouraging sign. The host of the conference and one of the editors, John Guilds, is the exemplar of the traditional standpoint on Simms and, greatly to his credit, has borne the battle for many decades, in which he has written the standard biography, edited various texts, and sponsored several volumes of essays. No one knows more about Simms than Guilds and he is, in that sense, a touchstone of Simms scholarship. But what drives Guilds is the old desire for recognition. These are the first words of this book: "The twentieth century is slowly according to William Gilmore Simms some of the recognition as a major American writer that had been granted him prior to the Civil War."[4] No doubt, much frustration is conveyed in that little word, "slowly." But the contributors are a motley crew and the subject matter, Simms and the frontier, is at some distance from the vexed matters of North and South, free and slave, so the pressure of the orthodoxy is much lessened.

There is no room to give very detailed considerations to the seventeen essays, except to note that they are a valuable mix of close readings and general analyses. The first section, in which David Moltke-Hansen convincingly sketches the evolution of Southern identity in Simms's time and in which Elliott West gives a lucid synopsis of the "new Western history" as it applies to the landscapes portrayed by Simms, is especially valuable. Moltke-Hansen sinuously evades the orthodoxy, and West, one suspects, does not know of it, so things begin refreshingly. Many of the remaining essays focus on particular texts, with no party line except the broad sense that Simms's game is worth the candle. Jan Bakker wins the award for greatest truculence. "Simms is American literature's first distinctly 'realistic' writer—not the postbellum Northern fictionalizer, John William DeForest. And I assert this canon-revising proposition without equivocation."[5] There are essays invoking contemporary literary theory, though nothing very adventurous. Bakhtin seems to have got to Simms criticism, but not poststructuralism, representations of the body, or the more exotic forms of postmodernism. On the whole, the essayists take Simms's politics for granted and seem more interested in the lineaments of his imagination, less in its legitimacy, though there is understandably some deprecation about his characterizations of slaves, Native Americans, and poorer whites.

Overall, the volume proceeds piecemeal, which turns out to be an effective strategy, perhaps even for the Simms crusaders. Essayists try to make this novel and that short story intriguing, which begins to make the reader less skeptical. There are many ways to persuasion, but it helps to be attentive to the strengths and weaknesses of an author. Consider Henry James. With an uninformed reader, there is little point in starting with *The Ambassadors* or any of the late novels. One can get lost in the wandering complexity of the Master's syntax and psychology. One has to begin earlier, with *Washington Square* or *The Aspern Papers*, where the reader can acquire a respect sufficient to carry him or her through to the more complex works. With Simms, it is otherwise, since he was a diffuse and undisciplined writer, as he himself freely confessed. Much was hit-and-miss. He changed, but he never grew more complex. His mix of precision and sloppiness was all jumbled in his paragraphs and stanzas. He was not an original thinker, but he had a marked energy, a rough capacity of sympathy, and he registered the ideological mutations of his culture (not merely Southern) with a fidelity almost suspect. With Simms, as with the Falstaff he admired and transmuted into his most notable creation, Captain Porgy, one must begin with the man and come to like the writings as his expression, warts and all. He is a Dickensian figure, and those who cannot weep at the death of Little Nell are perhaps well advised to stay away. And there is Simms's problem. For who weeps any more for Little Nell?

NOTES

1. On this, see Lawrence H. Schwartz, *Creating Faulkner's Reputation: The Politics of Modern Literary Criticism* (Knoxville: University of Tennessee Press, 1988).

2. Fletcher M. Green, "Resurgent Southern Sectionalism, 1933–1955," *North Carolina Historical Review* 33 (April 1956): 222–40.

3. William Gilmore Simms, "Writings of Cornelius Mathews," *Southern Quarterly Review* 6 (October 1844): 337–38.

4. John C. Guilds and Caroline Collins, eds., *William Gilmore Simms and the American Frontier* (Athens: University of Georgia Press, 1997), ix.

5. Ibid., 77.

Michael O'Brien, "The Flight Down the Middle Walk: Mary Chesnut and the Forms of Observance," in *Haunted Bodies: Gender and Southern Texts*, ed. Anne Goodwyn Jones and Susan V. Donaldson (Charlottesville: University of Virginia Press, 1998), 109–31. Reprinted with permission of the University of Virginia Press. Some passages of this were later used in Michael O'Brien, *Conjectures of Order: Intellectual Life and the American South, 1810–1860*, 2 vols. (Chapel Hill: University of North Carolina Press, 2004), 2:1185–97.

She knew the value of solitude for a writer, though she was very fond of society, whose brittle tensions were much of her subject matter. She liked to sit in her own room, designated and guarded as a retreat, which looked out on pleasant fields; there she would write, which she did with astonishing facility and speed, though she had trouble in finishing things, because she feared the world's opinion. She was very well read in the literature of the day, which offered confusing precedents, and she was prone to experimentation in matters of form; she was fastidious and a little cruel in the severity of her critical judgments. She had firm opinions that women needed an independent income. She herself was born to a comfortable estate, not quite the highest her society offered but close enough to give the opportunities of observing and mingling with the lofty and of becoming something of a snob. Yet she was troubled in the matter of parents and family. A father, in particular, later devastated with grief, was alternately charming and despotic towards her, which somehow hindered her growth into the prerogatives of adulthood; he became, for her, the symbol of an old order, whose destruction she survived and, intellectually, did much to subvert; she was to make him a central figure in her most important narrative. Her elder brother, to whom she was devoted, died young. As for her own marriage, it had satisfactions but many turbulences; her husband was involved in politics, mostly as an adviser to people more prominent than himself, and she liked in turn to advise him. Their sexual life was not a success: she had no children, which she regretted, and for this envied her sister, who was fecund. By the standards of her day, she was resistant to traditional gentilities and candid about the betrayals which characterized her contemporaries, while retaining a certain evasiveness about herself. She thought much about the relations between men and women, and amongst women, and had as much taste for female beauties as for male. She had many friends and few intimates.

She lived through a great war, which had a marked effect upon her sensibility and whose outcome destroyed the world into which she had been born. She kept a diary. She lived, for a while, in a place called Bloomsbury.

All the above statements are true of two women, Mary Boykin Chesnut and Virginia Woolf.[1] They are offered with some playfulness, since self-evidently there is very much which differed in their lives and sensibilities. Even these statements have had to be carefully phrased, sometimes to insinuate similarity when there is difference. Woolf finished many more literary ventures than Chesnut, who managed to publish very little in her lifetime, while Woolf feared critics far more than Chesnut, so much so that her bouts of illness were sometimes connected to trepidation about the reception of her books.[2] The literary precedents of 1880 in the American South and 1910 in England were different, though not abruptly so. Chesnut's critical judgments were privately expressed, while Woolf wrote abundantly for periodicals like the *Times Literary Supplement*. The father who troubled Woolf was her own father Leslie Stephen, while Chesnut was bedeviled by her father-in-law James Chesnut, Sr. But Chesnut's father Stephen Miller did marry twice, like Leslie Stephen, and both Virginia Stephen and Mary Boykin Miller were daughters of the second wife. Dick Miller, Mary's elder brother, died when he was seventeen and she was nine, while Toby Stephen was twenty-six and Virginia was twenty-four. It is hard to know whether Woolf's husband offered more satisfactions than Chesnut's. It is doubtful that her marriage was as catastrophically asexual as Woolf's, yet Leonard Woolf offered an intellectual and spiritual comradeship of which James Chesnut was incapable. On the other hand, childlessness was a more scarring burden in Chesnut's society than in that of Woolf, many of whose contemporaries were childless; in fact, her sister Vanessa Bell was unusual in their set for having offspring. Lastly, trivially, though both lived in Bloomsbury, Mary Chesnut's Bloomsbury was a long walk from the British Museum; it was a small house bearing that name in Camden, South Carolina, where she lived briefly during the Civil War.

Yet I do not offer these parallels just for play. There is value in binding together the experiences of these two women writers. Woolf's position as a woman in the landscape of literature has been carefully plotted, but Chesnut's remains obscure. I intend this essay as a contribution towards locating the South Carolinian in more than her present position, which is the literature of Southern history, and to suggest that literary critics might profit from considering where Chesnut's narrative techniques stand in the history of women and literature. To this end, it helps to begin with the matter of genre, a topic which has bemused the critical reception of Mary Chesnut.

As we now know from the edition of *Mary Chesnut's Civil War* published by C. Vann Woodward in 1981, the diary of Mary Chesnut is problematical. It is not, tidily, the diary which was published by, first, Isabella D. Martin and Myrta Lockett Avary in 1905 as *A Diary from Dixie*, then under the same title but revised by Ben Ames Williams in 1949. These editions claim it as a diary of contemporary events, straightforwardly set down during the Civil War, and under this impression historians for several generations used Mary Chesnut as a primary source. In fact, with varying degrees of incompetence, naïveté, and duplicity, these editors were cobbling together a diary from much more complicated and more interesting documents. As Woodward has explained, there are several sets of manuscripts. There is an original and incomplete Civil War diary, published as *The Private Mary Chesnut* by Woodward and Elisabeth Muhlenfeld in 1984.[3] There is a revised version of some sections, dated 1875, of about four hundred pages. There is a final, much longer version, dating from the early 1880s, which provided the copy text for *Mary Chesnut's Civil War*. There are fragments which offer differing versions of events. Virtually none of this was published during her lifetime.[4]

All this is confusing for those who like tidy and reliable evidence, or those who like their literature to exist as finite texts, published at a definite time by intending authors; that is, for most historians. What, they are inclined to ask, is Mary Chesnut now good for? Much of *Mary Chesnut's Civil War* is of limited use as evidence for the direct experience of the Civil War, because written two decades late. On the other hand, the mingling of the 1880s version and passages from earlier manuscripts mildly compromises its value as a specimen of American literature from the 1880s; whatever else *Mary Chesnut's Civil War* is, it is not quite what she would have published, if she had published.[5] As significantly, one can justly ask, what do we call this book, these manuscripts, this jumble? This is a practical matter, as well as an intellectual one. One must call it something in one's own discussion. Woodward has defined our range of options, as far as it touches genre: "memoir, autobiography, fiction, chronicle, history," as well as diary. None of these is adequate. Both Woodward and Steven Stowe, suggestively, have called it a palimpsest.[6] But this is more elegant than practical. My own preference is, simply, to call it a narrative journal, which conflates her own terms.[7]

Critics have differed over the reasons for this apparent jumble. Elizabeth Fox-Genovese, who has used Chesnut as an inferior foil to Louisa McCord, inclines to think it resulted from intellectual inadequacies. "The tension between her historical and private selves accounts for much of the richness and fascination of her diary," she concedes. "Yet ultimately she lacked sufficient control of her material to forge it into a coherent story."[8] Chesnut's editors, surprisingly, are circumspect about her reasons. They stress her experiments in fiction and memoir, ventures which were the prelude to the 1880s manuscripts, while being careful to insist on their failure. Woodward is most insistent that the palimpsest is a triumph, but does not say of what. It is not, one presumes, a triumph among palimpsests. On the whole, it seems to be argued that Chesnut blundered across her confusion of genres, because no one genre worked for her. I think this is only part of the truth.

It is my belief that Mary Chesnut knew what she was doing, which was partially to dissolve the principles of realism, that she understood her originality better than most of her critics have, and hence that a useful context for understanding her book is not only Southern women's diaries like that of Sarah Morgan but also the transition from novels like *Vanity Fair* to those like *To the Lighthouse*.[9] But, it must be confessed from the onset, this belief rests much upon inference. In understanding Chesnut, we are peculiarly hampered by a lack of collateral evidence. Her surviving letters are few and mostly unilluminating; she made bonfires of much of her correspondence.[10] She wrote no literary manifestoes, no prefaces, no afterwords. There are just the texts, which we must interpret, if we are to discern her meanings. So let me try to construct the pattern of inferences, which is made of several strands: her knowledge of modern fiction and history; the pressure of public events; the special consciousness of being a woman; her apprehension of instability; and her use of voices.

Like Virginia Woolf, Mary Chesnut mostly educated herself by omnivorous reading, though she did have some formal schooling, which Woolf did not. In fact, one of her richest pieces of writing, her unpublished novella "Two Years—Or the Way We Lived Then," remembers Madame Talvande's school in Charleston. She became accomplished in modern languages, in French and German, but seems to have read the classics only in translation.[11] Woodward makes much of her Anglophile reading. Indeed, in "Two Years" she writes of herself as "intensely English in all my sympathies." She read the usual English authors, old and very new, and one, Jane Austen, seldom read in America.[12] Russian literature was largely unknown to her, though there is the odd fact that in 1880 she offered the editor of the Charleston *News and Courier* a translation of a "novelette" by Pushkin, presumably taken from the French.¹³ The Germans feature more but did not matter much to her, with the usual exception of Goethe, and (a little) Schiller and Richter. These were fairly old-fashioned tastes, unlike those she had in French literature, which were more contemporary; Balzac, Sand, Dumas, Mérimée, and Sue, but no Baudelaire, Rimbaud, or Flaubert. Balzac was especially important; her narrative journal could be seen as a Southern *comédie humaine*, swarming as it does with vignettes of character, sensitive as it is about social nuances. But it is important to remember her taste for older French authors like Montaigne, Molière, above all, Pascal. She aspired to the epigrammatic, to distilled moments of wisdom or observation, which might help to comprehend life's hurly-burly; she scattered things like, "In a revolution shy men are run over. No one stops to pick them up," or "Jealousy of the past is most women's hell."¹⁴ In all this reading, she seems to have preferred narratives of social interaction with a marked edge, things which flirt with cynicism. This taste was summed up by Thackeray, her literary exemplar, to whom she gave a reverent eulogy:

> Thackeray is dead.
> I stumbled upon *Vanity Fair* for myself. I had never heard of Thackeray before. I think it was in 1850. I know I had been ill at the New York hotel. And when left alone I slipped downstairs and into a bookstore that I had noticed under the hotel for something to read.
> They gave me the first half. I can recall now the very kind of paper it was printed on—and the illustrations as they took effect upon me. And yet when I raved of it and was wild for the other half, there were people who said it was slow!! That he was evidently a coarse, dull, sneering writer, that he stripped human nature bare, made it repulsive, &c&c&c.¹⁵

This helps to explain her dislike of the usual feminine taste of the midnineteenth century, the literary domestic novel, which was for her too much the occasion for "piety and pie-making" and too little candid. Shakespeare, she once observed of *King Lear*, was good for "laying bare the seamy side—going behind the curtain of propriety.... He preceded Thackeray in that tearing off of shams. [Old] Mrs Chesnut set her face resolutely to see only the pleasant things of life and shut her eyes to wrong and said it was not there. The most devoted, unremitting reader of fiction I ever knew—everything

French or English that came to hand—would not tolerate Thackeray. 'He is a very uncomfortable, disagreeable creature.' "[16] In this, Chesnut's mother-in-law agreed with Leslie Stephen, who married Thackeray's daughter. Virginia Woolf was to remember: "When my brothers had gone to school, he still went on reading to my sister and me, but chose more serious books. He read Carlyle's *French Revolution*, and stopped in the middle of *Vanity Fair*, because he said it was 'too terrible.' "[17] As Stephen explained elsewhere of Thackeray: "A man may be called a cynic not as disbelieving in the value of virtue, but as disbelieving in its frequency. He may hold that the tender emotions have a smaller influence in actual affairs than easy-going people maintain, and that a purely virtuous person is a very rare phenomenon indeed."[18]

Chesnut's narrative journal is written in this spirit of discomfort, of pulling "ostrich heads out of the sand,"[19] of a disillusion which stops short of cynicism because life is too interesting in its mayhem. She lays bare much: old Colonel Chesnut's mulatto children, Buck Preston's cruel and innocent flirtations, sexually frustrated soldiers grabbing at their nurses, the murder of an old woman by slaves, the beating of a pregnant slave by a mistress, a man mimicking the grins of the dead to amuse a dinner table, another gleefully fishing out a tumbled oyster from between a startled woman's breasts, the incessant human folly of society.[20] Few are spared, including herself. In this, she differed from Woolf, who usually omitted herself from her own fiction, often mistrusted self-representation, and could speak of "the dominance of the letter 'I' and the aridity, which, like the giant beech tree, it casts within its shade."[21] But Chesnut is a character in her own narrative, one who is mocked as "the Explainer General," full of foible and weakness, shown "spinning my own entrails," taking her opium, exercising her "power to hide trouble." Though Chesnut policed these self-revelations and toyed with omitting herself, with being merely "objective," she confessed all but the most intimate.[22] She made it possible, for example, for us to understand the pain of her childlessness, though not its cause. Very early in her narrative, she writes: "I did Mrs. Browne a kindness. I told those women that she was childless now, but that she had lost three children. I hated to leave her all alone. Women have such a contempt for a childless wife." She confesses, baldly, "Of course, I know nothing of children. In point of fact am awfully afraid of them." And there is this, "Women need maternity to bring out their best and true loveliness," a commentary on herself, the belle who was never beautiful, but who admired feminine beauty extravagantly, even sensually. "Oh—I have been to see a delicious married beauty! So soft, so silly, so lovely, so kindly! Forbear!" Elsewhere, "Clear brunette she is, with the reddest lips, the whitest teeth, and glorious eyes—there is no other word for them."[23]

Fox-Genovese has argued that Chesnut's condemnations of slavery were untypical of her class and gender, which seems to me true, but also that they were untypical of her, which I doubt.[24] Mary Chesnut was often skeptical about her society and its ways; that is part of what her narrative journal is about, what her admiration of Thackeray meant. She poked fun at honor, for example: "The Hampton Legion all in a snarl about I forget what—standing on their dignity, I suppose. I have come to detest a man who says, 'My own personal dignity—self-respect requires—.'"[25] In "Two Years," she mocked the religious literalists: "Without a murmur, down on his knees went my late chatty interlocutor. I listened in amazement if I did not pray. / It was an eloquent appeal to the Almighty to keep his covenant. He had promised. We had his promise; he was a covenant God. There was his bond. We had it in black and white. Those exact followers of Calvin, they like documents legally executed—be the parties who they may."[26] Similarly she incessantly made fun of the rituals of courtship, condemned beauty for its ruthless hardheartedness, amused herself at the feebleness of conventional oratory, and savaged Southern integrity.[27] The list could be easily extended. No doubt, these skepticisms did not form a consistent critique of her society, which is part of Fox-Genovese's point.

Nonetheless one must confront the matter of Chesnut's attitude towards self and society. Like Thackeray, the historical novelist whose characters acted out their lives in real places and times, in colonial Virginia or near the battle of Waterloo, Chesnut acknowledged the reality of history, of things beyond the personal. The driving reality of the war which changed her life, destroyed her society, took away her ease, killed her friends, relatives, and enemies alike, was nonetheless exhilarating, what she struggled to call "objective." She started her original diary to do justice to its awful majesty.

At one level, she fashioned as good a book about the American Civil War as anyone—historian, novelist, poet—has produced. But its achievement is particular, and much shaped as literature by the dynamics of gender. Mary Chesnut was a woman, who understood (no doubt conventionally) that war was about more than men and women, or their relations. She wanted to touch that reality, to break out of the confined space of even a senator's wife, to realize "the very casques that did affright the air at Agincourt." She saw the war as her chance to be more than plain Mary Chesnut, the "childless wretch" who read modern novels.[28]

But did she break out, definitively? It has been rightly stressed that the form which she chose freed her from many of the conventions of the novel. But all forms have their constrictions. A disadvantage of hers was that it tied the narration of events to her presence, drew them into the drawing rooms where she stood and sat, to the streets where she walked, into the words which she heard. She had to be there, even if only as the ear into which stories and gossip were poured. She is at the center of the war as she narrates it. As has been observed, she was in many important places—Charleston at the bombardment of Fort Sumter, Montgomery during the establishment of the Confederacy, Richmond while it was a national capital—but she was not everywhere. Manassas was a story, not a shell exploding next to her. So her narrative journal has few Northerners in it, their nation is remote and unrealized. Lincoln appears because he is Jefferson Davis's rival, and she knew Davis. Sumner is there because her husband had berated the abolitionist in the Senate.[29] Ulysses S. Grant is a grim rumor, someone with whom those who vanish from her presence go to rendezvous. Hence hers was more a book about women than about men, and usually only about men in the presence of women. She knew this. When Fort Sumter was being bombarded, she wrote of it: "We hear nothing, can listen to nothing. Boom, boom, goes the cannon—all the time. The nervous strain is awful, alone in this darkened room.... We were all in that iron balcony. Women—men we only see at a distance now."[30] She realized her ignorance of what men did away from women: "They [women] always decry and abuse men. Now the men praise women. But then, when twenty men are together without any women, I am not there. So I can't say they are not even with us." She even saw the meaning of the war in a quarrel between the sexes: "We separated because of incompatibility of temper. We are divorced, North from South, because we hated each other so. If we could only separate—a 'séparation à l'agréable,' as the French say it, and not a horrid fight for divorce."[31] But the North would not have it: "They hate us so and would clasp us—or hook us, as Polonius has it—to their bosoms with hooks of steel. We are an unwilling bride." This image flowed into her vision of slavery, a thing which violated marriage because it gave concubines to husbands, but also a thing which explained marriage: "There is no slave, after all, like a wife."[32] Dissatisfied as a woman, as a wife, as a mistress, she was well prepared to comprehend the broken disillusionments of war, better perhaps than she might have understood success. Victory, it is true, might mean freedom for the South. But even this would be ashes:

> After all, suppose we do all we hoped. Suppose we start up grand and free—a proud young republic. Think of all these young lives sacrificed! If three for one be killed, what comfort is that? What good will that do Mrs. Hayne or Mary DeSaussure? The best and bravest of our generation swept away! Henry DeSaussure has left four sons to honor their father's memory and emulate his example. But those poor boys of between 18 and 20 years of age—Haynes, Trezevants, Taylors, Rhetts, &c&c—they are washed away, literally, in a tide of blood. There is nothing to show they were ever on earth.[33]

Defeat, she certainly knew, meant entrapment. Few moments are more chilling than that when, at the end of things in 1865, she has her husband, her warden and warrior, express the sentence, "Camden for life."[34] A door slams, at that instant, between her drawing room and the world beyond. In that room, she wrote her book. It is not surprising that it is, to a large extent, about that room.

But she peopled her room extraordinarily. It teems "through the astonishing vividness and reality of the characters," to use Virginia Woolf's phrase about Thackeray's *Pendennis*.[35] Chesnut rushes around the room, listening, talking. She goes to the window—"We are forever at the windows"[36]—and sees the men go away, turn the corner, come back with their stories and their wounds, or not come back. She scrutinizes them all, including the slaves: "I am always studying these creatures." Above all, there are voices.

The thing which most distinguishes the original diary from the narrative journal are the voices. These were much of what she added and wanted to realize. They embody her quasi-modernist leanings, *par excellence*, because they are fragmentary, intentionally so, I believe. People say things. Often we do not know who is speaking. One quotation does not always follow logically from its predecessor. Voices are not always answered. The profound and the trivial lie next to one another, unreconciled. Contemporary voices sit next to literary quotations, Medea is adjacent to someone called Albert.[37] Subject matters change abruptly. Consider this passage, long enough to give the flavor. It is February of 1865, she is in Lincolnton, North Carolina, and *inter alia* begins on the subject of Virginians.

These people are proud of their heroic dead and living soldiers—but are prepared to say with truth that [they] always preferred to remain in the Union and are ready to assure the first comers of Yankees that they have always hated South Carolina seceders and nullifiers as much as the Yankees do.

"You say Miss Giles is as clever as she is beautiful. Nonsense. Clever! She was out of the Confederacy and then came rushing in. Fool or mad, that was."

"Conduct of a fool. Most women atone for their sins when they marry."

"Spinsters and vestal virgins—how do you know? You have not tried it."

"We have ears to hear, eyes to see, and a heart to understand, all the same. Lookers-on see more of the game than players—&c&c."

F.F.'s have a dialect. Her cousin said "mighty little" for *very small*. She called a ball or a tea party "only a little company" and another form of the simple word "very" was "right much." And she lived in a house where Mrs. Mat Singleton used English as pure as that of Victoria Regina.

"How I like to hear Mrs. John Singleton's clean-cut sentences, every word distinctly enunciated."

"I should say she was the delight of her friends, the terror of her foes. I am afraid of those words dropped one by one with such infinite precision—drops of vitriol, sometimes."

Remember that night as the train stopped—a ponderous bank president filled the door of the car.

"What was the use of bank presidents? We have no money."

"He says he paid himself his salary in gold, so there is money somewhere for the stay-at-homes. He is a descendent-in-law of the pretender branch of the Stuarts."

"And he is as loud as a centaur."

"You mean *stentor*. He said, "Miss_____, yes, yes—I come for yer—Huddy come 'long.' Now, this was only a slovenly habit of speech. He writes admirably."

What a look she gave me then.

"Worse, that 'right much'—eh?"

"What did you do?" "Nothing." Terebene lamps do not disclose blushes.

> We had been bragging of South Carolina's purity of accent—Mrs. Mat's well of English undefiled, Mrs. Richardson Miles's sweetest and softest of voices, Miss Middleton's sweet low voice *and* wit *and* wisdom.
> "Galore."
> "Then came the rough boatswain's hoarse bawl."[38]

Who is Miss Giles? We are not told. She rushes late into the Confederacy, it seems, doubling for Virginia, foolishly marrying the Deep South, somehow unaware like a vestal virgin. The actions of Virginians bring up their speech, idiosyncratic and worthy of reproach. A bank president abruptly appears. Why? To point to fiscal dishonesty, partly. Mostly because, eventually, it is implied that he is a Virginian and his dialect is mimicked. Someone is offended. But who? Someone blushes. Why? For doing nothing. What required action? We do not know. South Carolina's linguistic purity is boasted of. But this is designated "bragging," so we know not to believe in it. "Mrs. Mat" is dangled before us in the words of Spenser's praise of Chaucer, Miss Middleton in Lear's commendation of Cordelia. Then a boatswain hoarsely bawls. Why? We are left to guess at the allusion. Throughout, the personal and the social are artfully interwoven, while she manages to convey the disjointed, crab-like quality of conversation.

Chesnut's narrative journal everywhere speaks that she understood Woolf's complaint that the three-decker novel let the definition of human character go unrecorded; out of evasion "spring those sleek, smooth novels, those portentous and ridiculous biographies, that milk and watery criticism, those poems melodiously celebrating the innocence of roses and sheep which pass so plausibly for literature at the present time."[39] This could pass for a description of most of the Southern literature which came Mary Chesnut's way in Camden in 1880.[40] Chesnut was aware that her times were beginning to demand a different narrative technique and may even have been emboldened by the new vein of realist writing, though mainly by its starker subject matter not its style.[41] Certainly she seems to have realized the shift more than, say, Augusta Jane Evans, whose novels, however much they dealt with subjects usually forbidden or inaccessible to women, held to a traditional narrative form. Chesnut knew that the matter of self was implicated in the sea-change, though she found it awkward: "Those Tarleton memoirs, Lee's memoirs, Moultrie's, Lord Rawdon's letters—self is never brought to the front. I have been reading them over and admire their honesty and good taste as much as their courage and cleverness."[42] Should self be hidden? This was a practical matter. Should the original diary, should the narrative journal be locked away from curious eyes? Sometimes, yes. Sometimes, no.

Why did narrative break down for Chesnut? It was not—I cannot say this with more firmness—because she was incapable of coherence. Her narrative journal is full of stories, vignettes, anecdotes, which are as coherently fashioned and told as any traditional Southern storyteller or Victorian novelist could wish. The tale of the "Witherspoon Murder Case," the old lady murdered in her bed by slaves, is a chillingly effective allegory which has stuck in the mind of generations of historians. The old patriarch, James Chesnut, is a character whom his daughter-in-law described and invented with stiletto care, a man more compelling by far than his counterpoint in Allen Tate's *The Fathers*, but a man who serves the same purpose, to stand as the "last of the lordly planters who ruled this Southern world." Chesnut admires him, hates him, knows his passing is for the good even as she regrets it; she shows him in all his strength and weakness, "blind, deaf—apparently as strong as ever, certainly as resolute of will."[43] The following scene about his grief is, I would contend, one of the more remarkable in Southern literature:

> Mrs. Chesnut was only a year younger than her husband—he is ninety-two or three. She was deaf. He retains his senses wonderfully for his great age.
>
> I have always been an early riser. Formerly I often saw him, sauntering slowly down the broad passage from his room to hers, in a flowing flannel dressing gown when it was winter. In the spring he was apt to be in shirtsleeves, with suspenders hanging down his back. He had always a large hairbrush in his hand.
>
> He would take his stand on the rug before the fire in her room, brushing scant locks which were shining fleecy white. Her maid would be doing hers, which were dead-leaf brown—not a white hair in her head. He had the voice of a stentor. And there he stood, roaring his morning compliments. The people who occupied the rooms above said he fairly shook the window glasses. This pleasant morning greeting and ceremony was never omitted.
>
> Her voice was "low and sweet" (the oft quoted). Philadelphia seems to have lost the art of sending forth such now. Mrs. Binney, Mrs. Chesnut's sister, came among us with the same softly modulated, womanly, musical voice. Her clever and beautiful

daughters were *criard*. Judge Hare said, "Philadelphia women scream like macaws."

This morning, as I passed Mrs. C's room, the door stood wide open. And I heard a pitiful sound. The old man was kneeling by her empty bedside, sobbing bitterly.

I fled down the middle walk—anywhere out of reach of what was never meant for me to hear.[44]

This is skill of a high order: the definition of time, the casualness of the opening ("I have always been an early riser" "sauntering"), the old ways observed by the young interloper, the man's vanity and indifference to all but his own ritual, his booming at his wife's deafness, their physical separation mitigated by the regularity of courtesy, the delaying paragraph (beginning "Her voice") so that we do not reach the climax too soon, the brevity with which the pitiful moment is portrayed, the anticlimax of Chesnut's recoil. There is a world of social history, and of character realized, in this story, which Chesnut perfectly understood.

One cannot convict Mary Chesnut of narrative inability. Her voices are artful, their incoherences intended. Why? Because she did not think that the world added up to a smooth story with an ordered moral. Rather, it was "full of strange vicissitudes, and in nothing more remarkable than the way people are reconciled, ignore the past, and start afresh in life, here to incur more disagreements and set to bickering again." In fact, Chesnut disbelieved for the reasons classically adduced to explain the onset of modernism. She had no faith in the old gods of Christianity, in the new ones of science, in the justice of her society, in the goodness of human beings and the probability of happiness for them. She did not even trust herself. But she knew that these skepticisms did not disavow the vitality of life—"so excited and confused—worthy of me"—but made it more urgent, more necessary to be portrayed.[45]

The evidence of her antebellum beliefs is so scanty, that one cannot reliably date the onset of these beliefs; my guess is that the Civil War deepened but did not create them, because they are not uncharacteristic of her contemporaries, that odd truncated generation which was just coming into possession of their world when the war came. Most appear in her narrative journal: William Porcher Miles, Henry Timrod, Paul Hamilton Hayne, Varina Howell Davis, Susan Petigru King, William Henry Trescot, James Johnston Pettigrew, L. Q. C. Lamar. Many of them were skeptical people, putting up with their privileged lot with a half-smile, very interested in the salon and scandal (some of which they occasioned), fashionable, witty, analytical, acting from necessity more than hope, a little sad. They were very conscious of themselves as a generation, at odds with but polite towards their elders, who in turn noticed: "Mr. Petigru said of that brilliant Trescot, 'He is a man without indignation.' He and I laugh at everything."[46] Above all, they were clever. This was her favorite adjective. "Agreeable men, clever and cultivated men, seem to spring up from the sands of the sea." "We discussed clever women who help their husbands politically." Trescot was "the very cleverest writer we have." Muscoe Garnett was "the best and the cleverest Virginian I know." Lamar was "the most original and the cleverest of our men." The word seems to have meant force of mind, touched with irresponsibility and wit. Cleverness was a social quality; it existed to be observed. Being assertive, it was usually associated with being a man. For a woman like Mary Chesnut, there was a price for laughing with Trescot: "Another personal defeat," she wrote about an incident in 1862. "Little Kate: 'Oh, Cousin Mary, why don't you cultivate heart? They say at Kirkwood that you had better let your brains alone awhile and cultivate heart.'"[47]

This burden of gender helps to make intelligible much of Chesnut's sensibility and may explain her resorting to a changed form of observance, which most of her contemporaries did not. We have no comparable postbellum writings from Trescot or Hayne: on the contrary, the effect of the war on men seems to have been to choke off the modest experimentation of the 1850s, to make skepticism unseemly.[48] Less public, less responsible for the blood, tucked away in Camden, Mary Chesnut escaped the crippling burden of piety. But there may be another, gendered reason for this. In Chesnut's society, journals were a literary form which women used freely, not exclusively for men wrote diaries too, but characteristically.[49] Chesnut poured all her genres, all her narratives into the form of the journal. In this she differed from Woolf, who kept genres distinct; the Englishwoman's diaries, letters, biography, essays, novels, were then and are now all gathered between different endpapers, firmly labeled. More, Woolf tended to separate out her own styles into these genres; the voice of the novels is more lyrical and experimental than that of the diaries, which are in turn distinct from the letters, which are direct, even plain speaking. Chesnut put all these together in one place, thus defying purity of genre and style. One is tempted to say that this was more radical, more defiant of the rules. But the temptation should be resisted, because one genre remained governing; the journal proved suitable, precisely because it had so few rules. The journal had long permitted authors, publicly or privately, to use history, memoir, autobiography, and fiction. It acknowledged only two imperatives: narrative must implicate self; the passages of time must be denoted.

For all this, one must stress that Mary Chesnut's achievement differs fundamentally from that of Woolf in *To the Lighthouse*. Chesnut dealt in articulated voices, Woolf in thoughts. "You have overheard scraps of talk that filled you with amazement," Woolf explained in 1924. "You have gone to bed at night bewildered by the complexity of your feelings. In one day thousands of ideas have coursed through your brains; thousands of emotions have met, collided, and disappeared in astonishing disorder."[50] Woolf's mature fiction seeks to capture this quality of internal character. But Chesnut kept disorder out of the mind, because she feared it, as well she might. Chesnut may have understood the instability of reason and madness, but she certainly refused to confront it, sometimes escaping by means of the oblivion of opium:

> There was tragedy, too, on the way here. A mad woman, taken from her husband, and children. Of course she was mad—or she would not have given "her grief words" in that public place. Her keepers were along. What she said was rational enough—pathetic, at times heartrending.
>
> Then a highly intoxicated parson was trying to save the soul of "a bereaved widow." So he addressed her always as "my bereaved friend and widow."
>
> The devil himself could not have quoted Scripture more fluently.
>
> [[It excited me so—I quickly took opium, and *that* I kept up. It enables me to retain every particle of mind or sense or brains I ever have and so quiets my nerves that I can calmly reason and take rational views of things otherwise maddening... {and have refused to accept overtures for peace and forgiveness. After my stormy youth I did so hope for peace and tranquil domestic happiness. There is none for me in this world.}]][51]

So Chesnut kept her voices out in the world, where they were attached to flesh and blood, where they were safer. Indeed, she seems even to have exported her own thoughts and attached them to others.[52] In this sense, Woolf was braver, in fracturing the line between the internal and external worlds, though she was to pay a terrible price for this courage.

Chesnut's flight down the middle walk, away from her particles of mind, reasonably disqualifies her from the modernist canon, as traditionally understood.[53] There are too many aspects of that movement to which Mary Chesnut would have been hostile. She had no notion of an avant-garde. There is no reason to believe that she would have looked on a Picasso painting or heard a Stravinsky score with equanimity. We are told, plausibly, that, "Modernist works frequently tend to be ordered, then, not on the sequence of historical time or the evolving sequence of character, from history or story, as in realism or naturalism; they tend to work spatially or through layers of consciousness, working towards a logic of metaphor or form. . . . [S]ynchronicity . . . [is] one of the staples of Modernist style."[54] Chesnut believed in history and studied character, as it happened in time. She would have recoiled from the proposition that older forms of mimesis were now irrelevant, even pernicious. She would not have thought it necessary to urge art as an ordering myth. She would have been too genteel to inhabit Henry Miller's tropics, though she might have managed an awkward laugh when Lytton Strachey pointed to that stain on Vanessa Stephen's white dress and asked, "Semen?"[55] On the other hand, she would have found Eliot's postbellum characterization of "the immense panorama of futility and anarchy which is contemporary history" intelligible. She would likewise have understood when Eliot argued that art is "not a turning loose of emotion, but an escape from emotion; it is not the expression of personality, but an escape from personality."[56] She would certainly have grasped the point when, in arguing for December 1910 as a turning point, Woolf explained, "All human relations have shifted—those between masters and servants, husbands and wives, parents and children."[57] But Chesnut could make her own case for an earlier turning point, a different social transformation. And she knew that literature responded to "fragmented utterances" and a "dislocation of parts."[58]

My argument is not that Chesnut is a modernist, but that, on the subtle and confused continuum which leads from the Anglo-American literary culture of 1860 to that of 1930, she is closer to the latter end than we have thought. The inceptions of modernism were overlapping and uneven: many members of the Bloomsbury group other than Woolf, writers like Lytton Strachey, were less radical about form than Chesnut herself; it was Roger Fry who observed that they were "the last of the Victorians."[59] For one must remember that Chesnut's narrative journal was written in the early 1880s; because she brings to life the early 1860s, there is a marked temptation to annex her to the sensibility of the mid-century and to neglect the evident fact of her intellectual and aesthetic growth between 1865 and 1880. Chesnut is nearer to the *fin-de-siècle* than we usually realize.

Why was she so "advanced"? This is elusive. But it mattered that her starting point, Thackeray, was, of all the great Victorian writers, least committed to the principles of realism. It was Thackeray, after all, who understood that, whatever fiction did, it did not mimic real life. He was an author who began his career by writing parodies, a man who debated genre and style: "We might have treated this subject in the genteel, or in the romantic, or in the facetious manner," he cheerfully explained to his readers in *Vanity Fair*.[60] Most importantly, Thackeray observed in *Pendennis*: "Ah sir—a distinct universe walks about under your hat and under mine. All things in Nature are different to each: the woman we look at has not the same features, the dish we eat from has not the same taste to the one and the other. You and I are but a pair of infinite isolations, with some fellow-islands a little more or less near to us."[61] Gregariousness in both Thackeray and Chesnut arose from this bleak insight; it was an attempt at island-hopping.[62] But Thackeray, like his admirer Anthony Trollope, had a strong sense of comity between author and reader which was alien to Chesnut. The men, with bluff clubbishness, talked to the reader over their port and cigars, even if they talked of isolation. Chesnut the woman never articulated a vision of her possible readers, was silent on their nature, was alone with her voices, and aspired to impersonality.

Hence much hinged on gender. Virginia Woolf, though she admired Thackeray, felt an unbridgeable gulf between herself and such as him. "It is useless to go to the great men writers for help, however much one may go to them for pleasure. Lamb, Browne, Thackeray, Newman, Sterne, Dickens, De Quincey—whoever it may be—never helped a woman yet, though she may have learned a few tricks of them and adapted them for her use," she wrote in 1929.[63] For men wrote assertively, with purpose and ambition. They commanded the genres of outwardness: history, political economy, travel writing, biography. Women were confined to fiction, the genre of enclosure, in "the common sitting-room," where they observed "human beings . . . in their relation to each other."[64] The mark of intellectual freedom for women would be the movement outward, out of the room, into the world. This is a beguiling interpretation, which has been very influential upon modern opinion. It makes much seem intelligible, provides a historical explanation of the transit from Jane Austen to Margaret Thatcher, from Elizabeth Ruffin to Hillary Clinton.[65] It is useful for understanding Mary Chesnut, who moved towards the genres of outwardness, but by the half-step of importing a teeming world into her drawing room and mingling the techniques of fiction and "fact." Yet Woolf intended that the world should also be understood as thought, and that the movement should be double, out into the world of facts, down into the realm of "myriad impressions—trivial, fantastic, evanescent, or engraved with the sharpness of steel."[66] Here too Chesnut took her half-step, by admitting the disorder of voices but quarantining their chaos above the stream of consciousness. This was a humane compromise, however nervously accomplished. She once wrote, in her original diary in 1861: "Talked all night—*exhausted*. & nervous & miserable today—raked up & dilated & harrowed up the bitterness of twenty long years—all to no purpose. This bitter world."[67] She died twenty-five years later, to the last writing, making sense of things, summoning vitality, transcending bitterness.

NOTES

1. The standard biographies are Elisabeth Muhlenfeld, *Mary Boykin Chesnut: A Biography* (Baton Rouge: Louisiana State University Press, 1981) and Quentin Bell, *Virginia Woolf: A Biography*, 2 vols. (London: Hogarth Press, 1973).
2. But see Stephen Trombley, *"All That Summer She Was Mad": Virginia Woolf and Her Doctors* (London: Junction Books, 1981) for a convincing skepticism about the nature of Woolf's "madness."
3. C. Vann Woodward and Elisabeth Muhlenfeld, eds., *The Private Mary Chesnut: The Unpublished Civil War Diaries* (New York: Oxford University Press, 1984).
4. C. Vann Woodward, ed., *Mary Chesnut's Civil War* (New Haven, CT: Yale University Press, 1981), xv–xxix (hereinafter *MCCW*). See also Woodward, "What is the Chesnut Diary?" in James L. Meriwether, ed., *South Carolina Women Writers* (Columbia: Southern Studies Program, University of South Carolina, 1979), 193–209.
5. Woodward, of course, has scrupulously distinguished passages from the differing manuscripts; see "Editorial Problems and Principles," in *MCCW*, liv–lviii.
6. "Mary Chesnut in Search of Her Genre," (1984) in C. Vann Woodward, *The Future of the Past* (New York: Oxford University Press, 1989), 252, 260; Steven M. Stowe, "City, Country, and the Feminine Voice," in Michael O'Brien and Michael Moltke-Hansen, eds., *Intellectual Life in Antebellum Charleston* (Knoxville: University of Tennessee Press, 1986), 314. It has been argued that the palimpsest is a characteristic form for female writers. Mary Lynn Broe has observed of Djuna Barnes that, "Her palimpsest texts, such as *Ryder* and *Ladies Almanack*, disrupt a masculine economy that would assign a single system of signification to each work": see Broe, "Djuna Barnes (1892–1982)," in Bonnie Kime Scott, ed., *The Gender of Modernism: A Critical Anthology* (Bloomington: Indiana University Press, 1990), 19. Somewhat differently, Gilbert and Gubar have written, "In short, like the twentieth-century American poet H. D., who declared her aesthetic strategy by entitling one of her novels *Palimpsest*, women from Jane Austen and Mary Shelley to Emily Brontë and Emily Dickinson produced literary works that are in some sense palimpsestic, works whose surface designs conceal or obscure deeper, less accessible (and less socially acceptable) levels of meaning. Thus these authors managed the difficult task of achieving true literary authority by simultaneously conforming to and

subverting patriarchal literary standards": see Sandra M. Gilbert and Susan Gubar, *The Madwoman in the Attic: The Woman Writer and the Nineteenth-Century Literary Imagination* (New Haven, CT: Yale University Press, 1979), 73. Since Chesnut did not, in my opinion, adopt a "surface design" that was patriarchal, I am unsure whether this analysis is directly relevant, though it is suggestive.

    7. "Bloomsbury. So this is no longer a journal but a narrative of all I cannot bear in mind which has occurred since August 1862" (entry for September 23, 1863): *MCCW*, 425.

    8. Elizabeth Fox-Genovese, *Within the Plantation Household: Black and White Women in the Old South* (Chapel Hill: University of North Carolina Press, 1988), 371.

    9. Charles East, ed., *The Civil War Diary of Sarah Morgan* (Athens: University of Georgia Press, 1991). I should acknowledge that, though I wrote the first version of this piece before rereading her essay, part of my argument is anticipated in Elisabeth Muhlenfeld, "Literary Elements in Mary Chesnut's Journal," in Meriwether, *South Carolina Women Writers*, 245–61, a paper first delivered at the Reynolds Conference in 1975.

    10. They barely support a master's thesis: see Allie Patricia Wall, ed., "The Letters of Mary Boykin Chesnut" (M.A. thesis, University of South Carolina, 1977).

    11. She seems to have known her Seneca; see *MCCW*, 302, on Medea.

    12. Elisabeth Muhlenfeld, ed., *Two Novels by Mary Chesnut*, Southern Texts Society (Charlottesville: University Press of Virginia, 2002), 191, 185.

    13. *MCCW*, xxiii. Russian novelists like Turgenev and Tolstoy were barely making it into English by the time of Chesnut's death.

    14. *MCCW*, 271, 449. When I first aired this essay as a paper to the Southern Intellectual History Circle in 1994, David Moltke-Hansen suggested the *Memoires* of the Duc de Saint-Simon (1675–1755) as a precedent for Chesnut. Although there were copies around in South Carolina—in 1826 the Charleston Library Society had a 1791 Strasbourg edition—references to Saint-Simon are surprisingly scarce in Southern writing of the early or mid-nineteenth century, even in places where one might expect a reference, and there seem to be none in Chesnut's works. Among the few who did mention Saint-Simon are: Francis Kinloch, *Letters from Geneva and France Written During a Residence of Between Two and Three Years, in Different Parts of Those Countries, and Addressed to a Lady in Virginia. By Her Father*, 2 vols. (Boston, MA: Wells and Lilly, 1819), 1:69; and Hugh Swinton Legaré, "D'Aguesseau," *Southern Review* 8 (February 1832): 399–443. See *A Catalogue of the Books Belonging to the Charleston Library Society* (Charleston, SC: A. E. Miller, 1826), 231.

    15. *MCCW*, 546.

    16. Ibid., 65, 761–62.

    17. "Impressions of Sir Leslie Stephen," in Andrew McNeillie, ed., *The Essays of Virginia Woolf. Volume I: 1904–1912* (San Diego, CA: Harcourt Brace Jovanovich, 1986), 128.

    18. Leslie Stephen, "The Writings of William M. Thackeray," (1878–79) in Geoffrey Tillotson and Donald Hawes, eds., *Thackeray: The Critical Heritage* (London: Routledge & Kegan Paul, 1968), 377. Doubtless because of his family connection with the Thackerays, Stephen's essay is very guarded about Thackeray's moral shortcomings.

    19. *MCCW*, 762.

    20. Ibid., 31, 72, 414, 368, 189–227, 646–47, 626, 484; on Buck Preston, passim.

    21. Virginia Woolf, *A Room of One's Own* (1929; London: Grafton Books, 1977), 108, where admittedly she is speaking about a man's writing. In this critical work, unlike her fiction, Woolf does represent herself, though evasively, collectively: "Here then was I (call me Mary Beton, Mary Seton, Mary Carmichael or by any name you please—it is not a matter of importance) sitting on the banks of a river a week or two ago in fine October weather, lost in thought" (9).

    22. *MCCW*, 172, 23, 29, 23.

    23. Ibid., 28, 488, 105, 572, 146.

    24. Fox-Genovese, *Plantation Household*, 335–65.

25. *MCCW*, 102.
26. *Two Novels by Mary Chesnut*, 204.
27. *MCCW*, 229, 231, 638–39.
28. Ibid., 32.
29. Nathaniel Russell Middleton to his son, undated fragment of autograph letter but perhaps the early summer of 1860, Nathaniel Russell Middleton Papers, Southern Historical Collection, University of North Carolina, Chapel Hill.
30. *MCCW*, 48.
31. Ibid., 25. Divorce was illegal in South Carolina.
32. *MCCW*, 84, 59
33. Ibid., 412.
34. Ibid., 792.
35. Virginia Woolf, "Mr Bennett and Mrs Brown," (1923) in Andrew McNeillie, ed., *The Essays of Virginia Woolf. Volume III: 1919–1924* (San Diego, CA: Harcourt Brace Jovanovich, 1988), 385.
36. *MCCW*, 186.
37. Ibid., 302.
38. Ibid., 743–44.
39. Virginia Woolf, "Character in Fiction," (1924) in McNeillie, *Essays of Virginia Woolf: III*, 436.
40. Consider this backhander: "In England Mr. Gregory and Mr. Lyndsay rise to say a good word for us. Heaven reward them. Shower down His choicest blessings on their devoted heads—as the fiction folks say" (*MCCW*, 72).
41. Both Anne Jones and Steven Stowe, after reading a preliminary version of this essay, suggested that Chesnut may have intended realism, that her fragmentary drafts may have been but preliminary to a more ordered final version. In the discussions at Myrtle Beach, Elisabeth Muhlenfeld helped my resistance to this interpretation by indicating how Chesnut, in revising her manuscripts, moved usually and deliberately to weaken coherence, not strengthen it. Even her punctuation, Muhlenfeld has argued, served this purpose: "A look at a holograph page of the Journal reveals that Mrs. Chesnut uses a unique system of punctuation, the effect of which is to reproduce as accurately as possible the mind casting back and forth over a day's events, stopping now and then to ponder, veering occasionally from the moment at hand to the associations it evokes. She punctuates almost exclusively with dashes of various lengths and with spaces which, on the manuscript page, give a very real feeling of spontaneous and unstructured thought." See Muhlenfeld, "Literary Elements in Mary Chesnut's Journal," 251. A better candidate as a realist is Susan Petigru King, as is argued by J. R. Scafidel, "Susan Petigru King: An Early South Carolina Realist," in Meriwether, *South Carolina Women Writers*, 101–15.
42. *MCCW*, 194.
43. Ibid., 814–15.
44. Ibid., 610.
45. Ibid., 29, 216.
46. Ibid., 36. Of the names mentioned, all were born between 1822 and 1830.
47. *MCCW*, 358, 365, 568, 309, 393.
48. Trescot's postwar eulogy for James Johnston Pettigrew, for example, is lamentably gilded, uncharacteristic of the mind which Chesnut described as bristling with bayonets: see William Henry Trescot, *Memorial of the Life of J. Johnston Pettigrew, Brig. Gen. of the Confederate States Army* (Charleston, SC: John Russell, 1870); *MCCW*, 325.
49. I have discussed this elsewhere: see Michael O'Brien, ed., *An Evening When Alone: Four Journals of Single Women in the South, 1827–67*, Southern Texts Society (Charlottesville: University Press of Virginia, 1993), 2–4.

50. Woolf, "Character in Fiction," 436. One must remember, however, that Woolf was not contending against realism, so much as locating reality at the level of consciousness: on this, see Astradur Eysteinsson, *The Concept of Modernism* (Ithaca, NY: Cornell University Press, 1990), 184.

51. *MCCW*, 29. The double brackets indicate material interpolated into the 1880s manuscript from the 1860s diary; the single braces enclose words that Chesnut herself erased, but her editor thought it useful to restore. This passage shows clearly her reluctance to be too intimate, too introspective.

52. Muhlenfeld, "Literary Elements in Mary Chesnut's Journal," 257.

53. One must remember, however, that recent literary criticism has, by insisting upon consideration of female writers, begun to change our understanding of modernism. It remains unclear whether the effect of this will be to expand and reconfigure modernism, or to end its usefulness as an analytical category of sufficiently broad application. On such issues, see Shari Benstock, "Beyond the Reaches of Feminist Criticism: A Letter from Paris," in Shari Benstock, ed., *Feminist Issues in Literary Scholarship* (Bloomington: Indiana University Press, 1987), 7–29; Gillian E. Hanscombe, *Writing for Their Lives: The Modernist Women, 1910–1940* (London: Women's Press, 1987); and Scott, *Gender of Modernism*, passim.

54. Malcolm Bradbury and James McFarlane, "The Name and Nature of Modernism," in Malcolm Bradbury and James McFarlane, eds., *Modernism, 1890–1930* (Harmondsworth: Penguin Books, 1976), 50.

55. Bell, *Virginia Woolf*, 1:124.

56. "Ulysses, Order, and Myth," (1923) in Frank Kermode, ed., *Selected Prose of T. S. Eliot* (London: Faber and Faber, 1975), 177; "Tradition and the Individual Talent," (1920) in T. S. Eliot, *Selected Essays* (London: Faber and Faber, 1951), 21.

57. Woolf, "Character in Fiction," 422.

58. "Modernism," in M. H. Abrams, *A Glossary of Literary Terms* (New York: Holt, Rinehart and Winston, 1981), 109.

59. Quoted in Ulysses L. D'Aquila, *Bloomsbury and Modernism* (New York: Peter Lang, 1989), 4.

60. William Makepeace Thackeray, *Vanity Fair: A Novel Without a Hero* (1847–48; London: Thomas Nelson, 1901), 52.

61. William Makepeace Thackeray, *The History of Pendennis: His Fortunes and Misfortunes, His Friends and His Greatest Enemy* (1848–50; London: Thomas Nelson, 1901), 176. On Thackeray and representation, see A. Savkar Altinel, *Thackeray and the Problem of Realism* (Frankfurt am Main: Peter Lang, 1986) and J. Loofbourow, *Thackeray and the Form of Fiction* (Princeton, NJ: Princeton University Press, 1964).

62. Many were surprised, because of his cynical reputation, to find that Thackeray was a sociable man: see, for example, John Esten Cooke, "An Hour with Thackeray," (1879) reprinted in Philip Collins, ed., *Thackeray: Interviews and Recollections*, 2 vols. (London: Macmillan, 1983), 2:256–64.

63. Woolf, *A Room of One's Own*, 83.

64. Ibid., 122–23.

65. On Ruffin, see O'Brien, *Evening When Alone*, 7–14, 57–106.

66. Woolf, "Modern Novels," (1919) in McNeillie, *Essays of Virginia Woolf: III*, 33.

67. Woodward and Muhlenfeld, *Private Mary Chesnut*, 44.

Michael O'Brien, "'The South Considers Her Most Peculiar': Charleston and Modern Southern Thought," *South Carolina Historical Magazine* 94 (April 1993): 119–33, revised from a talk given at the Gibbes Museum of Art during the symposium *Creators and Stewards: The* 18th Century *World of Henrietta Johnson and the Charleston Renaissance*. Reprinted by permission.

In 1850 Charleston exercised a marked influence upon Southern thought and culture. It competed with New Orleans as the definitive Southern city, inferior in commerce but superior in intellectual endeavor. Though other Southerners often resented and mistrusted the city, its force was undeniable. But by 1930 Charleston was marginal to the formation of Southern thought. Other Southerners seldom paid it even the compliment of resentment, but offered indifference or the affection one might offer to an eccentric uncle, lodged in a handsome house, who can no longer afford to buy Christmas presents for his relatives.

If one looks, for example, through the works of the Chapel Hill group, Charleston is almost invisible. Howard Odum, in his *An American Epoch: Southern Portraiture in the National Picture* of 1930, mentioned it now and again, most often in a rambling chapter entitled "The Glory that was the South" where it occurs in polite and gilded allusions to vanished antebellum splendors. Only once does Charleston occur as a present, as opposed to a past fact, when Odum includes it in a long list of Southern "port facilities."[1] By the time of Odum's magnum opus, his *Southern Regions* of 1936, Charleston had vanished completely, although this was partly because in this book Odum was concerned to devise aggregate statistical tables for Southern regions and subregions, and by his methods all Southern cities—not just Charleston—became invisible as units of analysis. Rupert Vance, Odum's chief lieutenant, did a little better in his *Human Geography of the South* in 1932, by noting a few aspects of Charleston's recent urban planning, especially its experiments in tax and zoning laws "to encourage recent movement to preserve and restore the city's fine old architecture."[2] But this was a mere seven lines in a fat book of nearly six hundred pages.[3]

If one expands from the category of Chapel Hill authors to consider the rest of North Carolina, the record is not much more encouraging. W. J. Cash placed Charleston squarely in the midst of his excoriation of the culture of the Old South.[4] "One almost blushes to set down the score of the South here," he wrote, with almost as many inaccuracies as clauses.

> If Charleston had its St. Cecilia and its public library, there is no record that it ever added a single idea of any notable importance to the sum total of man's stock. If it imported Mrs. Radcliffe, Scott, Byron, wet from the press, it left its only novelist, William Gilmore Simms, to find his reputation in England, and all his life snubbed him because he had no proper pedigree. If it fetched in the sleek trumpery of the schools of Van Dyck and Reynolds, of Ingres and Houdon and Flaxman, it drove its one able painter, Washington Allston (though he was born an aristocrat), to achieve his first recognition abroad and at last to settle in New England.[5]

That was all Cash had to say on Charleston's record, except for a brief inclusion of DuBose Heyward and of Julia Peterkin (not a Charlestonian) in Cash's account of the growth of Southern critical thought in the 1920s and 1930s. Here he was more benign, though not without a justifiable sting: "Mrs. Peterkin and DuBose Heyward, while exhibiting an enormous freshness in their approach to the Negro—they were the first Southern novelists to deal with him in recognizably human terms instead of those of the old convention—still retained considerable vestiges of sentimentality. Both were prone to see only the poetical or ingratiating aspects of the Negro's lot."[6]

Jonathan Daniels of Raleigh gave Charleston a little more attention in his *A Southerner Discovers the South* in 1938. The city, at least, gets a chapter.[7] In it, the movement of rich Yankees south and poor blacks north is discussed as a happy development. A few jokes are made, mostly the usual jokes about vales of humility and mountains of conceit, but one less usual: "there [are] only two kinds of South Carolinians, those who have never worn shoes and those who made you feel that you had never worn shoes." For the rest, Daniels's portrait was a benign one. He was evidently, and confessed to being, seduced by the city's architecture, its tradition, its people, its "ancient integrity" and "old-fashioned charm." He reproduced, in full, the epitaph which is engraved upon the tombstone of James Louis Petigru in the graveyard of St. Michael's.[8] He mused—as one is supposed to do in graveyards—on the vagaries of history and contemplated the contributions of non-Charlestonians (Petigru, Calhoun) to the city. He ended by hoping that a few of the qualities of Petigru and of Charleston's tradition—the latter he defined as "gay ... and graceful, even warm"—might survive to inform the direction of the New South.[9]

That is pretty much all that North Carolinian scholarship and social criticism had to say about Charleston in the 1920s and 1930s. This is not surprising. Chapel Hill's business, as it so often proclaimed, was the future. Charleston was no part of the future, except insofar as it might instruct New Southerners on manners or zoning laws. One might expect, therefore, the Fugitives and Agrarians to have been more sympathetic to Charleston, since they were dedicated to the Southern past and its resuscitation. To a very limited extent, this was so. There were some sympathetic exchanges between the Fugitives and the Poetry Society of South Carolina, with the latter (for a while) being something of the elder partner, by virtue of precedence and having sponsored the first Southern number of Harriet Monroe's magazine *Poetry* in April 1922. The Fugitives were at some pains to be respectful of the Charlestonian poets, whom Tate in 1923 described as "obviously an intelligent and talented group."[10]

Both John Crowe Ransom and Donald Davidson won prizes from the Society. There was even some discussion in 1924, when *The Fugitive* was in financial trouble, of merging with it.[11] Both Davidson and Tate wrote more-or-less sympathetic reviews of DuBose Heyward's poetry and prose.[12] Yet one has to put the emphasis on the "more-or-less." When they were still Fugitives and fleeing from the high caste Brahmins of the Old South—and what Southern Brahmin was more high caste than a Charlestonian Brahmin?—the Nashvilleans objected to the whole idea of Southern literature. They were concerned to derogate the local color which was undoubtedly and purposely present in a book like *Carolina Chansons*.[13] They were upset with Harriet Monroe and Heyward for speaking about poetry and the indigenous with such prescriptive enthusiasm.[14] Later, when they were Agrarians and disposed to think more kindly of the local, the Nashvilleans turned their earlier objections to local color into a more subtle objection to the kind of indigenousness espoused by Charleston. In both phases, however, Nashville was eager to strip Charleston of its early claim to be a molder of modern Southern literature. And we tend to forget the plausibility of that claim in 1922, when Harriet Monroe observed in her preface to the special Southern issue of *Poetry* that the Poetry Society of South Carolina was "exerting an influence which may yet be felt throughout the South" and thought it logical that Charleston, because of its "old culture," should offer such leadership.[15] We tend to forget, because Nashville was so successful in changing the rules of the critical game.

However, one must note a significant schism in the Agrarians' ranks. Davidson believed that Heyward was flawed by appealing too much to outsiders, by writing with an eye on New York. "I could easily have imagined," Davidson wrote in 1929 of *Mamba's Daughters*, "the book to have been written by some fly-by-night millionaire novelist from the Riviera or Gopher Prairie, who put his yacht into Charleston harbor for the winter season and picked up enough local color to fill out his contract for a fifteenth best-selling novel."[16] This was a polite version of what Davidson had written to Tate in 1927: "The sham stuff, like Hervey Allen and Dubose Heyward, is easy. They merely exhibit for a foreign audience; they employ the accidents and omit the essences. It is needless to say that the essences are not magnolias, niggers, and cotton fields."[17] Tate, on the other hand, saw matters exactly backwards, that Heyward was flawed by being too local, insufficiently alienated. Even in 1924, in a review of Heyward's *Skylines and Horizons* that is mostly indulgent, Tate observed that "other poets in the South whose work is less obviously local may have a stronger claim to eminence than Mr. Heyward."[18] In time, Tate would come to elaborate a theory of Southern literature which made a balance of belonging and alienation central to the creation of significant art. Belong too much and the writer is stifled. Belong too little and you have no subject matter. Charlestonians, it became conventional to assert, belonged too much. Nothing was to be hoped from them, no Faulkner, no Tate, no Wolfe. Indeed, by 1935, John Crowe Ransom had so refined his definition of the South that he could read Heyward and Peterkin completely out of its literature, since "a Southern literature ... will never be constituted by a local color."[19]

This difference of emphasis between Tate and Davidson was of a piece with a deep-seated difference in literary and aesthetic philosophy between them, one which led eventually to estrangement. Tate was the modernist, Davidson the semi-traditionalist. Tate was the cosmopolitan, Davidson the regionalist. Tate looked to T. S. Eliot, Davidson to Thomas Hardy. Tate looked to Virginia, Davidson to Tennessee. Tate cared for what the modern poet might (with difficulty) think of the Confederate dead, Davidson cared for the dead themselves. It is little to be wondered that Tate was resistant to Charleston. In fact, I am not sure he ever visited the city. But Davidson did, at least three times, first to appear before the Poetry Society in 1927, second to a Southern writers conference in 1932, later to work in the Charleston Library Society in 1948.

His first reaction to the city was deceptively warm. "I am a worshipper of Charleston for life. The courtesy, the charm, and also ... the unpretentiousness and friendliness of all the people captured me." He went out to Middleton Place, a heron flew down by the water; it was all very pleasant.[20] But his feelings in 1932 were very different. "The Charleston meeting," Davidson wrote to Tate, "was delightful on the entertainment side, but in other respects completely uneventful. There was no fighting at all; there was almost no discussion. My impression was that the Charleston committee, or Heyward at least, had judiciously oiled the wheels and arranged that there be no discussion of the sort that arose last year.... There was a little light chatter, and then we went to lunch. There was only one more talk meeting. It consumed about fifteen minutes..."[21] For an ex-Fugitive and present Agrarian, this was deeply unsatisfactory, for both groups had thrived on intense, sometimes rancorous, debate.

This discontent embodies a familiar skepticism, best expressed by modern scholarship in the various writings of Jane and William Pease, which argues that Charleston has had too much charm, but too little rigor.[22] Such a standpoint is best summed up, perhaps, in a passage of Evelyn Waugh's *Brideshead Revisited*. It is when Anthony Blanche, with stammering cruelty and honesty, is reproving Charles Ryder for the imposture of the latter's exhibition of Latin American paintings and observes that "simple, creamy" charm is a great cultural blight, which kills love and kills art.[23]

By 1948, Agrarianism was dead as an active movement and Davidson was one of the few original authors of *I'll Take My Stand* who stood by its contentions. It is of some interest, therefore, that his essay, "Some Day, in Old Charleston," published in the *Georgia Review* in 1949, was more sympathetic to Charleston, not less. In it, Davidson spins a little story about working in the Charleston Library Society, hearing the noise of a military parade, going out to watch with the librarians (Miss Mazyck and Miss Bull), reflecting on old regiments and their modern transformations, noticing and deprecating the eroticism of the drum majorettes. He has dinner with someone he calls "Mr. Charles," in a room with portraits of colonial and Revolutionary ancestors on the walls, and they discuss the vulgar novelty of North Charleston. Back at the Library Society, Davidson continues to muse on history. He speaks of Charleston's traditions, reaching back "continuously into its remote past," its continuity of "family, of family life, and family position—irrespective of economic status—[which] was in fact a great distinction of Charleston among old American cities; for elsewhere that continuity had been generally broken by one cause or another." He writes of its stability, the subtle balance of persistence and innovation: "The secret of Charleston's stability, if it was any secret, was only the old Southern principle that material considerations, however important, are means not ends, and should always be subdued to the ends they are supposed to serve, should never be allowed to dominate, never be mistaken for ends in themselves." He characterizes the Old South as "chivalrous, courteous, religious, conservative, and stable." He complains of modernity's alienating habit of abstraction. He argues—this is something of a trick—that drum majorettes are evidence of this abstraction. He goes on to invoke all the horrors of the modern world, among which are "the Communist Manifesto, the Atlantic Charter, and the reports of the President's committees on education, civil rights, and the like." By the penultimate paragraph, he has so warmed to his theme that he announces: "The terrible results of this process are visible throughout the world. Everywhere one looks there are ruins—the ruins of societies no less than the ruins of cities. Over the ruins stream mobs led by creatures no longer really human— creatures who, whether they make shift to pass as educators, planners, editors, commissars, or presidents, wield batons, dance dances, and flaunt their naked abstractions with exactly the same inappropriateness and destructiveness as does the drum majorette." He ends with a faint hope that Charleston may be able to resist these horrors, that it has a better chance than many.[24]

This apocalyptic explosion reflects the very bad mood Davidson was in by 1948, one which would worsen during the 1950s, when he ended up running a Tennessee version of a Citizens Council. The ground on which he was able to stand had grown so narrow that the strain was telling. In 1932, when he had written so lightly about Charleston, he had, at least, the community which was the Agrarians. By 1948, that was gone. He belonged to few things to which he wished to belong. In Charleston, he saw people belonging, even with a hope of resisting the horrors he saw in modernity. It gave him some satisfaction to see this, but much more anger, not at Charleston, but at what Charleston reminded him was wrong with the modern world, and (one suspects) with himself, an unwilling citizen of that world.

This problem of Charleston and alienation, tradition and literature, was to be summed up in 1968—from Tate's standpoint, not Davidson's— ironically by a Charlestonian, Louis Rubin. His essay, "Southern Literature: A Piedmont Art," is one of the more notable acts of parricide or matricide in Southern literary scholarship. In it, Rubin damns Charleston and the Low Country (and the Tidewater, for good measure) as sterile. He argues that all good modern Southern literature is a product of writers who lived at least a hundred miles from the coast. He explains this in various ways. The coast has had no universities of stature, and many modern Southern writers have been university-trained. Places like Charleston have bestowed a benign patronage upon culture and, by genteel kindness, prematurely stifled the sharp alienations which are necessary to creativity. Piedmont writers, on the other hand, were born in cultures which little valued them. Hence Wolfe was a better writer than Heyward, because Wolfe's mother ran a boarding house and Heyward's mother wrote poetry. Moreover, the fructifying theme of Southern literature was change, the transition from old to new, rural to urban, traditional to modern. Places like Charleston were already urban, yet not modern.[25]

This is a passionate essay, probably one of the more revealing in Rubin's oeuvre. If one examines the record of Southern literature from a neo-Agrarian standpoint, its reasoning makes a certain sense, though a European will find unpersuasive the proposition that the presence of culture incapacitates the continuing vitality of culture. But Rubin does help to lay bare the crucial issue of Charleston's relationship to much modern Southern thought. Consider the three standpoints I have just described. Tate had argued that a balance of alienation and belonging produced the best literature. Rubin seems to believe that alienation is the driving force of literature. Davidson abhorred alienation and wished for belonging. Charleston was a pawn in this game, for Charleston stood unambiguously for belonging, for continuity.

At least, for many non-Charlestonians, Charleston stood for belonging and continuity. To look at such writings is to get an impression of a Charleston which was unreflecting, self-besotted, dining in front of ancestral portraits at idiosyncratic hours of the day. This Charleston was beside the point of modern Southern culture, whether that culture was being defined by sociologists like Odum or modernist writers like Tate and Faulkner. Even Margaret Mitchell used Charleston as little more than a dreamy refuge, to which—at will—Rhett Butler might return to find the world's remnant of grace and charm, that is, a place without the vulgarities of Scarlett O'Hara. In this image of Charleston, Southerners saw a city in amber, immobilized. Given that the essential problem of modern Southern thought has been the comprehension of change, it is no wonder that Charleston was deemed a pretty irrelevance.

Of course, this external image was wrong, both as to Charleston's present and its past. In 1930 as in 1850, Charleston was changing, understood it was changing, thought about it, wrote about it. But the *quality* of that change did mark Charleston off from the South inhabited by Allen Tate and Donald

Davidson. Tate, though he hoped for better, believed that the Southern tradition was all but dead. The famously ambivalent, not to say obscure, conclusion to his "Remarks on the Southern Religion" in *I'll Take My Stand*—"How may the Southerner take hold of his Tradition? The answer is, by violence"—could not, I would venture, have been written by a Charlestonian in 1930. No more could a Charlestonian have written, as Tate did, "Since he cannot bore from within, he has left the sole alternative of boring from without."[26] For a Charlestonian had a tradition, had a city, was within and not without.

In one sense, Rubin was right, not in representing Southern literature but in representing the standards by which it has been canonized. Those standards have been defined more by people with a fugitive grip on tradition, people who moved from alienation towards literary images of belonging, by people like Tate and Faulkner. This has not been the position of the modern Charlestonian. This does not mean, necessarily, that the writing of modern Charlestonians has been inferior, but it does mean that critics like Tate had little chance of sympathizing with Charlestonian writing, for such literature was outside their experience, did not address their problem. For, however much Tate may have spoken of Southern tradition and celebrated the value of unthinking belonging, however often he may have echoed T. S. Eliot on the curse of the modern dissociation of sensibility, Tate invariably chose alienation when faced with a choice between alienation and belonging, because alienation was his experience of life. If Allen Tate had inherited an eighteenth-century house and borne the name of an ancestor who had signed the Declaration of Independence, instead of having his brother Ben buy for him, for a very few years, a ramshackle house on the Cumberland River, we would have had a very different theory about what creates great Southern literature.

Most Charlestonians, by contrast, have chosen belonging.[27] What is important to stress, what Tate and Rubin seem to misunderstand, is that Charlestonians have been fully aware of the choice. They just chose differently. Their circumstances made it very difficult to do otherwise. Being given an intact tradition and being given a broken one are different things.

This choice is neatly exemplified in a neglected novel of DuBose Heyward, *Peter Ashley*, published in 1932. It is not a novel which has received much attention, except by scholars of Heyward.[28] It is not fiction for which one can make great claims, but a pleasantly written historical novel about the great secession winter, neatly fashioned, intelligent, better than many of its conventional devices of plot (the fiery belle, the ambivalent aristocrat, the duel) might suggest. Most relevant, however, is that *Peter Ashley* is a meditation on alienation and belonging.

In it, a young Peter Ashley returns in late 1860 from his education at Oxford. He wishes to be a writer, to revive and strengthen the literary tradition of Charleston, to add to the lustre of Simms, James Legaré, Gildersleeve, Timrod, and Hayne. He is unsure about the merits of secession, inclined to Unionism in the spirit of James Louis Petigru and his uncle Pierre Chardon, who has been (in effect) his guardian and raised him to be an intellectual distant from and skeptical of society's demands. For a while, Ashley manages to keep that distance, to avoid joining a regiment, even to manage silence on the pressing issue of the day. He has several ambivalent confrontations with the institution of slavery, incidents which balance cruelty against paternalism. This private story is interwoven with the public events of the Ordinance of Secession and the siege of Fort Sumter. Eventually, Ashley accepts the logic of his culture and joins the army of the new republic of South Carolina, and also wins the girl. He does this at the sacrifice of his detachment, even his intellectuality.

There are several themes at work in this plot. One of them complicates my purposes, for Heyward argues that war itself makes individualism irrelevant, requires the surrendering of critical distance. "Always as a prelude to war there comes a time when the rhythm of the life of a people changes," Heyward writes. "A man sensitive to such influences can almost mark the hour that saw the passing of the old, the arrival of the new. Before this moment isolated events possess the power to disturb the forward measured swing of time, but the dominant beat persists. Destiny, while it is not subject to the will of the people, is at least influenced by it. Then suddenly the rhythm quickens. The human equation disappears. It is the event that determines destiny. . . . [F]or the individual the final moment of decision has arrived. There is no turning back. There is no standing still. He must conform or he must be destroyed."[29] Still, war is only the most dramatic instance of a permanent and deeper ambivalence for the intellectual, whether to choose the loneliness of skepticism or the warmth of conformity. Petigru is given a speech which explains the matter, of how and why Charleston tolerates the dissident.

> "My dear fellow, I am invaluable. I cannot even play the martyr. Like your uncle, I am of the Clan. We are too old to fight, anyway, and so instead of becoming dangerous, we are merely

eccentric. We are allowed to say what we please. Our resignations have not been requested by one of our clubs. We fulfill a civic function—we are Charleston's excuse for considering itself broadminded. If anyone accuses them of intolerance, they have merely to say, 'Intolerant? Ridiculous!—why, there's Petigru, there's Chardon.'"

Peter could not help laughing. "And you don't mind being alone?" he queried.

"I rather like it. Old age, my boy, and the crystallization of a naturally cantankerous nature. But it is different for you. Youth must run with the pack, or die of loneliness."[30]

In the end, Ashley refuses the loneliness, the skepticism. "Why theorize?" he asks himself at the end of the novel. "Theories were for those who had nothing at stake. As for himself, for St. John's, for South Carolina, they had created a life that was completely satisfactory, that had beauty, harmony, dignity, continuity. It was theirs. They asked only the right to enjoy their own, undisturbed."

In this novel, the choice is starkly put. Heyward offers the alternatives only of lonely detachment or mindless belonging. Perhaps in a novel of peacetime Charleston, he might have put it less severely. After all, in the novel, Ashley's exemplars—the John Russell's Bookshop set—surrender their independence to the needs of war, which means that in peace they had some independence. Still, the message is clear. Stay in the clan, or be destroyed. What distinguishes Heyward from Tate, *Peter Ashley* from *The Fathers*, is that Heyward had a clan. Indeed I suspect this novel can only be read with full appreciation from within the clan of the Charleston tradition. It has too many laconic Charlestonian touches. In Davidson's account of dinner in Charleston, the portraits on the wall are abstractly colonial and Revolutionary. In *Peter Ashley*, they are familial:

> Peter paused upon the threshold of the big Charleston drawing room and looked about him with that impersonal appraisal that only a protracted absence can render possible. He saw now in the familiar apartment with its Adam decorations, its mellow portraits, its dim, warm brocades, an intrinsic beauty that enhanced immeasurably his natural pleasure in the familiar setting. Grandfather Chardon was still an ancestor, but he was

also a Romney; and the two stiff little girls who had looked down upon his adolescent wonderings with prim disapproval were not only great-aunts Katherine and Amanda, but Thomas Sully at his best.

Indeed, it is this tone of warmth, almost of sensuality, which most characterizes Heyward's description of the Charleston tradition. On landing at the Harbor, for example, Ashley is met by various relatives: "There were Warings, Gadsdens, Rhetts, Elliotts, names that sang in his memory like old tunes. The lovely girl in the scarlet turban and modish barcelona, who dimpled up at him and wagered that he'd never guess her identity, turned out to be his cousin, Alicia Pringle."[31] These names—Romney, Sully, Waring, Elliott—invoke many images for those accustomed to Charleston, very few for those outside the clan.

So, no less than many other Southerners, Charlestonians deliberated the choice between alienation and belonging. Unlike many other Southerners, who spoke so much of place and the concrete, however, Charlestonians had a place which was exquisitely, sometimes excruciatingly, concrete. It was in the names, the cousins, the paneling, the marriages, the portraits, the institutions of the city. That this specificity was sometimes bemusing to the non-Charlestonian is exemplified in a letter written by Davidson to Josephine Pinckney in 1930. She had sent to him an essay on Southern conservatism, which was eventually to be published in the Chapel Hill symposium *Culture in the South*. She had expressed uneasiness, it seems, that her essay was too grounded in her experience of the Carolinas and Virginia, too little sensitive to other Souths. Davidson swept such considerations aside. "The South," he reassured her, "is pretty much the same everywhere, in spite of local diversities. It is just more so, here; and less so, there."[32] Pinckney, in her revision of the essay, borrowed a few of Davidson's anecdotes and offered not a few generalizations about Southern culture, but her essay is also notable for assembling characterizations of particular Southern locales: Birmingham, Chattanooga, New Orleans, Vicksburg, Richmond, and others. She refers to them as marking "local divergences," but her brief sketches show more care for idiosyncrasy than Davidson would have thought necessary to manage. On Charleston, for example, she wrote: "Charleston seems a trifle more austere [than New Orleans] in spite of its sunny climate and sub-tropical flowers; the English culture absorbed the French to a surprising degree, and after all the Huguenot was the French Puritan. Her peculiarities—and the South considers her most peculiar—are sympathetic to neither French nor American culture."

Charleston was an intact, but a weakened tradition. Josephine Pinckney understood that, for Charlestonians, "the economic pressure ... is very real."[33] The problem for her and DuBose Heyward's generation was how to effect change, while restoring and preserving tradition. The houses were still there, but they were rotting. Doubtless their generation could have chosen differently, could have chosen alienation and thereby have let the thing die. They need not have bothered with the task of historic preservation and allowed the Joseph Manigault House to disintegrate; its gatehouse could still be a gas-station rest room.[34] They might have focused more resolutely on the consoling anguish of modernist words. But they did not, perhaps at the price of their membership in the canon of modern literature. I doubt that, in full knowledge of this fate, they would have chosen differently.

But the critical standards which have marginalized Charleston are not immortal. It is becoming fair to hazard that the neo-Agrarian interpretation of Southern literature is in decline, perhaps moribund. The canon of Southern literature begins to change, to take previously marginal voices more seriously, most obviously the female and the black. To put it politely, the relevance of Nashville to these themes is modest. But the relevance of Charleston in the 1920s and 1930s, oddly enough for so elite a white culture, is much greater. For one thing, its interest in landscape and preservation is likely to seem less quaint to a younger generation reared on the environmental movement. For another, an unusual number of Charlestonian writers were women, and one of the great ventures of the city's literature was representing black culture. Whatever one may make of *Porgy*, it was an attempt at such a representation. For the business of Southern criticism in the next generation—above all, comprehending the relations between genders and races—Charleston may prove less irrelevant than it was made to seem in 1930.

NOTES

1. Howard W. Odum, *An American Epoch: Southern Portraiture in the National Picture* (New York: Henry Holt, 1930), 17–18, 22–23, 31, 35, 49, 42, 247.

2. Rupert B. Vance, *Human Geography of the South: A Study in Regional Resources and Human Adequacy* (Chapel Hill: University of North Carolina Press, 1932), 508.

3. The record of the Institute for Research in Social Science was better, if one considers South Carolina as a whole, not just Charleston. But, even here, the state tended to be viewed as a quaint survival, especially in its black culture. See, for example, Guion Griffis Johnson, *A Social History of the Sea Islands, with Special Reference to St. Helena Island, South Carolina* (Chapel Hill: University of North Carolina Press, 1930); Guy Benton Johnson, *Folk Culture on St. Helena Island, South Carolina* (Chapel Hill: University of North Carolina Press, 1930); and Newbell Niles Puckett, *Folk Beliefs of the Southern Negro* (Chapel Hill: University of North Carolina Press, 1926). South Carolina was sometimes included in the Institute's various studies of mill factories.

4. Cash was born in Gaffney, S.C., but made his adult mark as a North Carolinian.

5. W. J. Cash, *The Mind of the South* (1941; New York: Alfred A. Knopf, 1969), 95–96.

6. Ibid., 385–86.

7. Though, since Daniels was touring Southern cities, almost every major city did.

8. An epitaph that went through many versions, before it satisfied Petigru's memorialist and daughter. See James Petigru Carson, *Life, Letters, and Speeches of James Louis Petigru* (Washington, DC: W. H. Lowdermilk, 1920), 477–88.

9. Jonathan Daniels, *A Southerner Discovers the South* (New York: Macmillan, 1938), 324–33.

10. John Tyree Fain and Thomas Daniel Young, eds., *The Literary Correspondence of Donald Davidson and Allen Tate* (Athens: University of Georgia Press, 1974), 79.

11. Louise Cowan, *The Fugitive Group: A Literary History* (1959; Baton Rouge: Louisiana State University Press, 1968), 130, 137, 149, 223.

12. Donald Davidson, "An Author Divided Against Himself," (1929) and "Stark Young and Others," (1929) in Donald Davidson, *The Spyglass: Views and Reviews*, ed. John Tyree Fain (Nashville, TN: Vanderbilt University Press, 1963), 29–39; Allen Tate, "DuBose Heyward," (1924) in Ashley Brown and Frances Neel Cheney, eds., *The Poetry Reviews of Allen Tate, 1924–1944* (Baton Rouge: Louisiana State University Press, 1983), 15–17.

13. DuBose Heyward and Hervey Allen, *Carolina Chansons: Legends of the Low Country* (New York: Macmillan, 1924).

14. Cowan, *Fugitive Group*, 114–16.

15. Harriet Monroe, "Comment: This Southern Number," *Poetry* 22 (April 1922): 33.

16. Davidson, *Spyglass*, 31–32.

17. Fain and Young, *Correspondence of Davidson and Tate*, 191–92.

18. Brown and Cheney, *Poetry Reviews of Allen Tate*, 17.

19. John Crowe Ransom, "Modern with the Southern Accent," (1935) quoted in Michael O'Brien, *The Idea of the American South, 1920–1941* (Baltimore, MD: Johns Hopkins University Press, 1979), 132.

20. His reaction is deceptive, because our evidence is a letter to Josephine Pinckney, his hostess, to whom he was obliged to be polite. See Donald Davidson to Josephine Pinckney, 6 November 1927, Josephine Pinckney Papers, South Carolina Historical Society, Charleston. (I am grateful to Stephen Hoffius for bringing this manuscript collection to my attention.)

21. Fain and Young, *Correspondence of Davidson and Tate*, 272.

22. See William H. Pease and Jane H. Pease, *The Web of Progress: Private Values and Public Styles in Boston and Charleston, 1828–1843* (New York: Oxford University Press, 1985), and idem., "Intellectual Life in the 1830s: The Institutional Framework and the Charleston Style," in O'Brien and Moltke-Hansen, *Intellectual Life*, 233–54.

23. Evelyn Waugh, *Brideshead Revisited: The Sacred and Profane Memoirs of Captain Charles Ryder*, 5th ed. (1945; London: Chapman & Hall, 1947), 239.

24. Donald Davidson, "Some Day, in Old Charleston," (1949) in Donald Davidson, *Still Rebels, Still Yankees and Other Essays* (1957; Baton Rouge: Louisiana State University Press, 1972), 213–27.

25. "Southern Literature: A Piedmont Art," (1969) in Louis D. Rubin, Jr., *William Elliott Shoots a Bear: Essays on the Southern Literary Imagination* (Baton Rouge: Louisiana State University Press, 1975), 195–212. Harlan Greene reminds me that, in fact, Heyward's mother also ran a boarding house: see Frank Durham, *DuBose Heyward, the Man Who Wrote* Porgy (Columbia: University of South Carolina Press, 1954), 7.

26. Allen Tate, "Remarks on the Southern Religion," in Twelve Southerners, *I'll Take My Stand: The South and the Agrarian Tradition* (New York: Harper, 1930), 174–75.

27. Which is not to deny the relevance of those Charlestonians who expressed that more complicated act of belonging, expatriation.

28. Useful is a chapter on it in William H. Slavick, *DuBose Heyward* (Boston: Twayne, 1981), 125–41; see also Rosellen Brown, "On DuBose Heyward's *Peter Ashley*," in David Madden and Peggy Bach, eds., *Classics of Civil War Fiction* (Jackson: University Press of Mississippi, 1991), 117–30. Heyward's biographer has a low opinion of the novel: see Durham, *DuBose Heyward*, 91–95.

29. DuBose Heyward, *Peter Ashley* (New York: Farrar & Rinehart, 1932), 102–3.

30. Ibid., 213.

31. Ibid., 52, 48.

32. Davidson to Pinckney, 12 July 1930, Pinckney Papers.

33. Josephine Pinckney, "Bulwarks Against Change," in W. T. Couch, ed., *Culture in the South* (Chapel Hill: University of North Carolina Press, 1934), 40–51 (quotations on 47 and 48).

34. Charles B. Hosmer, Jr., *Preservation Comes of Age: From Williamsburg to the National Trust, 1926–1949*, 2 vols. (Charlottesville: University Press of Virginia, 1981), 1:248.

ALLEN TATE

A review of a reprint of Allen Tate, *Essays of Four Decades* (1959; Wilmington, DE: Intercollegiate Studies Institute, 1999), in the *Times Literary Supplement* (June 9, 2000): 26.

It is about twenty years since Allen Tate died. A reissuing of the 1968 collected edition of his essays shows that, for some, he remains contemporary. The judgment is, perhaps, idiosyncratic. Tate's poems are still read, though for little beyond the compelling "Ode to the Confederate Dead." The will to explicate the modernist density of his verse has much slackened. Tate liked to make fun of the "Confederate prose" of his ancestors, but his own poetry could be ineffective, with lines such as "No more the white refulgent streets" and "Sad day at Oahu / When the Jap beetle hit!"[1] Critics and historians of American literature tend to see him, parenthetically and unfairly, as a minor figure in the story of American modernism or as an unreliable fringe member of the New Critics; in both cases, he is thought more interesting for the life he lived and those he knew. His letters are invariably published as a correspondence with someone else, never alone. On the whole, it has been the Southerners who have kept his memory most alive, a fact which would not please him unambiguously, for he made efforts to keep himself from being swallowed up by that tradition. In the arrangement of these essays, he carefully left his six causeries on Southern culture towards the end of a long book, so that the reader would be impressed by Tate the critic of John Donne and Dante, before encountering Tate the student of John C. Calhoun. He also carefully suppressed many of his early Southern writings.

The Southerners who continue to engage him have fallen into two camps. There are the conservatives who are heirs to the Agrarians of *I'll Take My Stand* of 1930; it is they who sponsor this reprint. But Tate was a very wayward cultural politician, who was at turns liberal, quasi-socialist and neo-conservative, and regarded a consistent politics as beside the point for a poet. Moreover, the chronology of his politics is inconvenient: when young he was a social conservative but an atheist, and when old he was a liberal but a Roman Catholic convert. Nonetheless, he is firmly if inaptly lodged in the American conservative tradition, somewhere between Albert Jay Nock and Ayn Rand.

Liberal historians and critics, too, have sustained him. There has been much recent writing on the modern Southern intellectual and literary tradition. In his few deceptively laconic essays on the South—especially "The Profession of Letters in the South" (1935) and "A Southern Mode of the Imagination" (1959)—Tate had offered the most cogent and influential interpretation of the trajectory of the Southern mind. Anyone who wanted to say something new had to engage with him. And refutation was not easy, for Tate was sinuously complex and persuasive. Indeed he was, arguably, the cleverest Southerner of his century and one who, self-consciously, knew that his authority would derive from venturing many genres: poetry, biography, criticism, autobiography. That is, Tate had long since learned the lesson of Coleridge. But there are signs that this engagement begins to die away. Michael Kreyling's *Inventing Southern Literature* (1998) may be the last major effort of this kind in wrestling with the author of *The Fathers*. Younger critics grow bored with these fights, conducted by men with grey hair or none, and the feminist scholars whose world the South must begin to inhabit care little for such fathers, clever or otherwise.

Essays of Four Decades is divided into five sections, which pay no heed to dates of composition. One can jump, in a few pages, from 1952 to 1928 and then to 1949, which makes consistency elusive to discern. The first section consists of programmatic essays on the function of the critic and the nature of literature. Roughly, these placed Tate in the same camp as his mentor John Crowe Ransom (to whom the book is dedicated) and, less consistently, I. A. Richards. Literature is "the complete knowledge of man's experience," but cannot be carried into the world and is hence inutilitarian; it tells us who we are, not what we must do. Hence politics was the death of poetry, possibly of culture itself. The second section offers case studies of, among others, the metaphysicals (Donne), the Romantics (Keats), and the modernists (Yeats, Pound). Tate leaned to the metaphysicals, as had his friend Cleanth Brooks, but he was surprisingly sympathetic to the Romantics, and indeed said, "I, too, insofar as I am a poet, am a romantic poet." As a disciple of Eliot, Tate most identified with high modernism, though he preferred the term "contemporary." Form made meaning but not necessarily quality, so the critic had much discretion of judgment, which Tate exercised freely, even quirkily.[2]

The third section is least coherent; an essay on Poe, a group on three types of imagination (angelic, symbolic, unilateral), plus discussions of Eliot, Longinus, Johnson, and a defense of awarding Pound the Bollingen Prize, despite his anti-Semitism. The fourth section is his Southern pieces and the fifth reprints the prefaces to previous collections, beginning with the *Reactionary Essays on Poetry and Ideas* of 1936. The predominant theme is borrowed from Eliot; wholeness has been lost from human experience and we have only fragments, which we engage with a spirit broken by the advance of secular modernity, but an art which fleetingly reassembles meaning.

How do the essays read now? The old strengths are still visible: range, trenchancy, seriousness. The old contempts continue to be jarring: "the insincerity of the academic mind," the poverty of historicism, the immorality of science and sociology. His instinct as a critic remains convincing: the claims in his time for Poe, Dickinson, Eliot, Crane, and Pound vindicate Tate's judgments now, even if those for John Peale Bishop and Herbert Read do not. His mysticism about "the man of letters" has worn badly; Tate's self-important solemnity about the specialness of poetic knowledge has not so much been refuted, as lost in the tendency to see all knowledge as special and isolated. What is striking now, though, is how uneven and insecure was his prose. He aspired to be a mandarin writer, who should tell us what to think, we trusting to his erudition and discrimination. But he backed away from this tone with bizarre frequency. "We have no critical method"; "historical generalizations are beyond my competence"; "I have never considered myself much of a literary critic"; "I myself am a parasite dangling from a small twig of [scholars'] tree of knowledge"; "I blush in the presence of philosophers." He spoke of having "no talent for research" and "inadequate scholarship," and of having "to learn as I went along."[3] Some of this was an almost-Edwardian gentlemanly condescension for professionals, some was a sly denial of talents for which he had contempt. But the insecurity was real and came, perhaps partly from a mangled childhood, partly from an unstable life, which eventually took him unhappily into the English department at the University of Minnesota, which was no way for a Southern seer to live. The effect was to make his prose often congested and pretentious, unclear, and sometimes self-defeating. It got worse as he aged. Nonetheless, intelligence marked everything he did. He played a deeper game than his readers knew and, not only for those who love a puzzle, his persistence is assured.

NOTES

1. Allen Tate, *Essays of Four Decades* (1959; Wilmington, DE: Intercollegiute Studies Institute, 1999), 579; "Elegy: Jefferson Davis, 1808–1889" and "Ode to Our Young Pro-Consuls of the Air," in Allen Tate, *Poems* (Chicago, IL: Swallow Press, 1961), 89, 98.

2. Tate, *Essays*, 210, 452, 223.

3. Ibid., 143, 159, 229, 235, 448, 596, 579, 624.

These two pieces are, firstly, a commentary on Anne Goodwyn Jones, "The Cash Nexus," in Charles W. Eagles, ed., *The Mind of the South: Fifty Years Later* (Jackson: University Press of Mississippi, 1992), 51–57, both of which were given at the University of Mississippi's 1991 Porter L. Fortune Symposium to mark the fiftieth anniversary of the publication of W. J. Cash, *The Mind of the South* (New York: Alfred A. Knopf, 1941); and, secondly, a review of Paul D. Escott, ed., *W. J. Cash and the Minds of the South* (Baton Rouge: Louisiana State University Press, 1992), in *Journal of Southern History* 60, no. 2 (May 1994): 430–32. Reprinted by permission.

Anne Jones presents us with an unwonted Wilbur Cash. One is accustomed to think of the Carolinian in company with the likes of Thomas Wolfe or James Agee, to think of him in disordered press rooms, or sitting rapt and frustrated before an old battered typewriter, or lying stupefied with whisky in a bedroom of his parents' home. This Cash is an old familiar, comforting, crumpled. But Jones's Cash is quite another thing, spanking and modern, with no Panama hat but a smart French suit, a man with a glass of lucid Montrachet in his hand and the keys of a new Citroen in his pocket, a man talking sinuously of hegemony and fissures in a text. Is this plausible? Or, rather, since I would not wish to stand condemned as a positivist by speaking baldly of matters of fact, is this persuasive?

Any canonical author has to be read variously by differing generations as the price of survival. We live in a theoretical age, in which the inscriptions of ideology matter greatly. If Cash is to survive, a bargain must be struck between him and a different generation of Southerners, to whom Althusser might matter as much as, if not more than, Jonathan Daniels. It is to Jones's credit that she understands the necessity for this renegotiation. She has struck the most original note of any I have heard in this long year of anniversary.

What does this renegotiated Cash look like? He is a Marxist, parallel to the school of Gramsci. He is aware of genre and the subversive power of language. He is political, close to revolutionary. He is a theoretician, who challenges positivism. He is a son of the patriarchy, an admirer of energy and virile success.

Is Cash a Gramscian? If we define the essence of Gramscianism as, first, the broadening of the scope of Marxism by infusing it with Croce's Hegelianized idealism and, second, the elaboration of a sociology for the social influence of intellectuals and ideology, the answer might be yes. If we loosen that definition further and define Gramscianism as a meditation on the relationship between material conditions and *mentalité*, the answer is yes; Cash was interested in a similar meditation and came up with some cognate reflections. In this loose sense, a parallel between Gramsci and Cash helps us to locate Cash in the philosophical spectrum, to see that he stands more in the camp of people like Gramsci than, say, Swedenborg. But is the parallel worth more than this gesture of identification? I doubt it. I particularly doubt Jones's contention that Cash was "Marxist to the core." For the kinds of Marxism with which she attempts to associate Cash—those of Althusser and Gramsci—are not themselves central to the materialist tradition of Marxism, but heresies from or improvements upon it, depending on your standpoint. There is so much Hegelianism at *this* Marxist core, that to locate Cash there leaves his analytical status less, not more clear.

Even at the level of personality and character, the parallel of Gramsci and Cash is unconvincing. While it is true they shared sickly childhoods, in adult life they could not have been more different. Gramsci was lean, ascetic, unsentimental, ruthless, and prepared to make sacrifices for his creed. He led protesters at the gates of FIAT, commanded a great political party, was incarcerated because Mussolini feared the power of his mind. His ideology was rooted in the cool judgment which is concerned with action. Wilbur Cash was tubby, hedonistic as far as he could manage it, prone to crying with emotion, was the sort of person who goes to watch a labor strike not lead one, and probably could not have drowned a kitten let alone a capitalist. Wilbur Cash did not know the meaning of action, and (perhaps to his credit) did not have a mind which anyone needed to fear.

Moreover, Cash was a Southerner and Gramsci, I think, was not. It is true that he came from Sardinia, which some including Gramsci have included under the category "Mezzogiorno," which in Italian implies south because it means midday, the time when the sun shines. Sardinia, however, held an ambivalent status in the regionalisms of Italy; the island half faced towards Naples and Sicily, half faced the Piedmont with which it had been politically united under the House of Savoy before unification. Mostly, Sardinia faced inward, with little sense of identification with Italy, with an idiosyncratic history and political economy strongly marked by its long association with Spain.[1] Of that ambivalent status, Gramsci was aware. His 1926 essay on "Some Aspects of the Southern Question" bears its traces. At one point he includes Sardinia in the South, though in the same breath he makes a distinction: "The South can be defined as a great social disintegration. The peasants, who make up a great majority of its population, have no cohesion among themselves (of course, some exceptions must be made: Apulia, Sardinia, Sicily, where there exist special characteristics within the great canvas of the South's structure)." Later he elaborates on the distinctiveness of Sardinia: "The only region where the war veterans' movement took on a more precise profile, and succeeded in creating a more solid social structure, was Sardinia. And this is understandable. Precisely because in Sardinia the big landowner class is very exiguous, carries out no function, and does not have the ancient cultural and government traditions of the mainland South."[2]

But Gramsci himself was at great pains to shed any identity with the island. He faced towards Turin, where he went to university, where he worked and agitated. Certainly Gramsci was sensitive to the problem of the Mezzogiorno and his 1926 essay made a marked contribution towards reordering attitudes towards the social and political problem of the South. But, if one examines the rhetoric of that essay, the conviction grows that Gramsci was no Southerner. Throughout he speaks of the South and Southern intellectuals as the other, as something else, a phenomenon to be understood and challenged. He, Gramsci, is not a Southern intellectual, shows no interest even in claiming the status of an expatriate from the South. His identification is expressed when he talks of himself or, more commonly, of "us," who are "the Turin Communists." Thus he talks of Piero Gobetti serving as a link between the Turin Communists and the Southern intellectuals, between "us" and them.[3] And it was this same Gobetti who, from that mediating position, was to observe that Gramsci "seemed to have come from the country to forget his traditions, to substitute for the diseased inheritance of Sardinian anachronism an enclosed and inexorable effort towards the modernity of the city dweller."[4] So, on the whole, I am inclined to relieve Cash of the keys to that new Citroen, and allow that, at best, he might have taken the odd spin in an old Alfa Romeo, though far less often than he rode in a Chevrolet.[5]

What about the Montrachet? Would Cash, gazing towards the externalized plumbing of the Beaubourg Centre, be at home in the cafés of Les Halles? What was Cash's understanding of genre and language? Was or is his book "a nexus in which questions of fact and rhetoric are inseparably linked through the mediation of ideology"? The problem is that any text is such a nexus. *The Mind of the South, the Prison Notebooks, Alice in Wonderland*, the Manhattan telephone directory, all can answer present if we ask, is there a nexus in the room? That does not diminish the usefulness of Jones's insight, only its particularity. If, however, we ask a historical question, did Cash *intend* to subvert language and genre? I am inclined to answer yes to genre, no to language. I do think Cash intended to muddle the line between genres; he wrote history, sociology, journalism, fiction, sermon, all in the one book. I doubt he did this in full analytical self-awareness, by sitting down and saying to himself, "Today I shall deconstruct genre." But I think he had his story to tell, this rhetoric he painfully loved, and the discretions of genre did not bother him, had to be swept aside if the story and the rhetoric were to be expressed.

As to language, I think Jones misreads *The Mind of the South*. I doubt that Cash had any sense that language, words, metaphor, were subversive and unstable. On the contrary, his text cries out that words are to be trusted. Indeed they may have been the only thing Wilbur Cash did trust. Which is not to say he did not understand that reality was fluid, often indistinct, full of shadows and ambiguity, but I am convinced he felt that words could capture it, that reality in all its nuance could be expressed in language. He knew it was difficult, he found it in fact agonizing, but his agony did not reside in the sense that the venture was impossible, only in the fear that he might prove inadequate, as he had on that night with the coed.

Was his language political and revolutionary? Certainly he offered a swingeing condemnation of his culture and, on the whole, has spoken more to Southern liberals than to conservatives. One finds little of Cash in the literary criticism of the neo-Agrarian school, in Cleanth Brooks, Louis Rubin, C. Hugh Holman, and Lewis P. Simpson. Donald Davidson gave the book a fierce review on its publication.[6] Richard Weaver in 1964, it is true, expressed agreement with Cash's contention that "the Southern mind is one of the most intransigent on earth," but only cautiously to celebrate the fact.[7] Yet reform—let alone revolution—ought to be an act of creation, as well as destruction. Cash knew what he did not like, but had little precise idea of the social order which might emerge if his demolitions were successful. He admired critical thinking, but more for the excitement of the process, less for the ends. So, while I agree that he had a vision which was "in the direction of diversity, equality, and liberty" because he thought to inhabit such a world would be more interesting and less constraining, I do not think one can find in his writings a description of that world.[8] Would blacks be equal, unsegregated? Would women be freed from the role of the belle and the matron? Would society be agnostic? Would science be unfettered? Who knew? Certainly not Cash. And, to be fair to him, given his belief in the power of the savage ideal, it would have been wasted energy for him to have speculated and planned for such a world. It was not going to happen.

The trouble is, some of it has happened. Did Cash help this? Woodward has firmly said, no, *The Mind of the South* has incapacitated subversion and must be retired to the back benches of Southern thought if the business of change is to go forward. On this point, I think Woodward was right. Cash has been most admired by those of modest political agendas and of conservative epistemologies. He has had little to do with civil rights, the single greatest transformation in Southern life since 1941, and absolutely nothing to do with that other—far less complete—motion, feminism. The various conferences held this year have made the fact abundantly clear, that Wilbur Cash has almost nothing to say to blacks and women. For them, he is part of the problem of Southern culture, not—as his admirers think—the solution. Jones's paper reinforces this impression, explicitly by identifying his patriarchalism, implicitly by generously inscribing on his illegible theory a few inscriptions which postmoderns might sympathetically read. It is a generosity which I doubt too many of her feminist contemporaries share.

But Jones addresses something more subtle than explicit politics, language. I agree with her that Cash's prose and his politics are seamless, but I read both as more conservative than she does. Was his prose modernist? Perhaps, in some of his themes. But the rhetoric? Cash has always reminded me more of Charles Dickens than T. S. Eliot, more of *Little Dorrit* than *The Four Quartets*. *The Mind of the South* is a great Victorian narrative, with choking sentiment, brooding melancholies, much conversation with the "dear reader," lots of weather and landscape. Like Dickens, Cash followed the aesthetic counsel that one should never let the pace slacken, never underestimate the power of death and mourning, never use one adjective when three will do. Whatever else it is, *The Mind of the South* is a tear-jerker. One reason he is less read today than in 1965 is that all the sad young men, who once came anxiously out of small Southern towns into the timid new world of an urban South, do not come in such numbers now, needing Cash to comprehend their predicament.

Once, of course, Cash was often read to offer a model to prose. Bruce Clayton still feels the dignity and inspiration of this *exemplum* and states his case in the *coda* of his biography.[9] But I suspect the biographer grows idiosyncratic in this admiration, because the norms of Southern prose have drastically changed since 1941. How many recent Southern writers write like Cash?

Marshall Frady, perhaps. Who else? This is not because, as Clayton implies, Cash was a *real writer* and others are mere pigmy academics, stumbling around with their pedantries. The recent South has many prose stylists fully the equal of Wilbur Cash. One of them, John Shelton Reed, is at this conference. Rather, it is that recent Southerners do not *want* to write like Cash. The tone now is leaner, more ironic, less evangelical. How many in this audience would urge an aspirant Southern author to model himself or (even more problematically) herself on Cash? He has gone the way of Thomas Wolfe. The South of Cash's prose is, for his successors, an interesting place to visit, but not somewhere they want to live.

. . .

It seems they had a donnybrook in Winston-Salem, when they sat down to consider the fiftieth anniversary of *The Mind of the South*. (I was at the other Cash conference in Mississippi, which by comparison seems to have been the quiet, staid one.) To the astonishment of the professors, the public came in droves, which created a heady atmosphere. Celebration turned to multicultural mayhem. Acting as a catalyst, Nell Painter bluntly said that Cash was a racist and a sexist. Mumbling among themselves about these claims, the older white men "were hesitant to address questions of sexism and racism publicly," but finally protested by declaring the necessity of historical context. There were complaints from the audience that there were no white women on the panels. The academics even flagellated themselves by observing that, thank God, Cash was not an academic and knew how to write. Hodding Carter took after young people for doing little but watch MTV and being ignorant of the South, its history, its mind, and everything else. As Larry Tise was moved to observe, this was a "*happening*." I wish I had been there. Failing that, to read Paul Escott's "Afterword," which must be one of the more indiscreet summaries of a conference on record, is some recompense. [10]

Even the essays are pretty good. Bruce Clayton, the laureate of the anniversary's remembrance, does an efficient biographical number. Raymond Gavins, with equal economy, sketches the history of segregation in North Carolina. Bertram Wyatt-Brown gets very technical about the type of clinical depression which may have carried Cash off ("recent neurological findings suggest that certain genetically controlled chemical compounds may induce the malfunctioning of the neurotransmitter, neuroendocrine, and automatic nervous systems in the brain"), has opposition-crushing footnotes from medical journals, and tells us that "Nordic mental care specialists" (these are people from Scandinavia, not blond psychiatrists in Gainesville) have concluded that "schizophrenia and depression are much more frequent illnesses in the relatives of artists, writers, scientists, and mathematicians than they are in the general populace."[11] Richard King continues his fascinating meditation on the relationship between Southern thought and the political philosophies of modernity, in what is probably the book's most original essay. Nell Painter, undaunted by the men's room, says that Cash could not imagine her (black, female, feminist, Freudian, educated) and so, let's stop reading him; along the way, she says a number of trenchant things. Elizabeth Jacoway, more quietly but more devastatingly, hazards that not only was Cash impotent with white women but probably slept with black whores, which helps to explain why the view of gender in *The Mind of the South* is so peculiar and insistent. David Hackett Fischer compares and contrasts Cash and James McBride Dabbs, for no evident reason other than that both wrote books about the South, one in 1941, the other in 1964; nonetheless, despite this oddity of conception, one learns from Fischer.

There are then some essays which appraise the evolution of Southern studies since 1941, at least on politics and economics. These must have been impossible assignments, which most of the essayists seem wisely to have circumscribed. Merle Black gives a brief version of the recent political history of the region, much of which he has himself written. Gavin Wright offers a brisk and cool guide to the economics of slavery, cotton mills, and the years between the World Wars; he ends with thoughts on the region's lack of economic homogeneity. Jack Kirby combines a selective tour of post-1941 historiography with, valuably, an assessment of the fluctuating reception of *The Mind of the South*, whose heyday was the 1960s and whose audience was as much Northern as Southern. C. Eric Lincoln reminisces about coming-of-age in Alabama and the North as a young intellectual and a member of what he describes as the "countermind" of the black South.

Reminiscence is what works best in this volume, because this is what is left to say. There is not much, if anything, now unmolested in the facts of Cash's interpretation of Southern history; very few even bother to defend him on that score, and the title of this book, with its plural *minds*, argues with his fundamental premise. The sources for writing his life are not ample and have been mined by two biographers; unless new manuscripts come to light, it is unlikely that much more can be added.

What remains is what the literary critics call reception theory—who read him, who was persuaded, who was indifferent. Many of the essayists speak to this. And the verdict of this volume is clear. White men of a certain age were once overwhelmed by the experience of reading him, and still feel a lingering affection, sufficient to be pained when he is attacked or dismissed. Black Southerners find little of use or are positively repulsed. Gavins politely notes that Cash "could not penetrate the veil" of black life. Lincoln remembers, "I was part of the South, Cash's South, but by Cash's definition, I was not a part of the southern mind. Nor could I ever be."[12] White Southern women, if Jacoway is any guide, seem to be politely amused, a little sorry for his inadequacies. Suddenly Cash's view of Southern history is shrunken to a white male fantasy. This does not bode well for his survival. Perhaps not even Wake Forest will have the conviction to summon a centenary gathering. But, if it does and the contributors promise to be equally contentious (and if I can be sprung from a Cornish nursing home), I would like to go.

NOTES

1. John M. Cammett, *Antonio Gramsci and the Origins of Italian Communism* (Stanford, CA: Stanford University Press, 1967), 11.

2. "Some Aspects of the Southern Question," [1926] in David Forgacs, ed., *An Antonio Gramsci Reader: Selected Writings, 1916–1935* (New York: Schocken Books, 1988), 178, 181.

3. Ibid., 184.

4. Piero Gobetti, *Scritti Politici* (Turin, 1960), 1003, quoted in James Joll, *Antonio Gramsci* (1977; New York: Penguin Books, 1978), 89.

5. In fact, I suspect the South/Mezzogiorno matter is inessential to Jones's argument, which centers more on techniques of representation than on the social conditions that might have formed the ideology of Cash and Gramsci.

6. "Mr. Cash and the Proto-Dorian South," (1941) in Davidson, *Still Rebels, Still Yankees and Other Essays*, 191–212.

7. George M. Curtis III and James J. Thompson, Jr., eds., *The Southern Essays of Richard M. Weaver* (Indianapolis, IN: Liberty Press, 1987), 229.

8. At least, not in *The Mind of the South*. His collected journalism might tell a different story.

9. Bruce Clayton, *W. J. Cash: A Life* (Baton Rouge: Louisiana State University Press, 1991), 192–222.

10. Paul D. Escott, ed., *W. J. Cash and the Minds of the South* (Baton Rouge: Louisiana State University Press, 1992), 252, 244.

11. Ibid., 44–45.

12. Ibid., 37, 227.

> The first of these pieces is a review of C. Vann Woodward, *The Future of the Past* (New York: Oxford University Press, 1989), in *Journal of American History* 77 (September 1990): 627–28. Copyright © Organization of American Historians. All rights reserved. Reprinted with permission. The second is an essay written to mark Woodward's death and published as "Making the South New: Sympathy and Scholarship in C. Vann Woodward," *Times Literary Supplement* (May 5, 2000): 17. I have restored the final paragraph, omitted by the *TLS* (presumably for reasons of space).

This is C. Vann Woodward's third collection of his essays and represents the sum of those published in about the last twenty years. The short introduction, brief prefaces to the book's six sections, and two essays (on Reconstruction and Robert Penn Warren) are new; the rest is a reprinting, though sometimes of pieces obscurely published.

Here we have Woodward in his various moods and roles. Throughout he is the elder statesman, giving advice, urging the longer view, resisting fashion, though this role is most evident in his writings of the late 1960s. (In fact, he seems to have been an elder statesman from quite a young age.) Collaterally he is the critic of an American society nurtured in isolation and habituated to the myths of innocence; this was a stance intimated in *The Burden of Southern History* (1960) but amplified in essays occasioned by Watergate and the bicentennial of the Declaration of Independence. With the notable exception of his article, "The Age of Reinterpretation" (1960), which cheerfully argued that nuclear weapons and the abolition of "free security" was forcing the United States into a period of "the fortuitous, the unpredictable, the adventitious, and the dynamic," his tone is sardonic about upheaval.[1] Woodward's message is sad ambivalence, a voice which says: we have seen this disaster before, calm down, we may just scrape by, damaged but wiser.

There is Woodward the comparative historian, urging others to compare, noting their efforts, doing a little himself. He reprints, for example, a lively 1978 consideration of slave emancipations and postwar reconstructions, a long review of Peter Kolchin's *Unfree Labor*, and a new essay which uses comparisons to chide a Reconstruction historiography bent upon celebrating the vitality of radicalism and so hard put to explain the failure of Reconstruction. That failure, Woodward insists here, was ineluctable. He doodles puckishly with assorted "counterfactual playbacks" to illustrate his gloomy conclusion that most (not all) in the great effort of Reconstruction was likely to be for naught.

There is Woodward the intellectual historian, pondering the origins of the Southern Renaissance, reviewing William Safire's novel *Freedom*, trying to defend and identify the nature of Mary Chesnut's achievement, and meditating on Robert Penn Warren's use of and attitude towards historical writing. As an offshoot, there are essays which offer a conservative defense of the belletristic tradition of historical literature which turns its face towards a wider public (mostly in the form of *laudationes* for Henry Adams, Francis Parkman, Richard Hofstadter, and David Potter). In these days of linguistic turns and handstands, these are not formidable as meditations on the aesthetic philosophy of history. But they do have the merit of being the testament of someone who once wrote a masterpiece of American historical literature, and has earned the right to dispense advice on narrative.

Woodward has, I suppose, passed beyond criticism into the canonical. Even his failings have interest. Yet I confess I opened this book with some trepidation, for I had detected a certain failing of his critical powers in recent years and wondered if such a collection would dispel or confirm a suspicion unfocused by stray reading of his periodical writing. In the twenty years and more covered by this volume, Woodward made himself one of our more important critics, certainly one of our most influential. If not a Sainte-Beuve, he has been at least a Leslie Stephen, taking up a middling position in the fastness of the *New York Review of Books*, chronicling the rough and the smooth, year in and year out. As a critic, he has had failings. He has taken refuge in paraphrase. His taste of books to be reviewed has sometimes been odd. He has been cagey, whimsical, and arch. He has buried strong opinions in throwaway turns of phrase, such that innocent authors can think themselves well reviewed by Woodward, when in fact they have been quietly excoriated. There are traces of all these qualities here.

And yet I finished the book with a higher regard for his latest years than when I started. For one thing, he has usually been wise enough not to use certain pieces, those in which he coasted, or those where his prophecies went awry. But mostly I was struck with the coherence and tenacity of his vision. Woodward is a historian who knows what he thinks, and has known it for a long time. And the vision is compelling. When not on form, it is true, he inclines to wagging the professorial finger at those who have unaccountably forgotten or misunderstood what Woodward somewhere said and explained. But when he is most serious, when the context is compelling and beyond minor intramural skirmishing, he has a gift of wisdom and ironic moral exhortation. It is not unuseful in this strenuously earnest and reborn-Victorian intellectual culture of ours to heed a little cynicism grounded in compassion. I am not sure Woodward has always been true to his gift as a historian, as a *writer* of history, for he somewhere and somehow abandoned that path. But these essays show a devoted attention to and care for the discipline of history, which he has served well.

...

C. Vann Woodward died at his home in Hamden, Connecticut, on December 17 of last year. He was ninety-one, so he had lived a little longer than even Leopold von Ranke. The parallel is not extravagant. Woodward helped to fashion the understanding of American history in this century; his peers were Frederick Jackson Turner, Charles Beard, Perry Miller, and perhaps few or no others. Certainly he was the pre-eminent scholar of the American South and, if historians were still considered eligible for Nobel Prizes, he might have followed William Faulkner to Stockholm. Few historians acquire a moral significance for their culture, though many affect to try. For a while in the 1950s and 1960s Woodward seemed to explain to Southerners who they had been and what they might become, at a time when the South was enacting the moral crisis of American life. Martin Luther King, Jr., at the Selma March of 1965 called Woodward's *The Strange Career of Jim Crow* (1955) the "historical Bible of the civil rights movement," which was hyperbole, but also a benediction.[2]

The shape of his intellectual career was complicated, being so long. He began as a Beardian and neo-populist, someone who mistrusted capitalism, wanted to break down class and racial barriers, and hoped to rehabilitate the radical tradition lost in the 1890s. He fraternized with socialists and Communists, had African American friends, and twice when young traveled to the Soviet Union. On the whole, class mattered more to him than race, and race mostly as an implication of class. In the 1930s he drifted into a doctorate at the University of North Carolina, the most liberal of Southern campuses, out of no vocation for history but because he had a passion to write a biography of Tom Watson, the Georgia populist. Yet, between 1938 and 1955, he published four books which redesigned modern Southern history; of these, *Origins of the New South, 1877–1913* (1951) was his masterpiece.

The older history had been an apology for the status quo. It had offered hagiographies of Civil War generals and benedictions upon segregation. It had applauded the alliance which the Southern political and economic order had contracted with Northern industrialism, at the cost of making a colonial economy, guaranteed by the disfranchisement of dissident blacks and poorer whites. Woodward, rather, looked with a cold eye on the planter class and its attendant bourgeoisie. He noticed that progress had been promised and celebrated, but somehow had never come, if the statistics of Southern poverty did not lie.

At the moral center of Southern history, Woodward located not Henry Grady or Woodrow Wilson but the Populists, whom he saw as intelligent radicals violently repressed by a ruthless appeal to white supremacy, men who then turned sourly racist in their defeat. So Woodward's were books sympathetic to those who suffered and scathing towards those who governed. They are funny, sad, and disillusioned, though Woodward always tried to see where there might have been hope and "forgotten alternatives."[3] Still bleaker critics thought he saw them too readily, but his was a conscious political choice, shrewdly made. The South which Woodward imagined was contested, usefully fragile. "Southerners," he insisted, "unlike other Americans, [have] repeatedly felt the solid ground of continuity give way under their feet." By the mid-1950s, the social order of the 1890s was beginning to unravel: the one-party system was fragmenting, the cotton economy was dying, the Brown decision of 1954 intimated the end of segregation. (Woodward himself had advised the NAACP on its brief before the Supreme Court.) What he called "the Bulldozer Revolution," the really-New South, seemed to pose the end of the South itself and its disappearance into the waiting abstractions of American homogeneity.[4]

All this left Woodward in danger of losing a subject matter pertinent to his times. His essays in that decade are elegiac, a preparation for obsolescence. "The Search for Southern Identity" (1958) begins, "The time is coming, if indeed it has not already arrived, when the Southerner will begin to ask himself whether there is really any longer very much point in calling himself a Southerner."[5] There is evidence that he started to look around for another topic. He became interested in comparative history, in foreign perceptions of American culture, and wrote even on American foreign relations. Indeed he was never to undertake a sustained piece of research or writing again, though he started and abandoned a history of Reconstruction, and dickered with a large study of racism. As a historian he began to lose direction, but the changes he feared and welcomed were his remaking. The civil rights movement placed the South in the center of the national debate, made the understanding of slavery and segregation a matter of urgency, and pushed the region's imaginative interpreters to the forefront. Books were dug up, which few had noticed: a reverie called *The Mind of the South* by a suicide called W. J. Cash, a memoir called *Lanterns on the Levee* by a failed Mississippi poet, an old conservative symposium called *I'll Take My Stand*, and some lectures given in Charlottesville in 1954 on the origins of the Jim Crow system.[6]

Before this, Woodward had been much respected by the cognoscenti, but not especially famous. Historians can be as accomplished and gifted as they can manage, but the times alone can make them into public figures, thought by many to be great. Southern history had long been a backwater, compared to Western history or Puritan studies. But, in the 1960s, Americans cared about the origins of the New South, because many wanted to kill and others to remake it. Advising them required Woodward to manage a delicate balance between self-criticism and patriotism. His *Thinking Back* (1986) has three epigraphs. The first is from his friend, Robert Penn Warren: "History is not truth. History is in the telling." The second is from Faulkner: ". . . you dont love because: you love despite; not for the virtues, but despite the faults." The third is from Chaucer's "The Parson's Prologue": "But trusteth wel, I am a southren man."

By 1961, Woodward was at Yale, which he made the headquarters of Southern history. He was writing significant essays, mostly mining the parallel between Reconstruction and the "second Reconstruction." From the pages of the *New York Review of Books*, he found a national audience. He accumulated sonorous honors. Almost above all, he continued to have many graduate students, who became the Praetorian Guard to his Marcus Aurelius and whom legend was to dub the best and the brightest. In fact, many were to be strangers to intellectual celebrity, but not a few became very significant historians, in their own right: Louis Harlan, Willie Lee Rose, James McPherson, and Bertram Wyatt-Brown from his Johns Hopkins days; Daniel Rodgers, Mills Thornton, Thomas Holt, Steven Hahn, and Barbara Fields from his time at New Haven. Woodward was not an iron mentor, who parceled out the minor pieces of his vision to be elaborated by disciples, but rather someone who offered guidance, experience, breathing room, and an example. The more so after the death of his only child Peter from cancer in 1969, students became a sort of family. Woodward was fiercely loyal to them, and (with the odd exception) they to him. This relationship offered the prospect of a legacy and Woodward very much wanted to survive, even after his retirement in 1978. "In America," he once wrote, "historians, like politicians, are out as soon as they are down. There is no comfortable back bench, no House of Lords for them."[7] To sustain relevance and postpone neglect meant he had to work. For this effort, he fortunately had a strong body and an iron will. So he continued to write and review, he presided over the *Oxford History of the United States*, he edited the journals of Mary Chesnut, he traveled frequently to conferences, he remained an astute dispenser of patronage, and he cast his net widely to charm and help younger historians: most of this he sustained almost to within half a year of his death.

Though Woodward had acquired many critics, he had the wit to understand that a civilized dialogue with them kept his synthesis alive. Yet such remarkable tenacity created a strange distortion. He was intellectually closer to the Progressive era than to the intellectual climate of the 1990s. He never really understood feminism, mistrusted multiculturalism, was little influenced by the "new social history," and was a stranger to postmodernist theory. To Woodward, narrative was an art, not a cultural construct, something you learned from Francis Parkman, not from tangled French theorists. This was unsurprising for a man born ten years before the death of Henry Adams. In all logic, Woodward ought long since to have been discarded by his hurrying juniors. But his vision had been subtle and complex: most could find something to like, something to use, and his penchant for irony made him sinuously available from many perspectives. And Woodward had self-consciously located himself in the tradition; it could not be spoken of without reference to him. No doubt, his death will lead to a sharp reassessment. It is probable that the youngest historians have respected Woodward, because older historians have told them to do so, not because Woodward's work speaks directly to them.

He was an unusual Southerner. He was agnostic about religion, he took little interest in sports, he seldom told stories off the printed page, he listened, and he was a mumbling public speaker. In conversation, he worked by deflections: a raised eyebrow, an ironic comment, an allusion, a slight smile. Those not alert to nuance could miss his contribution altogether, and those who went to his lectures often went away bemused at his legend. In dress, he was old-fashioned Ivy League—tweed jacket, tie, and pipe—but dapper. Albert Murray once said that Woodward looked like the local insurance salesman, but a small-town bank manager in 1950 might be more apt.[8] His manners were formal and courteous, but they did not invite familiarity. At least one of his former students called him "Mr. Woodward," as in Charlottesville they still speak of "Mr. Jefferson."

Once, at a historical convention, someone tried to invite himself to a dinner Woodward was planning. This presumption was stiffly rebuked, and Woodward turned to his companion to say, "But I do not *know* this person." So, he was no Jacksonian who celebrated the pell-mell, but a mandarin who was often acerbic towards the second-rate, a man who thought the modern university had abandoned serious standards of scholarship and tolerance. He was largely indifferent to the Southern popular culture which enchants those who relish Elvis impersonators. The catfish restaurant he disdained: "When I was young, we used to throw them back." Still, he liked an evening martini, traveled with a flask, and was not without curiosity. In Oxford, Mississippi, when an evening party was once winding down and a visit to a local club was proposed, he went along. (He was then in his mid-eighties.) It was packed, reverberating with a "retro chick band" called the Bouffants, who did old Motown numbers. The Ole Miss students parted gravely to let the apparition of an ancient gentleman gain a view, and for a respectable time he stayed, smiling and puzzled.

Of all the pasts, he was least interested in narrating his own. He preferred to be a little mysterious and inaccessible. Unlike most Southerners, who talk about family without prompting, he was reticent about his own origins. The nearest thing to memoir which he ever wrote, *Thinking Back*, begins abruptly in the 1930s and buries his childhood in a few sentences. He had grown up in Arkansas in a comfortable middle class family and was descended from slaveholders on his mother's side, from Methodist preachers on his father's. I once drove him from Alabama to northwest Arkansas. We made a detour to Vanndale, where he had spent his early childhood. He had not been there for forty years, not since just before entering the U.S. Navy during the Second World War. Everything had changed: the sharecroppers' wooden shacks, the mules, the cotton gins, all had been erased, and he exclaimed much over this. But the cemetery was still there. We stopped at its gate. He said, "They are all in there." I asked, "Do you want to go in?" And he said firmly, with a grimace, "No."

NOTES

1. C. Vann Woodward, *The Future of the Past* (New York: Oxford University Press, 1989), 98.
2. Quoted in C. Vann Woodward, *Thinking Back: The Perils of Writing History* (Baton Rouge: Louisiana State University Press, 1986), 92.

3. This is the title of the second chapter of C. Vann Woodward, *The Strange Career of Jim Crow* (New York: Oxford University Press, 1955).

4. C. Vann Woodward, "The Elusive Mind of the South," in *American Counterpoint: Slavery and Racism in the North-South Dialogue* (Boston, MA: Little, Brown, 1971), 276; C. Vann Woodward, "The Search for Southern Identity," in *The Burden of Southern History*, rev. ed. (Baton Rouge: Louisiana State University Press, 1968), 6.

5. Woodward, "Search for Southern Identity," 3.

6. Cash, *Mind of the South*; William Alexander Percy, *Lanterns on the Levee: Recollections of a Planter's Son* (New York: Alfred A. Knopf, 1941); Twelve Southerners, *I'll Take My Stand*; Woodward, *Strange Career*.

7. Woodward, "Elusive Mind," 282.

8. Albert Murray, *South to a Very Old Place* (New York: McGraw-Hill, 1971), 21.

A previously unpublished paper given at the Organization of American Historians in Chicago, March 1996, on a panel convened to mark the thirty-fifth anniversary of William R. Taylor, *Cavalier and Yankee: The Old South and American National Character* (New York: Braziller, 1961).

This session occasions the third time that I have read *Cavalier and Yankee*. The first must have been when I was an undergraduate, or soon after. I have an indistinct sense that I read it, like many others at the time, as one in a congeries of books—Henry Nash Smith's *Virgin Land*, R. W. B. Lewis's *American Adam*, David Potter's *People of Plenty*, Daniel Boorstin's *The Genius of American Politics*—as American Studies-ish, national character-ish.[1] 1968 or so was a bit late to catch that intellectual moment at its flood. Doubts had begun to gather about the sufficiency of such an approach. Were novels enough? What was myth? Like most clever and obnoxious undergraduates, I sniffed the breeze, which was not blowing in Taylor's direction, and was inclined to accept destructive criticisms of older books, by way of making room for myself.

The second engagement was around 1980. I was beginning to be interested in the intellectual culture of the Old South, had started to read among its canonical authors, and begun to be impressed by a sophistication and modernity for which the secondary literature little prepared me. Some of that literature was almost comically inadequate and easy to dismiss. This was not the case with *Cavalier and Yankee*, which was and is a complicated book, not easy to pigeonhole. I managed to pigeonhole it, you understand, because I was bent upon polemic. But I was conscious that, in mentioning the book, I was dealing with only part of Taylor's arguments, those parts where he argues that the South was growing isolated from and ignorant of the intellectual developments of the nineteenth century, where he says that William Campbell Preston was a thoughtless Grand Tourist, and Hugh Legaré read little or no modern literature and frittered his time away on idle socializing. I detected some errors of fact, and smelled condescension towards people I felt did not merit it and wanted to protest. But, even then, I was conscious of not having addressed the full range of Taylor's arguments.

I seem to have been given a third chance.

The first thing to say is that, for a book written in the late 1950s by someone not a Southerner, *Cavalier and Yankee* is remarkably free from cheap caricatures. Of course, its basic standpoint is Yankee. The South is regarded as isolated, retarded, possessed of "cultural attainments" dubbed "negligible."[2] Southerners are more irrational than Northerners, are warped by repressing their guilt over slavery, form a collection of Hamlets, and are doomed by their unstable mix of impetuosity and doubt. *Cavalier and Yankee* was first a Harvard dissertation and it would have required a superhuman detachment in Harvard Yard then to have believed much other than these things. What is striking, however, is what is not said. There are no easy condescensions about race and slavery, little Unionist complacency, and little neo-abolitionist preaching. When quoting Emerson's and Henry Adams's uncomprehending observations about the South, Taylor does not endorse them. Indeed the book is remarkable for its sympathy for the Southerners it evokes, especially when he gives them an extended analysis. Moreover, as I suppose has often been noticed, for a book with the title *Cavalier and Yankee*, there are very few Yankees in a book crowded by Cavaliers. Taylor speaks of reconstructing the dialogue about North and South, yet the inventing of the North scarcely appears in comparison to the inventing of the South, which is attributed to Northerners and Southerners alike. One gets the impression that the book was intended to be more systematic, more sectionally balanced, but got deflected into being more exclusively Southern, the author being entranced by the Gorgon's eye.

On the face of it, this is an odd contradiction. Is there such a thing as a sympathetic neo-abolitionist book about the Old South? If so, how does this happen? One reason is adduced in Taylor's 1979 preface.[3] The civil rights movement had begun, he was finishing the book in Washington, it seemed that the isolation of the South was ending, it was a moment to err on the side of generosity. Moreover, as his references to Charles Sellers's *The Southerner As American*, the 1960 liberal symposium, indicates, this impulse to conciliate was mutual. Southerners were saying, we'll try to be well-behaved liberal Americans, if you let us back into the mainstream without the mandatory Yankee smack around the ears for past misdemeanors.[4] In that sense, *Cavalier and Yankee* was trying, as nicely as possible, to explain why antebellum Southerners had screwed up, while finding reasons to be optimistic that things in the present day, the 1950s, might go better. The smack was still there, but is so muffled by a velvet glove that one scarcely notices.

But part of the reason for the book's sympathy is structural, to do with the mix of Taylor's reading and his writing. My sense is that the disparagements of the South are the book's inherited bric-à-brac, absorbed from the standard historiography of the day, while the sympathy is Taylor's own. The secondary literature cited in Taylor's notes are a mixed bag. Some are fairly old—books like Orie Long's 1935 *Literary Pioneers*, Linda Rhea's 1934 biography of Hugh Legaré, Avery Craven's *Edmund Ruffin* of 1932, some of Clement Eaton's books, Cash's *The Mind of the South* of 1941—though fashions were less rapid in the late 1950s. A few things are new; Kenneth Lynn's *Mark Twain and Southwestern Humor* of 1959, Hubbell's *The South in American Literature* of 1954, Curtis Carroll Davis's 1953 life of William Alexander Caruthers, Stampp's *The Peculiar Institution* of 1956. But all these, with the partial exception of Hubbell's, were books written either by unsympathetic Northerners or apologetic Southerners. There is no earthly reason why Taylor should have seen any reason to disturb the reigning orthodoxy about the intellectual supineness of the South. Now and again, he came close. There is an oddly jarring passage, late in the book, where he observes, "The growing isolation of [South Carolina], like that of the South at large, was not the result of parochial ignorance or indifference to what was occurring elsewhere any more than it resulted from an absence of men of universal spirit. There were South Carolinians enough who were characterized by sophistication, a broad acquaintance with politics and a knowledge of history." It is hard to square this with the arguments earlier in the book. In fact, in general, the later one gets in the analysis, Taylor having worked his way through his texts, the closer he drifts to the argument for cultural distinctiveness. The last words of the book are, "Once it was *different* down there."[5]

Cavalier and Yankee is most remarkable for its independent reading of the original sources. Rereading the book, I got a strong sense of Taylor alone in a room with a small number of texts—*Swallow Barn*, *The Valley of the Shenandoah*, and *Woodcraft*—and setting down relatively fresh, fairly unmediated readings of those texts. I did not get a sense of a study stuffed with all the latest books and an author desperate to fit in with his contemporaries. That is, this is a 1950s book, not a 1990s book, which is one of its merits. Whatever else one may say in praise of the present day, indifference to contemporary intellectual fashion is not among those things. But methodological alertness is, and by those standards *Cavalier and Yankee* offers us its methodology or presumptions only episodically. They are scattered throughout the book, or only made explicit in the preface to the 1979 edition.

The key presumptions seem to be these. 1) The South and North were more alike than unlike, that "the idea of a divided culture" was or ought to be a discarded premise of historiography, though there were "certain important differences" between the sections, of which slavery was the greatest. Still values were, on the whole, shared. Hence 2) there was a tension between these similarities and differences, a tension which put Southerners in a state of anxiety. This was not so much guilt, more repression, which may be said to have warped their psychological development. 3) The North had its own problems, mostly with an accelerating materialism, which led it in turn to project upon the South some fanciful chivalric ideas. 4) Much became focused in debates about national character, and regional character. 5) It followed that one needs most to understand perception and emotion, "the dynamics of the legends rather than ... their literary origins or their degree of historical authenticity." Lastly, 6) novels are the best place to understand the emotional problem, because "the nineteenth-century novel was social and ideological history in microcosm," and such novels and tales "possess an element of free fantasy that is sometimes very revealing."[6]

Let me offer an image to summarize this argument. There are twin brothers, not identical, who share a house. One is a banker, dull and proper in morals but rich, if somewhat (not very) worried about his acquisitiveness. The other is a failing farmer, who resorts to the local brothel and has a certain charm, but who mistreats his farmhands. Derived from their common parenthood, much is shared by the brothers by way of tastes and inheritance. The strain of life and consanguinity, the claustrophobia of the situation, tells most upon the farmer, who lives in a pre-therapeutic age and so is not referred to a psychologist, paid for by his Blue Cross/Blue Shield. Instead, he talks too much, sometimes locks himself in his room, and writes fiction, until baffled by his derangements and frustrated by how bad his fiction is, he emerges and tries to throttle his brother and burn down the house. He succeeds only in burning down his own room, and is thereafter committed to an asylum. Much later, along comes a historian who sees a semi-ruined house, discovers the manuscripts, and tries to recover what happened from the evidence of these weird and tense narratives. There is talk that, if the manuscripts are read sympathetically, the brother might be released from the asylum, older but wiser, and be given a job in the bank. Thus the North, the South, the war, William R. Taylor.

There is not much point in arguing *in extenso* with these presumptions. I agree with almost none of them, but it would be invidious to lumber out the historiography of the last thirty- five years by way of refutation. I would only observe that ca. 1960 was one of the few, fleeting times in American history when it seemed plausible to believe that North and South did not have separate cultures, and even then you had to try really hard. (Although I should add that, when I began to think about the idea of the South in the mid-1970s, I too read Sellers's symposium and like Taylor found it made plausible an exploration of the history of perception. But I was old-fashioned in this reasoning.) Eugene Genovese did for social similarities between North and South by dragging slavery from the margins to the center; Eric Erikson's psychology went out of fashion to be followed by psychohistory *tout court*; the idea of a national character was rent by the social divisions of the 1960s; it became harder for even intellectual historians to wave aside the problem of social structure, let alone to suggest that the problem of society might be inferred from the "free fantasy" of a storyteller. Less obviously, with the onslaught upon the New Criticism, the novel began its long decline from cultural preeminence. We live now in an increasingly non-fictional age and few, outside of diehard creative writing programs, contend that most is revealed to us, if we lean forward in our chairs as a novelist speaks. Nowadays Faulkner is an industry, no longer a sage. As significantly, American intellectual history became more interested in formal intellectual paradigms, like the Enlightenment or Romanticism or civic humanism, and *Cavalier and Yankee* is notable for its indifference to such issues. It is a very *American* book, that is, it explains American events exclusively by means of American materials and thought; little which is exogenous matters, except for its ill effects. For example, it is argued that Southern fiction is weak because too much influenced by English literary models, whereas *Uncle Tom's Cabin* is strong because (as Taylor put it in 1979) "it became a refinement of a developing indigenous tradition."[7] Such an emphasis, too, has not been characteristic of more recent developments. Until multiculturalism came along recently, the transatlantic has been unusually important in recent historical literature, more so than at any time since Frederick Jackson Turner displaced Herbert Baxter Adams. And even multiculturalism has given us *The Black Atlantic*.[8]

Instead let me draw attention to some less-regarded aspects of *Cavalier and Yankee*, which seem to me important, if puzzling. The first is the odd sense, which grew upon me as I reread it, that this is a book much formed by the intellectual perspectives of the late nineteenth century, not merely by the obvious context of the 1950s. In a funny way, *Cavalier and Yankee* is more a book about Boston and Charleston in 1880 than about those same cities in 1830. Consider its strange claim that there were antebellum Southern Mugwumps. There is a long passage which mixes Hugh Legaré, Henry Adams, and Richard Hofstadter on the age of reform, a disquisition which talks much about displacement, about Federalists and Addisonians out of time. There is a section called "The Age of Anxiety." Open and shut your eyes rapidly and Legaré dissolves into William Dean Howells, the old man whose stuffy literary banquets are evoked at the beginning of Henry May's *The End of American Innocence* as the horror which preceded the liberations of modernism. Consider especially how much Taylor conflates the South with the plantation legend and the idea of the Cavalier and the Anglo-Saxon. Open and shut your eyes rapidly and John Pendleton Kennedy becomes Thomas Nelson Page. Consider how much Taylor makes of the counterpoint between Northern material growth and Southern disadvantage. Here James K. Paulding dissolves into Henry James, or perhaps George Gershwin, and one's mind turns to Northerners buying up old plantations on the Sea Islands. Francis Pendleton Gaines's book on *The Southern Plantation* of 1924 is much cited by Taylor, and it is a book which is most about the postbellum myths of the plantation. At one point, Taylor writes: "The fictional Southern plantation which Ellen Glasgow, William Faulkner and other twentieth-century writers inherited was principally the creation of two active periods of literary and social ferment. The first and most interesting of these lasted from about 1832 until the mid-fifties, when the literary energies of both North and South were drawn off into purely polemical writing. The second period lasted from about 1880 to the end of the century." These seem to be connected issues for Taylor, which is plausible enough for someone who had read Wilbur Cash.[9]

But *Cavalier and Yankee* does not simply understand 1830 as though it were 1880. Rather, the issues important in 1880 seem to be those which Taylor most recognizes in 1830. 1880 seems to have dictated an agenda, directed his eyes upon certain features of the Old South, made it difficult for him to see other features which had shrunk in significance by 1880. I would even hazard that his claim that the antebellum years were peculiarly preoccupied with the issue of nationalism smacks of the postbellum. Not that both periods were not obliged to think about the issue, but Taylor's sense that for an antebellum Southerner nationalism was anxious and obligatory is far more relevant to the years after Appomattox, than to those before the shelling of Fort Sumter, when the idea of the Union was far more tentative and so less fraught, because there was no compulsory idea of an American mainstream. Unfortunately, 1880 is an unsatisfactory standpoint for understanding 1830, not least because the South in 1880 made very much of the plantation legend, Cavaliers, and Anglo-Saxons, was economically disadvantaged, and felt impelled to defer to Northern mythology. The South in 1830, on the whole, saw plantations with cold realism or satire, was skeptical of the Cavalier theory, was less drawn to a sense of identity with Anglo-Saxons, was rich, and felt little need to defer to Northern opinion.

The second striking thing in *Cavalier and Yankee* has to do with its interest in outsiders. They appear constantly in this book, almost obsessively, I am tempted to say. To be well-born, an aristocrat, well-educated, to have traveled to Europe seems to be a terrible thing. It dooms one to sterility. To be ill-born, self-educated, parvenu, seems to make one intellectually fecund, if somewhat confused. In the former group, there is Legaré, Preston, Randolph. In the latter are almost all the novelists and storytellers, such as Wirt, Kennedy, Simms, Caruthers. Even Taylor's notable Northerners seem to be parvenu: Sarah Hale and Paulding, notably. I know nothing of Professor Taylor's personal history, indeed have never met him before today. But I began to wonder whether in Harvard Yard he had a bad time with Boston Brahmins and this book was his revenge.

This claim, that the Cavalier myth was sponsored by outsiders, gathers strength in the book in a rather piecemeal fashion, to the point where Taylor seems to have noticed that an emotional preference had grown into a thesis and felt obliged to proclaim it. But his respect for parvenu energy seems to have been at warfare with his judgment of their intellectual inadequacies, so at the last even the parvenu fails the test. They "were self-made men," he says, "provincial in their outlook and historically naive, who possessed no sure sense of any cultural tradition."[10] This seems to be an impasse; the aristocrat fails for too much tradition, the parvenu for too little. Failure must therefore abound. Indeed, this is a book peculiarly about failure. Taylor identifies failure and inefficacy, indeed is often cruelly blunt in identifying it, but somehow forgives it, understands it, is even drawn to it. Hamlet seems to be worth knowing.

These idiosyncrasies of standpoint help to explain this book's achievement. There are conventional ideas in *Cavalier and Yankee*, as there are in any book. But it has a very distinctive combination of ideas, which made it stand alone, and gave it an anxious, musing force. On every page there is intelligence, sometimes tumbling over itself. Taylor observed in 1979 that this book "produced few disciples," which is true enough. This is said with regret, and it is speculated that more methodological explicitness, as in H. Stuart Hughes's *Consciousness and Society*, might have evaded this fate.[11] I doubt it. It seems to me the nicest thing one can say about a book of substance, that it produced no disciples, because it means there was something induplicable in it, little which could be ripped out and plundered. You may recall the moment in Monty Python's *The Life of Brian*, when the crowd has denominated Brian as the Messiah and demands a blessing from him. He looks confused and irritated, but finally says, "Look ... You've got it all wrong. You don't need to follow me. You don't need to follow anybody. You've got to think for yourselves. You're all individuals." The crowd chants back, in unison, "Yes, we're all individuals." Brian tries again, "You're all different." They chant, "Yes, we are all different." In frustration, Brian varies the injunction to, "You've all got to work it out for yourselves." The followers agree, "Yes, yes!! We've got to work it out for ourselves."[12] These are disciples. They are best avoided, even if it is hard on one's vanity not to have them.

As I have tried to suggest, *Cavalier and Yankee* is most remarkable for its engagement with particular writers. The parts where the book takes off and is exhilarating are those moments when Taylor has his novel in hand, some biographical details, and thinks hard about what this writer meant, what he or she felt. Taylor seems to understand this as his strength, at least so I read his 1964 letter to Clement Eaton, which is quoted in the 1979 preface: "We watch one man (or woman) draw conclusions, conceive of ideas, change his (or her) mind, develop inconsistencies, struggle to resolve them, lose hope, etc. We see the process of historical change from the *inside out*, and our understanding of group behavior is increased in accordance."[13] Perhaps Taylor never quite reached the group, but he was extraordinarily good at evoking individual men and women's experience. I would particularly single out his passages on William Wirt, who was not an easy man to like. This freshness of scrutiny was *Cavalier and Yankee*'s greatest contribution. It made antebellum Southerners interesting, it helped to give them back a certain humanity, suggested subtlety and ambivalence, implicitly (more than explicitly) liberated a sense that the Old South was not unworthy of an intelligent historian's time.

NOTES

1. Henry Nash Smith, *Virgin Land: The American West as Symbol and Myth* (Cambridge, MA: Harvard University Press, 1950); R. W. B. Lewis, *The American Adam: Innocence, Tragedy, and Tradition in the Nineteenth Century* (Chicago, IL: University of Chicago Press, 1955); David M. Potter, *People of Plenty: Economic Abundance and the American Character* (Chicago, IL: University of Chicago Press, 1954); Daniel J. Boorstin, *The Genius of American Politics* (Chicago, IL: University of Chicago Press, 1953).

2. William R. Taylor, *Cavalier and Yankee: The Old South and American National Character* (1961; Cambridge, MA: Harvard University Press, 1979), 17.

3. Ibid., 1–9.

4. See Charles Grier Sellers, Jr., ed., *The Southerner as American* (Chapel Hill: University of North Carolina Press, 1960).

5. Taylor, *Cavalier and Yankee*, 261, 341.

6. Ibid., 16, 17, 21, 5.

7. Ibid., 6.

8. Paul Gilroy, *The Black Atlantic: Modernity and Double Consciousness* (London: Verso, 1993).

9. Taylor, *Cavalier and Yankee*, 55–65, 96–101, 3–8, 148; Henry F. May, *The End of American Innocence: A Study of the First Years of Our Own Time, 1912–1917* (1959; New York: Alfred A. Knopf, 1969), 3–8.

10. Taylor, *Cavalier and Yankee*, 340.

11. Ibid., 3.

12. Graham Chapman et al., *Monty Python's the Life of Brian (of Nazareth)* (London: Methuen, 2001), 72.

13. Taylor, *Cavalier and Yankee*, 4.

A review of Eugene D. Genovese, *The Slaveholders' Dilemma: Freedom and Progress in Southern Conservative Thought, 1820–1860* (Columbia: University of South Carolina Press, 1992), published as "Conservative Thought in the Old South: A Review Article," *Comparative Studies in Society and History* 14 (July 1992): 566–76. Reprinted by permission.

It has been thirteen years since Eugene Genovese published a book solely in his own name, and nine since *Fruits of Merchant Capital*, whose authorship he shared with Elizabeth Fox-Genovese. It is not impossible that our younger readers, as they used to say, know him only as a crotchety and conservative gentleman who, from a Southern fastness, occasionally lobs hand grenades into the debates over multiculturalism and political correctness, a man whom the *Village Voice* has felt it necessary to label a sort of Public Enemy No. 1, a man who veers between elaborate Southern courtesy and abrupt New York acidity. Our older readers will better remember from a generation ago the Genovese of *The Political Economy of Slavery* and *Roll, Jordan, Roll*: Genovese the radical, the enemy of Republican gubernatorial candidates, the historian who transformed the study of slavery and the Old South, who did more than anyone else to introduce Gramscian concepts of hegemony into American thought. Many might see his present conservatism as a deviation from his early radicalism. In fact, it is probably only an extension of a Marxism which always stressed order and discipline.

Those who measure their historians out in books will have reason to feel that Genovese has been silent for too long on his métier, the Old South. In fact, he has been engaged with Fox-Genovese in a venture as extensive as *Roll, Jordan, Roll*, which bears the working title of *The Mind of the Master Class*. This is intended to be an intellectual history of the Old South or, rather, of the slaveholding hegemony defined in his earlier books. For several years, sometimes in his name, sometimes in hers, sometimes in both, articles have been appearing which have been sketching pieces of the puzzle they wish eventually to define and solve. But these have often appeared in obscure places, so the lay reader will be forgiven for having missed them. Even the cognoscenti have sometimes neglected their significance. Thus scattered, these essays have not compelled an assessment or occupied a prominent place in the debate over antebellum Southern culture. *The Slaveholders' Dilemma*, being both a summary of those piecemeal articles and a down payment on the magnum opus to come, will presumably change this situation.

Genovese contends that the intellectual culture of the Old South has been seriously underestimated, that its intellectuals "matched their northern counterparts in learning and creativity," not perhaps in the novel, but in the study of legal theory and jurisprudence, political economy, theology, historical literature, and political theory, that is, in most of the serious endeavors of the American mind of the early nineteenth century. These intellectuals were not alienated from their society, but, in the most profound sense, its representatives. Genovese sees this intermeshing of thought and society as a strength in both, contrary to those who have damned the Old South as intellectually sterile precisely for its failure to generate alienation, to throw up Thoreaus and Melvilles. Genovese further believes that in the Old South reside the origins of that anti-capitalist Southern conservatism which forms so uneasy a part of the Reaganite coalition. Hence it is important to study those origins, partly as a matter of historical curiosity, partly because antebellum thinkers grappled with issues which Genovese believes to be still relevant: "We could, if we would, profit greatly from a reasoned engagement with the thought of Calhoun, Dew, Bledsoe, Thornwell, and others as we grapple today with the staggering problems of a world in headlong transition to the Lord knows what. The finest aspects of their thought, shorn of the tragic commitment to slavery and racism, constitute a searing critique of some of the most dangerous tendencies in modern life."[1] Their chief grappling was with the interwoven problems of progress, freedom, and social order. Herein lies the dilemma defined in Genovese's title. For antebellum Southern intellectuals represented a social order which was in but not of the modern world, which valued the ethics of intellectual and social freedom but needed slavery, which participated in transatlantic bourgeois culture but was mistrusted by it for anachronism. Caught in this contradiction, they came to realize that freedom and slavery, equality and hierarchy, liberty and order were not irreconcilable opposites between which history was inevitably making a choice in the name of progress, but were facets intrinsically related in any successful and functioning society. A devotion to freedom, they reasoned, can never release us from the fact of subordinations.

To explicate this dilemma, Genovese gives a close reading to a number of Southern intellectuals and their texts. He begins with Thomas Roderick Dew of Virginia, best known for his proslavery *Review of the Debate in the Virginia Legislature of 1831 and 1832* (1832) but most used here for his *Lectures on the Restrictive System* (1829) and the posthumously published *Digest of the Laws, Customs, Manners and Institutions of the Ancient and Modern Nations* (1852). By Dew, the theme Genovese wishes to explore is stated. Dew believed in progress, "reveled in the advances in learning, economic production, transportation, communications, even in morals, and he recognized the self-generating power of science of technology.... [T]he root of this welcome progress lay in the expansion of individual freedom." His *Digest*, predicated on the theme of liberty, was a sweeping history of the West. Yet, at the same time, Dew as a political economist, as a reader of Malthus and Ricardo and the gathering studies of modern urban and industrial society, understood that immiseration was everywhere and growing. He even conceded that slavery was likely to be ended, not necessarily by the moral challenge of antislavery, but by a competitive and cheap free labor system which would make the capital invested in slaves ebb away. Was this acceptable? Would society be morally advanced if all the world became Mayhew's London? Genovese sees this dilemma and choice as emblematic of the world view of the Southern intelligentsia: "Dew believed that the West faced a stark choice: It could continue a headlong progress that threatened to end in social catastrophe; or, it could effect a worldwide restoration of a servitude that threatened the end of civilization's progressive momentum. With a heavy heart he chose slavery, order, and stability." Genovese pursues the dilemma's nuances and ramifications through the writings of many figures, but notably John C. Calhoun, James Henley Thornwell, Albert Taylor Bledsoe, William Henry Trescot, and James Henry Hammond.[2]

The book, despite or because of its brevity, is a *tour de force*, written with concision and nuance. The argument is sustained with Genovese's usual driving cogency, in fact with a little more than his usual cogency. For it is well to remember that Genovese has characteristically been an essayist, and most of his books (perhaps not excluding *Roll, Jordan, Roll*) have been collections of essays necessarily prone to miscellaneous thoughts, and Genovese has not always resisted the blandishments of the form. However, though a fox in his choice of form, Genovese has been a hedgehog in his standpoint. But his quills, though as pointed, are not quite as they were, a fact which has gone unnoticed by many. Bashing the ingenu Genovese of *The Political Economy of Slavery* from 1965 is one of the minor sports of American historians, one easier to play than bashing the Genovese of the more complex *Fruits of Merchant Capital*. (Indeed, Genovese has peculiarly exercised his influence through the frequency with which, by accepting his questions, other historians have formed different answers which mimic his presumptions. No important modern historian has influenced more, and persuaded fewer, than Genovese.) The mature Genovese has accepted the view that antebellum intellectuals were envisaging their society as an alternative form of modernity; he has noticed a vitality in its intellectual culture when once he was oblivious of it; he has added (though very little here) women to his lexicon of Southern society; he has abandoned the claim that the Old South was prebourgeois. All these, and other changes, he has been careful to delineate, just as he has been handsome in his acknowledgments of those historians, who have forced him (no easy matter to so forceful a thinker) to amend. Still, he has stuck to an essential point, which underpins this book: antebellum Southerners were not members of a capitalist bourgeoisie, who happened to own slaves rather than debentures, for "the slaveholders, unlike conservatives in the North and abroad, explicitly identified the free-labor system itself as the source of the moral evils and forged a critique that struck at its heart." Moreover, though he defines the dilemma of choice between freedom and inequality, he still sees those who chose the path of inequality as the essential Southerners. As he and Fox-Genovese have elsewhere written, "At the core of their thought lay a belief in hierarchy, particularism, and the necessarily unequal interdependence of society's members."[3]

Though it is perilous to pigeonhole a historian whose accomplishments have been so various—he has always, for example, been notable as a legal historian and has claims to being a historian of religion—Genovese's contributions have been most marked in social history of an older dispensation, that is, to a history far closer to the political economy of the nineteenth century (of which Marxism is a variety) than to the so-called New Social History, which he has not infrequently excoriated for political naïveté and sentimentalism.[4] But, the occasional essay notwithstanding, most famously on George Fitzhugh in *The World the Slaveholders Made*, Genovese has not appeared systematically in the role of an intellectual historian, which he does here. It is a role doubtless logical for a Gramscian who has always stressed the importance of intellectuals in the dynamics of society, but nonetheless a role which has come late in Genovese's career.

But what kind of intellectual historian is Eugene Genovese? Clearly he is not interested in the various methodological issues which have perplexed intellectual historians in the last generation. They have worried about the status of thought, its epistemological foundations and consequences. They have puzzled over poststructuralism's relevance to history, taken linguistic turns (or not), and debated contextualism. These matters Genovese disdains. This is not always to his disadvantage, not least that he gets down to writing the history, rather than worrying about whether the history can or should be written. His briskness might usefully be imitated by the Hamlets of our intellectual history.

Nonetheless, not having a formal theory, Genovese has an informal one which might be characterized as part Antonio Gramsci, part Arthur Lovejoy: the former has given Genovese a social theory which the historian has often acknowledged, the latter embodies a view of the history of ideas which seems present by osmosis. Genovese takes particular intellectuals seriously, not for their idiosyncrasy, but for their representativeness. He shows very little interest in the immediate, as opposed to the general, personal, or social contexts in which texts are written. Rather, he reads texts and people through texts, more or less literally, and correlates them with what he believes to be the nature of Southern society. Genovese's world is not one in which meaning is problematical. Words mean what they say. Further, words not being contextualized, they are arrayed in a debate, imbedded in history but somehow independent of its immediate context. Thomas R. Dew, John C. Calhoun, Allen Tate, and Richard Weaver are locked together in this debate, which can be said to exist irrespective of whether Calhoun, Dew, and Tate ever read one another or accepted the terms of such a conversation. That is, Genovese writes the kind of intellectual history, damned by Quentin Skinner as ahistorical, in which Aristotle, Machiavelli, and Marx are involved in the oldest established floating seminar on politics and society in town.

Genovese himself is a member of the seminar, a participant prone to wagging his finger at others whose commitment to the assigned topic wavers. Throughout this book, he upbraids his Southern intellectuals when they talk of matters of minor interest to him. At such moments, they stand accused of obfuscating the issue, of trailing off "into some less than helpful remarks," of misunderstanding their own positions. Sometimes Genovese is stiffly censorious. "It would," he observes of Bledsoe, ". . . take little effort to demonstrate that, read in the context of his political theory as a whole, his indignant rejection of 'slavery in the abstract' conceded the essentials of the doctrine he was purportedly rejecting." Sometimes Genovese is indulgent. "Only one conclusion followed from Trescot's analysis, although he never fully articulated it," he writes elsewhere, before helpfully providing the conclusion which Trescot never felt it necessary to offer.[5]

At the heart of this seminar is the matter of power—who has it, where it comes from, how it is wielded, on whom it acts, who resists it. Power has long been Genovese's essential subject matter. In this he has been most the Marxist. At the beginning of his career he has chiefly interested in the wielders of power and the world they made. He then was drawn to those who resisted and who, by being locked in the struggle, made a power for themselves. He has now reverted to his early fascination with the master class, such that the slaves have dwindled to the odd clause. But power remains central.

So Genovese is the kind of intellectual historian who is interested in the ideology of power, and little else, unless it can be placed at the service of that subject matter. This can be seen in the opening sentences of this book: "These lectures were intended primarily as a contribution to intellectual history. The first question that might arise would therefore concern resonance. Did the intellectuals discussed here have much influence? Did they, as it were, speak for their people, in particular for the slaveholders?"[6] This is not the first question which would occur to most intellectual historians of the present day, unless they were students of "reader-response" theory. But the question does prompt a tidiness of focus which gives this book its cogency.

The cogency, however, is bought at a price, probably unimportant in a short book which might plausibly claim a discrete problem—"the link between freedom and progress and its implications for the defense of slavery"—as its province, but consequential for the promised *Mind of the Master Class*.[7] In *The Slaveholders' Dilemma*, the South is reduced to the slaveholding class, that class to its ideologists, those thinkers to the conservatives who addressed the matter of slavery and social philosophy in a spirit of social elitism. At each step, small acts of exclusion are made to enable the reader to reach the point where the essence of the South—the South as a locus of social power—can be read, in miniature, in passages of certain conservative thinkers. All Southern thinkers who were theologically liberal like James Warley Miles, or politically democratic like Andrew Jackson, or socially alienated like Hugh Legaré, or antislavery like Hinton Rowan Helper, or feminist like Sarah Grimké, or Jewish like Isaac Harby, are ignored. Genovese's South is Protestant in theology, Federalist in politics, slaveholding, unalienated in social philosophy. Certainly these criteria, if applied to Southern society as a whole, would exclude a majority of its inhabitants. But even for the narrower world of the intelligentsia, the list of people whom Genovese's analysis cannot accommodate is as long as, if not longer than, those whom it can.

One of Genovese's starting points, the intellectual vitality of the Old South, was a claim and appeal first made by other historians as a way of releasing curiosities, of commencing a cycle of reconsideration which might unravel a stale orthodoxy and enable us to see the full range and complexity of Southern thought. This was done, as Genovese paraphrases the point, because the claim of American intellectual historians to have grasped the nature of Southern thought was slight, they never having bothered to read the appropriate texts. (Most have done little more than read Fitzhugh with rubber gloves on, which has preserved a kind of purity, but at the price of historical understanding, which, after all, has little to do with purity.) Genovese has gone a long way in his writings and in other ways towards helping in the endeavor of reclaiming that complexity. Yet his own curiosity seems to have definite limits. Fiction and poetry interest him very little and his ventures into literary criticism are seldom illuminating. He neglects formal intellectual paradigms: this is a book where the Enlightenment, Romanticism, Scottish common sense philosophy—all matters of moment for Southern intellectuals—are absent. This indifference to abstractions other than the abstraction of society extends even to political philosophy of the Jeffersonian or Jacksonian variety, where Genovese seems to draw a blank. As absent are politicians who actually functioned on the Southern and American political scene (voting, being voted upon, having constituencies), as opposed to politicians who were detached meditators upon society. We see the Calhoun of the *Disquisition on Government*, but not the Calhoun of the upcountry hustings; this lacuna helps to explain a marked failure in this book to measure, not the fact, but the depth of Southern commitment to egalitarianism and democracy among whites.

About these limitations we need not overmuch complain. This is a short book, whose author might plausibly plead the necessities of omission. And one might reasonably ask, how many intellectual historians have made as much contribution to social history as this social historian has made here to intellectual history? As a delineation of a certain brand of influential conservative thought, it is exceptionally interesting. His characterization of Southern attitudes towards feudalism and the Middle Ages is trenchant. His discussions of Dew and Bledsoe are the best we have, for they grapple with the full range of their thought. On Calhoun, he is perhaps less original, though useful in extending the writings of Lacy Ford, who has stressed the "modern" side of Calhoun's thought.[8] I suspect Genovese misunderstands Trescot. By putting the analysis of class relations to be found in the 1850 pamphlet,

The Position and Course of the South, at the heart of Trescot's thought, Genovese turns the South Carolinian into a sort of Fitzhugh. My own reading, however, of Trescot's several writings is that he was far more interested in the political side of power than its social grounding. That is, as Trescot saw it, society created and molded power for young oligarchs like himself, thereby offering a role which a man fond of power and the intellectual pleasures of detachment might play. Though Trescot saw and described advantages in a slave society, his enthusiasm was far more muted and less sincere than Fitzhugh's, and far more flexible. He wanted to ride, booted and spurred, more than he wanted a particular horse. On James Henry Hammond, Genovese is shrewd, if one ignores the uneasy attempt to make Hammond a believer in Christianity.

One aspect of Genovese's characterization of Southern thought requires discussion. He grounds part of his discussion on the contention that antebellum Southern thinkers were defending slavery in the abstract. He has, therefore, some difficulty when his Southern intellectuals declined to take any such position. James Henry Hammond, for example, wrote in 1844 to Thomas Clarkson, the English abolitionist, "If you were to ask me whether I am an advocate of slavery in the abstract, I should probably answer, that I am not, according to my understanding of the question. I do not like to deal in abstractions." Genovese dismisses this passage as disingenuous, if not dishonest. "Now," he writes in full seminar finger-wagging mood, "Hammond knew perfectly well that the question concerned not philosophical abstractions but the specific issue of slavery abstracted from immediate circumstances, especially the matter of race." In fact, Hammond knew no such thing, but was making quite a different point, as his next sentences showed: "I do not like to deal in abstractions. It seldom leads to any useful ends. There are few universal truths. I do not now remember any single moral truth universally acknowledged. We have no assurance that it is given to our finite understanding to comprehend abstract moral truth." Here Hammond was being unusually radical. Not too many Southerners would have been willing to deny the universality of morality, though many, including Thornwell the Old School Presbyterian, would have agreed that it was not man's place, in God's order, to determine or grasp finalities. George Frederick Holmes, writing in 1843, probably took the more usual middle course of giving a little to universality, and much to contingency: "If the question of slavery were submitted to the consideration of slave-holders in the abstract, as implying permanent bond service between races of equal intelligence and equal degree in the scale of creation, there are few Southerners who would yield to the Northern Abolitionists in zealous and determined protestation against it. . . . [But] the point is not submitted to us as a new and abstract question—the institution of slavery is found in the midst of us." Abolitionism

> may meet us with the assertion that, if it be conceded that slavery would not be defended as an abstract question, we are liable to the charge of inconsistency, and convicted out of our own mouths. The general truths of morality are fixed and immutable, and are equally obligatory at all times and in all places; but those, which may be called secondary truths, and which are applicable to the details of the economy of society, are binding by the authority of the laws, dictated in a great measure by policy, expediency and necessity. These vary with the infinite variety of circumstances, and to this latter class does the question of negro slavery belong.[9]

This distinction between the abstract and the practical is not, as Genovese has it when speaking of Hammond, disingenuous or a sleight of hand, but one which goes to heart of the intellectual temperament and strategy of many, though not all, Southern ideologists. For many Southerners the word *abstract* came stamped with the burden of the eighteenth century's emphasis upon natural rights, a manner of thinking in which metaphysics decided morality, and morality would structure society. But historicism had sufficiently seeped into the Southern mind by 1840, that many were reluctant to speak of universal truths. Rather many Southern intellectuals appealed to history and to experience. History, they said, proves that slavery is a common human condition, usually beneficent. But this was not to say that history had always or would always compel a society to adopt slavery. Rather it was to say that history offered no decisive evidence against the immorality or inexpedience of slavery, and seemed to be offering decisive evidence against the morality and expediency of free labor.

So not all Southerners were willing to argue, as the abolitionists wished them to argue, on merely the ethical questions posed by natural law. Hugh Legaré, with his usual polemical briskness, dismissed this option as jejune. "Whether slavery is, or is not reconcilable with what is called by philosophers the law of nature, we really do not know. We find the greatest theoretical publicists divided upon the subject, and it is, no doubt, a very good thesis for young casuists to discuss in a college moot-club. We shall not undertake it, for we have no taste for abstractions."[10] Rather, many Southerners, including Hammond and Trescot, were aware that to rely upon history was to admit the possibility of flux. What history seemed to prove, history might disprove. By the same logic, what the Bible seemed to prove, a changed interpretation of the Bible or, less probably, a new Revelation by God, might disprove. Hence, curiously, it was precisely the rejection of the abstract and peremptory, which explains the great rigor of scholarship among Southern intellectuals, both secular and religious, which Genovese is at pains to show us. (And, by the same token, why Southern scholarship in the antebellum period was usually better than Northern.) If all causes were secondary, all were provisional, and vigilance was required. Hence, too, the willingness for each Southerner in each generation to run over the same arguments, to ensure that history was still on the South's side. Historicism is, intellectually, very labor-intensive.

In fact, the very dilemma which Genovese so ably and usefully delineates—the tension between freedom and power—occasioned the distinction between abstract and practical which he wishes to dismiss. For certainly many Southerners saw the agonizing choice which Genovese discusses. Unlike Dew and Genovese, both men of decisive intellect, those Southerners were very reluctant to choose. Many wanted to muddle through, hoping the problem would go away, that history or God would take care of it, and they would not be the generation that would pay the price of a choice. As it happened, they were disappointed. The choice was made. But their rejection of the metaphysical was so important because in metaphysics one must choose, one must resolve contradictions, one must construct a logically tidy world. The secondary world of history, on the other hand, evidences and permits untidiness. Southerners chose a middle path, a history and sociology brushed by religion and ethics, a religion and ethics brushed with history. This kept the anarchic implications of both at bay. That Genovese is insensitive to this aspect of Southern thought arises, perhaps, from his abhorrence of the middle path. He has usually preferred the decisive conservative or radical to the muddled liberal.

Perhaps part of the analytical difficulty lies in Genovese's view of the status of religion in Southern life. Some of the Southerners he discusses were less than orthodox in their Christianity, even skeptical. This fact Genovese is inclined to ignore or, worse, deny. Yet Calhoun rejected Calvinism and became a sort of freethinking Unitarian (his political secretary, Richard Crallé, was a Swedenborgian). Hammond once confessed himself "not a professor of Religion," valued Christianity as only a body of useful moralities, dismissed the Immaculate Conception, the divinity of Christ, and the existence of the Holy Ghost as superstitious mysteries. When he did dabble in religion, Hammond tried a little spirit-rapping.[11] Trescot, though he was a Christian, cannot be said to have shown marked piety, and was too fond of wine and jokes from eighteenth-century French memoirs to be other than incongruous in the company of James Henley Thornwell.[12] But Thornwell is Genovese's quintessential Southerner—he seems to have displaced Fitzhugh—and in this book skeptics are made to dwell in his shadow. For Genovese is very insistent that Southern society and its intelligentsia were one, and that both were orthodox in religion. That Thornwell, by being devout, represented a larger number of Southerners than Hammond, cannot be questioned. But intellectual history is not often, and not consistently, served by studying those thinkers with the big battalions, nor by conscripting the unwilling into the ranks; idiosyncrasy, not typicality, is its lifeblood.

I imagine many readers will find this book disturbing in its implications, and not know how to take its lessons. This confusion will be compounded by Genovese's occasional playfulness, which is echoed in his own description of one of his favorite thinkers: "Fitzhugh loved paradoxes, loved to shock, loved to put-on dog. But he also took himself seriously and meant to instruct." But what are we taught, out of this body of Southern thought? Certainly, we are supposed to repudiate market relations, as a system fatally prone to creating immiseration, inequality, and alienation. Even after the debacles of socialism in the Soviet Union and eastern Europe, some will find such a lesson still pertinent, though the ropes are crowded with those who are abandoning the ship of Marxism. We are, it seems, to discriminate among those systems of hierarchy which will best preserve some flawed measure of decent comfort and freedom. Yet Genovese does not tell us, here or elsewhere in his polemical writings, what system of inequality will work in mitigating the devastations of human nature, since manifestly the Old South's solution, slavery, cannot be ours. The Old South, after all, used the hierarchies which were to hand, which were inherited, which needed to be understood and elaborated. As Genovese himself writes of Thomas Dew, "With a heavy heart he chose slavery, order, and stability."[13] Remove "slavery" from the quotation and one has the essential message and mood of Genovese's own book. Yet Dew had, or so he thought, an order and stability to choose, the slaveholding Virginia he inhabited. For Dew, choice was an acceptance. I doubt that this is our situation. For us, choice would an invention, unless Genovese just wants us to accept George Bush's America. The difficulty is, what to invent?

Genovese urges us to eschew innocence, which is sound advice. But he is silent on the details of the realism he would have us embrace, and realism is nothing without details. In particular, he is silent on naming those who will pay the price of his realism, something which those he invites us to admire did not blush to do.

NOTES

1. Eugene D. Genovese, *The Slaveholders' Dilemma: Freedom and Progress in Southern Conservative Thought, 1820–1860* (Columbia: University of South Carolina Press, 1992), 2–3.

2. Ibid., 14, 18.

3. Genovese, *Slaveholders' Dilemma*, 33; Elizabeth Fox-Genovese and Eugene D. Genovese, "The Divine Sanction of Social Order: Religious Foundations of the Southern Slaveholders' World View," *Journal of the American Academy of Religion* 55 (1987): 212.

4. Notably in "The Political Crisis of Social History: Class Struggle as Subject and Object," in Elizabeth Fox-Genovese and Eugene D. Genovese, *Fruits of Merchant Capital: Slavery and Bourgeois Property in the Rise and Expansion of Capitalism* (New York: Oxford University Press, 1983), 179–212.

5. Genovese, *Slaveholders' Dilemma*, 98, 53, 83–84.

6. Ibid., 1.

7. Ibid., 41.

8. Lacy K. Ford, "Republican Ideology in a Slave Society: The Political Economy of John C. Calhoun," *Journal of Southern History* 54 (August 1988): 405–24.

9. "Two Letters on the Subject of Slavery in the United States, Addressed to Thomas Clarkson, Esq.," in Clyde N. Wilson, ed., *Selections from the Letters and Speeches of the Hon. James Henry Hammond* (1866; Columbia, SC: Southern Studies Program, 1978), 119–20; Genovese, *Slaveholders' Dilemma*, 91; George Frederick Holmes, "On Slavery and Christianity," *Southern Quarterly Review* 3 (January 1843): 253.

10. Hugh Swinton Legaré, "Hall's Travels in North-America," in Mary Swinton Legaré, ed., *Writings of Hugh Swinton Legaré*, 2 vols. (Charleston, SC: Burges & James, 1845–46), 2:284.

11. Drew Gilpin Faust, *James Henry Hammond and the Old South: A Design for Mastery* (Baton Rouge: Louisiana State University Press, 1982), 249, 261–62 (quotation on 249).

12. See, for example, William Henry Trescot to William Porcher Miles, 13 November 1853, William Porcher Miles Papers, Southern Historical Collection, University of North Carolina, Chapel Hill: this tells an anecdote, drawn from the life of Marie-Angélique, Duchesse de Fontanges (a mistress of Louis XIV), about a riddle told at Versailles to an innocent virgin, to which the answer was "a vagina."

13. Genovese, *Slaveholders' Dilemma*, 25, 18.

EDWARD AYERS

A review of Edward L. Ayers, *The Promise of the New South: Life After Reconstruction* (New York: Oxford University Press, 1992), in the *Times Literary Supplement* (February 26, 1993): 4.

When in 1971 C. Vann Woodward reissued his 1951 masterpiece, *Origins of the New South, 1877–1913*, he politely called for a new synthesis, to be undertaken by a younger historian "with another world view, fresher insights, and perhaps a different philosophy of history." Since then, he has been quietly waiting, not too dismayed that the call has been unanswered, drily observing not a few challenges gone awry. Now comes Edward L. Ayers, who confesses that Woodward's "book was never far from my mind."[1]

Certainly Ayers has a different philosophy. He prefers a "more active and intimate history" and is fascinated with instability, change, movement, contingency. He wishes to juxtapose voices and events, now "conversations on railroad cars," then words at "revival tents and juke joints," now a New Orleans prizefight, then a lynching watched, guardedly, "from a distance." The historian should go walkabout and deploy his microphone not only in public spaces, at Populist rallies and church services, but in private places where Southerners spoke painfully or gladly about their difficulties, in their love letters and account books. In less accomplished hands, this Bakhtinian philosophy would be a recipe for incoherence. Ayers makes it work remarkably well, partly by not pushing the strategy to its utmost conclusion. His voices are grouped, labeled, and tidied away in chapters. Scattered profusely are many stories, amiably told. I especially liked the Arkansas newspaper advertisement of 1900 which read, "Wanted at once, two good hustlers, either sex, to introduce and sell Lightning Vermin Destroyer."[2]

Ayers begins *The Promise of the New South* in 1880, when nothing in particular happened, and ends in 1906 with the Atlanta race riot. He clearly does not want to deal with Reconstruction, but instead intercedes a few conveniently vague years between its end and his beginning. Nor does he wish to cope with Southern progressivism; Woodrow Wilson shows up in this book only as a student at the Johns Hopkins University, and Theodore Roosevelt does not appear at all. Populism, however, seen as the greatest manifestation of the social and political insurgencies which swirled out of the New South's transformation, gets three strong chapters. These are written, one feels, out of a sense of duty, in what Ayers resentfully confesses to be "a more familiar style."[3] The heart of the book and the author are in those chapters where he discusses the myriad innovations of social and cultural life in the South of Coca-Cola. He is informative on religion, and rightly stresses the emergence of celebrity evangelists like Sam Jones, the ancestor of Billy Sunday and Oral Roberts. He is good on sports, the baseball teams in Augusta and Anniston which made Ty Cobb possible, the golf courses which Bobby Jones came to play on, the football teams founded by coaches like John Heisman of Auburn. He is best on the astonishing outburst of musical originality by which the South gave to the world the forms of jazz, the blues, and country music, and he has compelling sketches of such as Buddy Bolden, W. C. Handy, Scott Joplin, Charley Patton, and Fiddlin' John Carson.

On the more traditional subjects of New South historiography, Ayers is efficient rather than profound. He shows with what unevenness and uncertainty segregation evolved, by tracing the spreading enforcement of the disfranchisement of blacks and poorer whites, and he follows the ups and downs of party politics, at the end of which process the Democratic Party came to preside over a shrunken political domain. He lays much stress upon the rapid urbanization of the region. Indeed Ayers's South, although he deals with agriculture, is somehow and oddly urban. Though there is a chapter called "Out in the Country," it does not come until seven other chapters have lovingly detailed the growth of railroads, dry-goods stores, small and large towns, mills and mines. The grim and spreading blight of tenancy and sharecropping seems almost an interspersion.

This highlights a central difficulty of Ayers's vision of the New South. As a historian, Ayers is cheerful, engagingly so. He loves all the movement, the innovation, the idiosyncrasy, and has a gift for portraying it. He is not unaware of the region's inertia or insensitive to the innumerable tragedies of Southern life, its poverty, racism, and brutality. He names them all. But he has scarcely finished sombrely describing some horror, some strange fruit of lynching, when his eye is caught by a passing show, some bellowing evangelist or plucking guitarist, and he is off down the road after them, laughing infectiously. One follows him, more or less willingly, but it is hard not to cast an eye back on the abandoned tragedy, the man swinging from the branch, and reflect that there is something almost unseemly about this exuberance. And yet Ayers is right. The South is more than threnody. These Southerners did laugh and they were not "synonymous with the problems they faced"; part of the fascination of their history is such incongruity.[4] It is a decision of temperament whether this paradox is felt to increase or lighten the burden of Southern history.

Has Ayers displaced Woodward? There is much in *The Promise of the New South* which was ignored by Woodward: music, religion, consumer culture, sports. But *Origins of the New South* was quintessentially a synthesis, whose argument connected Reconstruction to the South after 1913 and refashioned our understanding of more than the years Woodward formally analyzed. Ayers has avoided this obligation as an avowed act of principle, and perhaps as a matter of prudence. He has not so much challenged Woodward as he has changed the subject. Probably the subject needs changing. In 1951, let alone 1890, there was no presidential candidate from Arkansas (Woodward's own state) who, wearing sunglasses, played the saxophone on a late-night television show, hosted by a black American from Ohio. *Eppur si muove* should be said even of Southern history.

NOTES

1. C. Vann Woodward, *Origins of the New South, 1877–1913* (1951; Baton Rouge: Louisiana State University Press, 1971), viii; Edward L. Ayers, *The Promise of the New South: Life After Reconstruction* (New York: Oxford University Press, 1992), vii.
2. Ayers, *Promise of the New South*, ix, 88.
3. Ibid., x.
4. Ibid., ix.

A review of V. S. Naipaul, *A Turn in the South* (New York: Alfred A. Knopf, 1989); it was published as Michael O'Brien, "An Intelligent Mechanism: Naipaul on the South," *Mississippi Quarterly* 43 (Winter 1989–90): 77–83. Reprinted by permission.

Gifted writers have been born in the South, more than they have been foreign visitors to it. In the nineteenth century, Dickens got as far as Richmond, before abandoning plans to go on to Charleston. Tocqueville sped rapidly down the Mississippi from Cincinnati to New Orleans, where he spent but three days, before hastening in five days overland to Washington. Of writers of the first rank, only Henry James has left us penetrating and original observations, preserved in *The American Scene*, of the region and its cities. It was all too common that Europeans used to come to New York and Boston, there to be enveloped by attentive coteries and to spin out their days profitably before realizing that the time for a Southern excursion had run out. Or, as often, the Northerners who offered themselves as cicerones would suggest that the South, a bleak and vicious place, held little interest. Only Thackeray successfully resisted these presumptions, and found himself more at home in the South than the North, so that he wrote not *The Bostonians* but *The Virginians*. By the late nineteenth and early twentieth centuries, the trade routes carried authors north and westward, for the pocketing of lecture fees. So it is a modest sign of the South's modest prosperity, that chance and economics begins to draw aliens in to record their observations. Even in 1968, when I first visited the South from England, I do not recall seeing another English face. As early as 1980, this had changed. I remember sitting in the airport at Atlanta, about to catch the newly established direct flight to London. In the bar, I suddenly realized, there was a Babel of British voices, Cockney, Glaswegian, Mancunian. A certain privacy abruptly dissolved.

It is too early to know whether V. S. Naipaul will be numbered among the immortals. But certainly few modern British writers have produced more compelling literature, fashioned with great pride in the vocation of letters. The book jacket of *A Turn in the South* proclaims (surely in the author's own words) that he was born in Trinidad in 1932, went to Oxford in 1950, then "he began to write, and he has followed no other profession." Naipaul has been marked by his interest in travel writing, though the British have long taken the form seriously. Arthur Young on France,

Charles Doughty on Arabia, Evelyn Waugh on Abyssinia, James Morris on Venice, these testify to a genre seriously ventured, even if the occasion has often been the interlude between novels, the need for rest and recreation, and the opportunity to tinkle silver into half-empty coffers. At the moment, travel writing is unusually popular in Britain. New books are commissioned, old ones reissued.

Travel works offer the temptations of autobiography. For some writers, the impulse has been irresistible. There is little of America in Chateaubriand's *Voyage en Amerique*, but a great deal of Chateaubriand. The thing seen can be lost in the person seeing. Naipaul himself has used travel as a means of self-discovery. One of his earlier books, *An Area of Darkness*, is a sharp account of his first encounter with India. Nowhere can one find a more unyielding, tactile, claustrophobic portrait of the sub-continent. But the stronger memory is of Naipaul, the son of Indians transplanted to the Caribbean, who tries to find a point of sympathy with India, and fails. In this 1964 book, one can see Naipaul's technique as a traveler and maker of books begin to be fashioned, a process which has ripened through later works such as *Among the Believers: An Islamic Journey* and *India: A Wounded Civilization*. Naipaul casts himself as a presence on every page: landing at the airport, talking to the taxi driver, sitting in the hotel, scrutinizing his feelings, trying to connect the thing seen with the person seeing. He is a tourist among the living. With the dead, he has little to do, except when those he meets care for history, as they evidently do in the American South. Though he has some taste for ruins, in the manner of Volney, as a reproach to human vanity, mostly Naipaul has very little interest in the history which embodies itself in buildings or museums. His comments in 1964 on the Taj Mahal were dismissive: "it is a building wastefully without a function; it is only a despot's monument to a woman, not of India, who bore a child every year for fifteen years."[1]

Above all, his travels are full of talk. Or, to be more exact, they are filled with interviews. Though his narrative is full of retrospective commentary, or memories of his emotions when listening, the recorded text of his conversations portrays a man saying only a bare few words occasionally. He seems unwilling to give much of himself away to those whom he meets, as though wishing to hoard himself up for the dialogue with himself that forms his books. But he evidently has a gift for putting others at ease, for eliciting their real voices. And he does this by self-abnegation, by a blank and innocent curiosity. Or, at least, that is the technique, the trick he uses when he travels, the pretense of the account. Naipaul hovers in the narrative, ushers voices on and off the page, and seems never to judge anyone but himself.

It is a technique which has advantages. It can and has produced marvelous vignettes. In *A Turn in the South*, a man named Campbell explains to Naipaul the Redneck as a species with a vigor and insight, a gustiness which Naipaul (with unwonted enthusiasm) calls "a great Theophrastan 'character,' something almost in the style of the seventeenth-century character-writers."[2] These passages will survive and inform our understanding of Southern culture. But much seems to depend upon chance. Naipaul lets his travels unfold almost by accident. He has not, Ruskin-like, studied Southern culture before visiting it. Few books are mentioned, except Louis Harlan's biography of Booker T. Washington. One person leads him to another, he has his interview, he moves on. Some people are dull, some engaging, some shrewd, some stupid. It is as though Naipaul wants the culture itself to decide.

This is not a bad idea. To have learned the scholarly predicates might only have led him to confirm them, to bump along in their ruts. But, remembering that Naipaul is a kind of oral historian and that the golden rule of interviewing is preparation, Naipaul's want of preparation leads to dead spots. He goes to talk to Marvin Arrington, the black president of the Atlanta City Council, but the interview is a failure. "[It] was partly my own fault, because when Arrington took off his jacket and urged me to begin, just like that, I could think of little to say. I had been hoping for a little chat beforehand; and hoping that during this chat I might see ideas or themes I might want to follow up. But this blunt request to get started filled my head only with what was most obvious."[3] Little of interest is said.

And the mechanics of the technique are suspect. Page upon page of verbatim conversation is transcribed. How were the words captured? No tape recorder is mentioned, only a notebook. Perhaps as a consequence, the voices can ring falsely. In Alabama, he observes to a native that Tuskegee is the rival of Auburn. "Sam Hinote smiled. I was a visitor; he was tolerant. He said, 'Tuskegee is a black school. But Auburn is not its rival. Auburn's rival is Alabama State University.'" Sam Hinote, one feels sure, said no such thing, but instead "the University of Alabama." And elsewhere, the feel of the language can be wrong. Would Anne Siddons the author have quite said, in reminiscence: "I was a young woman newly come to Atlanta and still deeply caught in that web of what is seemly and what is not"? Someone from Hampstead might speak like this. Still, on the whole, the voices ring true. But this may tell us as much about Naipaul's gifts as a mimic man and a novelist as about his accomplishments in shorthand. Recently Naipaul published *The Enigma of Arrival*, a novel about traveling to England and living in its countryside, in which the protagonist is a barely disguised portrait of Naipaul himself. Reading *A Turn in the South* and *The Enigma of Arrival* in short succession, as I chanced to do, is to suspect that the partitions between Naipaul the "factual" travel writer and Naipaul the "fictional" novelist may be thinner than he wants us to think.[4]

This leads to a further thought, qualifying an earlier observation. The guilelessness of his travels may be part of the illusion he wants us to grant. He evidently talked to more Southerners than find expression here. Some are given great space, some (even Eudora Welty) are scanted. Naipaul talked to Margarita Childs in Charleston, the grapevine tells me: Childs whose commitment to civil rights is longstanding. She is nowhere to be found in this book. Instead Jack Leland, an old journalist, stands as the symbol of Charleston, a man garrulously and unguardedly giving us the voice of well-meaning bigotry. The voice is coaxed along by Naipaul's trick of detached sympathy. At one point in Leland's chilling monologue, something has been said about growing residential segregation and Leland says, "And today we have a tremendous black section. And the old Charleston, peninsular Charleston, is sixty percent black and forty percent white. The public schools are ninety-five percent black." Naipaul's voice is heard, saying, "What a fate for a city that lived off the plantations!" Encouraged, Leland plunges on, the noose tightening. Oh yes, the housing projects are crime ridden, I'm good friends with the Negroes, old servants are loyal, slavery was a calamity, blacks have too many babies, in Haiti they killed the whites. One can feel Naipaul sitting with veiled eyes, his pencil racing.[5]

Naipaul is, by the cruelly inflexible racial standards of the United States, an oddity. Of Indian extraction, born in Trinidad, an Oxford graduate, an English author, he must have puzzled many to whom he talked. It seems to have puzzled him, where he stood, where he should sympathize. The warmest moment is his encounter with the philosopher of the Redneck. But he often speaks of being moved by the black plight. One old black woman tells him of segregation and observes that, "'People have changed. And now some of those people wouldn't believe that they were that cruel back there.'" Naipaul then writes: "It was such a good way of putting it. She didn't offer a personal forgiveness. She spoke of a larger change of heart. It was immensely moving."[6] But much of Naipaul's understanding of race was formed in Trinidad, where

Negroes were separate from Indians like himself, where black and brown were distinguished, where there was the master race of the white English: these races shared things, like cricket, but were clean different, mutually repulsive. Even the Indians themselves were divided by religion, Muslim and Hindu.

Walking through Atlanta, seeing so many black faces, Naipaul thinks about race.

> I was taken back to some of the feelings of my childhood in Trinidad. There, though most of my teachers were Negroes (brown rather than black), and though for such people (as well as for policemen, Negroes again) I as a child had the utmost awe and respect, and though in my eyes people like teachers didn't really have racial attributes but were their professions alone, yet the minute I found myself in an out-of-school relationship with them I became aware—a child from an Indian family, full of rituals that couldn't be transferred outside the family house, rituals and attitudes that had day after day to be shed and reassumed, as one went to school and returned home—I became aware of the physical quality of Negroes, and of the difference and even, to me, the unreality of their domestic life.

In *The Enigma of Arrival*, he writes of flying frightened and unsure from Trinidad to England for the first time, via New York. In Puerto Rico, they land. "There was a Negro in the hangar.... The Negro was from the little airplane. I asked him whether he was from Trinidad. Of course he was. I knew that. I had seen him in the plane. But I asked him. Why? Friendship? I didn't need that. I noted the falsity in my behavior."[7] There is a sort of falsity in his passages here about Southern blacks, a trying to be sympathetic, a failing to be so.

For Naipaul, as for C. L. R. James in his great work on cricket and imperialism, *Beyond a Boundary*, race is mixed up with colonialism and independence. Race is about Trinidad, and Nigeria, and India, about Nehru and Nkrumah. Naipaul's other writing, as with *A Bend in the River* or *India: A Wounded Civilization*, show how much he, as a colonial, learned and aspired to Englishness.[8] Fulfilling the dream of the scholarship boy, he went to Oxford, he became the metropolitan, even later a sort of country gentleman. He has had to rediscover the side of him which is from and about the Third World. But he goes there as a stranger, his ancestry giving him the right of criticism, his Englishness sometimes giving the impulse. He has been willing to see that being oppressed is not a guarantee of virtue, that liberators can become oppressors.

Little of this has much to do with the insular experience of American blacks, their attempts to identify with the Third World to the contrary notwithstanding, except that Naipaul brings a political skepticism to black politics in America and to the iconography of black history. This is hardest on Du Bois, whose *Souls of Black Folk* is condemned for pastoral excesses reminiscent of Richard Jeffries, and for "evasiveness and too-pretty ways with words." Laconically, Naipaul traces Du Bois's late career: "He left the United States and went to live in West Africa, in Ghana, a former British colony that had in independence very quickly become an African despotism, and was soon to revert to bush and poverty, exporting labor to its neighbors." This is a candid voice, speaking some truth. But it is also the voice of gentleman's clubs in London. Perhaps not curiously, Naipaul is most sympathetic with Booker T. Washington, whose *Up from Slavery* was a favorite with his father in Trinidad. For Washington represented a peace with the dominant culture, not a defiance, and embodied the strains and doubleness of the eager outsider become ambivalent insider. Rereading *Up from Slavery*, Naipaul sees this doubleness: "So many snares; so many people to please; so many contradictions to resolve; so many possibilities of destruction. The achievement was great. But at what cost. He died at the age of fifty-nine."[9] Naipaul was fifty-seven in 1989.

One theme has run through Naipaul's travel writing and his autobiography, a fascination with religion. This is most powerfully worked out in *Among the Believers* (1981), his journey through Iran, Pakistan, Malaysia, and Indonesia. Religion is part of his quarrel with India. For he grew up formally a Hindu, but devoid of belief. In *An Area of Darkness*, he remembers: "I had been born an unbeliever. I took no pleasure in religious ceremonies.... One ceremony was like another. The images didn't interest me; I never sought to learn their significance. With my lack of belief and distaste for ritual there also went a metaphysical incapacity, this again a betrayal of heredity, for my father's appetite for Hindu speculation was great." Like many unbelievers, he has a fascination with belief. And in the American South, there are an abundance of believers. His encounter with them forms almost a central theme for this book. Preachers, the devoted, the converted fall across his path, often reminding him of Iranian zealotry. At a black church, he writes, "I began to feel the pleasures of the religious meeting: the pleasures of brotherhood, union, formality, ritual, clothes, music, all combining to create a possibility of ecstacy."[10] But the possibility belongs to others, not to Naipaul. He likes to see those pleasures, but not for long.

Like most travel books, *A Turn in the South* is not intended much for those traveled among. Stendhal did not keep his *Roman Journal* for the benefit of Italians. By the same token, excerpts from this book first disported themselves in the *New Yorker* and the *New York Review of Books*. The literati of London and the North, with other things to do with their time, will (I suppose) read it for Naipaul's sake more than the South's. They will get not a bad primer of modern Southern voices. They will not learn much about its intellectual culture and will be sadly misled on its history. On the latter score, the errors are too numerous to mention or remember. It would be foolish to correct the Southerners he quotes, and by consensus in our time men of letters are permitted creative ignorance of history. But there is a fair range of political, religious, and social opinion here from within an area bounded by Durham, Charleston, Jackson, Tallahassee, and Nashville. Virginia is missing, as is New Orleans, Texas, southern Florida. Hence the Southerner himself will not learn much from Naipaul, but there is no reason why he or she should. If a lifetime cannot compete with the visit of a few weeks, matters are awry.

So the proper critical question may be, is this vintage Naipaul? I think not. It may be the most mechanical of his travel books. He has his techniques, he uses them, a book comes out. It is hard for such to be a bad book, for his intelligence is too restless and acute, his ear for voices too sharp, his eye for texture too perceptive. But Naipaul needs a point of contact with a culture, almost a personal grievance which will release his curiosity. He seems to lack this here. Feeling the absence, he does his best to simulate the emotion. He talks about the parallels between Trinidad the plantation slaveholding culture and the low country of South Carolina, he remembers "Negroes" from his youth, he recalls other attempts to comprehend the great mystery of the religious mind. But he is, while never labored, often unconvincing. He does not seem greatly to care. It is hard to think that Naipaul is much different for taking his turn in the South, and the best of his travel writing is about the interchange between himself and the world he sees, about learning and being changed.

NOTES

1. V. S. Naipaul, *An Area of Darkness* (1964; Harmondsworth: Penguin, 1968), 206; idem, *Among the Believers: An Islamic Journey* (London: Andre Deutsch, 1981); idem, *India: A Wounded Civilization* (London: Andre Deutsch, 1977).

2. V. S. Naipaul, *A Turn in the South* (New York: Alfred A. Knopf, 1989), 204.

3. Ibid., 55.

4. Naipaul, *Turn in the South*, 176, 41; idem., *The Enigma of Arrival: A Novel* (New York: Alfred A. Knopf, 1987).

5. Naipaul, *Turn in the South*, 93–98 (quotation on 93).

6. Ibid., 125.

7. Naipaul, *Turn in the South*, 57–58; idem., *Enigma of Arrival*, 105–6.

8. See C. L. R. James, *Beyond a Boundary* (London: Stanley Paul, 1963); V. S. Naipaul, *A Bend in the River* (London: Andre Deutsch, 1980).

9. Naipaul, *Turn in the South*, 152, 154.

10. Naipaul, *Area of Darkness*, 32; idem., *Turn in the South*, 15.

A paper given at a panel on Reed's work at the Southern Historical Association in Louisville, 1994, and subsequently published as Michael O'Brien, "An Episcopalian Imagination," *Southern Cultures* 7 (Spring 2001): 13–20. Reprinted by permission.

I am commissioned here to discuss the influence of John Shelton Reed. But on whom? On historians of the American South like myself? I am not sure John Reed has had any influence on historians, at least in the direct sense. Though his writing is suffused with a *sense* of history, there is remarkably little formal history in his work. Is it, instead, the case that his influence has lain in transmitting from his own discipline insights, theory, and technique, by which Southern studies has been enriched? Has Reed brought us riches from the world of sociology, which has made us see things anew? Well, not really.

Reed seems barely engaged with his own discipline, as if he does a bit of sociology now and again so that they will not revoke his citizenship and deport him to some Devil's Island for disaffected social scientists. Indeed, he is inclined to abuse the trade of sociology, laments that regional sociology is dead, except for him, tells other sociologists off for writing atrociously. Certainly, he has his polling data; all those graphs and maps and indices that define the shifting landscape of Southern identity. These facts he has passed along to us. And they are useful. It is pleasant to have a graph or a table. It is nice and formal. One can know, for example, that in Duluth in 1976 the ratio of Southern to American entries in the names of businesses listed in the Yellow Pages was zero, but had risen by 1988 to .03, whereas in Winston-Salem it had fallen from .84 to .81. You may wish to know this. I myself do not find it positively repulsive as a piece of information, but it does seem to me the intellectual equivalent of a pretzel nugget.

In truth, this is not a good time to be an emissary from sociology. The discipline, once so promising, has lost adherents, has drifted to the margins of the intellectual world. How many historians now read any sociology? Be honest. When did you last look at a sociological journal? When did you last pick up a book entitled *New Perspectives on Sociology and History*? When *was* there last such a book? Who would send a history graduate student to take courses in a sociology department? Does your university still have a sociology department? No, not a good time.

So, why should we care for John Shelton Reed's influence on historians? Well, we probably should not. I think he has had some role in reassuring modern South-watchers that their subject matter is not disappearing, a disquiet which much troubled historians of the South in the 1950s and 1960s. Any old graph helps to fend off the prospect, grim to some (not to me), that studying the South will become like studying Merovingian ascetics, the contemplation of vanished flagellations and unintelligible tombs. This has been of some moment, though I suppose historians would have found other ways to reassure themselves.

John Reed is important for other reasons, more compelling, more elusive. As he himself has been at pains to insist, the South requires constant reinvention to survive. What matters is less the land or the climate or some hard positivist thing called the South, but the social psychology of the persons who claim the title of Southerners. This is a matter of will. Those with such wills are important. Reed has been amongst the most successful of modern reinventors of the tradition, one of the people who helps us see what he tells us is around us. But, first, upon his own testimony, he needed to invent the South for himself, being an East Tennessean to whom such matters were not self-evident, except from the standpoint of Massachusetts and New York, where he was educated. Such a route has made him unusually sensitive to the processes of migration, modernization, change. Unlike many Southern conservatives, to whom the South is a sort of rock which survives the erosion of time and the Yankees, Reed views the South as made by the social processes of time and change, what erodes as well as what is eroding. At least, he argues this in principle, though it is at odds with another Reed notion, the South as a folk culture.

But what has he invented? A South fit for modern conservatives, mostly. I stress the word *modern*. Reed has been conspicuous for disassociating himself from some of the older traditions of that conservatism, which included racism. (As did, for that matter, the older traditions of Southern liberalism.) He has written with contempt of tying Southern identity to racist ideology. I do not doubt that, in many of the conclaves of Southern conservatism, Reed has often had to bite his tongue or speak his mind on these matters. Nonetheless Southern blacks are a shadowy presence on his Southern intellectual landscape, apart from the odd essay which documents the bare fact that they seem to begin to feel a sense of comity with the South, and apart from the occasional observation or the reiterated and marked enthusiasm for some aspects of black music. But liking to boogie is not the same thing as assessing the role of blacks in Southern culture, which Reed has conspicuously failed to do. So, his invention of the South is white. It is also, mostly, middle class and downwards. The great houses of the Battery in Charleston, the elegant squares of Savannah, the foxhunters of Virginia, the haute cuisine of New Orleans, these form little or no part of Reed's South. Reed is into barbecue and pickup trucks, into subdivisions in Charlotte and gas stations in Mississippi. Say "greens" to Reed and he thinks, not of putting in Bobby Jones's impeccable Augusta, but of collards. Because of this, he has quietly let drop another aspect of Southern conservatism: agrarianism. There are almost no farms or plantations in Reed's South. Everyone has gone to town, or, if they have not, whatever they do on the farm which concerns farming does not seem to preoccupy him.

These are distinguishing lacunae. What does it leave? Reed holds to a version of Southern nationalism-cum-regionalism oddly reconfigured into a defense of Southern whites as an ethnicity, an idea whose moment never seems to have come, which is just as well. As a foreigner, however, I notice that there is little of the screaming eagle complacency which disfigures so much American thinking, especially but not exclusively its conservative phases; Reed seems happy that the South be a culture among cultures, not more important, certainly not less, just itself. It is true he sometimes flings off the occasional xenophobic phrase. I note, for example, he uses the adjective "candy-ass British," but I do not think I am supposed to take this personally. Certainly someone who, in 1982 while giving a talk at Vanderbilt, could compare John Crowe Ransom with the Ayatollah Khomeini deserves credit for having the odd cosmopolitan impulse.[1]

Technically, one might call him a Herderian, as understood by Isaiah Berlin. Reed has a very old-fashioned belief in the reality of folk culture, its power, its persistence, its integrity. It is one of his few real links with Howard Odum, whom he wishes to respect as a precursor, but whose theory was so disorganized, whose prose was more so, whose influence has so vanished. From this grows a belief in states rights, not for reasons which John C. Calhoun might recognize (Reed does not seem to have a *political* theory), but because the folk are segmented into groups which cling together within the boundaries of state cultures. But not all Southern states are created equal in Reed's landscape; North Carolina is preeminent. He seems to be a laissez-faire conservative, though one more interested in the liberties of the citizen than in the possible economic benefits which might accrue from any free markets; the gimcrack economic optimism of the Reagan years seems to have put Reed into a very bad temper, if the essays in *Whistling Dixie* are any guide. One might surmise that his folk conservatism is reminiscent of

William Graham Sumner's, who was influential on Odum, were it not that Sumner was a pessimistic Social Darwinist and Reed persistently underplays the force of competitiveness, of struggle, of violence. Confronted with stark statistics about the level of murders, for instance, Reed insists that we be of good cheer. The Yankees, he says, tend to murder strangers, whereas Southerners murder their wives, husbands, friends, neighbors. I confess that the advantage of this has always eluded me. After all, one can do something about meeting strangers, but one is stuck with spouses and neighbors; it would be nice if they were not murderous. This disposition to look on the bright side of Southern identity is part of a pattern in Reed. He is, usually, a mild writer, without malice towards even the malicious. I say "usually," because an observer whose basic stance is that the world is going to hell and it is probably someone else's fault cannot always preserve a mood of benign charity.

This sense of impending cultural destruction, of course, drives his greatest gift, his wit. In truth, the Tory mind often turns to satire. Think of Jonathan Swift, Samuel Johnson, H. L. Mencken, Evelyn Waugh. Here is Reed's greatest influence; he makes us laugh and thereby makes us think. He collects eccentricity and calls it normality. His writing is a splendid montage of absurd anecdotes, crazy people, illogical premises, ridiculous conclusions, all which are adduced to demonstrate that Southerners are among the world's sanest people. There is wisdom in such a stance, an anarchic wisdom. To do this he has fashioned a prose of great distinction, rapid, conversational, crafted, illusory. It is a style full of real people lightly disguised, stories, self-awareness, self-mockery. Whatever one may think of his social opinions, with almost none of which I agree, this voice makes Reed a humane presence. It is a voice, ineradicably his own, which will outlast our own time, past the moment when the last RC Cola has been drunk. There is not a page or a paragraph in his mature writings, picked at random, which could have been written by anyone else; this is the mark of a master.

But, like many writers who offer us self-revelation, Reed deflects our gaze from what he is to what he wishes us to see. There is a ruse going on here. It is the illusion of this style that the author is a sort of good old boy, sitting on his porch, swigging his whiskey, going out the back to shoot hapless mammals. This is an imposture, carefully constructed. Consider one immovable fact. This man is an Episcopalian, who clings to the Book of Common Prayer, with all its stately cadences. More, he has written a book about the transformations in ritual in the Church of England, arising from the Oxford movement, during the nineteenth century. *Glorious Battle* is a book about chasubles and the reredos and stained glass and miters and confessionals and Te Deums and Sexagesima. What are we to make of this? In a brief essay on being an Episcopalian in *Whistling Dixie*, he adduces three reasons for his religious belief. One is "the splendor of the ruined Anglican liturgy, sacked and burned by indigenous barbarians of our own time." The second is inertia, that "remaining where I was planted makes very little statement at all, and that suits me just fine." He writes of "this vegetable aspect of my affiliation." Third is that, being vegetable and alienated from the barbaric aspects of modern Anglicanism, he has opportunities for "grisly humor."[2] I am inclined to suggest that, here, we are close to the heart of the matter. Underneath this scruffy exterior lurks a very high-caste Anglican, who thinks the world has gone to hell, but that it is full of amusement and energy. But it is an energy which has drained out of that Anglican world, never very remarkable for passion. Cranmer is long gone to his grave, Newman long since passed to Brompton Oratory. Little is left but vegetable habit within that tradition. So, what to do? Perhaps one needs to borrow energy, to wander the world to collect energy from others' energy of belief.

Consider this image. See Reed in a cool Gothic chapel, where he follows the incantations and raises his voice when the liturgy requires it. Then see him step out abruptly into a parking lot full of pickup trucks, their radios blaring country music. He does not hurry back in; he likes the contrast, it is invigorating. He gets to like the music, takes off his tie, goes with them to the barbecue pit, seeks to understand and capture their world's idiosyncrasy. He learns about them, acquires an ineradicable affection for them, sometimes (just a little) condescends to them in his laughter, reinvents them, *almost* becomes them. But, remember, that he is *not* them.

So, what does this make John Reed? Casting around for a useable parallel within the Southern tradition, my mind turns to Augustus Baldwin Longstreet and *Georgia Scenes*. These stories, too, were concerned with the absorbing oddities of Southern life, of fights, eye-gougings, storytellers, false gentilities and pretensions. But Longstreet was no frontiersman. He was a proper Methodist gentleman, with a Federalist ideology. The Federalist world was dying or dead; the frontier was vibrant. Longstreet came to take a perverse pleasure in it, and the conservative became the student of the vernacular. John Reed, too, has a Federalist imagination, has found the same solution, the same pleasure. But, when you read him, when you revel in those assiduously gathered stories about Conway Twitty and Brother

Dave Gardner, listen carefully. In the background is the faint sound of murmured words echoing off bare cherished choirs, words like "we have followed too much the devices and desires of our own hearts," and "Lord, now lettest thou thy servant depart in peace, according to thy word," and "Man, that is born of a woman, hath but a short time to live, and is full of misery. He cometh up, and is cut down, like a flower; he fleeth as it were a shadow, and never continueth in one stay." Such words matter more to him than they do to many of us, but we will not understand John Reed unless we train ourselves to hearing them, beneath the roar of drag racers.

NOTES

1. John Shelton Reed, *Whistling Dixie: Dispatches from the South* (Columbia: University of Missouri Press, 1990), 5; William C. Havard and Walter Sullivan, eds., *A Band of Prophets: The Vanderbilt Agrarians After Fifty Years* (Baton Rouge: Louisiana State University Press, 1982), 58.

2. John Shelton Reed, *Glorious Battle: The Cultural Politics of Victorian Anglo-Catholicism* (Nashville, TN: Vanderbilt University Press, 1996); Reed, *Whistling Dixie*, 218–19.

A review of Bill Clinton, *My Life* (London: Hutchinson, 2004), in the *Times Literary Supplement* (27 August 2004): 3–4.

Bill Clinton has written two books: a beguiling memoir of growing up in the South and becoming a young Arkansas politician, and a tedious account of being president of the United States. It is tempting to ignore the latter, by way of courtesy to the author, but unfortunately the two books may have an organic relationship, so the tedium will require an explanation.

The Southern coming-of-age autobiography is a genre, self-evidently intended by Clinton, who admires Willie Morris's *North Toward Home* (1967) and Thomas Wolfe's *You Can't Go Home Again* (1940). In such books, a young Southern boy grows up in an old house with an unkempt yard, is formed by a strong homely mother or (more rarely) father, goes fishing with friends, has eccentric relatives with startling stories, is influenced by imaginative teachers, and is scarred by evangelical religion. Eventually the boy becomes a man by dint of reading, talking, having sex under worrying circumstances, and going to college, all of which wrenches him away. For such men, literature becomes a meditation on the irreconcilability of what was lost and what gained in the movement between, what Clinton here calls, "big impersonal cities and small towns."[1]

It is usual, in such memoirs, to counterpoint the stable child with the disordered adult, but Clinton offers a reversal. His youth is portrayed as painfully mobile, but maturity as evenly accomplished, apart from mysterious lapses. ("Mystery" is one of his favorite words.) It is hard to quarrel with the first part. Before he was born as William Jefferson Blythe III in 1946, a freak road accident killed his father, who turned out to have had four wives and assorted children, all carefully concealed from the others. Virginia Cassidy Blythe (later Clinton, later Dwire, finally Kelley) was a doting mother but a working woman, who liked rouge, race tracks, booze, men, and casinos. His stepfather Roger Clinton was a car salesman, violent, abusive, and drunk. Bill Clinton, as the younger Blythe became, came to live in Hot Springs, not a typical Southern small town but a resort crowded with bathhouses, gangsters, invalids, hotels, and bookmakers. Such facts push Clinton towards Southern Gothic. But other facts do not. There was a kindly grandfather, affectionate black servants, the local movie house, the high school band, and helpful teachers who encouraged a gauche, overweight outsider of a boy.

Faced with this tension, Clinton prefers to be Willie Morris and turns away from being Flannery O'Connor. He claims that this choice was the choice of his childhood, when he repressed the stark pain of witnessing abuse beneath a display of normality. He became used to keeping secrets and offers now a defense of the habit. All of us, he says, are "entitled" to secrets: "They make our lives more interesting, and when we decide to share them, our relationships become more meaningful." The secret world is a haven and a respite, but also a burden and a shame: "the allure of our secrets can be too strong, strong enough to make us feel we can't live without them, that we wouldn't even be who we are without them." By this, the reader is primed for a meaningful relationship. But, after Daddy has had his last drunken binge, not another secret emerges, though Clinton coyly hints at hidden things and promisingly speaks of himself as sinful, but understandably evades specificity. Even when we know he has been sinful, and he knows we know, he is disappointingly prim and admits only to being "inappropriate," which is no sort of adjective for a Southern Baptist to use.[2] Even in these degenerate days, no sinner should stand up in a backcountry pew and exclaim, "Lord! Lord! I have been inappropriate!"

Still, the memoir bounces along very nicely for several hundred pages, as Clinton goes to college, serves as a junior aide for J. William Fulbright's senate office, takes up his Rhodes Scholarship, and works his way towards becoming governor of Arkansas in 1979. Indeed, if these pages had been published as a separate book, many would think that Clinton has contributed a classic of Southern political memoir. A Southern politician is supposed to be a good storyteller and, in these early pages at least, Clinton is. He is good-humored, can be pleasingly sardonic, and has the good sense to quote those funnier than himself. I particularly liked the story about the exchange between the ancient Mike Mansfield and the fairly ancient Fulbright, when Mansfield "asked Fulbright his age and Fulbright said he was eighty-seven. Mansfield replied, 'Oh, to be eighty-seven again.'" Better, perhaps, is Clinton's repetition of something heard in the Arkansas hills when he was running for Congress in 1974, a saying used to "describe someone you really don't like": "I wouldn't piss in his ear if his brain was on fire." Indeed, one of the better things about *My Life* is that no one has edited Clinton's Arkansas idiom, so the text is scattered with phrases like "along toward the end," "funny as all get-out," and "behaving as I'd been raised to do."[3]

Arkansas is physically large, but it has few people, so its politicians require stamina. David Pryor's rule was, "If you don't like catfish don't run for office."[4] Clinton quickly grasped that, to win elections, one must be indefatigably willing to visit every town, venture into every diner, pray in every church, and shake every hand. This played to his strength, even his need. Running away from the secrets of his childhood seems to have led him to run towards everyone else, at least for five minutes at a time.

But his political success had other roots. On the one hand, he was the modern politician *par excellence*, media savvy, poll conscious, cold blooded, tactical. On the other, he was the most traditional of Southern politicians, in the back room with the boys, playing a musical instrument to amuse the voters, electrocuting criminals, and calling down the blessing of the Almighty. In Little Rock the latter persona needed to predominate, in Washington the former, but there was never a moment when both were not present. In Arkansas, the political has been personal for a long time, and illogicality is cheerfully tolerated. This is a state, after all, in which a municipal judge once reproved an overly informed lawyer, "Young man, that may be the law of the state of Arkansas but it is not the law in my courtroom." In the same particularist spirit, the town of Sherrill in the early 1980s dispensed with local elections, on the grounds that nobody was much interested in running against the city officials, who had been hard enough to find, in the first place. The mayor explained, "It's not the way it's supposed to go, but it's the way we do it."[5]

Certainly, a floozy or two or three was not a problem. When I lived in Fayetteville in the 1980s, it was devoutly believed that the boy wonder had bedded every other woman in the state. One never actually met a woman who had been his lover, but somebody knew somebody else who knew something about a political rally and a motel and a married woman. None of these titillating rumors made any difference to his political prospects. Indeed, they may have helped to overcome the early prejudice that a politician with long hair and a wife who refused to adopt her husband's surname was, probably, unmanly. Arkansans came to know that Clinton had the political gift, had improved their state, and was deeply flawed, mostly by being indecisive, disorganized, self-serving, too willing to please, and prone to getting things right, but only eventually. They held their breath when he ran for president, because they knew that the Americans would rapidly discern the gift and experience the flaws, and no one knew how that twin discovery would turn out.

Important to Clinton's politics has been his religion, which explains him as much as it does George W. Bush. This is easy to lose sight of, because

Clinton supported abortion and gay rights, hung out with Hollywood stars, and was loathed by many evangelicals. One of the shrewder suggestions, in a book disappointingly thin on analysis, is that "the New Right Republicans ... hated me because I was an apostate, a white southern Protestant who could appeal to the very people they had always taken for granted." But, in fact, Southern Baptists are so decentralized and diverse that they do not have apostates, only those for whom one needs to pray. Clinton's faith is real enough: it started in his childhood, was confirmed by singing in church choirs and attending bible camps, and carried on into a White House where he and Al Gore, at their weekly lunches, took turns in saying grace. To be sure, he is a modern, urban sort of Baptist, the kind who has lost touch with the old savage insistences on guilt and original sin, on abjuring dancing, card-playing, and the devil's music. Clinton plays cards incessantly, likes to dance, listens to Oscar Peterson, and seems to think in country music lyrics, though he did not take a drink until he was twenty-two. The religion, rather, expresses itself in a stress upon community and family, a cloying sentimentality, an insistence on good works, a fear of mortality, and a theme of forgiveness. This last quality is most striking. In politics, there is rancor and, as Clinton has had every reason to know, the partisan bitterness has deepened in his lifetime. But there is scarcely an enemy, with the exception of Kenneth Starr, whom Clinton does not wish to forgive or to be forgiven by. In the moments after the news of Kennedy's assassination reached his high school, for example, he heard "an attractive girl who was in the band with me say that maybe it was a good thing for the country that he was gone" and he became angry. (There are frequent references to being angry.) In 1992, she came to a political rally in Las Vegas, was then "a social worker and a Democrat," and "I treasured our reunion and the chance it gave me to heal an old wound." Likewise, he is generous to the elder George Bush, Bob Dole, and even Newt Gingrich.[6]

One consequence of this religious instinct is some indifference to history and a curious blindness to cultural difference, surprising in a Southerner and a president associated with multiculturalism, but fairly normal for a Baptist. Only very occasionally does Clinton reach for a historical context. He sees himself, for example, as standing for the New South against the Old, as the heir of the civil rights movement, and as someone charged with healing the wounds of the 1960s. But, for the most part, little which came his way seems to require a historical analysis. He thinks in social problems, rapidly understood and solved by a policy decision. "Our job is to live as well and as long as we can, and to help others do the same," he writes in his last pages, by way of a summary sentiment. "What happens after that and how we are viewed by others is beyond our control. The river of time carries us all away. All we have is the moment."[7] This is not how Thomas Wolfe, let alone William Faulkner, saw time and the river. So Clinton is not a man haunted by what happened at Gettysburg, in the moment before Pickett's Charge. Southern history does not seem to be a burden, at all, for him. This casualness extends to Arkansan political history—he does not mention Jeff Davis, Hattie Caraway, Joseph T. Robinson, or Sid McMath—and even to his family. The kinfolk he met, he talks about, but not the family which lived in the more remote past.

Instead, when recounting the numerous people and places he has seen, what he observes are individuals, with particular qualities. Sometimes he offers engaging and discerning sketches (as with John McClellan and Boris Yeltsin), sometimes he manages only a lazy adjective, but he rarely reaches beyond the individual to their culture. When he is talking about his younger days in a fairly homogeneous place, this mode of thought matters less. But, for later global times, it leads to a flatness of vision, which seems intrinsic to Clinton's optimism. If everyone is basically the same, and most people are good, then little is intractable and there is no reason not to gather together at the river. However, in this same flatness may be the root of Clinton's racial tolerance. These memoirs show no especial knowledge of African American culture, apart from his liking jazz and admiring Martin Luther King, Jr. In *My Life*, names like W. E. B. Du Bois, Frederick Douglass, and Ralph Ellison are absent. It is that Clinton treats blacks like everyone else, as individuals worth knowing. In American culture, that undifferentiation constituted something remarkable.

For all that, Clinton is better read than any president since Woodrow Wilson. The evidence is richly scattered through the book: Gabriel García Márquez and Dylan Thomas, Carl Sandburg and E. H. Carr, Edmund Wilson and Hugh Thomas, William Styron and John Locke. Literature seems to work for cultural escape in Clinton's sensibility. He does not refer to Arkansan writers like John Gould Fletcher, Vance Randolph, Harry Ashmore, or Shirley Abbott of his own Hot Springs. However, authors get mentioned by Clinton more than they get discussed, and so the residue of his literary consumption is unclear. The early part of *My Life* may be the better, as memoir, because Clinton has read many good writers. But the later part casts grave doubt on that theory.

It is hard to understand how the ineptness of the last five hundred pages was allowed to pass to the printers, since its hopeless structure ought to have been simple enough to fix. Almost no chapter has a theme. Clinton proceeds week by week, month by month, year by year, and merely recites what happened. Sometimes five or six subjects are covered in a single paragraph. No doubt, surviving a miscellaneous procession of events and actions is the experience of being president, but telling the story as one thing after another squeezes out reflection. So *My Life* degenerates into a medieval chronicle, in which there is war in the Levant, malevolent conspirators, a beautiful maiden, friends willing to perish for the sake of the kingdom, and a deluge somewhere in the land (usually Florida). Here and there, as with the Lewinsky scandal, the impeachment, or the Palestinian-Israeli negotiations, he fashions something recognizable as a narrative, but then he is off again, appointing someone to a minor office, giving an unimportant speech in Utah, declaring a new national park, and having dinner in Warsaw. It seems his publishers tried to call a halt, for the acknowledgments speak chillingly of Clinton's editor persuading him to omit "countless names" from the manuscript.[8] Yet myriads remain. It is as though the prose is running for office and every name mentioned is logged as another vote.

Yet the literary habit of recording minutiae probably runs deeper. Two explanations present themselves, one psychological, the other political. It may be that the events, which culminated in the humiliation of the impeachment, were so damaging that Clinton cannot bear to step back and focus upon a larger pattern, though he clearly has the intelligence to do so. Certainly he invites the reader to hazard a cheap psychology. He is the president, after all, who in late January 1993 held a retreat at Camp David for his Cabinet and senior White House staff, "in which we were supposed to bond by sitting in a group, taking turns telling something about ourselves the others didn't know." (Lloyd Bentsen sensibly declined this offer and, as Clinton remembers it, observed that "if there was something about him the rest of us didn't know, it was intentional.")[9]

But a political explanation for Clinton's taste for minutiae is easier to demonstrate. It is well to remember that, with nearly twelve years service, he was a state governor far longer than any president in American history. For the sixteen others who reached the White House, their average gubernatorial tenure lasted a little over three years. Hence, as a politician, Clinton was unusually formed by the experience of being a governor, and so was peculiarly made by Arkansas. As it happened, its politics did not encourage an ambitious clarity of purpose, something Clinton tried in his first term and which led to his defeat in 1980. Rather, the state encouraged a politics progressive in tone and disposed towards the incremental improvement of social services, as long as change did not offend the state's traditional social values and its few but dominant businessmen, the so-called "Good Suit Club" of Sam Walton, Don Tyson, Jackson T. Stephens, and others.[10] As Diane Blair, who wrote so well on *Arkansas Politics and Government* in 1988, then explained, in Arkansas partisanship was of little importance; Republican voters were few in state elections, it was wise to complain about more liberal Democrats elsewhere, and political party meant almost nothing in gubernatorial-legislative relationships. Policy mattered less than manner, because the governor appointed few important state officials, had little power to effect policy, but had many opportunities to entertain. Almost above all, personal friendships were crucial.

Being governor taught Clinton to deal in small policies and medium-sized rhetoric, though he never ceased to pine for big policies and sweeping rhetoric, which usually got him into trouble. Later, Clinton's critics, seeing the same pattern in Washington, would joke about his offering the American people a "Nouvelle Deal." The president himself, naturally, preferred phrases like New Democracy and the Third Way, but these just denoted a negation or modification of ideologies which lingered from more ambitious times and places. Still, paying attention to many intelligent, small policies added up to a respectable presidency, which left the United States a more humane place. Unfortunately, a preoccupation with small things when writing an autobiography has less to be said for it.

NOTES

1. Clinton, *My Life*, 38.
2. Ibid., 46, 773.
3. Ibid., 96, 213, 106, 83, 653.
4. Diane D. Blair, *Arkansas Politics & Government* (Lincoln: University of Nebraska Press, 1988), 59.
5. Ibid., 195, 233.
6. Clinton, *My Life*, 863, 65.
7. Ibid., 952.
8. Ibid., i.
9. Ibid., 489.
10. The name was invented by John Brummett, in the 1980s a political columnist for the *Arkansas Gazette* and the most acute of Clinton-watchers in the state: see John Brummett, *Highwire: From the Backroads to the Beltway—the Education of Bill Clinton* (New York: Hyperion, 1994), 215.

INDEX

Abbott, Carl, 138
Abbott, Shirley, 255
abolitionism (and abolitionists), 12, 17, 30, 87, 100, 166, 205, 214, 224, 227, 229, 230
abortion, 254
abroad, 16, 20, 181, 225
abstraction, 22–23, 43, 46, 50, 65, 91, 104, 118, 150, 185, 208, 226, 228–31
Abyssinia, 238
Acadians, 32
Act of Union (1707), 29
Acton, John Emerich Edward Dalberg, first baron, 90
actors, xi, 22, 116
Adam, Robert, 189
Adams, Charles Francis, 149
Adams, Henry, 49, 84, 156, 206, 210, 214, 217
Adams, Herbert Baxter, 124, 217
Adams, John, 149
Addisonians, 218
affirmative action, 113
Afghans, 34
Africa (and Africans), 29, 34, 35, 42, 46, 57, 65, 87, 130, 242
African Americans, 18, 32, 35, 60, 63–65, 72, 74, 102, 108, 116, 127, 130–31, 133, 135, 138, 142–45, 207, 255. *See also* blacks; Negro
Agee, James, 197
Agincourt, battle of, 165
agnosticism, 200, 210
agrarianism, 100, 247
Agrarianism, Southern (and neo-Agrarianism), 20, 119, 130, 132, 182–86, 191, 194, 200
agriculture, 62, 64–65, 235
ahistoricism, 93, 95, 226
Alabama, 4, 12, 64–67, 87, 94, 97–98, 110, 120–21, 123, 126, 130, 203, 211, 239

Alamance County, North Carolina, 79–81, 85
Alaska, 8, 51
Albany, Georgia, 12
Aldington, Richard, 92
alienation, ix, 105, 183–91, 223, 227, 232, 249
aliens, 14, 27, 31, 64, 237
Allen, Hervey, 183
Allston, Washington, 181
Althusser, Louis, 197–98
amateurs, 103, 123–24
ambition, 12, 49–50, 55–57, 74, 81, 89, 90, 93–94, 106, 115, 175, 256–57
ambivalence, 34, 75, 102, 128, 131, 144, 187–88, 198, 205, 220, 242
amendments, constitutional, 56, 66, 69, 126
American Historical Association, 141
American Historical Review, 3, 115, 121–22
American Revolution, 46, 54, 126, 134, 143, 184, 189
ampersand studies, x
anachronism, 5, 29, 42, 100, 134, 199, 223
anarchy, 174, 231, 248
ancestors, viii, 45, 64, 70, 82, 98, 103, 125, 144, 184, 186, 187, 189, 194, 235, 241
Anderson, Benedict, 37, 140
Andrews, William L., 142–45
anger, 13, 15, 92, 185, 254
Anglicanism, 45, 249
Anglicization, 28
Anglophilia, 30, 33, 36, 37, 162
Anglophobia, 30–31
Anglo-Saxons, 26, 32–33, 35, 113, 218–19
Anniston, Alabama, 235
anthologies, 9, 19, 103, 116, 134, 139–45, 153, 176
anthropology, 31, 37, 128

antifeminism, 139
antiquity (and the ancient), 11–12, 36, 43–44, 46, 62, 79, 93, 111, 135, 181, 199, 211, 224, 252
anti-Semitism, 14, 195
anxiety, 30, 58, 59, 72, 73, 129, 141, 142, 201, 216, 218–19
Appalachia, 4, 38, 41, 156
Appiah, Kwame Anthony, ix, xii, 131, 139–40
Applebome, Peter, 16–17, 24
Applegate, Celia, 3–4, 6–8
Appomattox Courthouse, 20, 60, 109, 113, 218
Apulia, 199
Arabia, 238
archaeology, 90
Arendt, Hannah, 122
aristocracy, 98, 181, 188, 219
Aristotle, 110, 226
Arizona, 17
Arkansas, vii, 17, 113, 156, 211, 234, 236, 251–57
Armstrong, Louis, 11, 34, 74
Arnold, Matthew, ix, 15, 36, 62
Arrington, Marvin, 239
Ashmore, Harry, 255
Asia, 3, 5–8, 35, 46, 156
Astor, Viscountess Nancy, 32
Atlanta, Georgia, 41, 127, 234, 237, 239, 241
Atlantic Charter, 185
Atlantic Ocean, 18, 35, 109, 156, 217
Auburn, Alabama, 235, 239
Audubon, John J., 91
Audubon, Lucy, 87, 90–91
Augusta, Georgia, 94, 235, 247
Augusta County, Virginia, 71
Aurelius, Marcus, 209
Austen, Jane, 34, 162, 175–76
Australia, 10, 33, 67
Austro-Hungarian Empire, 27
autobiography, x, 79–83, 144, 161, 173, 195, 238, 242, 251, 257. *See also* memoirs
Avary, Myrta Lockett, 161
Ayers, Edward, 137, 234–36

Bagehot, Walter, 93
Baker, Jean, 57–58
Bakhtin, Mikhail, 157, 234
Bakker, Jan, 157
Balkans, 6

Balzac, Honoré, 88, 163
Bangladesh, 54
Banneker, Benjamin, 143
Baptists, 10, 113, 252, 254
Barbados, 100
Barnard, Frederick A. P., 87–88
Barnes, Djuna, 176
Barrett, Elizabeth, 93
baseball, 10, 235
Basingstoke, 24
basketball, 129, 139
Basques, 7
Baudelaire, Charles, 163
Beard, Charles, 86, 128, 207
Bechet, Sidney, 11
Beckett, Samuel, 116
Belfast, 7
Belgium, 54
Beluche, Renato, 87, 89
Bender, Thomas, ix, 114, 118
Benn, Tony, 70
Benson, A. C., 34–35
Benson, E. W., 34–35
Benson, Lee, 122
Benton, Thomas Hart, 58
Bentsen, Lloyd, 256
Berkeley, California, 19
Berlin, 10
Berlin, Isaiah, 75, 247
Bert (gardener), 80, 85
Beton, Mary, 177
Bevan, Aneurin, 28
Beverley, Robert, 123
Bible, 207, 231, 254
Binney, Mrs., 170
biography, x, 59, 83, 86–97, 110, 125, 149, 156, 169, 172, 175, 195, 201–3, 207, 215, 220, 239
biracialism, 74, 75, 104, 143, 145
Birmingham, Alabama, 12, 126, 190
Bishop, John Peale, 196
Blackett, Richard, 28, 30, 35
Blackheath, battle of, 6
blacks, viii, 4, 17–18, 20, 28, 34–38, 44, 47, 57, 61–68, 71–74, 90, 94, 96, 98, 108, 114, 117, 130–32, 143, 145, 154, 165, 177, 181, 191–92, 200–1, 203–4, 208, 217, 221, 235–36, 239–42, 246, 251, 255. *See also* African Americans; Negro
Blair, Diane, 257

260 INDEX

Bledsoe, Albert Taylor, 223–24, 226, 228
Bleser, Carol, 96
Bloomsbury, 160, 174, 177
Blotner, Joseph Leo, 96
blues, 11, 36, 129, 144, 235
Bolden, Buddy, 235
Boles, John, 140
Bonaparte, Joseph, 49
Bonaparte, Pauline, 49
Bonn, 15–16, 20
Boorstin, Daniel J., 213
Boritt, Gabor, 57–58
Bosnia, 79
Boston (and Bostonians), 20, 43, 109, 121, 149, 182, 217, 219, 237
Bouffants (retro chick band), 211
Bourbons, 51
Bowman, Rev. J., 34
Boyd, William K., 124
Brant, Irving, 96
Braund, Kathryn, 29
Brazil, 65
Brenner Pass, 95
Bretons, 6
Brewer, Holly, 28, 30
Bristol, 89
Britain (and the British), vii, viii, x, 6, 7, 9, 16, 22, 24, 26–37, 41, 50, 54, 80, 100, 133, 145, 237, 238, 242, 247. *See also* United Kingdom
British Museum, 180
Brompton Oratory, 249
Brontë, Emily, 176
Brooke, John M., 87–88
Brooks, Cleanth, 195, 200
Brown, William Wells, 34, 143
Brown vs. Board of Education, 208
Browne, Mrs., 164
Browne, Sir Thomas, 175
Browning, Robert, 93, 95
Bruce, Robert V., 58
Brugger, Robert, 94–95
Brummett, John, 257
Brussels, 15, 86
Buchenwald, 83
Buck, Paul H., 61
Buckle, George Earle, 96
Buell, Lawrence, 122
Bulldozer Revolution, 132, 208

Burckhardt, Jacob, 116
Burke, Edmund, 7, 46, 89–90
Burr, Aaron, 49
Burton, Vernon, 144
Bush, George H. W., 12, 232, 254
Bush, George W., 56, 73, 253
Butler, Rhett, 186
Byrd, William, II, 143
Byron, George Gordon, 181

Cable News Network, 10
Cade, Jack, 44
Café Paris, 31
Cairo, 33
Calhoun, John C., 3, 18, 86, 96, 104, 108, 144, 155, 181, 194, 223–24, 226, 228, 231, 247
California, 17, 51, 87
Calvin, John (and Calvinism), 59, 165, 231
Cambodia, 27
Cambridge, Massachusetts, 42, 109
Cambridge, University of, 10, 20, 34–35
Camden, South Carolina, 160, 167, 169, 172
Camden Society, 97
Camp David, 256
Campbell, Charles, 123
Campbell, Colin, 81
Campbell (redneck philosopher), 239
Camus, Albert 13
Canada, 7, 34
canons (and the canonical), 20, 97, 103, 110, 114, 116–17, 122, 137, 139–40, 142, 153, 157, 174, 187, 191, 197, 206, 213
capitalism, 55, 59, 91, 132, 198, 207, 223, 225
Capper, Charles, 116
Caraway, Hattie, 255
Cardiff, 28
Caribbean, 35, 38, 49–50, 87, 89, 106, 135, 238
Carlyle, Thomas, 15, 31–32, 86, 164
Carmichael, Mary, 177
Caroline County, Virginia, 88
Carpenter, Jesse, 103
Carr, E. H., 255
Carroll, Lewis, 199
Carson, Caroline, 15
Carson, Fiddlin' John, 235
Carter, Hodding, 202
Carter, Jimmy, 12
Caruthers, William Alexander, 215, 219

Cash, Wilbur J., 144, 180–81, 192, 197–204, 209, 215, 218
Catalans, 6
catfish, 211, 253
Cather, Willa, 156
Cerami, Charles A., 48–49
Chapel Hill, North Carolina, 10, 124, 127, 129, 180, 182, 190
Charleston, South Carolina, 5, 10, 12, 61, 88, 109–11, 162, 166, 180–93, 217, 237, 240, 243, 247
Charlotte, North Carolina, 247
Charlottesville, Virginia, 127, 149, 209–10
Charter Oak of Connecticut, 44
Chateaubriand, Vicomte François, 238
Chatelet, Pierre du, 80, 85
Chattanooga, Tennessee, 190
Chaucer, Geoffrey, 169, 209
Cherokees, 114
Chesapeake Bay, 135
Chesnut, James, Jr., 160
Chesnut, James, Sr., 160, 170
Chesnut, Mary Boykin, 23, 87–88, 91, 94, 96, 108, 143–44, 159–79, 206, 210
Chicago, Illinois, 9, 11, 64, 108, 124, 127
Chicago, University of, 18, 124, 127
Chicanos, 7, 113
childhood (and children), 11, 13, 28, 35, 56, 58, 80, 85, 132, 151, 153, 164, 173, 174, 196, 198, 209, 211, 238, 241, 251–54
childlessness, 159, 160, 164, 166
Childs, Margarita, 240
China (and the Chinese), viii, 12, 34, 46, 53–54, 114, 132
Chopin, Kate, 18
Chou-en-Lai, 55, 70
Christ, Jesus, 57, 232
Christianity, 44, 45, 59, 111, 171, 229, 23–33
Churchill, Winston Spencer, 32–33
Cincinnati, Ohio, 27, 87, 237
citizenship, viii, x, 27, 43, 54, 72, 133, 185, 245, 247
Clarkson, Thomas, 229
class (social), 4, 14, 33, 68–69, 70, 75, 80, 91, 92, 102, 105, 130, 165, 199, 207–8, 211, 222, 227–28, 230, 247
Clay, Henry, 59
Clayton, Bruce, 201–2
Clinton, Hillary, 175
Clinton, William Jefferson, 12, 106, 251–57
Cobb, James C., 25
Cobb, Richard, 94
Cobb, Thomas R. R., 88
Cobb, Ty, 235
Coclanis, Peter, 128
Cole, G. D. H., 6
Coleridge, Samuel Taylor, 195
Collège de France, 81
Colley, Linda, 29
Colombia, 87
colonialism, 4, 15, 28–30, 32, 42, 45, 50, 57, 85, 100, 106, 122–23, 128, 131, 134–36, 141, 143, 165, 184, 189, 208, 241–42. *See also* empire; postcolonialism
Coltrane, John, 74
Columbia, South Carolina, 13
Columbia University, 124, 127
Common Prayer, Book of, 248
Communism, 185, 199, 207
Concord, battle of, 41
Confederate States of America, 17, 28, 34, 58, 61, 67, 72, 82, 103, 128, 131, 144, 166, 168–69, 183, 194
Connecticut, 44, 87, 94, 207
conservativism, 17, 36, 46, 53–54, 67, 70, 74, 91, 113, 116–17, 125, 128, 134, 136, 139, 143–44, 155, 185, 190, 194, 200–1, 206, 209, 222–23, 225, 227–28, 231, 246–47, 249
constitutionalism, 18, 55–56, 58, 61, 65–68, 70, 72, 113, 155
contextualism (and contexts), ix, 16, 18, 43, 60, 66, 103, 116–17, 162, 202, 206, 217, 226, 254
contingency, 73, 75, 122, 136, 229, 234
conversation, ix, 20, 23, 34, 97, 117, 119, 149, 169, 201, 210, 226, 234, 238–39, 248
Conway, Jill Ker, 84
Cook, Ebenezer, 143
Cooke, John Esten, 10
Cooper, James Fenimore, 153
Cooper, Thomas, 96
Cork, 28
Cornwall, 6, 29, 204
cosmopolitanism, vii–ix, 119, 127, 183, 247
country-and-western, 11, 33
Crallé, Richard K., 231
Crane, Hart, 196
Cranmer, Thomas, 249

Craven, Avery, 155, 215
Crete, 11
Croce, Benedetto, 116, 197
Crummell, Alexander, 34–35, 37–38, 61
Crumpacker, Edgar D., 69
Cuba, 69
Culloden, battle of, 6
Cumberland River, 187
Curti, Merle, 115

Dabbs, James McBride, 203
Dabney, Richard Heath, 18
Dailey, Jane, 74–75
Daniels, Jonathan, 181, 192, 197
Dante Alighieri, 194
Darwinism, Social, 46, 248
Davidson, Cathy, 112
Davidson, Donald, 130, 182–90, 200
Davidson, James Wood, 103
Davidson, Jo, 58
Davis, Curtis Carroll, 215
Davis, Jeff, 255
Davis, Jefferson, 3, 17, 58, 86, 166
Davis, Richard Beale, 104
Davis, Varina Howell, 171
Declaration of Independence, 58, 60, 150, 187, 205
DeConde, Alexander, 51
defeat, 6, 49, 62, 113, 167, 172, 196, 208, 256
DeForest, John William, 157
DeLatte, Carolyn E., 91
Delta (of Mississippi), 4, 63–65
democracy, viii, 10, 26, 41, 45–46, 48, 54–55, 69–70, 105–6, 117, 119, 130, 151, 154, 227–28, 257
Democratic Party, 67–68, 70, 72, 74, 235, 254, 257
Denmark, 55
DeSaussure, Mary, 167
Detroit, Michigan, 132
Devon, 12
Dew, Thomas Roderick, 5, 223–24, 226, 228, 231–32
diaries, 37, 79–81, 85, 87, 96–97, 99, 101, 120, 144, 160–62, 165, 167, 170, 172, 176–77, 179
Dickens, Charles, 31, 158, 175, 201, 237
Dickinson, Emily, 176, 196
Diderot, Denis, viii

Dilthey, Wilhelm, 82
Dionysius of Halicarnassus, 111
divorce, 166, 178
Dodd, William E., 18, 124, 127
Dole, Bob, 254
Donegan, Lonnie, 28
Donne, John, 194–95
Doughty, Charles, 238
Douglass, Frederick, 34, 57, 60–61, 87, 108, 143, 255
Du Bois, W. E. B., 60, 74, 84, 130, 242, 255
Dukakis, Michael, 106
Duluth, Minnesota, 245
Dumas, Alexandre, 163
Dunglison, Robley, 149
Dunning, William Archibald, 124, 127
Durham, North Carolina, 243
Durkheim, Emile, 129
Dutch, 29
Dyck, Anthony Van, 181
Dylan, Bob, 255

East Anglia, vii, 29, 41
Eaton, Clement, 104, 215, 220
eccentricity, 180, 189, 248, 251
Edel, Leon, 86
Edelson, Max, 28–29
Edinburgh, viii
Edinburgh Review, 6, 31
Edwardian, 196
Edwards, Jonathan, 60
Edwards, Laura, 137
Egerton, Clyde, 129
Egypt, 79
Eire, 26–27, 54
Elgar, Edward, 26
Eliot, Thomas Stearns, 13, 23, 32, 117, 130, 174, 183, 187, 195–96, 201
elitism, 17, 36, 66, 68, 72, 97, 101, 105, 118, 130, 191, 227
Elizabeth II, viii
Elkins, Stanley, 125, 129
Ellington, Edward Mercer ("Duke"), 10–11
Ellison, Ralph, 255
Emerson, Ralph Waldo, 10, 15, 84, 106, 214
Emancipation Proclamation, 60
empire (and imperialism), x, 5, 8, 13–14, 29, 31–32, 34–35, 48–51, 55, 100, 105, 107, 109–10, 135, 241

empiricism, 57, 115, 122, 129
Engerman, Stanley, 128
England (and the English), vii, ix, 6–7, 9, 12–13, 21, 26–29, 34, 36, 41, 43, 53, 79, 87, 91, 96, 102, 107, 109–11, 113, 119, 142, 149, 156, 160, 162, 164, 168–69, 172, 177–78, 181, 190, 196, 217, 229, 237, 240–41, 248
Enlightenment, vii, ix, 31, 46, 59, 104, 111, 217, 228
Episcopalianism, 34, 113, 248–49
epistemology, 82, 116, 201, 225
Erikson, Erik, 217
Escott, Paul D., 202
ethnicity, 130, 137–38, 140, 247
Europe (and Europeans), vii–x, 3–4, 6–8, 10–16, 20–21, 24, 27, 29, 35, 42, 46, 49–51, 85, 94, 100, 104, 113, 121–22, 124–25, 131, 133, 138, 186, 219, 232, 237
evangelicalism, 17, 202, 225, 235, 254
Evans, Augusta, 144, 169
evolution, 33, 95, 97–98, 157, 203
exceptionalism, 46, 136
expatriation, 20, 130–31, 193, 199

Falklands War, viii
Falstaff, Sir John, 157
Fascism, 14
Faulkner, William, 4, 10, 14–15, 18, 33–34, 96, 108, 129, 153, 183, 186–87, 207, 209, 217–18, 255
Faust, Drew Gilpin, 87, 89–90, 128, 233
Fayetteville, Arkansas, 253
federalism, 3, 5, 7–8, 15, 27, 68–70, 100, 113, 154–55
Federalist Papers, 41, 144, 155
Federalists, 45, 69, 144, 155, 218, 227, 249
Ferris, William, 127
FIAT, 198
fiction, 24, 95, 98, 110, 122, 129, 131, 144, 153, 157, 161–64, 173, 175–79, 187, 193, 200, 216–18, 228, 240
Fields, Barbara, 209
Fife, 26
fin-de-siècle, 132, 175
Finkelman, Paul, 150
Fischer, David Hackett, 41–46, 140, 203
Fitzgerald, F. Scott, 10
Fitzhugh, George, 101–2, 107, 225, 228–29, 232

flags, 6, 41, 45
Flaubert, Gustave, 163
Flaxman, John, 181
Fleming, Thomas J., 48–49
Fleming, Walter Lynwood, 124
Flexner, James Thomas, 96
Fliegelman, Jay, 149–51
Florida, 50–51, 72–73, 123, 243, 256
Fogel, Robert W., 128
folk (concept of), 36, 41–47, 75, 91, 98, 102–3, 140, 144, 178, 192, 242, 246–47
Fontanges, Marie-Angélique, duchesse de, 233
Ford, Lacy K., Jr., 228
Ford's Theater, 60
Fort Sumter, South Carolina, 166, 188, 218
Foucault, Michel, 115, 118
Fox-Genovese, Elizabeth, 161, 165, 222, 225
Frady, Marshall, 202
France (and the French), vii, ix, 6, 18, 22–23, 26, 29–30, 33, 48–51, 55, 62, 70, 80–81, 87, 109, 111, 119, 123, 162–64, 166, 177, 190–91, 197, 210, 232, 237
Franklin County, Pennsylvania, 71
Fraser, Charles, 88
Fredrickson, George, 22
freedom, x, 12, 40–48, 55, 59, 76, 79, 87, 90, 97, 104, 119–20, 122, 141, 167, 175, 206, 222–25, 227, 231–33
Freehling, William W., 71
French Revolution, 55, 164
Freud, Sigmund, 95, 104, 129, 203
frontier, 57, 64, 156, 249
Fugitive poets, 182, 184
Fulbright, J. William, 12, 252
Fuller, Margaret, 83

Gaffney, South Carolina, 192
Gaines, Francis Pendleton, 218
Gainesville, Florida, 203
Gardner, Brother Dave, 249–50
Garnett, Muscoe R. H., 172
Garrison, William Lloyd, 56
Gates, Bill, 10
Gates, Henry Louis, 130, 139–40
Gatewood, Willard B., Jr., 90
Gavins, Raymond, 202, 204
Gayarré, Charles E. A., 123
Gaza Strip, 56

Geddes, Patrick, 36
Geertz, Clifford, ix, 104
gender, 4, 19, 66, 69, 75, 80, 84, 113, 118–19, 125, 127–28, 130, 137, 144, 165, 172, 175–76, 179, 191, 203
Genoa, 10, 20
Genovese, Eugene D., 93, 112, 125, 134–36, 217, 222–33
genre, x, 11, 83, 89, 94–95, 102, 110–12, 129, 134, 144, 154, 161–62, 172, 175–76, 195, 197, 199–200, 238, 251
gentility, xi, 84–85, 143, 159, 174–75, 186, 249
George, Saint, 45
George III, 43
Georgia, 6, 9, 22, 24, 37, 63–64, 66–67, 87–89, 94, 103, 123, 135, 207, 249
Georgia Review, 184
Germany (and Germans), viii, 23, 29–30, 32–33, 42, 46, 101, 109, 111, 132, 162–63
Gershwin, George, 218
Gettysburg, battle of, 60, 82, 153, 255
Gettysburg Address, 4, 41, 59
Gettysburg College, 57
Geyl, Pieter, 86
Ghana, 131, 242
Gibbon, Edward, 84, 93
Gilbert, Sandra M., 176–77
Gildersleeve, Basil, 15, 96
Giles, Miss, 168–69
Gilman, Caroline, 144
Gilroy, Paul, 35
Gingrich, Newt, 12, 254
Ginsberg, Allen, 84
Gittings, Robert, 92–93
Gladstonianism, 31
Glasgow, 28, 237
Glasgow, Ellen, 218
Gobetti, Piero, 199
Gobineau, Arthur de, 13
God, viii, 59, 119, 137, 165, 202, 229, 231
godlessness, x
Goethe, Johann Wolfgang, 163
Goldman, Eric, 86
golf, 36, 64, 235
Gombrich, Ernst, 44
Goo-Goo Clusters, 130
Gopher Prairie, 183
Gore, Albert, Jr., 73, 254
Gothic, 14–15, 46, 65, 84, 129, 249, 251

Göttingen, 15
Grady, Henry, 3, 61, 208
Gramsci, Antonio, 104, 197–99, 204, 222, 225–26
Grand Army of the Republic, 18, 61
Grant, Ulysses Simpson, 17, 55, 166
Grantham, Dewey W., 141
Gray, Richard, 24
Greek, 111
Green, Fletcher, 134, 155
Greene, Harlan, 193
Greene, Jack, 106, 135
Greenville, Mississippi, 15, 26, 36
Gregory, Mr., 178
Griffith, D. W., 11
Grigsby, Hugh Blair, 101
Grimke, Frederick, 101
Grimké, Sarah, 137, 227
Grimké, Thomas Smith, 111–12
Grummond, Jane Lucas De, 89, 94
Guardian (newspaper), 35
Gubar, Susan, 176–77
Guelzo, Allen C., 58–60
Guggenheim Foundation, 20
Guilds, John C., 156
guilt, 14, 19, 89, 137, 214, 216, 254
Gulf of Mexico, 109
Gwin, Minrose, 142–43, 145

Hahn, Steven, 209
Haiti, 49–50, 87, 240
Hall, Jacquelyn Dowd, 128
Hamburg, 33
Hamden, Connecticut, 207
Hamilton, Alexander, 49
Hamilton, J. G. de Roulhac, 124
Hamlet, 214, 219, 226
Hammond, James Henry, 87–90, 96, 128, 143, 224, 229–32
Hampstead, 239
Hampton Legion, 165
Handy, W. C., 235
Harby, Isaac, 227
Hardy, Thomas, 92, 183
Hare, Judge, 171
Harlan, Louis, 209, 239
Harper, Frances Ellen Watkins, 144
Harrington, James, 36, 43, 116
Harris, J. William, 142–45

Harris, Katherine, 72
Harris, Trudier, 142–43, 145
Harris, William C., 58
Hartz, Louis, 24
Harvard College, 61, 68, 130, 214, 219
Hawaii, 51, 86
Hawthorne, Nathaniel, 153
Hayne, Mrs., 167
Hayne, Paul Hamilton, 96, 171–72, 188
Heath, D. C. (publishers), 144
Hegel, Georg Wilhelm Friedrich, ix, 79, 103, 115–16, 125, 133–34, 197–98
hegemony, 17, 20, 28, 110, 113–14, 118–19, 197, 222
Heidelberg, 132
Heineccius, Johann Gottliebb, 117
Heisman, John, 235
Helper, Hinton Rowan, 227
Hemings, Sally, 84, 128
Hemingway, Ernest, 10, 15
Henneman, John Bell, 102
Henry, Robert, 111
Henry VII, 6
Herder, Johann Gottfried, 247
Herndon, William, 60
Heyward, DuBose, 180–93
Higginbotham, Sanford W., 134
Highlander Folk School, 36
Hilton Head Island, 36
Hindi, 33
Hinduism, 113, 241–42
Hinote, Sam, 239
historicism, 76, 89, 101, 111, 117, 121, 196, 230–31
Hobbes, Thomas, 42–43, 116
Hobsbawm, Eric, 4, 24
Hobson, Fred, 142
Hofstadter, Richard, 206, 217
Hoggart, Richard, 24
Holden, W. W., 88, 91
Hollinger, David A., 116, 118, 140
Hollywood, California, 11, 254
Holman, C. Hugh, 200
Holmes, George Frederick, 5, 96, 229
Holmes, Oliver Wendell, 61–62
Holt, Thomas C., 74, 209
Holy Ghost, 232
Hong Kong, 6
honor, 48, 165, 167

Hooper, Johnson Jones, 143
Horton, George Moses, 143
Horton, Willie, 17
Hot Springs, Arkansas, 251, 255
Hotspur, Harry, 26
Hotz, Henry, 13
Houdon, Jean-Antoine, 181
Houston, Texas, 12
Howells, William Dean, 69, 218
Hönnighausen, Lothar, 16
Hubbell, Jay B., 103, 113, 215
Hughes, H. Stuart, 219
Huguenots, 29, 32, 191
Hume, David, viii, 23, 82, 137

Illinois, 88, 90
India (and Indians), 6, 27, 31, 34–35, 46, 238, 240–42
Indian Mutiny, 35
Indiana, 18, 69
Indians (Native Americans), 29, 32, 45, 48, 127, 131, 142, 144, 154, 157
Indonesia, 242
Iowa, ix, 87
Iran, 242
Iraq, 51
Ireland (and the Irish), 9, 26–29, 32, 54
irony, 60, 62, 108, 135, 144, 185, 202, 207, 210
Irving, Washington, 153
Isaac, Rhys, 150
Islam, 241
Israel, 256
Italy (and Italians), ix, 6, 12, 15–16, 30, 65, 71, 100, 111, 198, 204, 243
Ivy League, 17, 108, 127, 210

Jackson, Andrew (and Jacksonianism), 10, 69, 80–81, 86, 96, 211, 227–28, 243
Jacobs, Harriet, 108, 117, 143–44
Jacoway, Elizabeth, 203–4
Jamaica, 34
James, C. L. R., 35, 241
James, Henry, 10, 12, 86, 157, 218, 237; *Aspern Papers*, 12, 157
James, William, 107, 118
Jamestown, Virginia, 29, 32, 134
Japan, 10, 15, 87, 125
jazz, 11, 16, 33, 36, 235, 255
Jeffers, Robinson, 156

Jefferson, Thomas (and Jeffersonianism), 10, 15, 28, 48–51, 55–56, 69, 84, 86, 96, 108, 123, 128, 134–35, 143, 149–51, 228
Jews, 29, 32, 227
Jim Crow system, 63, 66, 73–75, 141, 207, 209. *See also* segregation
Johns Hopkins University, 124, 209, 234
Johnson, Guion Griffin, 192
Johnson, Lyndon Baines, 12, 32
Johnson, Michael P., 90
Johnson, Robert, 4, 21
Johnson, Samuel, 195, 248
Jones, Anne Goodwyn, 22, 178, 197–202
Jones, Bobby, 235, 247
Jones, Sam, 235
Joplin, Scott, 235
Joyner, Charles, 90
Jung, Carl, 129
Junkers, 71

Kames, Lord Henry Home, 111
Kandahar, 34
Kantrowitz, Stephen, 74–75
Kato Zakros, 11
Keats, John, 92, 195
Kelley, Virginia Cassidy, 251
Kennedy, John Fitzgerald, 58, 254
Kennedy, John Pendleton, 31–32, 143, 215, 218–19
Kentucky, 34, 88, 90, 98
Kenyans, 34
Key, V. O., 4
Khomeini, Ayatollah, 247
King, Martin Luther, Jr., 12, 36, 73–74, 108, 137, 144, 207, 255
King, Richard H., 122, 129, 203
King, Susan Petigru, 144, 171, 178
Kirby, Jack, 203
Kissinger, Henry, 70
Kloppenberg, James, 106, 114
Kolchin, Peter, 22, 53, 125, 205
Kousser, J. Morgan, 66
Kreyling, Michael, 18, 195
Ku Klux Klan, 44, 128
Kuhn, Thomas, 88
Kukla, Jon, 48–50

labor, 28, 32, 63–64, 126, 138, 198, 224–25, 230, 242

Labour Party, 28
LaCapra, Dominick, 116
Laffite, Jean, 89
Lagos, 34
Lamar, Lucius Quintus Cincinnatus, 171–72
Lamb, Charles, 175
Lambert, Franklin, 28–29
Lampedusa, Giuseppe, 13
language, 7–9, 18, 26, 29, 33, 51, 84, 87, 103, 111–12, 115, 118, 129, 150–51, 156, 162, 197, 199–201, 239
Las Vegas, Nevada, 254
Lasithi region, 11
Latin America, 125, 138, 184
Latin language, 5, 42, 111, 117
law, 27, 29, 59, 65, 68, 70, 72–73, 89, 101–2, 111, 150, 180, 182, 224, 230, 253
Law, John, 93
Lawrence, T. E., 92
Leamington Spa, 33
LeConte, Joseph, 87–88
Lee, "Lighthouse Harry," 169
Lee, Robert E., 17, 20, 55, 60–61
Legaré, Hugh Swinton, 15, 96–97, 101, 104, 109, 213, 215, 217–19, 227, 230
Legaré, James M., 188
Leibniz, Gottfried Wilhelm von, viii
Leland, Jack, 240
Levant, 256
Levine, David, 58
Lewinsky, Monica, 256
Lewis, Jan, 150
Lewis, Jerry Lee, 30
Lewis, R. W. B., 213
Lexington, Massachusetts, 41
Lhasa, 7
liberalism, 13, 42, 54–55, 59, 74, 125, 128, 134, 155, 194, 200, 207, 214, 227, 231, 246, 257
Liberia, 34, 57
liberty, 41–46, 48, 51, 55, 200, 223–24
Liberty Bell, 41, 43
Lieber, Francis, 101
Lieber, Oscar, 101
Lincoln, Abraham, 4, 8, 56–61, 155, 166
Lincoln, C. Eric, 203–4
Little Rock, Arkansas, 253
Liverpool, 28
Livingston, Robert, 48, 50
Locke, John, 41, 116, 255

Lodge Force Bill (1892), 68
Lomax, John, 36
London, 20, 29, 31–35, 109, 151, 224, 237, 242–43
London, Jack, 12
Long, Earl, 124
Long, Orie W., 215
Longinus, 195
Longstreet, Augustus Baldwin, 249
Lost Cause, 123
Lott, Trent, 55
Louisiana, 8, 48–51, 66–67, 87, 102, 123
Louisiana State University Press, 124
Louisville, Kentucky, 126
L'Ouverture, Toussaint, 49
Louvre, 96
Lovejoy, Arthur O., 103, 226
Loyalists, 45
Lucian, 120
Luftwaffe, 13
Luxembourg, vii
lynching, 14, 17, 64–65, 75, 234–35
Lyndsay, Mr., 178
Lynn, Kenneth, 215

Macaulay, Thomas Babington, 31, 144
Machiavelli, Niccolò, 116, 226
MacLean, Nancy, 74
Madison, James, 4, 23, 49–50, 94, 96, 134, 144, 150, 155
Madrid, 50
Maine, 81
Malaysia, 242
Malone, Dumas, 96
Malthus, Thomas, 224
Manassas, battle of, 166
Manchester, 36, 237
Manhattan, 95, 199
Manigault, Joseph, 191
Manly, Basil, Jr., 101
Manly, Louise, 103
Mansfield, Mike, 252
marginality, 16–18, 21, 56, 64, 106, 128, 131, 180, 191, 217, 245
Márquez, Gabriel García, 255
Marshall, John, 134
Marx, Karl (and Marxism), 116, 125, 129, 197–98, 222, 225–27, 232
Maryland, 34, 67, 87

masculinity, 56, 128, 176
Massachusetts, 17, 41–42, 45, 94, 109, 246
materialism, 198, 216
mathematics, 87, 102, 149, 203
Mathews, Cornelius, 156
Mathis, Ray, 87
May, Henry F., 218
Mayhew, Henry, 224
Mazzini, Giuseppe, 100
McCarthy, Mary, 122
McClellan, John, 255
McCord, Louisa Susanna, 96, 144, 161
McGregor, Ewan, 84
McKinley, William, 51, 69
McMath, Sid, 255
McPherson, James, 209
Mead, Margaret, 122
Medea, 167, 177
Melungeons, 132
Melville, Herman, 10, 153, 223
memoirs, 57, 84, 130, 139, 161–62, 169, 173, 177, 209, 211, 232, 251–52, 255. *See also* autobiography
memory, 27, 43, 60, 83–85, 133, 135, 167, 190, 194, 238
Mencken, H. L., 248
Mephistopheles, 49
Mercer University Press, 89
Mercia, 26
Mérimée, Prosper, 163
Merovingians, 246
metaphor, 154, 174, 200
metaphysical poets, 195
metaphysics, 103–4, 118, 230–31, 242
Methodists, 34, 113, 211, 249
metropolitanism, 29–30, 103, 153, 241
Mexico, 8, 31, 50, 109
Mexico City, 31
Mezzogiorno, 16, 71, 198–99
Miami University, vii, 113
Michelet, Jules, 23, 116–17
Michener, James A., 87
Michigan, University of, 18
Middle States, 3, 41
Middleton, John Izard, 15
Middleton, Miss, 169
Middleton Place, 184
Midi, ix
Midlands, English, 41

268 INDEX

Midwest, 3, 13, 132
migration, vii, 22, 27, 29–30, 35, 38, 41–42, 45, 50, 64, 126, 132–33, 138, 140, 246
Miles, James Warley, 227
Miles, Mrs. Richardson, 169
Miles, William Porcher, 171
Miller, Dick, 160
Miller, Henry, 174
Miller, Mary Boykin, 160
Miller, Perry, 103–4, 115, 207
Miller, Stephen, 160
Milton, John, 5
Minerva, Owl of, 4
Miniver, Mrs., 33
Minnesota, 48, 132
Minnesota, University of, 196
Mississippi, 3, 15, 20, 55, 63–64, 66–67, 87, 112, 114, 123, 132, 209, 247
Mississippi, University of, 26, 127, 129, 202, 211
Mississippi River, 49, 237
Missouri, 34
Mitchell, Margaret, 145, 186
Mobile, Alabama, 13
modernism, 9–10, 56, 86, 104, 143, 167, 171, 174, 176, 183, 186, 191, 194–95, 201, 218
modernity, 123, 132, 185, 196, 199, 203, 213, 225
modernization, 4, 25, 246
Molière (Jean Baptiste Poquelin), 163
Moltke-Hansen, David, 157, 177
Momigliano, Arnoldo, 89, 92, 95
Monroe, Harriet, 182
Monroe, James, 48
Montaigne, Michel Eyquem de, 163
Montana, 48
Montgomery, Alabama, 94, 166
Monticello, 4, 149, 151
Monty Python's the Life of Brian, 220
Monypenny, William Flavelle, 96
Moore, Harry Estill, 6
Moore, Rayburn, 96
Morgan, Sarah, 162
Morris, James, 238
Morris, Willie, 251–52
Moscow, 21
Moultrie, James, 169
mourning, 79–80, 154, 201
MTV, 202
Mugwumps, 217
Muhlenfeld, Elisabeth, 177–78

multiculturalism, viii, 4, 9, 17, 19–20, 34, 37, 112–14, 131, 134, 140, 202, 210, 217, 222, 254
Munslow, Alan, 122
Murray, Albert, 210
music, 11, 17, 33, 36, 102, 129, 144, 170, 235–36, 242, 246, 249, 253–54. *See also* blues; country-and-western; jazz; rhythm-and-blues
Mussolini, Benito, 198
Myrtle Beach, South Carolina, 178
myth, 26, 32–33, 174, 205, 213, 218–19

Nabokov, Vladimir, 84
Naipaul, V. S., 35, 237–43
Naples, 198
Napoleon Bonaparte, 48–50, 52, 86
Nashville, Tennessee, 36, 105, 182, 191, 243
National Association for the Advancement of Colored People, 208
National Endowment for the Humanities, 127
Negro, 13, 102, 130, 139, 181, 192, 230, 240–41, 243. *See also* African Americans; blacks
Netherlands, 54
New Delhi, 33
New England, 3, 41–43, 45, 87, 104, 106–7, 181
New Orleans, Louisiana, 10, 30, 48–50, 80, 87, 123, 180, 190, 234, 237, 243, 247
New York, 11, 20, 43, 48, 87, 107–8, 114, 121–22, 149, 153, 163, 183, 222, 237, 241, 246
New York Public Library, 15
New York Review of Books, 206, 209, 243
New York Times, 16
New Yorker, 243
Newcastle, University of, 10, 36
Newman, John Henry, 175, 249
Nicaragua, 27
Nietzsche, Friedrich, 116
Nigeria, 27, 34, 53, 241
Nixon, Richard Milhous, 70
Nkrumah, Kwame, 241
Nobel Prize for Literature, 207
Nock, Albert Jay, 194
Nordic, 203
Norfolk, Virginia, 88
Norfolk Rising (1549), 44
Norse, Old, 42
North Carolina, 10, 79–80, 87, 88, 101, 123, 132, 139, 167, 180, 182, 202, 207, 247
North Carolina, University of, 207

North Dakota, 50
Norton, W. W., 134, 142
nostalgia, 31, 74, 124
Nott, Henry Junius, 111
Nott, Josiah, 13, 31
Notting Hill, 34
novels (and novelists), xi, 13–14, 38, 59–60, 69,
    84–85, 108, 110, 129, 154, 157, 162–63, 165–66,
    169–70, 172, 176–77, 179, 181, 183, 187, 189,
    193, 206, 213, 216–17, 219–20, 223, 238, 240
Novick, Peter, 115, 118

Oakes, James, 136
O'Connor, Flannery, 10, 252
Odense, 10
Odum, Howard W., 3, 6, 128, 180, 186, 247–48
O'Hara, Scarlett, 186
Ohio, vii, 27, 236
oligarchy, 54, 229
oratory, 60, 93, 111, 150–51, 165
O'Rourke, Jemima, 79, 81
Osborne, John, 13
Osterweis, Rollin G., 104
outsiders, 22, 183, 219, 242, 252
Owsley, Frank Lawrence, 103, 108, 124
Oxbridge, 91
Oxford, University of, 15, 188, 237, 240–41
Oxford English Dictionary, 6
Oxford History of the United States, 210
Oxford Movement, 248–49

Page, Thomas Nelson, 218
Page, Walter Hines, 31
Painter, Nell Irvin, 202–3
Pakistan, 34, 54, 242
Palestinians, 256
Palladio, Andrea, 149, 151
Pandemonium, Hall of, 5
Paris, viii, 11, 15, 20, 48–51, 149, 151
Parkman, Francis, 206, 210
Parrington, Vernon Louis, 107
Pascal, Blaise, 163
passports, 22, 27, 132
paternalism, 58, 188
patriarchy, 75, 128, 141, 149, 170, 177, 197, 201
patriotism, 7, 42, 45, 49, 123, 209
patronage, 30, 186, 210
Patton, Charley, 235
Paulding, James K., 218–19

Pease, Jane H., 184
Pease, William H., 184
Pennsylvania, 43
Percy, LeRoy, 26, 36, 65
Percy, Thomas, 144
Percy, Walker, 1, 14, 129
Percy, William Alexander, 13, 15, 36, 63
Peterkin, Julia, 181, 183
Peterson, Norma Lois, 87
Peterson, Oscar, 254
Petigru, James Louis, 172, 181, 188–89, 192
Pettigrew, James Johnston, 101, 171, 178
Philadelphia, Pennsylvania, 149, 170–71
Phillips, Caryl, 35
Phillips, Ulrich Bonnell, 18, 94, 103, 127–28,
    130, 132
Picasso, Pablo, 174
Pickett's Charge, 255
Piedmont (Appalachian), 63–64, 94, 125,
    185–86
Piedmont, kingdom of, 198
Pierce, Charles Sanders, 118
Pinckney, Eliza Lucas, 144
Pinckney, Josephine, 190–92
Pippin, Horace, 58
Pitt, William (the elder), 43
Pittsburgh, Pennsylvania, 41
plantations (and planters), 34, 42, 63–64,
    68, 87, 93, 100, 125, 139, 154, 170, 177, 208,
    218–19, 240, 243, 247
Plutarch, 89
Plymouth, Devon, 13
Pocock, J. G. A., 93, 116–17
Poe, Edgar Allan, 14, 18, 58, 143, 195–96
Poinsett, Joel Roberts, 15
Poland, 46
Polonius, 166
Polybius, 89
Pontchartrain, Lake, 94
Popper, Karl, 76
populism, 10, 63, 66–67, 75, 130, 207–8, 234
Porgy, Captain, 157
Porter, Roy, 16
positivism, 115, 197, 246
postcolonialism, 29–30, 50. *See also*
    colonialism; empire
postethnicity, 19, 140
postmodernism, ix, 9, 18–19, 112, 114, 125, 129,
    132, 137, 142, 157, 201, 210

postsouthern, 18
poststructuralism, 18, 112, 114, 116–17, 157, 226
Potter, David M., 127, 206, 213
Pound, Ezra, 195–96
Presbyterianism, 28, 113, 229
Presley, Elvis, 10, 28, 32, 211
Preston, Buck, 164
Preston, Captain, 41
Preston, Dickson J., 87
Preston, William Campbell, 213, 219
Pringle, Alicia, 190
progress, 62, 102, 115–16, 126–27, 208, 223–24, 227
progressivism, 10, 67, 100, 106, 155, 224, 234, 257
Prokopowicz, Gerald J., 58
proslavery argument, 32, 45, 57, 104, 119, 143, 153–54, 223
Protestantism, 28, 113, 227, 254
Prussia, 62, 65, 71
Pryor, David, 253
psychobiography, 94
psychohistory, 217
Public Broadcasting Service, 81
Puerto Rico, 241
Pulitzer Prize, 20
Puritans, 12, 135, 191, 209
Pushkin, Alexander, 162
Pyrenees, 109

Quakers, 43, 155
Queens' College, Cambridge, 34
Quincey, Thomas de, 175

Radcliffe, Ann, 181
radicalism, 36, 115, 117, 125, 172, 174, 205, 207, 222, 229, 231
Raleigh, North Carolina, 181
Ramsay, David, 123, 144
Rand, Ayn, 194
Randall, Henry Stephens, 149
Randolph, John, 30, 49, 70, 96, 219
Randolph, Vance, 255
Ranger, Terence, 4, 16
Ranke, Leopold von, 116, 207
Ransom, John Crowe, 20, 32, 36, 182–83, 195, 247
Raper, Arthur, 63

Rawdon-Hastings, Francis, 1st Marquess of Hastings, 169
Read, Herbert, 196
Readjusters, 74–75
Reagan, Ronald, viii, 223, 247
Reconstruction, 17, 32, 53–56, 62, 65, 67, 69, 72–75, 102, 123–24, 205–6, 208–9, 234, 236
Redcliffe plantation, 94
Rednecks, 239–40
Reed, John Shelton, 109, 128–29, 133, 202, 245–50
Rehnquist, William, 73
Remini, Robert V., 86
Renaissance, 117, 151
Renaissance, Southern Literary, 145, 206
Republican Party, 67–69, 72, 74, 222, 254, 257
republics (and republicanism), 8, 27, 36, 45, 49, 51, 56, 80, 88, 106, 119, 167, 188
Revere, Paul, 42
revolution, 4, 45, 55, 150, 163, 197, 200
Reynolds, Joshua, 181
Rhea, Linda, 215
rhetoric, x, 21, 80–81, 83, 92, 108, 111, 122, 144, 150–51, 199–201, 257
Rhett, Robert Barnwell, 167
Rhodes Scholarships, 252
rhythm-and-blues, 10, 11
Ricardo, David, 224
Richards, I. A., 195
Richmond, Virginia, 41, 74, 101, 166, 190, 237
Richter, Jean Paul, 163
Rimbaud, Arthur, 163
Roark, James P., 90
Roberts, Oral, 235
Robinson, Joseph T., 255
Rockefeller, John D., 32
Rockwell, Norman, 58
Rodgers, Daniel T., 209
Roman Catholicism, 28, 54, 113, 136, 194
Romanticism, 31, 46, 59, 81, 85, 94, 100–2, 111, 133, 195, 217, 228
Rome (and Roman), 15, 24, 42–43, 93, 111, 243
Romney, George, 190
Roosevelt, Theodore, 51, 56, 234
Rorty, Richard, 75, 104, 122
Ross, Dorothy, 114, 121
Ross, Sul, 87, 89
Rousseau, Jean-Jacques, 10
Rubin, Louis D., Jr., 22, 185–87, 200

Ruffin, Edmund, 88, 96–97, 215
Ruffin, Elizabeth, 175
Rushmore, Mount, 56
Rusk, Dean, 12
Ruskin, John, 239
Russia (and Russians), 53, 65, 125, 162, 177
Ryder, Charles, 184

Safire, William, 206
Saint Cecilia Society, 181
Saint George, 43
Saint George Tucker Society, 138
Sainte-Beuve, Charles Augustin, 206
Saint-Simon, Louis de Rouvroy, duc de, 177
Sandburg, Carl, 255
Santayana, George, 85
Sardinia, 198–99
Sark, Isle of, 26
Sartre, Jean Paul 116
Satan, 5
Savannah, Georgia, 43, 94, 247
Savoy, House of, 198
Scandinavia, 36, 203
Schiller, Friedrich, 163
Schlegel, August von, 46, 111
Schlegel, Friedrich von, 111
Schlesinger, Arthur, Jr., 29
science (and scientists), viii, 6, 9, 11, 18, 49, 62, 101–3, 110, 171, 196, 200, 203, 224, 228, 245
Scotch-Irish, 29, 32
Scotland (and Scots), 6–7, 9, 26–29, 31–32, 36, 109
Scott, Walter, 59, 181
Sears-Roebuck, 44
segregation, racial, 13, 32, 34, 61, 63, 73–75, 137, 202, 207–9, 235, 240
Sellers, Charles Grier, Jr., 214, 217
Selma, Alabama, 12, 73, 207
Seminoles, 137
Seoul, 7
Shakespeare, William, 26, 163
Shalhope, Robert E., 88
sharecropping, 64, 68, 211, 235
Shelley, Mary, 176
Sherman, William Tecumseh, 4, 13, 61
Sherrill, Arkansas, 253
Sherwood Forest, 44
Shields, David, 143
Shiloh, battle of, 4, 17, 124

Siddons, Anne, 239
Sidney, Algernon, 36
Simms, William Gilmore, 96, 108, 143–44, 153–58, 181, 188, 219
Simpson, Lewis P., 18, 200
Singleton, Mrs. John, 168
Singleton, Mrs. Mat, 168
Sitia, 11
Skinner, Quentin, 42–43, 88, 104, 116, 226
slaveholders, 13, 44, 102, 211, 222, 225, 227, 232, 243
slavery, 12–14, 17, 30–32, 34–35, 38, 45, 50, 53–58, 60–61, 63, 69, 73, 88, 90, 93, 96–97, 100, 102, 104, 106, 124, 128, 130–31, 135, 138, 143–44, 150, 155–57, 164–67, 170, 188, 203, 205, 209, 214, 216–17, 222–32, 240, 242
Slovenes, 7
Smith, Adam, 28, 31
Smith, Ashbel, 87, 89
Smith, Cotton Ed, 17
Smith, Henry Nash, 213
Smith, John, 143
Smith, Lee, 129
social science, 114, 192
socialism, 6, 36, 194, 207, 232
sociology, x, 36, 86–87, 90, 103, 128–29, 132, 186, 196–97, 200, 231, 245
Socrates, 21
South Carolina, 13, 29, 36, 66–67, 69, 79–80, 87–88, 90, 100, 101, 112, 123, 132, 144, 160, 169, 177–78, 181–82, 188–89, 190, 192, 215, 229, 243
South Carolina College, 111
Southern League, 9
Southwest, 113, 215
Soviet Union, 6, 10, 207, 232
Spain (and the Spanish), 29, 48–51, 53, 111, 123, 154, 198
Spencer, Elizabeth, 15
Spenser, Edmund, 169
St. Louis, Missouri, 41
St. Petersburg, 7
Stamp Act, 41, 45
Stampp, Kenneth, 215
Stanton, Lucia, 150
Starr, Kenneth, 254
Statue of Liberty, 41
Stein, Gertrude, 122
Stephen, Leslie, 160, 164, 177, 206

272   INDEX

Stephen, Toby, 160
Stephen, Vanessa (later Bell), 160, 174
Stephens, Alexander H., 61
Stephens, Jackson T., 257
Stephens, Lester, 87
Sterne, Laurence, 31, 175
Stevens, Thaddeus, 57
Stewart, Dugald, 103
Stith, William, 123
Stockholm, 207
Stoicism, 14
Stoppard, Tom, 116
Stowe, Harriet Beecher, 217
Stowe, Steven, 161, 178
Strachey, Lytton, 90, 92–93, 96, 174
Strasbourg, 177
Stravinsky, Igor, 174
Stuart dynasty, 17, 29, 168
style, xi, 18–19, 44, 59, 142, 169, 172, 174–75, 192, 202, 235, 239, 248
Styron, William, 255
Sue, Eugène, 163
Sully, Thomas, 190
Sumner, Charles, 137, 166
Sumner, William Graham, 46, 248
Sunday, Billy, 235
Supreme Court, U.S., 66, 73, 208
Swedenborg, Emanuel, 198, 231
Swift, Jonathan, 92, 248
Sydney (Australia), 20, 33
Sydnor, Charles, 155

Taiping Rebellion, 53
Taiwan, 54
Taj Mahal, 238
Tallahassee, Florida, 243
Talleyrand-Périgord, Charles-Maurice, 49–50
Talvande, Anne-Marie, 162
Tarleton, Banastre, 169
Tate, Allen, 20–21, 23, 32, 104, 112, 129–30, 136, 144, 170, 182–87, 189, 194–96, 226
Taylor, John, 88
Taylor, William R., 104, 213–20
Tazewell, Littleton Waller, 87–88
Teich, Mikuláš, 16
Tennessee, 66, 123, 183, 185
Tennyson, Alfred, Lord, 31, 59
Teutonic, 31

Texas, 50–51, 67, 87, 89, 132, 243
Thackeray, William Makepeace, 23, 31, 162–65, 167, 175, 179, 237
Thatcher, Margaret, vii–viii, 175
theology, 96, 143, 223, 227
Theophrastus, 239
Thomas, Dylan, 255
Thompson, John R., 31
Thoreau, Henry David, 223
Thornton, J. Mills, III, 209
Thornwell, James Henley, 96, 223–24, 229, 232
Thurmond, Strom, 70
Tibet, 6
Ticknor, George, 15
Tidewater, 65, 88, 125, 185
Tillman, Benjamin, 74–75, 128
Timrod, Henry, 143, 171, 188
Tise, Larry, 202
Tocqueville, Alexis de, 116, 237
Tokyo, 33
Tolpuddle Martyrs, 37
Tolstoy, Leo, 177
transatlantic, 12, 135, 217, 223
transnationalism, ix–x, 3
Trescot, William Henry, 31, 171–72, 178, 224, 226, 228–29, 231–33
Trinidad, 36, 237, 240–43
Trinity College, Cambridge, 35
Trinity College, Durham, North Carolina, 124
Trollope, Anthony, 175
Tucker, George, 215
Tucker, Henry St. George, 70
Tucker, Nathaniel Beverley, 70, 94
Tudor dynasty, 17, 29
Tunbridge Wells, 34
Turgenev, Ivan, 177
Turin, 199, 204
Turks, 132
Turner, Frederick Jackson, 207, 217
Turner, Nat, 137
Tuscaloosa, Alabama, 12, 88
Tuskegee Institute, 239
Twain, Mark, 153, 215
Twitty, Conway, 249
Tyson, Don, 257

Ulster, 7, 27
United Kingdom, 7, 27, 37

United States Information Agency, 22
University of North Carolina Press, 124
Utah, 256
utilitarianism, 59, 86

Vance, Rupert, 36, 129, 180
Vanderbilt University, 247
Vanndale, Arkansas, 211
Vatican, 96
Vendée, 80, 85
Venice, 12, 238
Versailles, 233
Vicksburg, Mississippi, 4, 190
Vico, Giambattista, 23
Victoria, Queen, 31, 168
Victorianism, 31, 34, 59, 92, 104, 170, 174–75, 201, 207
Vidal, Gore, 49
Vienna, 10, 95
Vietnam, 6
Virginia, 5, 18, 29–30, 32, 34, 36, 60, 62, 66–67, 70, 74, 87–89, 94, 100–1, 123, 125, 134, 150, 165, 167, 172, 183, 190, 223, 232, 243, 247
Virginia, University of, 149
Volney, Constantin, comte de, 238
Voltaire, François-Marie Arouet, viii–ix
Voting Rights Act (1965), 74

Wales, 9, 26–28
Walker, Juliet E. K., 90
Wallerstein, Immanuel, 93
Waltham, Massachusetts, 109
Walton, Sam, 257
Ward, Brian, 28, 33
Waring family, 190
Warren, Robert Penn, 15, 20, 205–6, 209
Warsaw, 21, 256
Warwick, University of, 10
Washington, Booker T., 239, 242
Washington, D.C., 12, 60, 66, 68–69, 123, 214, 237, 253, 257
Washington, George, 42, 56, 96, 134
WASP, 113
Watergate, 205
Waterloo, battle of, 165
Watson, Charles S., 154, 156
Watson, Thomas J., 65, 207
Waugh, Evelyn, 184, 238, 248

Weaver, Richard M., 104, 200, 226
Weber, Max, 93, 129
Webster, Daniel, 18, 31
Webster-Ashburton Treaty (1842), 31
Wedgwood, Veronica, 93
Weimar, 15
Welty, Eudora, 18, 129, 154, 156, 240
Wessex, 26
West (American), 3, 49, 107, 151, 157, 209
West, Benjamin, 42
West, Elliott, 157
West Country, vii
West Indies, 34
West Virginia, 139
Whiggery, 10, 43, 69, 91
White, Hayden, 116
White House, 30, 254, 256
white Southerners, 4, 17–18, 35, 60–61, 64–69, 72–75, 100, 102, 108, 112–13, 130–32, 139, 143, 157, 204, 208, 228, 235, 240, 246, 247, 254
white supremacy, 22, 74–75, 100, 132, 208
whites, 22, 26, 34, 57, 61–63, 69, 141, 191, 202–3, 241
Whitman, Walt, 61
Wigan, ix
Wigen, Kären, 5–8
Wilford, Hugh, 28, 33
Wilkinson, James, 49
William and Mary, College of, 5, 32, 110, 135
William and Mary Quarterly, 135
Williams, Ben Ames, 161
Williams, Hank, 130
Williams, Tennessee, 15
Williamsburg, Virginia, 32, 110, 135
Wilson, Douglas, 57, 150
Wilson, Edmund, 255
Wilson, Woodrow, 18, 31, 46, 60, 96, 124, 208, 234, 255
Winfrey, Oprah, 56, 81
Wingspread Conference, 114, 118
Winston-Salem, North Carolina, 202, 245
Wiregrass region, 65
Wirt, William, 219–20
Wisconsin, 69
Witherspoon Murder Case, 170
Wittgenstein, Ludwig, 82, 116
Wolfe, Thomas, 183, 186, 197, 202, 251, 255
Wolff, Larry, 16
Wood, Marcus, 28, 30

Woodward, C. Vann, 4, 12, 15, 17, 20, 24, 66–67, 73, 75, 96, 125, 127–29, 132, 134, 136–37, 144, 161–62, 176, 179, 201, 205–11, 234, 236
Woolf, Virginia (formerly Stephen), 122, 160, 162, 164, 167, 169, 172–79
Worcester, battle of, 44
Wordsworth, William, 94
Wright, Gavin, 128, 203
Wright, Patience, 151
Wright, Richard, 20
Wyatt-Brown, Bertram, 202, 209

Yaeger, Patricia, 22
Yale University, 17–18, 20, 104, 127, 209
Yankees, 14, 18, 41, 104, 107, 168, 181, 213–15, 217–20, 246, 248
Yazoo (Mississippi), 63–64
Yeats, William Butler, 195
Yeltsin, Boris, 255
Yorkshire, 29
Young, Arthur, 237
Young America, 153–54
Younge, Gary, 35

www.ingramcontent.com/pod-product-compliance
Lightning Source LLC
Chambersburg PA
CBHW021835220426

43663CB00005B/262